W9-CBD-292

THE OPERATOR

Center Point
Large Print

Also by Kim Harrison and available from Center Point Large Print:

The Peri Reed Chronicles
The Drafter

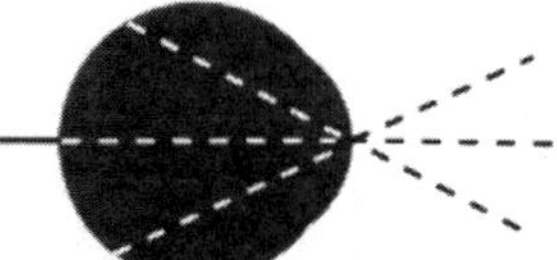

This Large Print Book carries the Seal of Approval of N.A.V.H.

THE OPERATOR

KIM HARRISON

CENTER POINT LARGE PRINT
THORNDIKE, MAINE

This Center Point Large Print edition
is published in the year 2017 by arrangement with
Pocket Books, a division of Simon & Schuster, Inc.

This book is a work of fiction.
Any references to historical events, real people, or real places are used fictitiously. Other names, characters, places, and events are products of the author's imagination, and any resemblance to actual events or places or persons, living or dead, is entirely coincidental.

The text of this Large Print edition is unabridged.
In other aspects, this book may vary
from the original edition.
Printed in the United States of America
on permanent paper.
Set in 16-point Times New Roman type.

ISBN: 978-1-68324-297-0

Library of Congress Cataloging-in-Publication Data

Names: Harrison, Kim, 1966– author.
Title: The operator / Kim Harrison.
Description: Center Point Large Print edition. | Thorndike, Maine : Center Point Large Print, 2017.
Identifiers: LCCN 2016056408 | ISBN 9781683242970 (hardcover : alk. paper)
Subjects: LCSH: Large type books. | GSAFD: Fantasy fiction. | Suspense fiction.
Classification: LCC PS3608.A78355 O64 2017 | DDC 813/.6—dc23
LC record available at https://lccn.loc.gov/2016056408

For Tim

ACKNOWLEDGMENTS

I'd like to thank the readers who stuck with me, trusting the storyteller, and my new readers who took a chance.

CHAPTER ONE

"Ah, ma'am? Please don't touch the car," the man with the glass tablet said, and Peri flicked her eyes to him, acknowledging his words as she lifted the handle of the hundred-thousand-dollar car. Immediately it opened, the door making a soft hush of sound that meant money well spent as she slipped inside and let the leather seats enfold her.

"Ma'am?"

It smelled new, and her eyes closed for a moment as she almost reverently set her hands on the wheel, smiling as her shoulders eased and an odd relaxed tension filled her. It was sleek, sexy without being over-the-top as if confident in its power and comfortable under the spotlight. Its red color went deep, showing shadowed layers that only an off-the-assembly-line paint could deliver. A two-seater, it looked fast, with wide tires that had ample turning radius in the wheel wells and an antenna array panel to plug in just about anything now or in the future. The sound system was adequate at best, but the onboard computer display was big enough to be useful and glass compatible. Much of it was plastic, though, and Peri's nose wrinkled.

"It looks as if it was made for you," the man

said, the annoyed slant to his brow belying his smile as he stood just outside and held his tablet like a fig leaf.

Peri tossed her straight black hair out of her eyes, her smile real as she looked up at him. “I bet you say that to everyone.”

He rocked closer. “No. Only those who look like they belong in it.” He cleared his tablet, and the car’s logo ghosted into existence on the clear glass. “Well?”

Angling her slim form, she smoothly got out before he had a coronary. Immediately the chaos of Detroit’s auto show beat anew upon her, the air smelling of ozone and popcorn, and the rhythmic thump of ambient electronic dance music from the live stage pounding into her. Content, she sent her gaze up to the multitude of cameras set to record and identify, secure in the knowledge that the swirls of black smut she’d painted on her face would keep her anonymous.

She wasn’t alone wearing it—face paint had become to Detroit’s auto show what big hats and mint juleps were to Churchill Downs. Both men and women sported well-placed dots and swirls to disguise themselves as they checked out the competition or just avoided being tagged and sent literature. As she was dressed in black leather pants and a cropped jacket with a silk shell and six-inch black boots, the paint made her feel especially flirty and powerful. Sexy.

She turned back to the coup, thinking it was cheating to show it in a paint job that you couldn't get from the factory. "How do you get around the weight issue of the batteries? You've got them in the front, but the drive tram is in the back. The weight isn't over the wheels, and it's going to turn as if it was on pudding."

His interest sharpened. "It's not an issue at posted speeds."

Peri nodded, and he winced as she ran a hand caressingly over the car's sleek lines—all the way from the front to the back. "Over posted speeds is when you need the control, though. Acceleration?"

"Zero to sixty in four-point-two seconds," he said, tapping his tablet awake.

"Battery only, or warming engine assist?" she asked, and he smiled as he brought up the literature. Ten steps away, a printer came alive with the stats.

"Engine assist. You can't break four seconds on just battery."

"A Mantis can."

The man looked up. "I mean a real car."

Peri eyed him from under a lowered brow. "You're saying a Mantis isn't a real car?"

"I mean," he tried again, flustered, "a car you can actually have. If you're looking for speed, have you considered—"

"Sorry. No thanks." Peri stepped out from under

the hot spotlights and into the milling crowd, snagging a tiny flute of champagne in passing. Her dress and attitude parted the way, and her warm feeling of satisfaction grew as the tingle of alcohol slipped into her. It was nice to know she still had the best. *Ahh, life is good.*

"Why do you tease them like that?" a voice said at her elbow, and she spun, hand fisted.

But the man had dropped back as if expecting it, mirth crinkling the corners of his brown eyes. The brief protest of the surrounding people subsided as they pushed past and around them—and were forgotten.

"Silas?" she questioned, her gaze flicking to the messenger drones at the ceiling, worried a high-Q might be hiding among them. Then her eyes dropped to his tall, body-building form. His cashmere coat across his wide shoulders made him even more bulky, but his waist was trim and his face clean-shaven. The white of salt from the street rimed his John Lobb shoes, and he grimaced when she noticed. "What are you doing here? How did you find me?" she said, shifting into the lee his body made when someone jostled her.

Taking her empty flute and setting it aside, he pointed to a nearby communal area set up with tall tables and rentable connections to get a message outside the no-Internet-zone needed for security. "I've never known you to miss the opening of the

Detroit auto show," he said as they walked. His low voice at her ear slipped through her like smoke, staining the folds of her mind and bringing a thousand unremembered moments with him to hover just beyond recollection. "I like your hair that length."

It was quieter among the tables, and Peri touched the tips of her jet-black hair just brushing her shoulders. She'd let it grow. No need to cut it. Slowly she levered herself up on one of the high stools. He'd been watching her. That was probably where her itchy feeling had been coming from, not that she'd had to close her store on a Monday to hit opening day.

The hot-spot connection found her phone and chimed for her attention, and she turned the rentable link facedown. Silas looked tired. There was a familiar pinch of worry in his eyes as he levered himself onto the seat across from her. He laced his thick hands together, setting them innocently on the table, but she could smell the hint of gunpowder on him; he'd been to the range recently. A black haze shadowed his jawline, and a memory surfaced of how it would feel if she ran her hand over it, delighting in the prickly sensation on her fingertips. Behind him, people in extravagant dress and having enough technology to run a small country mingled and played. She'd come to lose herself among them, to pretend that it was hers again for the day. She missed the feeling of being in control so surely that the rest of the world seemed a fantasy.

I shouldn't have come here. I made a mistake.

A misplaced anger seeped into her, pushing out the doubt. She'd made a place for herself, a new life, found a new security that didn't hinge on anyone but herself. "Are you alone? Is Allen with you? Damn it, you do realize you might have blown my cover?"

"It's nice to see you, too. Yes, I'm fine," Silas said dryly, and she slumped, looking past him and into the crowd for anyone watching without watching. Sighing, Silas scratched the side of his bent nose, his focus blurring as if remembering a past argument. "I might not have been the best agent, but I know better than to go to your coffee shop. As for Allen, I don't particularly care where he is. I've not been in contact with him since"—he hesitated, lip twitching—"you quit."

She had left, and he'd found her. *So not good.* "Stay away from my coffee shop." Heart pounding, she slid off the stool.

"Peri. Wait," he said, voice weary. "I only came to give you your book back," he said, reaching past his coat to put one of her journals on the table.

Her breath caught, and she stopped, recognizing the leather-bound tome. It had been painstakingly pieced back together, the damage pressed out as best as possible, but it was still obvious where the bullet had torn into it. Kind of like her life.

It was from her last year in Opti training, an entire twelve months of memories intentionally erased from her mind so she could successfully bring down the corrupt Opti from the inside. The United States' clandestine special ops program was gone, and the diary was her only link to why she had done it. Her pulse quickened at the answers that might lie in the pages. Why she hated blue sheets, why silver Mustangs made the scar on her pinky itch, why the scent of chocolate chip cookies left her melancholy. There were answers in the pages, guarded by demons she feared would tear apart what little self she'd managed to pull back. Her ignorance made her vulnerable, but it also made her safe.

Hand to her cold face, she backed up, her footing unsure on the thick carpet. "I'm not that person anymore," she whispered. Damn it, she was going to have to rabbit. If Silas had found her, anyone could.

"Peri."

He pulled her to a stop. Anyone else would have gotten her heel through his instep, but she hesitated, letting him draw her back. Breath held, she looked up at him, her soul crying out for what she'd left behind. She'd liked who she'd been, and the wrongness of that still woke her in the night when all was quiet. Silas had been a big part of that, not the worst, but a part nevertheless.

"I'm not asking you to return to the person you

were, just understand her," he said. "It's been almost a year. You have to stop hiding from this. You won't ever be free of it if you don't come to grips with what you've done, the good and bad."

"Is that your professional opinion, Doctor?" she said, yanking out of his grip. Her wrist stung, but she refused to look at it.

Silas's jaw clenched as unknown thoughts flitted behind his eyes. Her chin lifted, daring him, and with a frustrated grimace, he turned away. "Never mind. I made a mistake. I shouldn't have come. You take care of yourself, Peri."

"You, too," she said as he walked away, hunched and unseeing. His tall frame and wide shoulders were tight under his coat as he wove through the lights, bare skin, and beautiful people. With a feeling of having won, she watched the crowd take him, but it shifted to worry as her fingers traced over the book in indecision, until finally she picked it up.

A business card from the Georgia Aquarium slipped out, falling to the floor. It wasn't Silas's name on it, but he'd likely be using an alias. Next to it was a hand-printed phone number. She stared at the card for a moment before turning and walking away, leaving it to be lost in the clutter.

To know what she had done might destroy everything she had made for herself. It was easier to ignore it, keep pretending she was happy and hope the lure to return to the power and prestige would never be stronger than the loathing of what she'd turned herself into to get there.

But she wasn't sure she could do that anymore.

CHAPTER TWO

"Babe, why don't you wear that clingy black top anymore? I like how it makes your little breasts into gotta-have handfuls."

"Stop. Right there." Brow furrowed, Peri eyed Jack over the noisy *schuuuck* of the milk steamer as he sat before the coffee shop's cash register and worked a crossword puzzle on his tablet. Beyond him through the large windows, a January snow sifted down in a sedate hush, the unexpected pristine white beautiful until it hit the ground and was churned into a slushy brown by steady foot traffic and slow cars. She knew the top in question, and though she'd never wear it again, she couldn't throw it away. It was good for dinner out and breaking in all at the same time. Finding that combination was hard—even if it had been ages since she'd done either.

"That apron isn't hiding anything," Jack continued, clearly enjoying her irritation as she looked down at the cream-and-black cotton that said uniform. "You think these suits are here for your glass four-gen connection?"

"I said stop." She hadn't seen Jack in three weeks—not since some fool kid had tried to pull a stab-and-grab. She'd thought Jack might be gone for good. Yet there he sat at her counter, looking like sex incarnate, his expression earnest in question as his blue eyes watched her, half-lidded behind his tousleable blond hair. His stubble was thick—just the way she liked it—and she could imagine the whiff of electronics he so excelled in. My God, he'd been good. They both had been. *Maybe he's here because I saw Silas.*

That had been four days ago, but her diary—hidden among her cookbooks for the first three days—had kept him at the forefront of her thoughts until she'd given in to the nauseating will-I, won't-I and cracked the binding last night. That she'd found nothing in the first few pages but classes and grades had been both a shock and a relief. Just the briefest mention of Allen and Silas. Apparently Silas had been so stricken by his girlfriend's death that he hadn't seen her as anything other than a chair that wasn't empty. It was obvious her naive self had been honored to have been chosen to help rout out the corruption in Opti, perhaps a little egotistical even. But most special ops agents were. They had to be to survive.

Embarassed by her past gullibility, she took the to-go cup, sashaying around Jack to pluck a sheet from the store's printer in passing. "Leave," she muttered as she headed to a window table.

Did someone make a pass at me and I didn't notice? she wondered, her fingers rising to touch her felt-pen pendant as if it were a security doll. The one time that had happened, she'd nearly broken the man's wrist, catching herself before causing permanent damage; the man's lawyers made more than he did, which was saying a lot. Hand clenched around the pendant, she went over the last few hours. They were all accounted for. Every last second. *Why is Jack here?*

Chuckling, Jack returned to his crosswords, ignored by the impeccably dressed business clientele scattered about the upscale coffeehouse.

Peri had worked hard to divorce herself from her past, and yet she still found herself breathing in the expensive cologne of the suits she served as if it were a drug. She eyed their leather briefcases and high-end purses, knowing their cars were as shiny as the fob resting beside their state-of-the-art phones and tablets, all so new they smelled of factory. She knew the simplicity she'd built around herself was a lie as she lured in everything she missed, all the while pretending she'd made a clean break from what she didn't want to be, what she couldn't be. Even so, she'd been able to ignore it until Silas had shown up.

I'm sick, she thought as she stopped before a thin man in a suit. "Headed out, Simon?" Peri asked, and he glanced up from his tablet, startled. It was hard to tell by looking, but he was worth between eight and ten million depending on the day. She'd done a search on him the first time he'd come in, worried he might be someone he wasn't. "How about a refill?"

The early-forties man waved closed the weather map on his tablet, his brow still holding his worry for the coming snow. "Yes, thanks, Peri. You know me better than my wife."

She set the cup beside the rental-car fob, her focus blurring when his faint Asian accent brought a flash of memory of hot sun and smelly river. Bringing herself back with a jerk, she glanced at Jack. He'd been there. She was sure of it. Even if she didn't remember it. "That's because I see you more than she does. Going home this weekend?"

The man blinked as he rolled his tablet into a tube and tucked it in a front pocket. "How did you know?"

Smiling, she handed him his ticket from the printer, and he laughed. "I almost forgot that. Your phone dies one time at the terminal and you never trust it again. Thanks. I'll see you on Monday." But she'd known he was leaving before the printer had come alive. His socks were the same he'd worn yesterday, his hotel card wasn't in his phone case when he'd paid, and his hat was in his satchel, not sitting on the nearby chair with his coat like it had been every other morning.

The scent of his cologne rose as he began to gather his things. A longing—an ache almost—filled her, and she reached for his coat, the lapels still damp from the snow. Anyone watching would assume she was angling for a bigger tip as she held it for him and slipped it over his shoulders, but her eyes closed as she breathed in the smell of linen, stifling a shiver at the sound of it brushing against silk and the clicks of his weather-inappropriate dress shoes on the worn oak floor. She was a God-blessed junkie, and she took sips of her poison where she could. *First class from Detroit to New York will have breakfast.*

"See you next week," Simon said, saluting her with his coffee and heading for the door.

"Watch yourself out there. It's a jungle," she said in farewell, but he was gone, the door chimes jiggling behind him. In an instant he was lost in the snow-slow maze of cars and foot traffic. She smiled at the big-engine cars pushing their way through the snow. The electric vehicles Detroit was known for tended to vanish in winter, replaced by the beefier combustion engines she'd grown up with until the temps pulled out of the negatives. Seeing them on the road, getting the job done, made her feel connected, home.

An emergency vehicle went past, lights flashing but siren off, and she felt her past creep up behind her.

“He’s not your type,” Jack said, standing too close to be ignored.

Peeved, she turned and walked through him, muttering, “How would you know?”

She shuddered as she passed through the hallucination, the structured mental scaffold designed and implanted to keep her from going insane when two conflicting timelines had been left to fester in her mind. Whether Silas’s fix-on-the-fly had worked was debatable. After all, she *was* hallucinating. That the illusion was familiar was beside the point. That it took the form of her old partner, the one she’d put in jail for corruption before she went ghost, was a bad joke.

Illusion Jack had been present on and off for almost a year, the hallucination so complex and intricately tied to her intuition that it had developed a weird, independent intelligence of sorts, causing him to show up when she was stressed and searching for answers.

And it bugs the hell out of me he’s right most of the time, she thought, her motions abrupt as she rinsed the few pastry dishes before piling them in the bin to return to the restaurant next door. It wasn’t Simon she was lusting for. It was the scent of untried electronics, the whiff of exclusive perfume, the confidence a big bank account and a golden parachute bought. God help her, but she missed it.

Jack slipped up behind her, breathing in her ear

to make the lingering scent from Simon and the sight of his and her hands together in the soapy bubbles bring back an unexpected memory. It was night; she had been feeling good. Jack had been especially clever. There'd been danger . . . soap on her fingers, a fast car, pulled shoulder, an adrenaline-fueled smile on Jack's face, a folded printout in his hand—it was what they'd come for. She hadn't cared what or why, only that they'd done something insanely cunning to get it.

Pulse fast, she rubbed the white porcelain with a cold rag as if she could wipe the images away. She'd made a memory knot of that to survive when everything else was gone. Why?

"Because you loved me," Jack whispered. "And you don't want to forget it. Ever. It's what you are. Stop trying to be this small thing. We were unstoppable. Tell me it wasn't good."

She couldn't say that, even to herself. Lips in a thin line, she rinsed her hands, wishing the guilt would sluice away with the cold. Jack was a crutch: the planner, her security net, a link to a life she wasn't going to live again. She wouldn't be the person she was good at being. The power and charisma were toxic. The status had been an illusion. Her life had been a lie, and it was too easy to use her and give her a shake to erase it all like a living Etch A Sketch.

Peri snapped a clean towel from the rack, and Jack dropped back to recline against the register.

His face was suddenly clean-shaven now, and he was wearing something trendy and expensive that showed off his narrow waist. “Go away,” she muttered, glancing over the coffeehouse as rush-hour traffic began luring her clientele into the slushy streets. “No one needs you anymore.”

“You need me.” Jack followed her gaze to the buses and taxis. “Or I wouldn’t be here. Something is wrong, you just don’t know what yet.”

Carnac, the store’s cat, jumped onto the counter, and Peri absently fondled his ears as she sourly remembered her enthusiasm from her diary’s pages, eager for the chance to prove herself and use her skills to do something no one had done before. She had changed so much that it was like reading someone else’s thoughts.

“You look sexy when you bite your lower lip, you know that?”

Peri’s brow furrowed. “Go. Away.”

Jack blew her a kiss. “You don’t really want me to leave, or I’d be gone already. I’m bringing everything back, babe. So slow it hurts. You want to remember. It’s who you are, who you have to be. This?” He flicked a coffee mug. “This will kill you.”

She knew her face still held her anger when the door chimed a greeting and her attention went over Jack’s shoulder. Breath held, she turned away. *Allen. Effin’ fantabulous. That’s why Jack is here.*

Sighing, Jack pulled himself straight and turned to the door. "Son of a bitch. Just once I'd like to warn you that you're in real danger, not that one of your old boyfriends is back."

"Allen was never my boyfriend." She was talking to herself, but she couldn't stop.

"Whatever."

Jack was gone when she looked up, and Allen had taken a seat at one of the window booths, the snow still on his shoulders. His back was to her to give her the illusion of control, but his neck showing from under his short haircut gave away his tension. She must have seen his silhouette or the car he drove earlier. And Jack, her intuition made real, had come to warn her. *Thanks a hell of a lot, Silas.* But it was unlikely Silas would have told Allen where she was.

Carnac stared at at the man, tail switching. He'd never liked Allen. Hands steady, she poured a cup of coffee, putting it in a to-go cup because Allen *wasn't* staying. Light brew: the man was a wuss when it came to coffee. Damn it, if he was trailing trouble, she was going to be pissed.

"I should have opened a flower shop," she muttered, weaving through the tables.

Her breath came in fast when a young woman suddenly stood, knocking the coffee. Both of them gasped, Peri from the surprise, the woman from twelve ounces of hot coffee down her pristine white blouse.

At the woman's flash of pain and shock, instinct kicked in.

The world blinked a sharp-edged blue, and suddenly Peri was three steps back, the woman still sitting as she leaned to get her rolling pen, accidently pushing it just out of her reach. Breathing the blue sparkles of hindsight deep into her lungs, Peri held the unspilled coffee tight to her chest, stepping on the pen to stop it, then giving it a little nudge to roll back to the woman's reach before she could stand.

"Thanks!" the woman said. Her relief was a little too much for the small courtesy, and Peri's intuition pinged. But then the world flashed red as time caught up—and she forgot.

Peri blinked, finding herself standing before a woman smiling up at her. She had Allen's coffee pressed against her chest—and no clue why she'd stopped. "Ah, all set?" she asked, scrambling. She'd drafted and rewrote the last three seconds, maybe four, losing them. Why?

"Yes, thank you," the woman said, holding her pen up as if it meant something.

From behind the register, Jack put a hand to his forehead, dramatically wailing, "Oh, you spilled coffee all down your front and spotted my brand-new pumps! You *stupid* coffee girl!"

Half-understanding filled her, and Peri frowned. Great. Allen shows up, and she drafts. He would have seen it, being an anchor and trained to not only remember but bring the rewritten timeline back into her memory as well. Resolute, she crossed the floor as the woman put on her coat and left. Jack didn't know anything she didn't, but he—or Peri, rather—was getting good at piecing things together from the smallest of clues.

Silent, she stood across from Allen and set the cup down hard enough to spill. His brown eyes held nothing as he looked from the CNN broadcast at the ceiling to wipe the puddle away, his thin hands knobby from being broken and made strong in hand-to-hand. He was in a suit, but he wore it uncomfortably, as if he'd rather be in a BMX racing kit or a harness to climb a rock or jump out of a plane. His dress shoes were soaked and salt-rimed . . . and he smelled fantastic.

Hand passing once over his snow-damp black hair, he leaned back to look her up and down, no smile on his narrow, long face. "You do know you just drafted?"

She hated looking ignorant. "I didn't want coffee down my front."

A smile threatened. "It was her front, but close." Concern pushed out his hint of pride in her. "Are you okay? How many unfragmented drafts do you have making holes in your brain?"

How about I use a bullet to make a hole in yours?

Her shop was emptying as it grew closer to nine, most of the patrons using the at-table option to settle up using phone cash, the p-cash app made for their high-tech glass devices both easy and secure. He'd timed it perfectly. "How did you find me?"

He lifted a shoulder and let it fall. "Process of elimination. I know Detroit is your city and you're sitting over an old medical dump."

I should have stuck with sipping the barium syrup, she thought, but at least she knew the residual contamination from the illegal dump had covered the radiation marker Opti had given her. Her year would be over come June, and then she'd truly be free.

"I'm not looking right now to hire help to wash dishes," she said loudly, ticked he might have blown her cover. "Thanks for stopping in. Have a nice day."

He grabbed her sleeve as she turned, and she stifled the urge to palm-break his nose. She'd only end up drafting to fix it. She'd always been a softie like that.

"Jack is missing," he said.

Peri reached for the table, slowly sitting as vertigo threatened. Missing? The real Jack, not the hallucination based on him. Possibilities she'd denied pushed to the forefront, and she shoved them back down. "H-how long?" she stammered, putting a cold hand to her warm face.

"Two days. He was recently moved to a government facility and was boosted in transit."

"Bill?" she said, but her mind was on Jack, not their handler. The bear of a man had vanished cleanly when Opti fell apart. *Damn it. Damn it all to hell.* She'd said no. Why did she have to keep saying it?

"That's my guess." Allen's hands were in his coat pockets. He was waiting, just waiting. "I could use some help cleaning this up."

"Not my problem." Emotion pushed her to her feet, panic not because Jack was free, but because a tiny glowing spot of want had fanned to life, faint from having been denied, but growing stronger.

"You've been marked," he said, stopping her again. "You aren't safe anymore. The alliance is gone, but I've been working with the government to try to bring Bill in. If we can—"

She put a gentle hand on his shoulder that was all threat. "I don't do that anymore."

Unwilling to be bullied, he pushed her hand off. "You have skills no one else does."

"Go find another one. The psych wards are full of us," she said bitterly. The few remaining patrons were leaving fast, girding themselves against the snow and finding the door as traffic thickened. "I'm not going to work for the government, not even to tuck the bad back into hiding." She was flushed, hating it.

"Bill wants you," he said. "That's why he boosted Jack. He wants you, and he's not afraid to send a drafter to bring you in."

Fear slid through her, and her focus sharpened on Allen's worry. You never sent a drafter after another drafter. The risk was too great that one of them would end up dead, and they were too rare to waste like that.

"You ever hear of Michael? Michael Kord," Allen asked. "He was a rising drafter when you were in Opti. Here, I've got a picture of him."

The name was familiar, and curiosity drew her eyes down. "I remember this guy," Allen said as she scanned the grainy surveillance photo of a tall, clean-shaven man with short black hair. It had been taken in Detroit; she could see the elevated rail in the background. "Bill was grooming him to take your place. Encouraging all sorts of interesting behavior."

Peri's brow furrowed, a slim finger hovering over the photo as a memory tickled the top of her head. *Something about birds . . .*

"Bill is a manipulative bastard," Allen said, still looking at the photo. "But he doesn't discard someone who might make him money someday."

Like me, she thought, shaken. "I remember him," she whispered, the photo bringing her thoughts into focus. He was a dark man, thin but not gaunt. Attractive. Hispanic? He liked his sunglasses and his car. *Birds.* The single memory she had of him was of him drafting to kill the pigeons who'd spotted his ride.

"You remember Michael?" It was a shocked utterance. "That was in the year I erased. Do you remember . . ."

Her gaze lifted from the photo. "Anything about you?" she asked dryly. "No. I didn't make any memory knots of you." She backed up, not knowing what to do with her hands. Michael must have really pissed her off for her to have made a memory knot that would survive a wipe. "You want anything else? I like to mop before the lunch crowd comes in."

"Memory knots?" he questioned. "Jeez, Peri, you know better than to play with those."

He needed to leave. She could be out of here in forty-five seconds if she had to, but a more gracious exit—one with the money to move fast—required some privacy. "That will be fifteen-eighty for the coffee," she said, hip cocked.

Allen's lips parted. "Are you kidding?" he said loudly, and the last patron gathering his things snorted. It was Cam—Scottish descent but all American, ruggedly beautiful and with a sharp mind and enough personal charisma to draw her. He was heading for the register, unusual for the tech-loving man. For some reason, he didn't like using his p-cash app to pay at the tables anymore, but maybe that was her fault.

Hand on her hip, Peri pointed to the very

obvious sign over the register. Everything was fifteen-eighty: every size, every variety, every day. No refills unless she felt like it. She was a lousy bookkeeper, and this made it easy as well as keeping the place smelling of money. "You're not buying a cup of coffee, sir," she said mockingly. "You're buying a secure place to check your email in a pleasant setting." And it was secure. She made sure of it every day.

"I bet you still take cash, don't you?" he said as he reached for his wallet. "Good God, I'm in the wrong business."

"Then why do you keep trying to get me to come back to yours?" she said pointedly. "I'll get you your change." Taking the proffered bill, she strode to the register.

Flustered, she barely acknowledged Cam when he slid his own twenty across the stainless steel counter and she absently made change. "Thank you," she said when he dumped it all in the tip jar. "Do you want one to go?"

"Peri, is everything okay?"

She looked up, truly shocked at the concern in his melodious voice. Following his nod to Allen, she slumped. "Oh. Yes. He's an old business associate trying to lure me back. He gets under my skin is all."

Cam's eyebrows rose. "Oh!"

Oh? Head tilted, Peri eyed him. "Oh, what?"

The young stock market analyst smiled faintly,

too confident to be embarrassed, but close. "I thought he was an old boyfriend you might need help encouraging to leave. I still could help—if you want."

A smile, real and grateful, spread across her face. The kindness felt anything but small. "Thank you," she said, touching his hand so he'd believe her. "I'll be fine. It's just business."

He frowned, clearly not convinced. "I'll call you later."

She shut the register, Allen's change in her grip. "You don't have my number."

Cam's expression became crafty. "I would if you'd give it to me."

At that she laughed, the clear, unusual sound bringing Allen's head up in surprise. "Out. Go make money. But thank you. You totally just made my day."

He sighed in playful regret, giving Allen a sharp look as he headed into the snow. Slowly Peri's smile faded. Change in hand, she crossed to Allen and dropped it on the table. "Have a nice day. Bye-bye now."

"Who was that?"

She watched Cam cross the street and hail a cab, its solar-gathering paint white to indicate it was available. Even as she watched, it shifted to black as he slipped in and was gone. All Detroit cabs had the controversial paint job, illegal outside of the city but standard on her first-year Mantis.

Detroit did what it wanted. "I stole his car once. He's no one."

"You *stole* his car?"

"Yeah, but he never found out because I put it right back." Seeing Allen waiting, she added, "His p-cash PIN is the same as his door lock. It was an Audi. This year's. I borrowed the fob and drove it around the block while he drank his coffee and watched his CNN. No harm, no foul." God, it was nice. Not as nice as her Mantis, but nice.

Allen rose, his lanky athleticism looking disheveled after Cam's precise business attire. "Why didn't you try one at the dealership?" he asked as he stacked the coins atop the paper bills.

"Because they check your name against your address, and if I'd given them my real one, they would've sent me literature."

"Peri, why won't you help me?" he asked suddenly, and her tension slammed into her. "You're good at this. We need you, if for nothing else than tucking Michael away. No one but you has even a chance at it."

"No thanks." She went behind the counter, finding strength there.

"Peri Reed!" Allen exclaimed, clearly frustrated. "You tell me why you won't come back, and I'll leave forever. The truth."

"The truth?" she echoed, not sure her soul could handle any more truth. "It's too easy to use me," she added, backing up a step, arms over her middle. "Why do you think I'm hiding over a medical dump? Jesus, Allen. I trust Bill more than some new governmental task force. With Bill, I know it would be all about the profit, sent to assassinate some poor schmuck who invented a new way to make electricity so Bill could sell it to the highest bidder. At least Bill would make me think I'd offed a drug dealer. If I go back to work for the government, even for one job, they will wipe me back to my sixteenth birthday and fill my head with whatever past they want. Either that, or they'll tuck me away in a cell until they need me again."

"I wouldn't let them do that to you," he said, sounding insulted, but the fear was too real, tingling in her fingertips. Behind him, rush-hour traffic started and stopped, awkward from the rising snow. *No wonder Cam had taken a cab today.*

Peri reached for a dishcloth, agitated. "Don't take it personal. I don't trust anyone. This is not my fight, and I'm not going to draw attention to myself. As long as I don't play the game, I'm not a threat. Everyone leaves me alone. Right?" Which was debatable, but she was going to stick with it—at least until Bill showed up, a smiling, flirting Jack in tow. But she'd be long gone by then.

Her attempt at pretending she was normal had failed. Normal people didn't worry about chunks of time being destroyed and replaced by false truths—manipulative and damaging truths.

"You're afraid?" he needled, and her face warmed.

"Maybe I just don't care."

Allen's eyes narrowed. "Fine. You can keep the change," he said tightly, pace stiff as he strode to the door, yanked it open, and vanished into the busy street.

Her shoulders slumped as she listened to the door chimes clink and the secondary alarm system click on in the silence. "I generally do," she said. She didn't mind lying to Allen; the guilt was because she was lying to herself.

It wasn't that she didn't care. She did. But she couldn't risk going back. The lure was too much, the fear too real. She teased herself with the power she'd once had, existing on the fringes, hoping that with little shots of it she might build up her resistance—all the while knowing it was a lie, that the ache would never go away, waking her in the small hours when only Carnac lay purring to distract her.

The truth was she'd liked working for Opti. She needed the thrill of lives being in the balance of her skills and chance; lived for the fast cars, sexy clothes, rigorous training that pushed her to her limits, and the smart man at her elbow. She liked it so much that for three years she ignored the signs that she was someone else's weapon until it was rubbed in her face—and as much as she hated it, she still mourned the loss of everything she had once had.

She had become a part of the corruption at Opti without even realizing it. Because of her, people had died—they died so someone she'd never met would have a fraction better profit, or buy an election, or bring virus-carried death to a region another country wanted to exploit.

And even knowing all of that, even steeled against it, she didn't know whether she could resist the choice if it was put to her again, the risk of being manipulated into something foul aside.

CHAPTER THREE

"He should be out by now," Latisha grumbled as she looked up from her rifle's scope, adjusting the night vision before returning to squint at the coffee shop. "If he stays too long, she's going to spook and run."

"My princess of paranoia is already running," Bill said, the faint accent he cultivated to give himself more class at odds with the old van, and Jen, almost unseen in the back doing her drug calculations, nodded in agreement. Her long blond hair was almost white where the glow of the tablet caught it, and her face even paler.

"It's like a fortress in there," Jen said, the young psychologist and low-level anchor still in the dress suit she'd been wearing when he'd sent her in to evaluate Peri's state of mind and get a weight estimate. "The glass is bullet resistant. The doors are reinforced. There might be a way in through the upper apartment. It must have cost a fortune. What is she so scared of?"

"Herself." Bill fiddled with his ring, the heavy metal sporting a raised Opti logo. Jen thought about that for a moment, then went back to her calculations. Realizing the ring had turned into a nervous tic, Bill laced his hands and looked across the dark, slushy street. Three blocks over, the street zoned to service the surrounding business area was alive with jazz and late dining, but here it was still. Peri would use the front door. She was too intuitive to not know they might be there, too proud to not face them head-on.

A hum pulled his attention up, the streetlight catching a glint of shiny plastic. Bill reached for the radio. "I said all drones on the ground. Minimal presence. Minimal!"

"It's not ours," an anonymous voice came back, and Bill frowned at the carrier logo.

"She doesn't know that," he growled. "It's after sunset. Bring it down."

"Yes, sir."

"For Christ's sake, Bill. I'm not done yet," Jen complained, and Latisha grinned, gum snapping as the blond woman hustled to finish her calculations. Bill leaned forward, watching the black silhouette against the lighter darkness, satisfied when an almost subliminal pulse flickered over the van's electronics and the drone dropped like a rock. From the back, Jen sighed, her motions slow as she restarted her tablet and began her calculations again, the tactical EMP flick having taken out her glass-based technology as well.

A high-Q drone wouldn't have gone down, and satisfied it was a carrier—illegal on the streets after dark—and not local security disguised as one, Bill settled back into the seat. His three-piece suit kept him from feeling the cold coming in Latisha's open window, but he leaned to turn the van's heat warmer when Jen pulled her light jacket tighter about herself. Her silk blouse was untucked, and a thin strip had been ripped from the bottom, now fixed and fluttering from one of the nearby trees to give Latisha an indication of the wind.

Sending a drafter to down another drafter was chancy, but this, too, was an evaluation. Latisha would dart Peri when Bill had the proof to back up what he already knew: Peri was the more effective agent despite Michael's considerable drive and skill. The antidrafting portion of the drug would take effect immediately, but the sedative needed time to work. Michael would keep her occupied until it did.

Uncomfortable, Bill shifted his bulk. The seat was too small for him and his lip curled at the ugly vinyl. He'd be concerned if he wasn't already confident of the outcome. Peri was a bitch and difficult to work with, but Michael still had his own agenda, not yet tempered or tamed. Even with the safeguards that Opti's chemists had built into their latest miracle—currently sitting in Jen's med pack—he didn't trust Michael with it. Bill knew how to manipulate Peri—hell, he'd given her most of her hangups and coping techniques. Michael . . . not so much.

"Thank you," Jen said, having noticed the new warmth, and Latisha frowned, anxious for her ammo. It was late, and the cold wind funneled between the buildings kept the dog walker's head down and his pace fast. The coffee shop was empty but for Peri and Ron. A thrill spilled through him. Waiting was the second-best part. Seeing Peri's face when she realized she was in his stable again would be the first. No one left him. Ever. She'd thank him someday.

"Ron is out," Latisha said softly, her low voice filling the van. Her rifle was cradled in her thin hands, scarred thumb caressing it through the holes in her gloves. "Jen, I need those darts."

"Hang on," she said tersely. "I'm guessing at how much adrenaline will dilute it, and it's not exact. I'll make up a half-dose dart to follow it with in case the first isn't enough, all right?"

"Holy shit," Latisha swore, jerking Bill's attention up. "Look at the size of that coffee."

Vinyl creaked as Bill leaned forward, his eyebrows rising when he spotted the dark shadow picking his way down the walk to where Michael waited. It was a venti, and if the man couldn't hold his bladder the next half hour, Bill would shoot Ron himself.

Jen pushed forward between him and Latisha, her light perfume spilling over him. "Are you kidding?" she whispered, her shirt hanging open. "He can't possibly handle all that."

"Can't blame a person for trying," Latisha said, smiling wickedly as her gaze rose from behind Jen's shirt.

Bill's breath hesitated as his thoughts realigned and the question of why the onetime Olympic sharpshooter would never agree to drinks with him was answered. Then he smiled back. It was hard to find fault with someone who liked the same things he did.

His expression slowly relaxed when he realized Ron was coming their way. Fingers made thick from hand-to-hand, he reached for the radio. "Michael? Talk to me."

The circuit popped open. "The useless son of a bitch used his phone to pay for it," Michael said, his anger obvious. "You take him. He's yours. I'm doing this alone."

"He used his phone?" Jen exclaimed, and

Latisha leaned to open the side door as Ron approached. "You can't muddle p-cash."

"Maybe if you wouldn't keep insulting my best anchors, you'd have a good one!" Bill barked, then caught his temper. Rubbing his forehead, Bill searched for strength. Drafters were prima donnas. They tended to shut down if you yelled at them.

Cold air shifted his short hair as Ron lurched in, the electronics-laden van barely rocking. "You used p-cash?" Jen demanded, and the man hesitated, eyes wide in alarm.

"It's fifteen dollars a cup! No one told me to carry that much cash."

Bill's shoulders tensed. Ron was Michael's third anchor in two months. He'd known he wouldn't last long since Michael preferred his anchors curvaceous and willing to extend their working relationship to the bedroom, but he'd been hoping to get at least one task out of him.

"This is intolerable," Michael said coldly over the radio, unaware or, more likely, not caring that Ron might hear. "I'm beginning to wonder if you secretly want her to escape, Bill."

Peeved, Bill thumbed the connection closed. Everyone on-site was at least a low-level anchor. Calling it off wasn't an option. Helen was getting impatient for a live trial.

Aghast, Jen smacked Ron's shoulder. "You idiot."

"It doesn't matter," Ron cajoled, his ears reddening as he hunched, his head inches from the ceiling. "She's running. She may look like she's closing up for the night, but there's a cat carrier behind the counter and the printer is unplugged." Knowing he'd made a mistake, he extended the huge coffee to Bill. "It's really good."

Latisha chuckled. "For fifteen dollars, it had better have my aunt's *special* water in it."

"And it's possibly drugged," Bill said sourly. "Ron, you just bought yourself a permanent desk. Peri won't look up the number, but the authorities investigating her abduction will."

"But," the man fumbled, face darkening in the dim van. His expression abruptly shifted when he figured it out. "Ah, shit." Falling back into the long bench seat, he stared at the silent equipment, disgusted. "I could go back in and dart her while her back is turned," he said, knowing this was the last time he'd ever see the field.

Latisha chuckled, thanking Jen when she handed her the darts. Bill was tempted to let the idiot do just that. "What a capital idea," he said as he watched Peri at the register. She looked smaller than he recalled. "You don't think she has a handgun? She can shoot first, ask questions, and draft later to fix a mistake."

Ron shrank down, embarrassed.

"You're right that she's coming out," Bill added, his tone distracted. "If our own beloved Allen

Swift was there this afternoon, she knows her anonymity is blown and is running."

Jen threw her long-empty cup into the trash, clearly wishing she could chance Ron's abandoned venti. "It was Swift. How do you think I found her? She's sitting on a medical dump to hide the tracker you gave her."

A real smile lifted through him as he recalled Peri's bullheaded bravery when she chose to be chemically tagged for the chance to blow Opti all to hell, but it soured fast. Seeing her emptying the trash and washing other men's dishes didn't give him the satisfaction he'd been hoping for. As much as a pain in the ass as she was, she was better than this. It'd feel good to have her back. Anchors were expendable, but he did try to make lasting relationships with his drafters. Usually.

Peeved, he thumbed the circuit open. "Michael. Your call."

"I can down her alone" came back immediately.

Bill seriously doubted it, and he wondered who would draft first: Michael, who drafted only as a last resort due to a mistrust of the anchor who would bring his memory back, or Peri, who had none and would suffer permanent memory loss. "Okay, we're a go," he said, and he could almost feel the tension rise as small pockets of his people readied themselves for 125 pounds of unforgiving quick fists possibly coming their way.

Latisha was humming a creepy southern lullaby

to her rifle as Peri turned the "Open" sign around and pulled the shade on the thick glass door. Her humming ceased. "Cat carrier is on the counter," she said softly, her words jerking through Bill. "Big purse next to it. Here we go."

"Ready, Jen?" Bill asked, and the woman muttered she was, restraining harness jingling as she checked it. Bill leaned forward. He wanted to get out so he could see better, but contented himself with a pair of night goggles, adjusting the contrast until they could handle the overhead light bathing everything in a goggle gray-green. She'd fight until she downed Michael or was bested, and if that happened, she'd draft and run. If Latisha missed, they'd have to track her down like a rabbit.

"What if she goes out the back?" Ron asked.

Bill's nose wrinkled at the stink of the man's sweat. "She has too much pride to retreat," he said as Peri turned off the lights before picking up her purse and cat carrier and heading for the door. His anticipation quickened. The best prey were those who were hunters, and Peri was a savage when cornered.

Latisha steadied her rifle, tracking Peri, though she wouldn't shoot until Bill told her. Bill held his breath as the faint tinkling of the door chimes sounded. Large purse over her shoulder, Peri set the cat carrier down on the piled snow to lock the door.

"I love this part," Jen whispered as Peri bent to pick the carrier back up, and a flash of desire, misplaced but potent, snarled like knots through Bill. He'd been a field agent once—that's how he knew Peri wanted to come back. She couldn't stay away any more than he could.

"There's my girl," Latisha said, then jerked her finger away when Peri abruptly threw the cat carrier into the shadows, grunting in the effort.

"Son of a bitch!" Michael shouted, falling into the manicured bushes with the carrier on his chest. The sound of breaking dishes came loud through Michael's live mic, a sliding crash as he shoved the heavy, dish-laden carrier off him and got up.

Bill's breath came fast and held. His grip on the goggles tightened when Peri jumped at Michael, her slim fingers reaching for her boot knife even as she landed on him, pinning him to the icy walk. "Where is he? Right now!" she shouted, so loud that he could hear it before Michael's open mic could bring it to him.

"Son of a—"

She flicked the knife, nicking the skin under his eye and then shifting it to his throat to keep him unmoving. Bill smiled, proud of her when her expression changed in recognition. "You're Michael," she said, the words out of synch with her lips. "Who's with you? Bill?"

Pressed into Bill's back, Jen made a soft noise of

disappointment. “I would’ve thought he’d have lasted at least a punch or two.”

Bill lowered the goggles. “Michael knows her idiosyncrasy about only killing people who kill her first. It will get interesting now.”

Michael was laughing, thinking her self-imposed rule a weakness. The derision would only make Peri that much more determined. “Peri Reed,” he mocked. “You changed your hair.”

“There she goes!” Jen exclaimed as Peri lurched off Michael to flee, and Bill put a hand on Latisha’s arm to stop her.

“Wait,” he whispered as Michael scrambled after her. Still on the ground, he caught Peri’s ankle and gave a yank. Peri turned even as she fell, her first kick missing. Michael still had her foot, though, and she used it to drag herself closer before he could break it, nailing him right in the chest with a boot heel.

Swearing, Michael let go. His foot flashed out, knocking her Glock into the road, where it skittered into the far gutter. Angry, he was on her in half a second, flinging her knife away and pinning her to the sidewalk. “Little soldier girl, playing army,” the man said.

Bill’s lips turned down in disappointment, but with a curious flip of vertigo, the world flashed blue and he was back a second in time, watching Peri roll away instead of reach for her knife. An instant of red coated his vision, and time meshed.

“Did you see that?” Jen exclaimed, her perfume strong as she leaned between them for a better look. “She hop-skipped to keep her knife!”

“Don’t shoot her!” Bill exclaimed when Latisha readied her rifle. Eyes glued to the pair, he watched Peri score on Michael before the man backed off, reassessing the threat and the bloody line she’d scratched into him in warning. Peri was darting glances into the night, looking for them, knowing Michael wouldn’t be here alone.

“I thought you said whoever resorted to drafting first was the poorer agent,” Jen said, and he waved his hand impatiently for her to shut up so he could hear them.

“That hop-skip was tactical, not escape based.”

Peri and Michael were circling, making Bill breathless. Watching her work had always been a pleasure. “You walk away. I walk away,” Peri said, voice small through Michael’s mic. “No one dies.”

Michael was grinning, an almost childlike anticipation on him as he misjudged his own worth. He wouldn’t understand until he was choking on his own blood, laughing probably, at the rare occurrence of being wrong, his ego greater than his true capabilities. But as Michael was truly gifted, he could be excused. Bill never should have brought him into the program, but drafters were so rare, even a psychotic one was useful.

“Right,” Michael said, giving away his intention a fateful second before attacking.

She was ready, blocking his front kick with her palm, blocking his straight punch with her scarf, then using it to tangle his next spin kick and yank him off balance. Pride warmed Bill. She was keeping her distance as she looked for another way out. She didn’t like to kill, avoided it when she could, called it a failure when she was forced to.

Still tangled, she gave him a shove and he fell on the ice, not rolling fast enough to entirely evade her jab to his thorax. It caught him on his cheek, and she spun to her feet before he could get a grip on her.

Michael had stopped laughing. His expression was ugly as he rose and felt his bruised face. Disappointment filled Bill, and he watched now only to see how she would bring him down. “Offer is still open,” Peri said even as she looked into the sharp black-and-white of a snowy night for the best way out.

“Michael, get back so we can dart her,” Bill said into the radio, not surprised when the man launched himself at her in a silent rage.

Like the artist she was, Peri pivoted, smacking the back of his knee in passing. Michael’s leg crumpled, and she caught his arm, jumping two seconds back when he got a grip on her.

Bill watched in a blue-sheened world as again

she kicked his knee, this time shoving him into the lamppost. Time caught up, flashed red, and Michael hit the post with a dull *thwap.*

Stunned, Michael reeled, trying to stay upright. "You little bitch!" he shouted, and she straight-kicked him back to hit it again.

"Oooh, twice in a *row,*" Jen said in admiration.

Latisha watched, her finger far from the trigger. "Did she do what I think she did?"

Bill nodded. "The hop-skips?" he asked. "Yes. They both know they're happening until after they're done, and then they forget."

"How can she not know?" Latisha asked in awe. "It's beautiful!"

"It is, isn't it." He was watching through the goggles, slightly queasy at the tiny shifts in time. "It's hard to notice little jumps in the heat of it all."

And yet she kept doing it, making Michael more and more incensed as she chipped away at him. Bill knew he should stop it, but he didn't, wondering whether Peri was enjoying the chance to use her skills as much as he was enjoying watching her work. He jerked, thinking it might be the end when she got a foot between his and she yanked him down. He'd seen that look in her before, and he could hardly breathe as they fell together, Peri following him into the street.

Michael was after her dropped knife, but she reached it first, eyes alight as she threw it at him even as she rose. Michael didn't even notice it lodging under his knee, and motions graceful, she jumped at him, her foot landing squarely atop the hilt, jamming it deeper.

That he felt, and she fell to the salt-wet pavement as Michael gasped. Jen cried out a warning when he kicked at her like a playground bully. She rolled, jumping back half a second to roll sooner so he'd miss. In a silent rage, he followed her, but she'd found the broken dishes, and she raked a shard across his face when he got too close.

"My God. She's cutting him to shreds!" Jen said.

It was over. "I'm calling it," Bill said tightly, his pride in Peri eclipsed at the embarrassment that he had ever thought Michael might have had a chance. He was good, but Peri was the queen of last chances.

"You want me to dart her?" Latisha said, eyes wide. "He's out of control."

Grim, Bill shook his head. "Shoot him first."

Jen scrambled for the back to make another dart for Peri, but Bill knew there was no time, and the half-dose dart Latisha had wouldn't be enough even in the best of situations.

Motion fast, Latisha sighted down the scope. "This isn't going to drop him." Three heartbeats later, the puff of air shocked through Bill. Michael bellowed, furious as he pulled the dart out. Peri's head came up. She was going to run. She had to.

Bill thumbed the radio on. "All backup," he said calmly. "Bring her in."

"You son of a bitch!" Michael exclaimed, and Peri leapt for the darkness. Four men were tight behind her. "She's mine. Mine!" Michael shouted. He was beginning to stagger, but he swung at the man trying to drag him away, and they both sprawled into the slushy gutter.

It was three to Peri's one now, and as Latisha looked for an opening, Peri sent the most eager back with a front kick, spinning to hit the second with a crescent kick. He stumbled, going down, but the first had recovered and grabbed her about the waist from behind.

"That was dumb," Latisha said as Peri broke her attacker's nose with her head, then probably a rib when she threw him over her shoulder to hit the curb. Red splattered fantastically across the snow.

"Get Michael down!" Bill shouted into the radio when the idiot staggered up and pulled a man off Peri. Recovered, she did a fast palm strike, hitting Michael's nose. Disgusted, Bill threw the radio at the dash as Michael fell back in the shrubbery, blind from the tears and blood. "Shoot her, too," he demanded as he reached for the door and got out. "I want her down. Now!"

Irate, Bill jogged to the street, Ron tight behind him. If Michael got ahold of her, he'd kill her. Bill's thick hand smacked into his hip holster, and he pulled his weapon. "Peri Reed! Stand *down!*"

Peri spun. Behind her, the man she just kicked fell into the snowbank, clutching his ribs. She poised, her thoughts almost visibly tumbling through her: recognition, hatred.

"It's time to come home," he said softly, and then guilt joined her expression.

The hesitation was her undoing. With an audible thump, the second, half-dose antidrafting/sedative dart thunked into her arm, right through her coat.

Peri frantically pulled it out, but the damage had been done. "No," she groaned, no longer able to draft her way out of the mistake. Ron stupidly rushed her.

"Wait!" Bill called, one hand outstretched, the other raising his Glock. It felt small in his hands, and he hoped the sight of it might slow her down enough to listen. He'd bought a half hour of police ignorance, but a gunshot would negate that.

Slow from the drugs, Peri spun, slamming her foot into Ron's face. A dull crack of his neck breaking made Bill wince, and then Ron fell, dead before he hit the ground. "I don't want to come back," Peri rasped as she staggered. "That's your warning, Bill. Understand?"

But she'd seen his Glock and the drug had done its job, and he shook his head. "Don't make me shoot you, kiddo. You can't draft your way out of this. Not for another hour at least. Besides, I have something you want."

"You son of a bitch," Michael slurred as he tried to claw his way upright using the lamppost. "You promised it to me!" he exclaimed, slipping back down to the slush and filth.

"You want to remember, yes?" Bill said, motioning for the tightening circle of agents to back off before they spooked her. She was like a wild horse, untamed and ready to run. "Be your own anchor? No one telling you what's real and not?" he added, hiding a zing of excitement when her gaze slid to Michael, still rambling in a dangerous, drug-induced tirade as he lashed out at anyone coming near. "I can give you that now," he said gesturing at the van. "Let's talk."

Peri's eyes shifted from him to Michael, weighing the man's drugged rage against Bill's confident, welcoming smile. Slowly she rose to her full height, trying to hide the sedation, such as it was. "No cuffs."

"No cuffs," he agreed, knowing her quick agreement was only half due to wanting the increased privacy and time to metabolize the drug to make escape easier. He was her handler; she was fighting ten years of conditioning. She might not trust him, but she'd listen if she thought she had a way out. She didn't. Her need to remember had chained her. All that was left was her realizing he was making her a god.

"Good girl." Bill's grip tightened on the Glock. "After you." He lifted his head. "Back off!" he shouted. “I want everyone to stand down! And clean up this site. We are to be gone in forty seconds!”

“I’m not your girl, Bill,” she whispered breathily. Her pace to the van was slow to hide the effects of the sedative. The six men bracketing her followed at a respectful distance. She was free to kill and maim, and they had to hold without damaging her. Such was the rarity of her skill. Such was the pearl of his Peri.

“I’m going to make you perfect, whether you want it or not,” he whispered as he holstered his Glock, anticipation pooling in him.

One of his cars was pulling up, a second one behind it. Sirens sounded, faint in the distance. Even without gunplay, his window had been compromised. “Get him out of here,” he said, gesturing at Michael. Only now did two men approach, efficiently bundling him into the first car. There was a bellow of anger, and Bill smiled, thinking Peri’s knife had just come out.

Her rifle uncocked and hanging over an arm, Latisha ambled forward. Peri’s wet scarf was in her grip, and a smile quirked her lips as she watched Peri be escorted to the van. “Did that go well or not? I can’t tell.”

“One dead? Yes. It went well,” he said as Ron was zipped into a bag.

“Mr. Heddles? What do you want to do with the cat?”

"Cat?" Bill turned to the agent holding Peri's zipped purse. There was a wildly moving shape inside. *Carnac,* he thought, eyebrows rising. "Let it out of the bag," he said, taking the tattered, slush-soaked journal the man had tucked under his arm. It was one of Peri's. She'd want it back, and having it on his person might keep her from running a few precious seconds more.

Bill strode to the van, leaving others to collect Peri's Glock and broken dishes. He was heady with the anticipation of working with her again. Even better, Helen would be pleased, and with that, she'd get off his back and let him work.

CHAPTER FOUR

Peri stiffened at the collective soft intake of breath of the agents surrounding her as she walked right past the van. Safeties clicked off, and her eyes narrowed. Hands moving slightly away from her sides, she turned. Bill was waiting by the van's open door, his expectant expression wary. The woman Peri had spilled coffee on this morning was inside, and Peri's lip twitched. *How long have you been watching me, and who gave me away?*

"I'm not getting in that van," she said, and Bill took a slow breath. She hated vans. Nothing good ever happened in a van. Well, almost nothing. "You want to start this all over again?" she asked as the men surrounding them became more severe.

Bill put his hands in his pockets in a show of impatient annoyance. "You have to agree we need to vacate," he said, voice rumbling, and she glanced past them to the approaching lights.

"You wanted to talk, we can talk," she said. "There's a dance club on the corner. You. Me. That's it."

The woman in the van drew back, clearly nervous, but Bill rocked back and forth on his heels, considering it. "Give me the Evocane and accelerator," he said to the woman in the van, and her blue eyes widened.

"Bill," she protested, and he grimaced.

"Do it," he said tersely. "I want everyone out of here. I'll find my own way home." His smile returned as he looked at Peri, but his assurance fell flat on her. "We both will."

Not likely, but we can play it like that, she thought, shifting her balance when the blond woman vanished into the van, reappearing immediately with two prepped syringes, one blue, one pink.

"That's not enough Evocane," Bill said as he took them, dropping the capped syringes behind his coat and in his suit coat's pocket. Peri stiffened, seeing her diary already there, lost in the fight and now in his possession. "She needs a half cc," he added, frowning at the men surrounding them, fidgeting at the approaching siren.

"Seriously?" The blond woman's gaze darted to Peri. "That's a lot of synapses. I thought she could only draft forty seconds."

Bill nodded. "It's not how long, it's how far she reaches." His expression shifted as the remaining cars left. There were only the six men surrounding them and the two women. "Give me the Evocane vial, Jen. Go. If we aren't back in an hour . . ." He smiled, his teeth catching the streetlight as he handed the nearest man his Glock. "We'll be back in two."

The slim blond woman reluctantly gave him a vial, and Bill tucked it away. "Come on, Jen," the woman behind the wheel demanded, and Peri inched forward as their security broke up and let them pass. The men got into the van, and it drove off even before the door rolled shut.

Peri watched it bounce and jostle back onto the road, vanishing quickly. She turned to Bill, listening to the night and feeling the chill through her coat. It wasn't unusual for Bill to take a personal hand in dealing with his drafters. He'd been her handler since she'd graduated from Opti Tech. But still, it felt odd, just her and him, in the cold, in the dark.

Bill stood before her and waited, wisely giving her a moment to assess the situation. They both knew she couldn't draft. Bill had her on weight and was as good as if not better than her at hand-to-hand, enjoying hitting things into submission whereas she used it only to evade. The smell of spent gunpowder still lingered, but she'd seen him give his Glock to one of his security. She could run, but the lure of what he hinted at was too much to walk away from—and Bill knew it.

Not to mention he's got my diary, she thought, the idea he might read about the year she had studied and prepped with Allen and Silas to bring him down intolerable.

"Shall we go?" he finally said as the sirens became loud, gesturing to the nearby bright lights at the corner and the dance club.

I am such an idiot. "You first," she said, and amendable to that, he turned on a heel, taking a moment to stomp the snow off his shoes when he reached the salted sidewalk. She'd lost her scarf somewhere, and it was cold.

"I want to apologize for darting you with Amneoset," he said as she came even with him, staying a little behind and to the left. "But you wouldn't have listened if I had just walked in and ordered a coffee. Besides, I had to find out who was better, you or Michael."

She said nothing, her eyebrow going up as she looked askance at him.

"Okay, you're right," Bill conceded as they

passed under a streetlight. "But you have to admit he has skills."

"Skills? He's psychotic. You should have thrown him back into whatever psych ward you got him from," she muttered, knowing that most drafters were found there. She'd been an exception, her wealthy mother overreacting to a small incident, her fuss getting Peri recognized by Opti and brought in *before* she was labeled insane by well-meaning health-care providers who had no capacity to accept that what she was experiencing was real.

"*You,* though, are the best," Bill said as if she'd said nothing. "*My* best operative I've ever had the privilege to train. No, the best I've watched evolve, because this is who you are, Peri. You are perfect. Beautiful, deadly, perfect. She wants you for the live trial. To make sure it works before accelerating the rest. I just want you back where you belong."

She. He had said "she." Someone else was pulling Bill's strings, funding him now that the government wasn't. That van had looked rather tatty for Bill.

"I want to make you into a god," he said, and she snorted in disbelief, stoically crossing against the light when they reached the corner. But Michael had seemed to believe it was possible, so possible that he had been incensed that she was getting it and he wasn't. You couldn't fake anger like that. Psychotic or not. Perhaps Bill was playing them both, though.

Head down and hands in his pockets, Bill paced quickly beside her, his steps totally out of synch with hers. "I know what you're thinking, but if I wanted to wipe you and start over, I could have done it already."

"So you say," she admitted, glancing back at her coffee shop as the cops drove by, slow with searchlights from the car playing over the scuffed snow spotted with blood. She couldn't go back, but she'd known that before she'd locked the door and threw the cat carrier full of dishes at Michael. They'd let Carnac go. He'd be okay, but it bothered her. "How did you find me?"

Bill chuckled. "It wasn't easy. I never thought you'd use a medical facility to hide your radiation marker. It was Allen, and let me tell you, it's been a test of patience, letting him range as he wanted this past year. I knew he'd eventually bring me to you."

Allen. But she was glad it hadn't been Silas who'd blown her cover. Hunching deeper into her coat, she thought of her diary, wanting it back. Before them, noise and laughter spilled into the street as they neared the line of cold women with bare legs and men stoically listening to them complain, waiting for their chance to go in.

"I'm going to need to know if you want to work with him again by the end of the week," Bill said, adding "Allen" when she looked up, confused. "Personally, I think it's a mistake, but that could only be my wish to beat the hell out of him. Seriously, if you want him, let me know before I give in to myself. Otherwise, Jack is available."

"I'm not working with either of them," she whispered, shivering from more than the wind coming in from across the Detroit River. She stopped. They had reached the front door. "You have nothing I want," she said, his confidence turning her stomach.

"Yet here we are." With a cool confidence, he handed the doorman a large bill. The velvet rope dropped, and he crossed it as the crowd complained. He turned when he realized Peri was still on the sidewalk. "We broke the memory barrier, Peri. It took almost forty years, but we can do it." He hesitated, a thick hand extended. She knew how it would feel, curving around her waist, and she frowned. "Are you coming? It's just talk."

Her arm ached where the dart had stuck her, and she felt queasy from the lingering Amneoset, but her foot was by far worse, the swelling in her ankle beginning to make walking difficult, even in her boots. She could run. He had no weapon—apart from the lure of memory.

Head down, she came forward, sidling out of his reach as she went in.

Immediately the feel of the place washed over her, the electronic music with its steady heartbeat soothing her as much as the muggy body heat. It was crowded, people standing at the bar and around small tables. Face paint had been utilized far beyond its original intent to thwart the facial recognition cameras—a fashion statement more than a defiant gesture.

Feeling out of place, she ran a hand down her coat, the expensive material now coated with a grungy film of wet street dirt. Her slacks and sweater under it would make her look like a frump. That Bill was impeccably groomed didn't help, and she eyed his somewhat water-fat face cleanly shaved and his graying hair dyed black as he gave his outer coat to the coat check and arranged for one of the quieter booths on the upper floor terrace overlooking the stage and bar.

Again, she was struck by how ill his suit looked on him. Oh, it was tailored to a high-price perfection, giving where it should and tight where it ought to be, but Bill's calm exterior covered a cold, calculating cruelty. Some of her patrons had that look as well, but with Bill, there was no understanding of accountability to temper it. It made him into the thug he'd started life as despite his ongoing efforts to cover it up.

She shook her head at the man offering to hang up her coat as she took it off, and Bill smiled as if fond of his little paranoid creation. Bothered, she pushed past him, following the host through the crowd to the stairs. "That's my girl," Bill said, a hand finding its way to the small of her back. She'd say he was being a gentleman, but she knew he was checking to see whether she had a weapon she hadn't pulled on Michael, stymied by her coat now over her arm.

Stim tabs crunched under her feet as she went up the stairs. Colored lights spun, making the smoke at the high ceiling glow in bands of moving red and gold. It was an upscale place. You could order at the table and pay at the table, but real people brought out the drinks, flashing real skin, unlike the holographs on the stage and dance cage.

Unbuttoning his suit coat, Bill slid into the booth made for six, spinning the menu to himself. His Opti ring looked tight on his thick finger as he ordered something. Seeing her still standing, he patted the bench next to him in invitation.

Peri pulled her eyes off her diary and sat down, keeping space between them. It was quieter here, the noise from the dance floor being deflected. Still, the thump from the bass pounded into her, tightening her tension. This was wrong, but she had to know.

"Nothing but the best for you, kiddo," Bill said, sighing as he set the syringes on the table before them like the carrots they were. "I ordered champagne. Lucky for you, nothing in these will interact with the alcohol, and we need to celebrate."

Peri set her coat aside. Across the open space

over the dance floor, there were booths of partying people. No one was close enough to see the syringes, and even if they could, it was unlikely anyone would care. It was that kind of a place. "What are they?" she asked.

Clearly pleased with himself, Bill settled the flats of his arms on the table and leaned toward her. "Forty years of research," he said, pulling back when their champagne arrived in a bucket of ice. "Already? I can see why you favor this place. Good service."

Her jaw had added itself to her list of aches, but the fight was clear in her memory, meaning she hadn't drafted more than a second or two. That she might be missing chunks didn't hold the same impact it had a year ago, but still, to remember . . .

The pop of the cork made her jump, and she scanned the place as the sweet amber gurgled into the glasses. She liked the vantage point. Worst case was that she had five minutes before Bill's people would be coming in the back, replacing the servers and the bouncers, and the building would be his. *I wonder what Cam would think if he could see me now,* she thought.

"Peri?" Bill prompted, and she took the glass he was holding out. Lip curled, she set it down, not appreciating his clumsy attempt at manipulating her, patently obvious as he tried to remind her of everything she once had: the privilege, the clothes, the excitement, the above-the-law confidence that she'd taken for granted was hers and always would be.

And yet . . . "How does it work?" she asked, hating herself.

His lips curled into a satisfied smile. "The pink is the accelerator. One cc intravenously will chemically destroy the synapses that cause you to forget a draft," he said calmly, tapping his glass to hers before taking a sip. "You only need to administer it once, but you have to dose yourself up on Evocane first or you'll have a psychotic episode the first time you draft, and what's the point of that? Fortunately the Evocane is much easier to administer. Half a cc right in your muscle, like an insulin shot." He smiled. "I insisted it be easy," he said as if she should thank him for it.

"Drafters can't hold twin timelines," she said, head shaking in denial. "That's why we forget in the first place." But if they had found a way to eliminate the memory loss, she'd be dependent on no one. She'd be whatever she wanted to be. *I'd become even better at what I'm good at, a cold-blooded killer.* Her hands had become fists, and she forced them to relax. "How long have you been able to do this?"

"Successfully? Not long. We've been able to eliminate the synapses that prevent an altered timeline from moving from short-term to long-term memory since the sixties."

She licked her lips, watching the bubbles rise in her untasted drink. “They went mad.”

“To the individual,” Bill said, seemingly to be truly regretful. “But as most of them had come to Opti mad to begin with, it was written off as a failed therapy. It was most vexing, I understand, so they shelved it until Evocane was developed to arrest the hallucinations and accompanying paranoia.” He touched the syringe with the blue drug. “It stops it dead in its tracks. Keeps you sane.”

“I won’t be your tool again,” she said flatly, and Bill’s exuberance dulled.

“You are vulnerable, kiddo,” he said as he set his glass down. “Always have been, even with an anchor at your side to bring your memory back. You know it. I know it. Frankly, I don’t blame you for abandoning us. We failed you.”

She swallowed hard, not wanting to admit the ugly truth behind why she’d run. “That’s not why I left.”

“No?”

Her hands clenched when he reached behind his suit coat and took her diary out from an inner pocket. It was all she could do to not rip it from him when he flipped through it, stopping at a random page. “ ‘He says I forget nothing,’ ” he said, reading her words aloud. “ ‘That it’s still there, just the way to recall it derailed, and if I follow my instinct, I will never go wrong. But seeing him mourning the loss of Summer, even now, six months after she passed, maybe it's better to forget.' "

She could hardly breathe as he closed it and tossed her soul carelessly to the bench out of her reach. "Vulnerable," he pronounced. "But no more, Peri. Let me give your freedom to you. Lying to you was a mistake. You're smart enough to handle the truth. But this?" He touched the waiting syringes. "You want this. It's your choice."

"Choice?" she barked out, her anger sparking as she recalled how they'd wiped her year after year, concealing that she was working for a corrupt man under the guise of a government-run organization. "You have no right to talk to me of choice."

"Don't you get it?" he said suddenly, a flicker of his anger showing. "There's no longer a need to scrub you. Ever," he said, his eyes riveted to hers. "I *want* you to remember. Everything and always. You can work with someone or alone. But you will work for me. I have your memory, Peri. Right . . . here," he said as he set his hand possessively on the two syringes.

I don't want to come back. I don't want to have to kill out of necessity. "Keep it," she said. "We're done here."

She stood, jerked to a halt when Bill caught her. Peri looked down at his hand's meaty thickness about her thin wrist. She knew from experience she couldn't pull free, but a quick jab to his eye would get him to let go. Bill knew it as well, and still, he was there, holding her.

"Do you think me stupid?" he growled, hunched as he dropped his benefactor mask. "That I'd send my men away if I wasn't sure? Let you walk free when I could have you in cuffs, tied to a chair? Stop being foolish," Bill said, his voice settling in her gut, heavy and unyielding. "I have what you want, Peri Reed. I'm giving it to you. Why are you being so stubborn?"

He let go, and she rocked back, catching her balance. "Sit down," he demanded, and she did, heart pounding.

"I've seen you with your clientele," he said as he took up the blue syringe, gauging the amount of liquid in it. "Breathing in their power like a drug, pretending to be that small thing." He was scornful, and shame pricked at her because it was true. "You'd like to pretend you walked away from us, your morals washed clean. Rescuing the daughter of the head of the alliance?" His gaze went to hers, holding it. "Everyone believes you lured Opti into a trap so the alliance could hopefully end us, but we know it was a lack of action that made that decision. You didn't tell the alliance we were coming. That's why I trust you. Am I wrong?"

Her silence was answer enough.

Bill nodded, his expression empty. "We've

made progress in the year you've been on leave," he said as he took the blue vial out of his pocket. "I understand your desire to work without an anchor. Fair enough. It must be intolerable for someone so proud to be reliant upon another." He flicked the cap off the blue syringe, and it clattered on the tabletop. "Now you won't have to," he said, filling the syringe to the half cc mark.

Breathless, she froze. Oh, God. He was offering her everything she ever wanted. But Opti used anchors to control drafters. If they were taking them out of the equation, they must have something else now, something more secure that wouldn't be swayed by love, or fall asleep, or simply forget. Something that came in little blue and pink vials, maybe.

"Your skip-hops were impressive," Bill said as he pushed her sleeve up to expose the hard muscle of her shoulder. "You were never one to sit idle. I won't let you need, Peri. I promise."

It's addictive? she thought in horror as he framed her shoulder with his thick fingers. And that, of course, was the control. They had only to withhold the maintenance drug and she'd do whatever they wanted. She wouldn't be a god. She'd be a tool, a piece of ammo. Whoever held the source of that blue liquid held the power, not her.

"Welcome home, Peri," Bill whispered, that needle descending.

That stuff was not getting into her. Peri's breath came in smoothly. Reaching, she grasped the neck of the bottle of champagne and swung it. Bill pulled back, but she'd anticipated it, and the bottle hit him square on the side of the head, right where she wanted.

Bill's startled jerk collapsed to nothing as his eyes rolled back and he slumped, syringe clattering to the grimy floor. Pulse fast, she eased him down on the long bench. Leaning, she grabbed her diary before sending her hands into his pockets, looking for a weapon, cash, anything, since they'd confiscated what she'd walked out of her coffee shop with.

No one even noticed, and as her fingers rifled through Bill's pockets—taking the wad of cash from his wallet before dropping the flexible metal case on his chest—a myriad of emotions flooded her, all shoved to the background to deal with later. They had a cure. It would make her perfect but would turn her into a slave. *This is so bad for my asthma,* she thought as Bill groaned and reached for his head.

Pissed, Peri grabbed his hand in a submission hold, bending until he grunted, his eyes flashing open. She had to lean in with all her weight. His wrist had been broken more than once. "Listen to me, old man. Listen real good," she said when he focused on her in anger. "I don't do this anymore. Now, I'm going to walk out of here. You can either watch me go or try to find me again, but the first will be cheaper, cleaner, and have the same result as the last. Got it?"

Bill's lips pressed into a thin line, but she'd seen him angrier than this. She added a twist to his wrist, and pain pulled his expression into a snarl. "You'll be back, Peri. You are my best. I'll wait for you, but not forever. You don't have forever. You've only got a week."

Ticked, she slammed his head against the wall to knock him out. Heart pounding, she stood and looked down at the dancing people. Even now, no one had noticed them. *I'm not going to be his weapon.* But the chance that she might remember her drafts was irresistible, and after a second of indecision, she leaned under the table, grimacing at the tacky floor as she retrieved the syringes and recapped the Evocane. Taking the blue vial as well, she stuffed it behind her shirt, where it made a cold, hard spot against her middle.

Grabbing her journal, she turned and walked out. "Anchor in a can," she muttered, the crash of adrenaline making a nauseating slurry. Conflicted, she held her arm to her middle, pressing the vial to herself. A part of her wanted to inject them both that very second. To remember her drafts would free her, make her dependent on no one. But the chance she might be hooked on a maintenance drug for the rest of her life, a slave to whoever held its source, was too great.

Silas, she thought. He could tell her if it was true. If it was safe.

You'll be back resonated in her mind, and she stifled a shudder, even as she felt the pull.

Never.

CHAPTER FIVE

"I told you to stand down." Bill's voice was soft, heavy with irritation as he stood with his back to Michael, his feet in the sun streaming in over his rented office space, hands clasped behind his back as he looked out over Detroit. "You did *exactly* what I told you not to, and now you have a cracked rib and a possible concussion."

Michael shifted in the worn chair, trying to find a position that didn't cause his chest to ache. Bill no longer had a government-funded med wing to send him to, and he wasn't about to take anything over-the-counter that might interfere with his ability to draft. The heat from his finger wasn't registering on his phone's screen, and he pressed harder. "I'm fine," he muttered, distracted.

"Fine isn't task-ready," Bill said caustically. "I *told* you to give us a shot."

Tired of Bill's griping, Michael looked up from deleting old emails. Watching Bill try to be professional was a riot. The large man's Bronx accent showed when he got pissed, and though he might eat imported chocolate and drink expensive wine, Michael doubted he could tell them apart from Hershey bars and Budweisers. "Have you got a new anchor for me yet?" he asked, allowing a hint of his annoyance to show. Ron had been an insult. Buying a cup of coffee with his phone? If Peri hadn't killed him, he would have. The low skill level of available anchors said more than the fifth-floor office and reduced resources that Bill was on the skids, trying to make it work and find a way back to his lost power. And for that, he needed drafters.

Bill's hands clenched, then released as he turned, and Michael hid his smile behind a quick rub under his nose. He could tell it was all Bill could do to not grab his phone out of his hand and throw it across the room. Egging the man on had become Michael's favorite pastime.

"We're having trouble finding someone who complements your profile," Bill said.

Michael continued to delete emails, knowing it would piss off Bill even more. "Translation," he drawled, stopping himself just before touching his sore nose. "You can't find anyone with enough balls for the job. You know what? That's fine. I won't need one after you accelerate me."

Striding to his desk, Bill yanked open a low drawer and set a heavy bottle thumping down upon it. "I agree Ron wasn't optimal, but you have to start trusting your anchor."

"Please. The man was a joke." Still focused on his phone, Michael sent out a text to a woman he hadn't seen in three months. "I don't want another anchor. I want the accelerator." Michael's lips curved down as an old jealousy rose, thick and cloying. "Giving it to her wasn't the deal."

"Deal? The deal was it goes to the best," Bill said, pointing at him with his empty shot glass. Expression twisting, he set the shot glass down and took a swig right from the bottle. "You were off your game, Michael."

Bullshit. Michael's eyes narrowed in anger. "You interfered. Darted me. Took me out of the equation. And now you expect me to be all scotch and cigars with you? I'm not buying into this. Give me a reason, or I'm taking a vacation. Right now."

Bill scrubbed at the bridge of his nose.

"How many drafters you got, Bill?" Michael asked, knowing the few still at large were lying low, like he should be. But he liked it too much. This was who he was, and anything less felt dead.

When Bill looked up, his frustration was safely back in check, but Michael could see it, simmering just under the surface. "I like you, Michael," he finally said, and Michael stifled a rude snort, knowing "like" had nothing to do with his sitting in Bill's office. "I'm not going to risk your mental health until I know it's safe, and you'd better hope to God we get your guinea pig back, or you'll never be accelerated."

"Good story. I'd stick with that." Head down, Michael went back to his messages. He'd thought Bill would have written her off once she'd run again, but the man was obsessed. He always had given the ladies preferential treatment. Peri Reed would have to be dead before he'd get advanced, and Michael wasn't that patient.

"Will you put that bloody hell thing away. I'm talking to you."

Sighing, Michael rolled it up and tucked his phone into a front pocket. "Yes, Dad."

"You are a bloody hell piece of work," Bill snarled, his accent becoming worse as the alcohol took a stronger grip. "I won't risk you until I have more assurance it's not going to rot your brain in the long term."

"I got news for you, Bill. I'm not going to die in a bed."

"We still don't know if the maintenance drug remains effective in the long term."

"Just admit you'd rather give it to her." Michael tapped his fingers on the worn fabric of the chair, unsure of what to do with his hands now that his phone was gone. He knew he sounded petulant, but he'd refused his pain meds, and his chest hurt every time he breathed.

"It's not ready, you're not ready," Bill said, and

Michael's eyes narrowed, an old anger surfacing. "We wait."

"You *want* me dependent on someone else," he prompted, his breath going shallow when Bill's silence told him he was right. He sat up, slowing when his ribs ached. "I read her file. I know what you did to her. Wiped three years of her memory to keep her useful. Gave her a false one. Twisted her into an obedient bitch who'd die for you. I'm not letting you do that to me."

"That's where you have it wrong." Bill's face was empty of emotion. "Peri would never die for me," he said. "It's the thrill she'd die for. The chance to outwit the odds. She's perfect."

Michael jiggled his foot impatiently. He knew the feeling, but he didn't like that she might share it with him, that she might understand. It was his feeling, not hers. "A perfect pain in the ass," he muttered.

Jerked back to the present, Bill curled his lip. Motions rough, he took another swallow from the bottle. "She's perfect," he said again. "And if she'd just accelerate herself and realize I've turned her into a goddess, she'd come home."

She has the accelerator on her? Michael froze at the sudden realization. That little nugget of information hadn't reached him. "She has it?" he said as Bill set the bottle down with a sharp click. "Has she used it?"

"I don't know."

It was terse and distracted, and Michael settled himself deeper into the cushions, not liking the uncertainty.

"Stay away from her." Bill's expression was empty, and for the first time, Michael couldn't read what was going on behind his eyes. "She'll kill you if she feels threatened. I'll accelerate you myself when we know it's safe. You understand me? You're all I have left, Michael, and I'm not going to risk you. Not on this. Let Peri bear the danger."

Kill him? Doubtful, but he'd seen the med wing where they kept the people they'd tried the accelerator on, retired drafters or those with the ability to draft but too far gone to be reintroduced to society. It was deathly silent and ugly. "I hear you," he said, and Bill moved his bulk from behind the desk, the grace of it reminding Michael that Bill could still break men's heads like boards. His past wasn't as pretty as he pretended, and if he kept pushing, he'd remind Michael of that.

"Do you?" Bill leaned over Michael, almost pinning him to the chair.

Michael looked up, pushing the older man out of his space with a single finger. "I just said I heard you. Why am I here? I've already been debriefed."

Bill's lips twitched at the hesitant knock at the door, pushing himself up and away from Michael. "Come!" he shouted, then turned back to

Michael. “I’m glad we have this understanding,” he threatened.

I understand I’m the only drafter you got left, old man, and that you gave the accelerator to an AWOL. Michael looked at the door as it opened, but it was only Jack, and he settled back, dismissing him. The blond man had once been Opti’s star anchor, but he was little more than an accessory now, skilled but useless without a drafter to glom onto. “If you think I’m taking Jack as my new anchor, you’re sorely mistaken,” Michael intoned, reaching for his phone as a message came in. It was that woman, telling him to get bent, and he smiled as he tucked his phone away. *Worth a shot.*

“Hey, hi,” Jack said, scanning the room before taking the chair beside Michael’s, scooting it an inch or two away before settling down. “The feeling is mutual, Bill. There’s no way in hell I’m going to pair up with Michael.”

“Good.” Bill poured a second shot glass and pushed it across the desk to Jack. “That’s not why I called you in.”

“Then why?” Michael asked, his mind only half on the conversation. *Bill gave the accelerator to Reed? Let her walk away with it?* No, this crap about wanting her back as a test subject was just that.

“Because Jack knows what Peri might do next and what resources she might have that I don’t know about." Bill sipped his scotch. "Jack was her anchor for three years. He ingrained most of her hangups, knows her better than I do. If anyone can second-guess her, it's him, and we need to keep tabs on her as this runs its course."

Michael propped his ankle on a knee, using the pain from the knife jab to center himself. "Why am I here, then?"

"You're here because you, Michael, are *not* my best despite your ego-ridden belief, and you need to better yourself. She brought you down with about six skip-hops. When we're done here, Jack will take you down to a training floor and walk you through it. Listen and learn."

"Fuck you, old man." Michael glowered at them, putting his foot back on the floor. Bill wasn't trying to bring her in. He was seducing her back, toying with her, giving her little bread crumbs so when she did return, she'd think it was her idea. Bill had no intention of accelerating him. And he wouldn't until she was dead and he had no choice.

Oblivious to his thoughts, Bill chuckled when Jack leaned to take a shot glass and clink it with Bill's. "So . . . do you think she'll accelerate herself?" Bill asked, sitting back against his desk to make the wood creak. "She's got a week's supply of Evocane with her."

Jack sipped the old scotch, clearly appreciating it. "Self-administer? Not a chance," he said, cradling the glass to his middle as if it was his soul. "The woman is scared to remember, scared to forget. And she doesn't trust you."

Bill scrubbed a hand across his clean-shaven face, his focus distant. "But she will. Once she calms down, has a good think, and realizes what I've given her, she'll come in."

Michael unrolled his phone and checked his news feed. *Not if I find her first.*

"Maybe, but you shouldn't have let her take an entire week of Evocane," Jack said.

"You gave it to her, or did she take it?" Michael asked, satisfied when Bill pointed his shot glass at him to be quiet. *If I kill her outright, Bill will be so pissed he'll cut me loose.* He'd threatened to do it before when Michael had "accidentally" put a student in a coma during finals. The bastard had been ruining the curve. But that didn't mean Peri wasn't going to die.

"You don't think she's going to dose herself once she feels safe?" Bill asked Jack.

Jack shifted uneasily. "She's going to want someone with her to put a clamp on her conditioning against being alone. I'm guessing she'll try for Silas."

"Who?" Michael said, not liking that they were for all intents ignoring him.

"Dr. Silas Denier," Bill echoed, and Michael recalled the bear of a man who had won the genetic lottery to have brains and brawn in equal, substantial measure. He was the one responsible for developing the slick suits they had all trained in, and Michael's lip twitched, remembering the cramping paralysis that simulated a gunshot.

"He's not an agent," Michael said, tapping his knee to make it pulse with pain in time with his thoughts. *Kill Peri. Not my fault. Become a god.* "He's not even an anchor."

"Technically, no, but he can defragment jumps," Jack said. "And Peri trusts him. But it's his research that will attract her. With the right lab and access to the proper tools—"

"You think he might try to pick the Evocane apart?" Bill interrupted. "Not likely. It took Helen's tech rats five years to put it together."

Jack nodded, setting a leg upon his knee. "She doesn't know that, and until that hope is eliminated, she won't come in. Tracking her down will be iffy, but we don't have to. Silas will need a substantial lab to even look at it. There are maybe a handful in the U.S. with the resources he's going to want. We find the lab, we find Silas, and then we find Peri."

Bill was nodding, leaving Michael almost choking in disbelief. Why were they even trying to get her back? She was uncooperative, impulsive, and not a team player. She'd been gone a year, and her ghost was still better thought of than him. "And then what?" Michael said, hiding his bitterness. "Wipe her back to nothing and start again?"

Jack leaned forward, his enthusiasm laughable. "Bill, she doesn't need to be wiped. She wants to come home. You know it. That's why you chose her for the live trial. She just needs to realize what you're offering her."

"I *chose* her because Helen insisted I use my best drafter, and Peri is that plus expendable," Bill said, glancing at Michael as he slipped his bulk from the desk, but the lie was obvious to Michael. Taking the heavy bottle back to the drawer, Bill shoved it closed with his foot. "That, and the woman has been without an anchor for almost a year. She has the skills to work independently despite our efforts to prevent it. The only thing she's scared of is herself."

"I can work independently," Michael said, his gut tightening when Bill gave him a weary glance and sat down behind his desk and tapped his laptop awake. *Son of a bitch.* Cowardly old men who couldn't think past what worked before. He didn't even *want* an anchor.

"As it stands, she has both Evocane and the accelerator." Bill's brow furrowed as he scanned the screen. "And you say she won't self-administer. I can't wait the months it might take for Denier to realize how complex it is."

"You can always just dart her with it, can't you?" Jack said.

Bill shook his head, eyes still on the screen. "The accelerator has to be given intravenously, and only when there's Evocane already in her system to buffer it."

Good to know, Michael thought, resolving to go down and quiz the nurses in the med wing. A little wine, a little food, a little sedative . . .

"Not the accelerator but the Evocane," Jack said, and Bill looked up, clearly intrigued. "I mean, it's addictive even without the accelerator, so just get her hooked on it and she'll come in once the cravings kick in."

"That has merit," Bill said, and Michael steepled his fingers, imagining how pissed Peri would be if Bill forced all Evocane's sins on her without any of the accelerator's lofty heights.

"She's not as good as you think," Michael said coldly.

Bill pulled his chair closer to the desk, peering at the screen as he carefully one-finger-typed something in. "She is twice the drafter you'll ever be," Bill muttered, and Jack came around the desk so he could see the data scrolling across the holoscreen from the front. "And it's not because you don't have talent, Michael. You could be the best if you would apply yourself. Show a little trust."

It was like that, then, he thought, seething. Angry, he stood.

Bill looked up. "Where are you going? I want you to work with Jack this afternoon on developing those skip-hops."

Michael forced his expression smooth. "Later. I need to soak my knee." Striding to the door, he stiff-armed it open and paced into the hallway, headed for medical.

Fuck Bill. He'd find Peri, take the accelerator for himself, then kill her twice. With the accelerator in him, he'd finally have the pleasure of remembering both her deaths.

CHAPTER SIX

"So I says to him, I spent thirty-five bucks on it. It's chic, not slutty!" Jack said in a high falsetto. "He's *such* a low-Q."

Peri's attention dropped from the high ceiling to the woman Jack was commenting on, her miniskirt too high, her gum snapping, and her pink hair teased out to look like the sacrificial XX chromosome in a horror flick. Her friend was just as nonconforming, but in leather. Who knew what had brought them to the Georgia Aquarium. Not the fish, certainly.

Peri's stomach gave a pang, and she followed the scent of fried food across the wide expanse to the second-floor cafeteria. She hadn't eaten on the Detroit/Atlanta express, wanting to stretch Bill's cash as far as she could. "Am I clear or not?" she asked.

Jack snorted, his light stubble and the not-really-there cup dangling between his fingers making him look casually alluring. “Babe, I only know what you know. It’s your decision.”

“Stop calling me that.” Tossing the aquarium’s information pamphlet into the recycle bin, she headed for the tunnel that led to the big tank. Twenty minutes in the great room/lobby watching the casual stance of the uniformed security and listening to Jack make up conversations for the patrons had left her reasonably sure she was unremarked upon and unnoticed.

According to the pamphlet, the big tank was the size of a football field, the viewing panes almost two feet thick to hold back the massive pressure. It was impressive, and she wondered how Silas had wrangled his way into working here. He had a unique skill set, but tending fish wasn’t among them. Maybe he’d lied on his résumé, having the smarts to back up whatever claim he’d made.

High above her at the lobby ceiling, a flight of holographic rays swam in a majestic array, garnering an awe-filled *Oooo* from the incoming patrons. Peri tried to blend in as she entered the tunnel leading to the large exhibit. There weren’t many single people here, and she’d come in with a school group, playing the part of a parent chaperone until passing the metal detectors.

Her empty stomach pinched as she dodged around two women with empty strollers. Schoolkids with aquarium encounter tablets darted back and forth, scanning the codes at each enclosure as if they were on an Easter egg hunt. She sent her fingertips to brush the vial and syringes still tucked behind her shirt to reassure herself they were there. The thought to take the accelerant rose like black guilt. To recall her drafts would be freeing, but remembering both timelines would lead to paranoia and then death. That a drug could prevent that sounded too good to be true.

But then again, I am already hallucinating, she thought, giving Jack a sidelong glance as he casually walked beside her and dropped his not-real cup into the trash in passing.

The tunnel to the observation theater had occasional bright spotlights and small tanks designed to soothe the claustrophobic, but it was the odd clear light that pulled her around the last curve, not the chance to see whale sharks. According to the pamphlet, "Dr. Sley" was available at noon on the weekends to answer questions. Silas knew as much about fish as she did, which was zero. It was probably the psychology degree that had gotten him the job. Being able to profile a room quickly, then having the physique to be useful in a security situation, was not to be overlooked in a room with over six million gallons of water behind the window. *He was good with the public, too,* she remembered, focus blurring when the sound of excited kids became louder.

She paused as she rounded the last curve, her eyes rising to the huge observation window. Children talked and shouted, their high voices soaked up by carpet and acoustic panels as they darted back and forth before the three stories of glass fronting her like a movie screen. Table-size fish swam sedately in a tank so long that it was hard to find the back, but it was the light that stunned her to stillness, and she stood, lips parted as a memory tried to surface.

Clear and sliding into the ultra blue, the light cascaded over her, the harsh yellow filtered by tons of water to let the softer shades and wavelengths express themselves. It was like nothing else, as unforgettable as it was impossible to describe, and her pulse hammered. She'd seen this before, and when a flight of rays flew before the window, she choked.

Images flooded her of warm water, the taste of rubber in her lungs, the feel of it between her teeth. There'd been someone with her. *Jack?* she wondered, feeling him silent at her elbow, not knowing. The emotions tied to the memory were that of love.

Had loved him? she thought, blinking fast as she looked away, unable to bear it. If she had, it had been a lie. Jack loved what she gave him, not who she was. That wasn't love at all.

"No, they're too big to be eaten," a familiar voice said, and her attention dropped to Silas standing at the bottom of the auditorium-like room, his bulk looking small against the backdrop of blues and grays. "The whale sharks are fed shrimp and fish from a boat. I suppose if they got hungry enough they might try, but fish that small wouldn't be put in the tank to begin with."

"Why are you still here?" Peri said, irate at Jack's presence, then even more angry for Silas having put him there. The illusion was gone when she lifted her chin, and she breathed easier.

Ten-year-olds clustered about Silas to make his iron-pumping physique look even more blocky. His waist was trim, though, and his black hair had a wash-and-wear style that suited him. Seeing him in a uniform-like polo shirt with a name tag and blah black pants made her smile, knowing the man liked his clothes classically trendy and unique. The polyester weave pulled a little across his shoulders, and her smile grew. She always felt small beside him.

"Who has another question?" Silas asked, and her pulse jumped.

Arms over her middle, Peri called out, "Have you ever swum with the rays, Dr. Sley?"

His head snapped up, shock and pleasure crossing him. But it vanished as he glanced at the security cameras in the high corners. "Yes I have," he said, and Peri flushed, both embarrassed and relieved he wasn't angry about how they had last parted.

"Thank you, everyone, for your questions," Silas said, his professional voice louder now. "Jose on my right can answer any others you might have. Enjoy your day at the Georgia Aquarium, and don't forget to go up to the second level for a top-down view of the tank."

Her chest hurt as he fended off a few more questions and made his way over, eyes never leaving hers. Last night, she'd read a few more pages of her diary before guilt had closed the binding on her thoughts concerning a long-ago afternoon at the range. Short version: Allen's cluster sucked, but Silas had opened up to three-word sentences. Her growing attraction to him had been obvious, almost as obvious as his pain at Summer's death. Seeing her own hopeful expectation against his indifference had been depressing. So was knowing how the story was going to end.

Forcing a smile at him now, she sent her fingers to the journal jammed into her back waistband like an evil touchstone, needing it even as she dreaded it. Silas had always told her emotion was never lost like memories, but what she'd read felt as if it had belonged to someone else, someone unrealistically ambitious and naive. Vain. *Had I really been that oblivious?*

"Peri Reed," Silas said warmly when he was close enough, his hand on her elbow surreptitiously leading her out of the camera's easy view.

Head tilted, he eyed her a telling second or two, clearly wanting to give her a hug but hesitating.

Head down, she slipped her arms around him and leaned closer, breathing him in as her eyes shut. "You were right. I needed to see what I forgot," she whispered.

Emotions long suppressed eked out of the cracks of her resolve as his hold on her tentatively strengthened into a raw vulnerability. He was warm and solid, and with the clear light behind him, a knot around her soul eased. She took a deep breath, and they exhaled together.

Lungs empty, she pushed back to see the light in his eyes teasing a smile from her. She never felt comfortable alone, despite her year of self-imposed exile. But it was more than that. She might not remember it, but he was an anchor, a fixed point of stability. And she trusted him, not just to tell her whether Bill's drugs were what he claimed, but trusted him.

God knew why, even if she didn't.

"I didn't expect you to come all the way down here," he said, his hand rising to hover over the soft swelling on her jaw, gained last night. "You found the card I left you, then?"

Peri winced, taking his hand before he could touch it. "That's not why I'm here."

Silas's focus shifted, scanning the faces behind her. "Is it Jack? Is the construct breaking apart?"

Her mind jumped to the vial and capped

syringes behind her shirt. "Jack is fine," she said softly. "I'm in trouble, so he's in and out, but he's not aggressive and feels stable. Is there somewhere we can talk?"

Silas sighed. "When are you not in trouble? My office." Hand on her shoulder, Silas directed her through a second tunnel, dodging strollers and schoolkids lingering over the smaller exhibits. The lobby was even more crowded with the dolphin show getting out, but his touch was familiar as he angled her to a service door. "Hey, I'm sorry about the car show. I shouldn't have surprised you like that," he said as he unlocked it and they went up a sterile set of stairs. "Have you, um, read it?"

Guilt washed through her, then relief as the door shut and sealed them in a new quiet. "The first couple of pages," she said. "Can you look at something and tell me if Bill was lying?"

"Bill!" Silas barked out. His steps faltered on the stair, and he drew her to a stop, eyes again going to her jawline, this time anger behind them. "He found you? Jesus, I'm sorry, Peri. I was so careful. Why do I suck at this!"

"It wasn't you." Bottom lip between her teeth, she strode up the last stairs and pushed open a fire door to enter a wide corridor. "Everyone found me." The hall was empty, and she slowed as he caught up. Tugging her shirt out from her pants, she found the vial and syringes. "What do you know about these?" she asked as she held them out. "Bill called the pink one an accelerator. He said it would let me remember. Without an anchor."

Silas's jaw dropped, his eyes darting from the syringes to her. "Bill . . . Peri, did Bill inject you with this? It's not supposed to exist."

His rush of fear hit her hard, and the first tendrils of disappointment that it wasn't safe tightened her chest. "He tried to," she said. "The blue one is some kind of maintenance drug to stave off the paranoia."

A soft scuff jerked her attention to the end of the hall, but it was only Jack, leaning against the wall to look sexy and mildly threatening. Silas had followed her attention to the empty corridor, and she shook her head to tell him it was nothing.

"Let me see it." Calmer, Silas took the vial, reading the label as he started them back down the aisle again. "It's probably the same stuff I read about in my graduate classes. Opti developed it in the sixties, then shut it down when everyone in the live trials died of paranoia-induced suicide. You say the blue one is a maintenance drug?"

Fear settled to a slow burn. "He called it Evocane?" she said, hoping it might mean something to him, but he shook his head. "It's Bill's latest attempt to convince me to come back," she added, and Silas's hand clenched around the vial. "He thinks that if I don't have to trust an anchor,

I'll run right home to him." She shoved her anger down, anger that Bill would try to use her again, try to lure her back with promises of her past, the power and above-the-law status she had enjoyed. Guilt swarmed out, smothering it. The things she had done . . . There was no rationalization that would justify her actions. Ignorance was not an excuse when it was willful. "He also implied Evocane was addictive," she added softly.

"No doubt." Silas jiggled the vial in his hand as they walked, tucking the capped syringes into a shirt pocket. "If it's addictive, you'll be less likely to draft when your levels are low and avoid any mental issues. I've got a few basic chemical tests in my office. Let's check it out."

"Thanks," she whispered as he stopped before a wide door. It looked like a closet, but DR. SLEY was written on a piece of curling masking tape stuck to it. "Sley?" she questioned as he used a card to unlock it.

"My aunt's married name," he said as he opened the door and gestured she go first into the long, narrow room stuffed with equipment and stacked boxes. "I'm using her son's social security number. I've been in hiding, too."

Nodding in understanding, she gave Jack a look to stay out before going in deeper. Everything was organized. It only looked cluttered because there was so much stacked to the ceiling. Why he was here was obvious, though. The end had a round window onto that same big tank. The flickering, soft light spilled over his untidy desk and rolling chair. A stained, empty cup of coffee sat beside the edge, almost falling off. The space was small, but it didn't feel cramped.

Silas was silent, the soft click of the door shutting behind him, obvious. "Have a seat," he said as he took a bottle of test strips from a drawer. Peri perched herself on the edge of the desk chair, rolling it back to give him more room. Her eyes strayed to the porthole, her angst rising. What if it was true? It would make her refusal to go back to Bill even harder.

"I know what you're thinking," Silas said, his voice holding warning as he rested his rump on the corner of his desk and shook out a test strip. "But it was nasty stuff in the sixties, and in Bill's hands, it's probably been made worse."

"That's why I'm here, Doctor," she said sarcastically, her interest sharpening when he carefully decanted a drop from the syringe onto the test strip and grunted in surprise.

She scooted closer to the edge of the chair. "What?"

Squinting at it, he frowned. "Most neural addictors fall in a narrow pH range, which, I'm sorry to say, it does. But the real nasty ones have a faint nitrite level." He pointed to a second test strip. "This one takes a while."

She sank back. It was like waiting to see

whether the pregnancy test strip would turn blue. Not that she'd had much experience there. In the tank, a diver swam by, fish following him to eat the algae he was scraping from the wall. Her suspicion pinged, and then she quashed it. If Bill had tracked her here, he wouldn't be looking for her from the wrong side of two feet of glass.

Still sitting on his desk, Silas pushed back until he hit the wall. Now it felt cramped, and she scooted her feet under her chair. "So . . . how have you been doing?" Silas asked.

Her eyes flicked from the test strip to him and she shrugged as his worry went right to her core and settled. He still loved her. Too bad she didn't remember loving him. "Okay, I guess."

"Seeing anyone?"

Seriously? "No, but I stole some guy's car last month for a joyride. Does that count?"

Silas chuckled. "For you it does. Nice?"

He looked comfortable and content, and her gut tightened. "The guy or the car?"

Shrugging, he took the test strip and compared it to a chart on the bottle. "Which one attracted you first?" he asked, the idle question anything but.

Pulse fast, she leaned to look, but the colored squares meant nothing to her. "The car."

Anxious, she waited as he studied it. Big hand scrubbing his mouth and chin, he shook his head. A sensation of obstinate demand blossomed. She wanted to remember, damn it. "Maybe the side effects aren't that bad," she said, and Silas stiffened.

"Bill's been tweaking this for who knows how long, tweaking it to control drafters," he said as he threw the strip away. "The most dangerous people on the face of the earth. You aren't touching this until I'm sure it's not going to kill you if you stop taking it."

Her lips parted at the new thought. "He wouldn't dare," she said, not sure whether she was more angry at Silas as he tucked the syringe back into his shirt pocket and out of her reach, or Bill for trying to con her into taking it. "We're too valuable."

"Not if you go rogue." Wide shoulders slumping, he lost his anger. "Sweet Jesus, Peri," he said softly. "There's nothing wrong with you the way you are, but if you want this, give me the time to check it out and make sure you're not selling yourself to whoever has the best lab."

Nothing wrong with her? She could reset time, but not remember it. Bitter, she turned to the tank, arms over her middle as she toyed with the idea of shoving him into the clutter and taking her drugs back. The ability to remember her drafts was in his pocket—and she wasn't a coward. "Thanks for your input," she said. "Can I have my stuff back, please?"

Jaw slack, Silas stood. But then his resolve grew. "Sure. You mind if I come with you to put the pieces back together again when this blows up in your face?"

Shocked, she hesitated. "You want to come with me?"

The desk phone rang, and she jumped. "Peri?" he questioned, ignoring it. "Don't think. Yes or no. Will you slow down enough so that I can keep up with you and keep you alive when you do something stupid?"

He wanted to come with her? "Uh," she fumbled, turning to the hammering on the door.

"Silas!" someone shouted, and then the door beeped and opened, and a young man all but fell in. "Silas. Tod is looking for you."

Peri backed up into the shadows as Silas casually lifted the ringing phone from the cradle and set it back down. "Mark, this is Peri. Peri, Mark."

"Hey. Hi. Silas, you need to get your butt downstairs. Tod is freaking out. The CIA is here. They say you're part of a terrorist . . ." Mark's eyes shot to Peri. "Holy shit! She's a terrorist?"

Peri sighed. The CIA? *Damn it, Allen. I am capable of making my own decisions.*

The phone was ringing again. Wrapping the cord around his thick hand, Silas yanked it out of the wall. The need to leave swelled. Peri eyed the bumps the syringes made in Silas's pocket, wanting them back. She edged past the desk, and Mark scrambled backward into the hall to make room. "Is there a service entrance out of here?" she asked.

In the hall, a bored, feminine voice called loudly, "There is. We'll be leaving through it shortly, Agent Reed. I'm Special Agent Beam, CIA. Could you come out with your hands where I can see them, please? You, too, Dr. Denier."

"You have the wrong man," Mark said to the unseen woman. "That's Dr. Sley."

Peri looked at Silas, his hands clenched and his jaw set in frustration. "This is so bad for my asthma," he whispered, and she started at her familiar phrase coming out of his mouth.

Mark yelped as he was yanked out of the doorway. "Go. Downstairs. Now," the woman said, and then the soft patter of sneakers on the tiled floor followed by the squeak of a door.

Silas sighed. "Allen?" he guessed.

She nodded. "He came to see me a few days after you. He's working for them in the mop-up, and apparently he thinks I should, too. Sorry. I think I blew your cover."

Silas's fists eased, but anger lingered. "Don't worry about it. I'll go first."

"No, I'll do it." Mood bad, Peri strode forward. Her hands weren't in the air, but they weren't near her body, either. Opti had been an autonomous agency in the U.S. military, so it was no surprise the CIA was fronting the cleanup. The CIA, like the rest of the world, had been oblivious to the unique talents that Opti fostered, hiding them under lies and need-to-know. And no one had needed to know—until now.

Her eyebrows rose as she found only one official-looking woman waiting. Allen was beside her, an odd expression of grim persuasion on his face. *One? They'd sent one agent?* That was either really insulting or flattering as all hell that they might actually treat her like a person.

"Thanks, Allen. You're a real peach," Peri said dryly as the African-American woman in her ugly black skirt and white top eyed her, feet spaced wide and sidearm unsnapped. "If you think I'm going to let you talk me into this, you are sadly mistaken. I forget things. I am not stupid."

"Peri, this is Agent Harmony Beam," Allen said, clearly trying to smooth things over, but Peri could tell he was worried she might blow this all to hell. "She's part of the new WEFT program. World Enumeration Federal Taskforce?"

Harmony? Isn't that a little flowery for the CIA?

"Agent Reed?" As if knowing her thoughts, Harmony gestured. "We have a car waiting."

Peri grimaced as the woman looked her up and down in evaluation, attention lingering on her scraped jaw. "Same old Allen," Silas said, his thick arms crossed over themselves. "She told you no, and you dragged her into it anyway."

"This is not my fault," Allen said, angry.

Peri looked askance at Silas. "Notice how it's

never his fault, but he's always front and center of it?"

"It's not my fault!" Allen exclaimed. "The CIA has *always* known where you were. I'm the one who's been keeping them off your back." His eyes narrowed in affront. "Both of you. They know about the Evocane and accelerator," Allen added. "They've been able to look the other way until Bill tried to snag you—"

"You didn't tell me he tried to abduct you," Silas interrupted, his gaze returning to the scrape on her jaw, and Peri shrugged. It hadn't seemed important.

"But when Bill tried to snag you," Allen said louder, "they had no choice but to bring you both in. Peri, they need your help," he added, softer now. "Bill isn't the only option here. They have the facility to re-create Evocane. Will you be reasonable and listen for once? Not all my ideas are bad."

But reasonable wasn't one of her favorite words, and not when she wasn't wearing the only gun in the room. Lips pressed together, she weighed the risk of drafting and forgetting the last few minutes against her need to run and disappear. She'd worked for the government before. All it took was a well-placed dart and a handgun to her gut to get her in a cell. And once there, there she would stay, trotted out to do their bidding when they needed her if she wasn't outright erased.

"I'm retired," she said flatly. "End of story."

"Yes? Someone thinks they can fix that." Harmony's low voice held disdain. "I need an answer, Reed. Are you with us or not?"

Temptation rose at the thought of a secondary source of Evocane. But it was too easy to use her. She could trust no one, especially the government. Then Peri stared when Silas cleared his throat and dipped into his pocket. "Silas," she seethed. "What are you doing?"

"I can't believe I'm saying this, but Allen is right." Eyes averted, Silas handed the syringes and vial over to Harmony. "I need the lab, if nothing else. I won't let them wipe you. If it's between Bill and the CIA, I take the CIA."

Allen was nodding, but they both seemed to have forgotten door number three existed, and her desire to run swelled. That is until Harmony dropped the drugs into a belt pack. "Thank you, Dr. Silas. Agent Reed?" Harmony prompted.

Peri looked at the hallucination of Jack, alone and unseen by all but her a short distance down the hall. He was rubbing the bridge of his narrow nose, but as if sensing her attention, he dramatically gestured for her to make a break for it. For three long heartbeats she considered it, eyeing Harmony's hard calves. She could obviously run. Her hair was clipped too short to grab, and her body was built for endurance and speed. And there was that handgun.

"Please," Harmony said insincerely, her dark eyes glinting.

Peri eyed the pouch where Harmony had stashed the syringes. That she might never forget again almost hurt; she wanted that freedom so badly. "You said you had a car?"

It wasn't a yes, but it wasn't a no, either, and Harmony gestured for her to go before them down the hall. Silas fell in beside her, then Allen. Harmony was last—at least until they passed two more agents who filed silently in behind them.

Not so on her own, then, Peri thought, finding a compliment in there somewhere. "Thanks a hell of a lot, Allen," she said, giving him a dark look.

"Right. Like you had a lot of options once Bill found you," he said.

"You're a security threat, Reed," Harmony said as they continued down the hall. "Once Opti ID'd you, we could no longer let you pretend you were a barista. Personally, I think this entire exercise is a mistake. If I had my way, you'd all be permanently jailed in a purple hell."

No doubt. But that Harmony knew that a particular shade of purple stunted her ability to draft only solidified that this was the remnants of Opti remake. "I'm not a barista. I'm an entrepreneur providing a needed service."

"You are a risk," the woman insisted as they picked up two more suits who radioed in their position. "Able to be programmed and erased at will. Allen Swift said you might be amenable to helping us, and we will investigate that option until you prove it to be the error it is. That we have something you need is not much of a comfort to me."

"Help with what?" Peri questioned, but she had a good idea.

"We're having difficulty acquiring a drafter named Michael Kord," Harmony admitted as Allen bobbed his head, clearly encouraged by Peri's interest. "He's aligned himself with the remaining corrupt Opti faction, and it's proving difficult to bring him in."

Michael again. "Sending a drafter to get a drafter isn't a good idea."

"It's not my call." Harmony's jaw was clenched. "If it was, I'd open the door and let you walk." Harmony pushed open a wide double door, and cool, cement-scented air blew in to shift her hair. There was a black car idling in the middle of the emptied lot. Beyond it was Atlanta, already hot in the afternoon sun. Smiling like an evil cat, Harmony gestured for Peri to do just that. "Please."

Harmony was indicating the car, but Peri could tell she was hoping Peri would go for the street beyond so she could shoot her in the back.

"At least you're not in a cell," Allen muttered.

Peri hesitated, wanting to run but needing what they had more. Not in a cell? Not yet. Not until they got what they wanted. Then they'd incarcerate her for the rest of her life, using Bill's wonder drug as both their carrot and their stick.

Bitter, she ran a hand over her hair, thinking she needed to cut it. Jack was gone, and it made her feel abandoned. "Sounds like it's the same offer Bill gave me," she said.

Beaming sarcastically, Harmony gestured again. "That's what I told them."

She had little choice, and Peri smiled insincerely. "Looks like I'm your girl."

"Ahhh, shit," Harmony swore softly, and Peri strode forward, the suits at the outskirts scrambling to get to the car before she did.

Fantabulous. Just effin' fantabulous. She was working for the God-blessed government again.

CHAPTER SEVEN

The air was on—the air was always on in Atlanta—and chilled, Peri settled deeper into the white leather couch, feeling forgotten in the informal, glassed-in meeting area between the CIA labs and their adjoining offices. Harried interns hustled amid the low-partitioned office space. On the other side were three labs, only one of which was lit. The central area where she waited was a cross between a lounge and a conference room, and being three stories down, it had direct access to the parking garage through the nearby elevator.

So far, everyone was ignoring her. Impatient, Peri rubbed the soft swelling on her jaw where Michael had struck her. The entire area had the open layout of an Opti facility, and she wondered whether her master password would work.

Her new glass-technology, WEFT-supplied phone hummed with an incoming call, and she cautiously picked it up off the low coffee table. She'd given WEFT one of her alternate, low-use phone numbers to rebuild her account. Until today, only two people had known that particular exchange—her mother's care facility and her bank—and her pulse quickened at the unfamiliar number. *Bill?* she thought as she answered the call with a hesitant "Yes?"

"Peri?" came a soft-spoken, masculine voice, and she had to think twice.

"Cam?" she finally guessed, mystified. "Where did you get this number?"

"From your cat's collar," he said, and Peri's eyes closed in a slow blink. *And Carnac.* "Are you okay? I found him outside your shop. You're not open today, bu-u-u-ut you probably know that."

A crash from the lab jerked her attention up. "Are you *trying* to kill her?" Silas shouted, neck red as he fronted a belligerent man in a lab coat.

"The residues will build up on her synapses and give her MS!"

The chemist in question dramatically dropped his tablet on the counter and stalked out. Uneasy, Peri held the phone closer as the unknown doctor hit the elevator button hard and turned his back on her while he waited. "Um, what are you doing with my cat?" she asked Cam.

"Feeding him," Cam said, and she swore she could hear Carnac purring. "He was still there when I went back after lunch, so I picked him up. He looked hungry. Are you okay?"

Peri glanced into the lab where Silas was still reaming out some poor tech, blurry behind a huge holographic wave screen detailing what looked like a neurological pathway. "No, but I will be. Hey, could you do me a favor? Two favors?"

"Sure. What?"

The elevator dinged cheerfully, and the slighted chemist stalked inside and hammered at the button to close the door. "Could you watch Carnac for me for a few days, ah, weeks?"

"He's housebroke, right?"

"Of course he is," she said, then added, "As long as you give him a cat pan."

"Mmmm," Cam muttered. "And two?"

"Could you forget you have this number?"

"Peri, whatever trouble you're in, I can help."

"Um," she stammered, embarrassed now. "It's

really sweet of you, but I'm okay. I'll tell you about it when I pick up Carnac. Okay?"

"Yea-a-ah," he hedged. "You're coming back, right?" he asked, clearly not believing her.

She was silent, thinking of how long it would take Silas to reverse-engineer the Evocane. "Sure," she said, hoping she was telling the truth. "Of course. Thanks. I owe you big. Bye."

She ended the call before he could say anything more, staring at the empty screen and trying to decide whether she was going to keep it or not; it was likely bugged.

Foreboding crept through her, and she wasn't surprised when the elevator dinged and Jack got out of it, looking so good in his Armani suit and day-old stubble that she didn't care that the elevator hadn't truly opened and the happy eighties music filtering out from it was all in her mind. Something had flagged her subconscious that a threat was looming, and Jack had come to warn her. Either that, or one of her old boyfriends worked at the CIA and was on his way down.

The illusion pretended to shoot her with his finger before he sat beside her, his shirt untucked and top button undone. He looked fabulous, and she harbored a growing sensation she'd seen him like that before, probably with a glass of wine in his hand after a successful task. She understood the wine now. It probably hadn't been easy lying to her day after day that their jobs were legit.

Nah, she thought as the hallucination gave her a sideways grin. He just liked his wine.

"Why are you here?" she whispered so whoever was behind the camera in the corner wouldn't think she was talking to herself.

"The longer you sit here, the harder it will be to slip them." Leaning back, he dropped an ankle on a knee. "Me, I'd bug out. Find a hole. Leave Silas to do what he does best. Wait for Silas to find you. He will, you know."

It was a good idea, but if she left, they might kick Silas out of the lab. The chance that he could reproduce the maintenance drug was worth hanging around for.

"But you never listened much to me, did you?" he said.

"Clearly more than I should." The elevator dinged again—this time for real. Allen's voice filtered out even before the door opened, and she stretched her arms in a façade of confidence across the back of the couch. The silver doors opened. Harmony strode out, followed by an older man in a suit and tie. It was there Peri's attention lingered, recognizing his wealth and privilege—the expectation that his word would be acted on without question.

"Oh look. Your new leash holder," Jack said, rising to help himself to a coffee from the narrow table against the wall.

The man's shoes were high-end, and she

breathed deeply, looking for the scent of cologne. His Burberry suit was perfection even if it was a bit stiff, woven from black and white threads to give the illusion of gray. He'd gone gray with his tie as well, lined with white and silver. His piercing blue eyes undimmed by age took everything in with efficient swiftness. Peri pulled her arms back to herself, unconsciously accepting his authority until Jack snorted and she shifted her posture to one less accommodating.

"Mr. Steiner, this is Agent Peri Reed," Allen said as he pushed ahead of Harmony to do the introductions. "Peri, this is Mr. Steiner. He'll be directing your involvement in bringing in Michael Kord and Bill Heddles."

Peri stood, slowly extending her hand. "Steiner," she said, thinking the sound of his suit sliding over itself was soothing. "Nice sandbox you have here."

He shook her hand, his eyes showing no emotion. "Thank you."

Her attention strayed to Jack, and he shrugged his opinion. It was obvious that Steiner relied too much on what other people told him. But she probably should play nice if she wanted to keep Silas in his lab.

Allen, ever the political grease, jiggled on his feet nervously. "Ah, I've been telling Steiner what I know of Michael. They've been monitoring him for six weeks."

"Really." There were chairs surrounding them, but no one was sitting down. "How long have you been watching me? Did you see my abduction the other day? What did you think? I should have killed Michael and walked away by the looks of it, but then we wouldn't be here having this conversation. Maybe you would have sent me a big, fat check if I had."

"I read the report," Steiner said smoothly, but she'd seen his flash of ire, and the need to bait him was irresistible—if Jack laughing at the coffee counter behind him was any indication. "I'm pleased you agreed to help us capture Michael," Steiner finished evenly.

"Agreed?" Peri smiled brightly to make Allen cringe at what might come out of her mouth. "That implies I had a choice. I had a choice?"

"Sir." Allen adjusted his glasses, giving her a look to shut up. "What she means—"

"No, I'm curious," she said, not flinching under their stares, her thoughts on the adjacent garage and her chances at simply walking out. "What are you going to do with Michael and the rest of us drafters once you find us? Put us in camps? Science labs?"

"Peri, stop it," Allen said outright.

But she was learning so much, and she watched in interest as Harmony tried to get her superior's attention. Steiner was impervious to the woman, focused on Peri, the man clearly knowing she was seeing how far she could push before someone pushed back.

"What happens to Michael afterward isn't your concern," Harmony said, and at that, Peri's fake good mood vanished. Harmony saw it leave, and there was a rush of motion as the woman stepped in front of Steiner. Tension sang in Peri, and she glanced at the camera, wondering who was behind it watching.

"It's very much her concern," Steiner said, and Harmony flushed when he physically moved the woman out from between him and Peri. "I'd be uncomfortable if she didn't ask. Reed, the entire branch of the CIA was kept in the dark about Opti's special skills until Opti was shown to be corrupt and other heads were put in charge of disbanding it."

"Thanks to Peri," Allen muttered.

Behind him, Jack shook powdered cream into his coffee. "He's got that right."

Steiner sighed at the raw emotions. "If drafters were any other group of people, it wouldn't matter," he said, noticing Peri looking over his left shoulder at Jack. "But every one of you is highly trained and unwilling to live quietly."

"I was working in a coffee shop," Peri accused. "That's not exactly noisy."

"You were gaining the trust of high-profile people who had their fingers on the pulse of the economy. Your ability to steal secrets and sell them was unparalleled."

“I was giving them a secure place to work, not stealing their secrets,” she said, peeved.

“You were surrounding yourself with everything you lost,” he said, and she met his gaze, unwilling to drop her eyes. “That you limited your guilty pleasure to that is why you’re here and not in the Opti-designed cell that waits for Michael.”

“You want me to bring him in so you can jail him?” she asked.

Steiner’s lips curved into a smile. “You’ve done worse to those who deserve it less.”

She took a step closer, not liking that he was right. Harmony stiffened. Behind him, Jack set his coffee down and mirrored Peri, pinning the older man between them. “Not when my name was on the next cell over,” she said. Steiner probably had access to all her records, knew more about what she’d done than she did herself. Peri had no defense other than a paper-thin, plausible deniability. She might have been manipulated into her actions, but Michael liked hurting people. She’d seen it in his eyes in front of her coffee shop.

“Your help in the matter will not go unnoticed,” Steiner said.

“My cell will have a window. Gotcha.”

“Peri,” Allen whispered. “Will you give him a chance?”

“I’m listening,” she said, her thoughts on the stolen vials.

Steiner made a small noise as if she'd passed some sort of test, but he rocked back to glance behind himself, searching for whatever Peri kept looking at, the man oblivious to Jack frowning at him. "The alliance's dewy-eyed idea that the drafters would come in when Opti fell apart was a poor one," Steiner said. "They predictably scattered, most going into hiding as you did. We're finding those who use their skills for monetary gain by reputation. That is, when a crime goes unsolved, we can figure out who did it by your quirks of methodology. WEFT has been tasked with bringing them in. I'm focusing on problem drafters first. It's my hope to find you all before your abilities become common knowledge."

"Yes, the world knowing about us would be a problem," she said bitterly.

"How do you think the common man will react if it's suddenly known that a small demographic can change the past?" Steiner accused. "You think they'll listen rationally? Take you in as the next evolutionary step of mankind and celebrate you? No. They'll believe whatever lie makes them feel justified in hunting you down. They'll not only kill you but go after your parents, siblings, and anyone else they think you've infected."

"Infected!" Jack exclaimed, but Peri didn't like the hallucination giving voice to her outrage. *Is he threatening my mother?*

"It will be genocide, Agent Reed," Steiner continued. "And you will be at the center of it. I'm trying to avoid that by bringing in drafters as they reach my notice. If a drafter's actions don't become an issue, I have no reason to bother them apart from the request that they remain childless."

Her eyes narrowed. "And if we don't like that last part?"

"We'll insist." He hesitated. "And *why* do you keep looking over my shoulder?" Steiner asked, anger finally reaching his voice.

"I'm watching the monster creeping up behind you," she said cryptically, and Allen cringed, knowing she was talking about Jack.

Peri had never wanted a family, but to force the issue didn't sit well, and when Jack began to pace, Peri sat down. "I'm still listening," she said, and Allen exhaled, clearly relieved.

Steiner stiffly lowered himself into the chair across from her, the empty expanse of the glass table between them. "Bill Heddles sent Michael Kord on task this morning. They have abandoned the Detroit facility and Bill needs immediate funds to set up anew."

I bet Bill is happy about that. "Okay." Peri glanced at the photos that Harmony had taken from a shiny blue file folder and spread across the low table.

"His flight is for St. Louis," Harmony said, pictures spinning to land in front of her where Peri stopped them with a quick hand. “We won’t know until he boards the plane, but he’s probably going to be there with this woman. Her name is Jennifer.”

She pointed down, and Allen bent at the waist, peering at the razor-sharp images. “She was in the van when they tried to snag me,” Peri said.

“You spilled coffee on her, too,” Allen said, clearly relieved that Peri wasn’t baiting Steiner anymore.

“Due to his current lack of resources, we feel Heddles might be on-site as well,” Harmony said. “If he is, we bring them both back. Think you can handle that?”

And then I’m in my cell until they need me again, she thought, jerking as her eyes lit upon a photo of Jack among the rest. Steiner cleared his throat knowingly at her reaction, and she slumped, settling back as if she didn’t care. But the damage had been done.

“You think Jack might be there, too?” Allen said as he picked up Jack’s photo.

“He was your last Opti anchor, right?” Harmony questioned suspiciously.

Peri nodded, her eyes lifting from the photo to Jack standing before the coffee urn. Setting his mug down, Jack crossed the room to peer over her shoulder. “I don’t remember that being taken,” the hallucination said.

Harmony's head shifted back and forth. "Sir, her flight risk is too high. Reed stays here."

"Excuse me?" Peri began to laugh, but it was bitter even to her ears. "You think I'm going to run away with Jack? Do your homework, Agent Beam."

"You are a flight risk," Harmony insisted. Frustrated, she turned to Steiner. "It's bad enough I have to work with Swift."

"You came to me," Allen muttered.

"Seriously?" Peri pulled the photo from Allen's hand and threw it in the trash. "You honestly think I'm going to trust Bill? Go running back to him? You think I like losing chunks of memory and being remade into whatever suits him? But I can see why you might be worried. *Your* great plan is to commit a slow and morally comfortable genocide on a new kind of human."

Steiner's expression was placid, but mistrust had tightened the corners of his eyes. Behind him, Jack took his photo from the trash and propped it up on the coffee counter. Peri didn't want to know the mental gymnastics going on in her head right now. The photo was still in the trash. She knew it. But there it was, in Jack's hand as he carefully wiped off a smear of coffee from it. *Maybe I'm not over him as much as I thought.*

"Peri shot and left Jack for dead when she found out he and Bill were using her," Allen said, indignant. "She's not going to go back to him or Opti."

"Yeah, that hurt, babe," Jack said, carefully shifting the photo to catch the light.

"Sir, this is my team. We've worked together for over a year. I don't want to add a new element," Harmony protested. "Besides, her radioactive tag will give us away."

"At this point, it takes four hours for enough radiation accumulation to ping a meter," Steiner said, clearly not caring. "That's deemed acceptable."

Jack sipped his coffee, saying, "If Harmony goes alone, she's dead and you know it."

Why do I care? Peri thought, but it was obvious she did. Or maybe she just wanted to crush Harmony's misplaced confidence. "You don't have the ability or skills to bring in a drafter alone," she said, and Harmony rounded on her.

"I brought you in."

Peri inclined her head. "I was cooperating."

Flushed, Harmony stood her ground. "How can you possibly know what I'm capable of?"

"You don't know what I'm capable of, either," Peri shot back. "You can't go against a drafter. You can't possibly."

Harmony took a breath, expression dark and her anger obvious. Steiner cleared his throat, cutting off her next words. "Harmony, may I speak with you a moment?"

"No!" she blurted, then caught herself. "Sir. I mean, yes. Yes, of course."

Eyebrows high, Steiner stood and gestured for her to step a few feet away.

Jack leaned over Peri's shoulder, whispering, "I don't think she likes you."

Hand waving, Peri pushed the hallucination away, and Jack vanished. "Good Lord," Peri muttered, glad he was gone. "What did I ever do to that woman?"

Allen chuckled as he sat beside her, and she shifted to keep from sliding into him. "You want the short list, or long one?"

From by the elevators, Harmony said loudly, "She is here until Denier figures out the Evocane, and then she will accelerate herself and run. Sir. She is a risk, not only a flight risk but to the safety of everyone on my team. She could draft and forget everything but being Bill's girl."

"Which is why I want you there," Steiner said. "We need her to draw them in. Allen is there in case she drafts. Get over whatever issue you have and work with the woman. If she tests clean for the presence of the accelerator, she goes."

"Sir." It was flat this time, and Peri smiled an apology when the woman glared at Peri and walked into the open office areas.

"Don't you love being the bait in the dumb-ass trap?" Clearly disenchanted, Allen stood as Steiner made his way back to them. Peri rose as well, uncomfortable that Harmony was right. The risk of being wiped was real. The chance she might chuck it all and run—even without the accelerator and Evocane—was real. She'd acquired new skills in eleven months, rubbed out the worst of the engineered mental blocks against being alone and the patterns of behavior that made her easy to find. But the chance that Silas could reverse-engineer Evocane and she could remember her drafts . . . that was real as well.

"Give Denier a blood sample before you leave the floor. We depart at eight p.m. tomorrow," Steiner said, blue eyes hard. "Tell Harmony what you need."

Her thoughts on Silas, Peri asked, "Is there any way we can go earlier?"

"Intel has Michael at the site at three a.m. We'll have you in place by two."

He turned away, and Peri cleared her throat. "An hour for recon?"

Steiner hesitated, his face expressionless. "Recon is there already. You can read the report on the plane. Harmony is in charge. No three-strike rule. You piss her off, and she kicks you back here. Understand?"

"Absolutely," she said, but he was already walking away.

Allen sighed as he sat down again. "Congratulations?"

Focus distant, she took Jack's picture out of the trash and blotted the coffee away. "If you say so." They'd had some good times. Lots of them. That she couldn't remember them was a small point. The emotion was still there. *Am I making a mistake?*

Anxiety rose, and she hid Jack's photo under the rest. The unease that Steiner had left behind was growing, and her eyes strayed to the elevators. "I should run and just keep running."

"Yeah, there's a good idea."

Eyes narrowing, she toyed with the idea of shoving his foot off his knee. "I'm not a child. I can make good decisions."

Oblivious, he rubbed his ankle. "Yeah? How is running a good decision? You can't make good decisions when you don't remember everything."

Her urge to shove his foot off his knee shifted to breaking his nose. But then she'd draft to fix it. Maybe if she had let Bill pump that crap into her, she might have the pleasure of remembering it. "Excuse me," she said tightly. "I need to give Silas a blood sample."

"Peri . . ."

Back stiff, she walked away, shivering as she entered the lab and the cold Silas had it at. Allen wouldn't follow her in here, where Silas was king, and her shoulders relaxed as she found him clustered before a wave screen with his technicians, looking over a hormone schematic.

"Hey, hi," she called out, and he looked up, smiling. "I'm leaving at eight tomorrow night. If they shut you out, call me." *And then I'm gone.*

"Peri." Finger up to ask for a moment, he gave the technicians a last instruction before tugging his too-tight lab coat straight and heading her way. "I doubt they're going to do that. They want to know how to make Bill's wonder drugs as much as you do, and I had access to the old research. How was the, ah, meeting? Everything okay?"

She glanced out the big plate-glass window to where Allen dejectedly waited for her, slumped in the white cushions. "About what I expect. It's a snag and drag. I've done worse than bring someone in who didn't want to come." Never another drafter, though.

"I meant are you okay working with Allen?"

Unable to meet his eyes, she shrugged. "As long as he doesn't try to dress me in pastels again." Depressed, she sat on a lab stool. "Allen is a such a dick." Silas laughed, and she stared at him. "What's so funny?"

"You are." His smile was soft as he leaned against the counter. "Half our conversations used to start that way. You liked him best, attracted to his drive and goal-oriented personality."

"Well, I don't remember it," she said sourly, thinking that didn't jibe with what she'd been reading in her diary. But she'd gotten only a few weeks into it.

A technician nervously edged forward, and Silas casually took the ticker tape of data he handed him. "That was hard for me to deal with," he admitted, voice distant as he unrolled his tablet from his pocket and pressed the bar code to the screen to upload the data. The entire tablet flashed blue to indicate a successful transfer, and he threw the tape away. "They can't apprehend Michael without you. You know that."

Nodding, she shifted the stool back and forth, thinking about her diary. Clearly something had shifted from what she'd read to the end, and a new desire filled her to find out when—and more important, how—his depression over Summer had shifted to jealousy, and then perhaps . . . a shared desire?

"Be careful," Silas said, oblivious to her thoughts. "I mean it, Peri. Allen isn't that good of a field anchor. Steiner thinks all anchors are alike, but if you draft, whatever you lose is gone."

"I can deal with it," she said distantly, then remembered why she was here. "Steiner wants a blood test to make sure I'm clean of the accelerator."

"Huh."

Silas was frowning at the new data on the screen. "What?" she asked flatly, and Silas straightened, his concern making her uneasy. "Is there a problem?"

"No. It's the preliminary breakdown of the Evocane," he said, brow furrowed. "Indications suggest the Evocane will have some nasty side effects. I mean, why is there a sodium uptake inhibitor in there?"

Her diary forgotten, she stilled her chair's motion. "Side effects?"

Silas's frown deepened. "I'm sure the chemical architects balanced everything out on paper," he said, his casual voice confused as he studied the tablet. "But the human body isn't a test tube. I know you want this to work, but this stuff is ugly. I can't let—"

"It's too soon to start talking about me taking it or not taking it," she interrupted, her stomach clenching. "Maybe I should just run. I'm good at that."

Silas exhaled heavily, his fingers slow as he closed down his tablet. "I don't think you should. I think you need to do this. All the way to the end. One hundred percent."

She sat where she was, stunned. "You want me to be the CIA's new toy?" she said indignantly. "Risk WEFT pumping me full of this stuff instead of Bill? You know as soon as I get Michael, I'm in the cell next door."

"Because they think you're a weapon," he said, his expression thick with concern. "This is your chance to prove them wrong."

She laughed bitterly. "I am a weapon."

"No, you're skilled. There's a difference."

His eyes pleaded with her, their pinched heartache familiar. She wanted to believe it, but she knew better. "When you can be made to forget, used by the highest bidder or most favorable lie or blackmailed, you're a weapon. Harmony is right," she said. "I'm a risk."

Silas touched her shoulder, and she stifled a surge of emotion. "You are a person. Convince the policy makers that you're trustworthy."

Her eyes fell from his. "Convincing Harmony of that isn't going to happen."

"She's just jealous." Silas gave her arm a quick squeeze before letting go.

"Of me? That's a laugh."

"Up until recently, Opti was hogging all the funds and resources," he said as he shuffled through a drawer. "You got the good tasks, the new gadgets," he added as he found a sterile finger lance and a blood-draw film. "And for what? Because you won the genetic lottery? Finding that out was hard. Harmony is good, from what I hear. And then you show up again, stealing her first chance to prove it."

Grimacing, she held her hand out. "And this is my fault?"

He swiped through his tablet's apps, shrugging as he pulled up the right one and set the blood-draw film on the softly glowing box. "Bringing Michael in will be the easy part. Convincing

Steiner you did it regardless of the carrot he's holding is harder. Okay. Little poke."

She steeled herself for it, eyeing the crimson drop before pressing it to the blood-draw film, the tablet recording her fingerprint for identification at the same time the film accepted her sample. "This is a waste of time," she muttered.

"Not if it makes Steiner feel better," he said, and Peri snorted as she took the sterile pad Silas handed her. He really was an odd mix of iron-pumping, lab-coat-wearing, PhD-holding psychologist. "Go get Michael. I'll pick the Evocane apart. If it's not safe, I'll make it safe. Promise."

He always makes it sound so easy. "Thank you." Rising up on tiptoe, she gave him a kiss on the cheek, finding a compliment in his suddenly tight expression. "Wish me luck."

Without a single glance behind her, she walked out.

CHAPTER EIGHT

"I have this, Swift. Go sit. I'll show you both when it's all compiled. Okay?"

Peri looked up from her phone as Allen dramatically dropped the CIA-issued tablet onto the tiny cocktail table Harmony had settled herself at. Motion oddly unsteady for the athletic man, he wobbled his way to the front of the jet and all but fell into the scarred, leather-bound chair across from her.

"And I thought *you* were a control freak," he muttered, making Peri smile as she rested the flats of her arms on the much wider conference table.

The jet had once shuttled VIPs in the early 2000s, still serviceable but its luxuries faded. Its leather was scarred with age and there was a noticeable lack of USB outlets. The lavatory was more spacious than she was used to, and a universal etherball kept them in contact with the web throughout the flight. Made up to seat twelve comfortably, it was still a nice little jet despite its age, everything that had once made it special now outdated even if it was still functional.

Sort of like me, Peri thought as she picked at the tacky-bottomed tray of desiccated cheese and crackers across the table from Allen. She'd changed into her upscale black suit less than an hour ago, going further to cut her hair to a functional ear length, and she brushed the black strands back, her guilt rising almost as fast as her anticipation. She'd taken pains to distance herself from this—the clothes, the haircut, the sensation of rising tension—and the same patterns she was resurrecting to keep her alive now felt like a trap.

Frustrated, Peri set her phone aside and put her forehead on the table. Her new felt-tip pen pendant swung out to clink on the faded wood, discolored from a thousand spilled martinis. Her breath came back hot and stale, and she turned her head. Out the oval window across the aisle, the sky had faded from deep blue to a black nothing, thick clouds blocking the ground.

Her open satchel sat on the wide leather seat under the window, the corner of her journal showing past her carefully folded street clothes. Frowning, Peri leaned across the aisle to pull the entire bag to her. Bringing her diary hadn't been a stellar idea, but leaving it in a CIA locker where anyone could find it was even worse, and besides, Silas's comments in the lab were bugging her.

She glanced at Allen pretending to read his latest rock-climbing magazine, his tablet making his face glow. She hadn't remembered that he didn't like to fly. It was unexpected from the adrenaline junkie who liked his bikes off-road and his sports extreme, and she smiled as she settled back with her diary, thumbing past the slow progression of tests, exams, and trials of the first trimester until she got to where she'd left off.

> Allen rented a skiff today, and we went out on Lake St. Clair. Big twenty-footer, with a tiny kitchen and a bed in the bow. Toward sunset, Allen spilled wine all over the cockpit, then fell in while getting a bucket of water to rinse it off. I think he did it so I'd come in after him and I'd

have to choose between wet clothes and wrapping myself in a beach towel for the sail in, but Silas cut the dinghy loose and we sailed on, leaving him sputtering and swearing. We went back to get him about an hour after it got dark. He was pissed, but honestly, it was the only time out there that didn't have Allen flapping his lips about something or other, usually about how we could beat everyone else in the next trial. The man never stops thinking. Plotting, Silas says, but I have to admit between Allen's underhanded strategies and Silas's tech innovations that make them work, we're staying ahead of the curve.

We're not winning any friends, but our supervisors are running this last year in training as if it's a freaking island where people are getting voted off, and I intend to be standing on the beach when this is over. I want that task. Silas needs it or he's going to kill himself with guilt. Allen . . . I can't tell if Allen wants it because he believes in bringing down the corrupt faction of Opti, or if he's looking for the job security that will come from this one task. I don't care. If he can keep doing what he's doing, we have a chance.

Silas and I watched the sun set behind

> Detroit, not saying a word. I think he appreciated the silence. I am such a chicken squirt. I should've done something other than put my head on his shoulder, but I was afraid I'd screw it up, and it's nice to see Silas doing better. He still has his moods, but he'll let himself enjoy something occasionally now. I love his laugh. I don't think I'll ever forget the sound of it, mixing with the waves and slapping sails when Allen dragged himself into the dinghy and we just kept going.

But she *had* forgotten, and feeling ill at opportunities lost from silence, she closed her journal, unable to read more. Why hadn't she made a memory knot of that? She had written about it so clearly she could almost see it. But the answer was obvious, sitting across from her and flipping through his magazine with little clicks from the tablet. Allen had burned that year from her mind. He would have taken extra care with that memory.

Cold, Peri carefully hid her diary under her clothes and zipped the satchel up. She couldn't find it in herself to be mad at him. She'd wanted it, fought for it, and a frown furrowed her brow. She was still wearing it when she looked up to find Harmony standing right before her.

"My, aren't we happy," Harmony said, her face

expressionless as she dropped two of the three CIA tablets on the table. “I’ve got your intel ready.”

Allen shut his magazine down and reached for his packet. “Finally.”

Exhaling slow and long, Harmony took the chair farthest from Peri. She’d changed into a blah navy pantsuit, her shoulder holster empty for the moment. Though it was off-the-rack and lacking the style of Peri’s outfit, she nevertheless looked professional. “Top pages are building schematics,” Harmony said, eyes on Allen as he eagerly flipped through them. “Everblue is in an industrial park between the airport and the city. Lots of room. Slow response time. Security is high, but it was put in after the fact and there are major holes.”

“Which we can use to our advantage as much as Michael,” Allen said, studying the last page where the electronic fence was detailed out.

Peri pulled her tablet closer, flipping past the grainy, probably drone-obtained cover photo of a standard warehouse/manufacturing facility to find the rough building blueprint and see where the exits were. Not liking them, she put her lower lip between her teeth and studied the air ducts and considerable upper crawl space. Though Everblue’s facility looked like a one-story, it was really three apart from the big hangar where the heavy machinery was. “Generators?” she asked, not bothering to decipher the diagrams Allen would be more familiar with.

"No," Harmony said. "City hookup. Intel says no need to cut it."

Depending on people she'd never met before felt wrong in about three different ways. "Live guard?" she asked.

"Nothing we can't work around." Harmony reached for a piece of cheese as if it was guilt itself. "There's a three-hour window between on-site presence. I told you, we have this."

Peri was starting to feel like the punch line to a joke, coming in at the last minute. Allen was taking it even worse, a born plotter, and she could see him chafing, torn between trying to replan everything and dealing with the stress of being a team player and trusting someone else. She, though, didn't have a problem making waves. "Are you sure?" she asked.

Harmony's chewing slowed. It was the only indication of her mood. "Yes."

Emboldened, Allen leaned forward. "What if Michael cuts the power? Shouldn't we—"

"My team is already there," Harmony interrupted. "You, Swift, are to stick with Peri in case she drafts. That's it."

"I can do something other than catch Peri when she falls," he muttered, eyes returning to his tablet.

"Not today, Swift," Harmony said, her fake mood of nonchalance wearing thin.

Peri leaned in, the flats of her arms aggressively on the table. "What does your team have in case you're wrong and we're interrupted by a stray guard or employee coming back for his or her phone?"

"I'm not wrong," the woman insisted indignantly.

Allen tossed his tablet to the table. "What am I here for? What is *she* here for?" he added, pointing to Peri. "You're the team leader, right? Use your tools. Don't lock them up in your tool chest because they might get scratched."

Harmony's jaw clenched, then relaxed. "Okay," she said, voice even. "Allen, if there are any unexpected guards, they're your responsibility as long as it doesn't interfere with you anchoring Peri."

"Check."

Allen takes care of any unexpected guards? What kind of a plan is that? That closed-in feeling was growing. Peri took enough crackers and cheese to make three mini sandwiches, knowing that for whatever reason, Harmony felt as if she couldn't. "What is Michael's target, anyway?" she asked, crumbs falling onto Harmony's intel.

"Ah . . . some kind of carbon filter," Harmony said, her attention on the crumbs.

Carbon filter? "And you think this is a legit task, not a trap?"

Allen slumped deeper into his chair. "And it was going so well, too."

"Not that it matters," Harmony said tightly, "but he's stealing proprietary information concerning a new process to modify existing autonomous carbon scrubbers used to collect airborne carbon into a usable form, in essence making fuel from the air. It lowers CO_2 levels and supplies a clean fuel to pay for itself. If Bill can secure it, the oil and gas companies will pay through the nose to keep it out of production." Clearly irate, Harmony turned back to her notes. "It's not a trap. It's a game changer."

That it is, Peri mused as she thought through the ramifications. "You're right," she said, and Allen looked up, shocked. Peri frowned at him. "What?" she said sharply, brushing the crumbs to the floor. "She is."

"*I* never said she was wrong." Allen hunched over the schematics. "What's the plan? Wait until Michael goes in, then use the building to contain him until we can bring him down?"

Harmony crossed her arms over her middle as if expecting him to protest. "That's it."

That's it, Peri thought. They were going to die. All of them. "Michael has been known to draft up to a minute," she said, not knowing why she was telling Harmony this. They could use everything she said to capture her as well. "If you don't have Amneoset, you're going to have to dart him with the sedative when he's rewriting time. Otherwise, he'll just draft his way out of it."

"Rewrite," Harmony echoed, eyes on a cracker as she carefully snapped it in two and ate the smaller piece. "What difference does it make?"

Allen chuckled and went back to flipping through the schematics, and Peri was satisfied that he'd find a way out when it all hit the fan. "You can't draft within a draft, so a rewrite is the only span of time you have to make something stick," she said, thinking Harmony should know this already. "You dart him with anything other than Amneoset, and Michael will simply rewrite time to avoid getting hit, and that includes being shot. Amneoset is wicked fast, but a sedative takes time before it shuts down the ability to draft, and that's all he needs."

"And that, Agent Beam," Allen said distantly, stylus between his teeth, "is why Steiner wanted me here." He looked up, taking the stylus out. "I'm the only one besides Peri who can tell you when you're in a rewrite. It's not hard to bring down a drafter when the timing is right. Unfortunately, you're a three-dimensional person, and only someone who can *see* in four has a hope of bringing down someone who *lives* in four."

Harmony brushed the crumbs from her, clearly trying to keep the distaste out of her expression. "Fine, so we sedate him during a rewrite. It shouldn't be hard after that," Harmony said, and Peri sighed. "You don't agree?" Harmony said provocatively.

"Stopping a drafter from jumping doesn't negate them," Peri said. "It's like shooting someone in the foot and expecting him to drop down dead."

"No, we just fall down and roll around a lot," Allen grumbled, eyes still on his tablet.

Harmony's lips pressed together. "Then what do you propose we do?"

"Offhand? I don't know," Peri said honestly. "There're too many variables, and I usually leave the planning up to my anchor. It'd be easier if I had something more lethal than an empty boot sheath, though."

Her phone was buzzing, and Peri pulled it to her from across the table. *Cam.* Damn it, if Carnac had run off, she was going to be ticked.

"Go ahead and take it," Harmony said as she stood. "I need to make a call."

"I'm familiar with anything you have," Peri offered, knowing Harmony was likely going to clear the ingoing assets with Steiner. "And Michael will be, too." Shoulders tense, she muttered, "We aren't just magic ponies."

Motion stiff, Harmony made her way to the rear of the plane, settling herself in an aisle seat where she could watch everything, her phone already to her ear.

Smirking, Allen went back to the blueprints. "I don't know why you have such a hard time making friends."

"Hey." Peri hit the connect button. "I'm not the

one being stingy with the assets." Hardly taking a breath, she said, "Hi, Cam. What's up?"

"Good afternoon." Cam's cultured voice eased into her like melted chocolate, sweet, bitter, and addictive. "Should I let Carnac out if I won't be awake to let him in until morning?"

"Ah, sure," she said as Allen made a sad sound and focused on the intel. "Just make sure you leave a dish of water by your door."

"The only reason I ask is that he didn't come back last night when I called. He's here now, but I'm worried he might try to go back to the coffeehouse."

An unexpected heartache went through her at the missing rhythm of her coffeehouse, and she ate another cracker, not hungry. "If he came back once, he'll come back again. You must be feeding him something he likes."

"I took him into the store, and he picked it out."

She could hear a coffee grinder, but it was low volume. He ground his own coffee? "You took him into the store?"

"Why not? People were taking their dogs in. And that's another thing. The bag says half a cup per ten pounds of cat. He's not eating it all."

"You can leave it out," she said, smiling from the mental image of Cam holding a cat up to the shelves and looking for a response. "He'll eat when he's hungry."

"I thought so." There was a slight hesitation, then, "What time zone are you in?"

"Huh?" Shocked, her eyes flicked to Allen, who'd caught the question as well.

"The only reason I ask is because I don't want to call you at three in the morning. By the sound of it, your jet is too small to be going to the West Coast. Still Eastern?"

"Ah, Central." Damn, he was good. "How—"

"I traveled a lot for a while. You get to know the sound of the engines. Are you okay? Need anything?"

Allen was silently laughing, and she made a face at him to keep quiet. "I'm fine," she said, embarrassed. "It might take me longer than I thought, though." Harmony was digging in a back locker, and the duffel bag she'd just dropped in the aisle held promise. "Ah, I've got to go," she said, not liking that her pulse had quickened at the thought of some firepower. "Thanks again for watching Carnac. He means a lot to me."

"No problem. Talk to you later."

"Bye." She hit the end icon. Allen was watching her sourly.

"He's going to be trouble," he said, perking up when Harmony's duffel hit the table with a familiar, comforting set of sliding clinks and thuds.

"He's just a guy watching my cat." Peri leaned forward when Harmony opened it up to show several Kevlar vests, handguns, and three dart rifles. "Which one is mine?"

"Doesn't matter." Harmony stood over them, brow furrowed. "The vest isn't optional."

She hadn't worn a vest since graduating Opti's boot camp, and she wasn't starting now. It would take a head shot to stop her from drafting, and a vest wouldn't prevent that. But Allen reached for one, eyes widening in pleasure. "Yes, ma'am!" he said as he picked out a handgun first, checking the clip. "These don't shoot darts. Can we kill him?"

"Not even if he kills you first. The Glocks are for emergency only." Expression closed, she sat. "Peri, is a ring chip okay? I can put it on a wristband instead if you want. It should be close enough."

Peri looked up from checking the dart rifle's chamber to find it empty. The heavy slickness of the instrument was soothing, though. "Chip?"

"The firing chip," Harmony said, then hesitated, her eyes brightening. "You don't have these? Or did you just forget."

"No," Allen mused. "This is new. A firing chip?"

Smug, Harmony reached for a Glock. Using a tiny tool from a small kit, she opened the hilt. "It's German. We've had it for a while. The chip has to be within two inches of the butt or the weapon won't fire. We're the first large-scale trial for the company who makes them. You haven't heard of this?"

It was obvious by her self-satisfied smile that she knew they hadn't. "Not that it was available in the States." Setting the rifle aside, Peri took the ring Harmony was extending. It was thick, like a class ring, and she put it on her index finger, where it almost fit. It was a great idea. If she lost the weapon or it was taken from her, it couldn't be used on her or sold.

"Ha." Allen took off his watch and handed it to Harmony to be fitted. "I never thought I'd see you with finger bling, Peri."

"Me either," she said sourly. Harmony was clearly in a better mood, and Peri's suspicions deepened. "I'm assuming there's a tracking chip in it, too?" she asked, and Harmony brightened.

"Obviously."

Peri's hand clenched into a fist and she eyed the ring with WEFT imprinted on it along with a serial number. "Well, at least it's not in my ass."

Allen's laugh choked off at the sudden turbulence. Harmony froze, her detailed work to get the chip onto Allen's watch interrupted. "We're landing," she said, checking her phone before shoving the empty satchel under a seat. "We move right to the warehouse. Steiner says Bill has pushed Michael's timetable up."

The jet was jostling in the unsettled air to make Allen grip his armrest. "Now?" he blurted, suddenly pale. "I thought we weren't going to be on-site until two in the morning."

"In and out." Harmony checked her hopper before sliding the weapon away. "Bill changed his plans. We adapted. The locals won't even know we were ever there."

This was getting better and better. Peri eyed Allen for his opinion, but he was too preoccupied by the jostling. "Why did Bill change his plans?" she asked, and when Harmony shrugged, Peri's unease strengthened. "We need to take a step back and find out."

"There's neither the need nor the time." It was quick, and Harmony looked ticked. "We go now. I'm sorry we can't check in and get a nice meal and a swim first."

Peri's lips parted. "Meal and a swim?"

Harmony eyed her past Allen clenching the armrests. "You want to stay in the jet?"

"You want to get shot?" Peri snapped.

"One more word and you don't leave the airfield," Harmony said, interrupting her.

"This is a mistake." Peri pushed back into the seat as the jet kissed the tarmac and Allen sighed in relief. If Michael's jealousy didn't kill her, then Harmony's pride would. And needing to draft to come back from that would really piss her off.

CHAPTER NINE

"How many people are out here?" Peri slung her dart rifle, cold fingers brushing her Glock to reassure herself she had it. January in St. Louis wasn't warm. At night in an open field dotted with industrial buildings, it was positively frigid. Her frown deepened at the government van parked in the shadows behind the warehouselike building. It was disguised as a local furniture mover, the panels caked with too much dirt to not be suspect. *Should have used salt and grime, not mud.*

"Eight." Kevlar vest showing, Harmony handed her a radio and earpiece. She was little more than a voice in the freezing blackness. "We're on channel B."

"Eight?" The cold from the cinder-block wall Peri was pressed against was seeping into her. "Why are *eight* people out here?"

"Because that's my team." A glow blossomed as Harmony fiddled with her phone, clearly the medium the radios were working through. Shadow heavy on her face, Harmony glanced at the radio still in Peri's hand. "You know how the radio works, right?"

"I know how a radio works." Peeved, Peri dropped the wireless receiver in a pocket and fitted the earpiece. Satisfied, Harmony closed out the app, and her phone and her face went dark.

It was nearing midnight, the night cloudless and gripped with a cold too bitter for snow. Traffic had slowed on the adjacent expressway. And whereas Peri would usually say midnight was too early for a B and E, the place was deserted, nothing but open flat land spotted with light manufacturing and service roads rimed with salt reflecting back the moonlight.

Peri eyed Harmony's Kevlar vest, wishing now she'd taken one if for nothing more than another layer. Allen looked warm enough in his. "Do you seriously expect you can have eight agents out here and not alert Michael to your presence?" she grumbled as she blew on her fingers, and Harmony's posture stiffened. "You don't think Bill has the guard on his payroll? That your men have been spotted and word sent back? Good Lord, you don't leave a multibillion-dollar piece of equipment in a manufacturing facility with a three-hour security window. This is a setup. They know we're here. They moved the timetable up to put us off balance."

"Thank you, Agent Reed," Harmony said, then louder to the agents already on-site, "Can we get inside, maybe?" and one jogged away.

"Agent Reed" echoed in her ear, and Peri started. "This is Steiner. I'll be monitoring the airwaves during this task. I trust you can keep the chatter to a minimum. I remind you that this is Agent Beam's task. Understood?"

Peri took the piece out of her ear and dropped it into her pocket. "I'm not questioning your methods," she said. "But thinking that Michael doesn't know you're on-site is ridiculous."

"I expect that he does," the woman said as she touched her earpiece. "Try to not let him kill you." She thumbed a button on her radio. "Viper moving in."

"Viper?" Peri muttered disparagingly. "*I've* never needed a code name."

Allen's slim hand landed warm and heavy on her shoulder. Leaning close, he pushed her to the fire door now propped open by an agent. "You've never worked with more than one other person before," he said, looking eager behind his thick glasses and faint stubble.

This was not how she did things, but she followed Harmony into the hangarlike building, appreciating the warmth. She couldn't help but feel as if she were shooting a lion who'd been tied down the evening before, all the while the lioness circling behind her.

Peri halted at the outskirts of the small group, hands in her armpits to warm her fingers as she scanned the heavy machines in rows and the cranes silent above them. A squatty mushroom-shaped container the size of a bus sat under a spotlight, and she figured it was the carbon condenser. There were too many people here. She liked her tasks simple. Fewer moving parts meant the less that could break.

"Allen?" she whispered, and he sidled up to her, squinting in the dim light.

"Just go with it. You might like this new army."

Doubt it. Not happy, she pulled him aside as Harmony stood with another agent and looked over the latest info on their tablets. "Michael is sitting somewhere, laughing at us."

"You want to ditch the posse and find him?" Allen asked, and she nodded, eyes flicking to Harmony. The woman would be pissed, but they were underestimating Michael. Badly. They were treating him as if he played by rules, and it was going to get them killed.

Peri straightened when Harmony came up to them, eyes bright. "Offices are through the double doors at the far side. Heat map indicates that's where he's at. Let's go." Peri didn't move, and Harmony jerked to a stop after two steps. "You want to show me how good you are?"

Allen jiggled her elbow to say something, and Peri took a breath, biting back her first sarcastic response. Then she turned and walked away.

"Hey!" Harmony barked out, hardly above a whisper. "Where are you going?"

Peri spun, wanting an end to it. "With Allen to find that surprise guard. Do I need a chip to fire the dart gun or just the Glock?" she asked, wanting to be sure, and Harmony frowned.

"Just the Glock. Michael is that way," Harmony said, pointing.

"You can go *that* way. My gut tells me to go *this* way." Peri pointed in the opposite direction. "Or don't you want to show me how good you are?" The man who had let them in flicked his eyes from one to the other, and Peri pushed into Harmony's space. "I'm not turning on you. I'm hunting. Or don't you trust me?"

Harmony's eyes narrowed. "Check in every five minutes. Wear your radio."

"Sure." As Allen fidgeted, she fitted her earpiece and turned the volume to zero. Finished, Peri jogged across the flat expanse, jerking out the earpiece as soon as the dark took her. Allen was close beside her. Emotion tightened her gut and gave her a slight headache. It wasn't because she'd stood up to Harmony and slipped her leash. No, it was because she was working.

"I'm surprised she let you out of her sight," Allen said, looking over his shoulder when they reached a small fire door.

"She thinks she's giving me enough rope to hang myself." Peri eased the door open and slipped into a dull hallway lined with doors.

"Are you?"

Peri sighed. "Probably." It was warmer, and her pulse was fast. Both ways looked equally unpromising, but she turned to the left and the heavier scuffs on the floor. "You think he's in the lab?" Allen guessed, looking at his schematic on his phone as they loped along.

Peri searched her intuition, not surprised when she saw Jack cross the top of the hallway and vanish to the right. He had a yogurt cup in his hand, scraping out the last bits. "Lunchroom," she said, breaking into a jog. "Call it a gut feeling."

Allen looked up, tucking his phone away and lurching to come even with her. "Why would they be in the lunchroom?"

"Because the walk-in freezers hide heat signatures," she said, turning the corner to find a double set of doors with BREAK ROOM stenciled on them. She slung her rifle and slipped her new CIA handgun from its holster. Allen did the same. "I ever tell you about the time I got caught by the Russian mob in a dance club in Florida?" she whispered, peeking in past the cracked doors to a silent, shadowed lunchroom. Jack was there, getting a soda out of the machine. "They trusted their technology more than a set of real eyes.

She slipped inside, easing to the wall to make room for Allen, tight behind her. "Believe it or not, I can fit in one of those tiny wine coolers."

Jack turned from the vending machine, a bottle of pop in his hand. "She smelled like cheap red wine for a week," he said, and Allen started, jerking Peri to the side.

Lips in a wide grin, Jack dropped the bottle to reach for his weapon. Red fizz sprayed the walls, and Peri gasped when Allen shoved a table over to hide behind. There was a muffled pop of Jack's silencer, and a louder crack of Allen's slug. "Bill!" Jack shouted, finger to his ear and running for the hall. "She's in the lunchroom!"

And then Jack was gone.

Red fizz continued to spurt and hiss, and slowly the bottle settled until red sugar gurgled in a flood and finally stopped.

Bill is here. Shocked, Peri peered above the edge of the table. "I thought he was a hallucination," she stammered, and Allen, busy changing his clip to a magazine, looked up.

"What?"

"A hallucination," she said again. "I saw him in the hallway, and I thought he was a hallucination!"

Irate, Allen took her weapon and changed her clip to a magazine as well. "You like it here, or you want to move?"

"Kitchen," she said, lurching forward when the doors to the hall exploded inward.

Head down and gripping Allen's arm, she ran for the swinging double doors. There was no option to stand and fight. There was only trying to find a more secure spot. Bill hadn't come alone either.

"Good God, how many people are out here?"

Allen said, right behind Peri as they went past the silent industrial kitchen counters. There'd be a service door after the dishwasher.

They weren't going to make it.

Shouts sounded behind them, and the almost inaudible puffs of high-projectile darts. Allen cried out. Peri shoved him into a corner and turned, firing with a rhythmic satisfaction, pushing them back. "You hit?" she shouted, firing off another round, *pop, pop, pop, pop.* "I said, are you hit bad!"

"Shoulder." Allen's hand lifted from his shirt to show a dart graze. "Damn, these hurt more than a direct lodge."

Relief spilled into her, then worry. "If you say so." *Pop, pop, pop.* She ducked down, not feeling as secure as she might. It was her bullets to their darts, but a dart could be just as lethal as a slug. Men were shouting, but they were safe for the moment, trapped between a walk-in fridge and a service counter. Between them and the attackers was a huge stove and more counters. Grimacing, she fitted her earpiece back in and thumbed her radio. "Harmony?" she said, not *ever* going to call her Viper. "We're pinned down in the kitchen!"

Allen's eyes showed his worry when a garbled response came back. There was actual gunplay at her end, and then Harmony shouting "Get out! Get out now!" Peri's attention fixed on Allen's, but she froze when Michael's voice slithered into her ear, icy and clear. "Peri. I'm going to kill your team. Then I'm coming for you."

She jumped at the pop of a gun. *Harmony . . .* But Peri could hear the woman grunting in anger in the background, struggling. It hadn't been her taking the hit. Not yet.

Allen jerked his earpiece out. "They knew what they were up against."

"No they didn't."

Eyes pinched, he looked at the ceiling. "Upper level is open. If we can get in it, we have free access to the entire complex." Allen's attention shifted behind her. "Down!" he shouted, handgun rising as a man in Opti gear sprang from an adjacent counter and shot at them.

A hammer slammed into her chest, hardly shifting her though her insides felt as if they had exploded. Gasping, she fell back, legs askew. Allen hit the floor, his hand pressed to his chest as blood leaked past his Kevlar vest. It was never meant to handle what had hit it.

So much for the darts, she thought, fear lighting through Peri as the call went out that they were down. Down and dying. Someone kicked her rifle and Glock away. Men ringed them, afraid to touch her.

Allen groaned in pain when they were pulled up and apart, his legs sliding across the linoleum. Her vision swam as she lifted her head, the pain familiar as it radiated out, but Peri smiled through it, the blood leaking past her fingers indescribably warm. Her eyes met Allen's, and at his nod, the slow buildup of pressure in her mind peaked, eddied, and then overflowed.

With a satisfied, agonized smile, Peri breathed in the rising blue sparkles and shifted the timelines back.

CHAPTER TEN

Bill's thick fingers waved the scrolling images on the screen to the trash to bring up a new set. His joints were knobby from being broken too many times in his martial arts practice, but wave technology with its holoscreens and light sensors was adaptable, and his hand's inflexibility didn't slow him down as it did with the rapidly outdating glass technology.

Standing against the wall and away from the door, he puffed out his cheeks in thought, glad he'd taken the time to shave on the plane. He was of the same mind as Peri that a poorly dressed thief was a lowbrow thief, and that was not the impression he wanted to give the WEFT force headed his way—even if he was in a tight spot financially.

Helen's money had set him up in a shadow of what he was accustomed to. His office was tatty and his hired muscle was only street-rated, easily surprised and shocked into immobility. He missed his combat-ready force. There was a growing need in him to walk away, to start small and grow. But for that, he needed money, money that wasn't tied to a woman who thought science was her biddable bitch. Good thing he knew how to find it. This one task would allow him to cut his ties with Helen as well as start Peri on the path to bring her home. He did value efficiency.

The images of St. Louis's industrial park were hard to decipher in the dusk, but a glint of light caught his attention, and he zoomed the borrowed high-Q drone's eye onto the building. Satisfaction rumbled through him as he found the WEFT force. Two cars and a van. No movement on the grounds. They were likely already inside.

"Find them?" Michael asked as he swiped through his phone. "I got word forty seconds ago that they were in the building."

Stifling a surge of pique, Bill closed the link and looked up at the five men in combat gear waiting for direction. Michael was behind Everblue's CEO's desk, feet on the imported wood as they waited for the download to finish. The scratches from the dish shards across his face were almost healed, but the cut Peri had dug into the man with her knife was red-rimmed and raw-looking under his eye. Bill knew it bothered Michael just by the fact he had refused to cover it.

"Feet off the desk," Bill said, shoving them off.

"You'd get there faster if you embraced new technology." Michael resettled himself, but his feet were on the floor, and Bill's tension eased.

"How much longer?" Bill asked, and Michael tilted his phone to check. A curious sensation tripped up Bill's spine. The sale of the carbon scrubber would set him up in an autonomous building with tighter security and the influence he was accustomed to, but it was the chance that Peri might show that had him here.

"Still scooping it up." Michael set his phone down.

"It would go faster if you would stop checking your email every five minutes."

"It's not my email, it's a first-person shooter game." Michael eyed him. "Why am I here? You're not letting me do anything."

"You're here so you don't fuck everything up," Bill said, vowing to stop swearing when Michael chuckled. "You're like a five-year-old helping Mommy in the kitchen," Bill muttered, and Michael's mirth vanished. "It would be easier if you were somewhere else, but then I'd have two messes to clean up instead of one."

Frustrated, Bill motioned for three of the five men to do a sweep. They moved out with a relieved quickness, not liking Michael's cold unpredictability any more than Bill did. He was starting to believe the smart man had realized he wanted Peri not as a test subject but working, and that he had no intention of accelerating Michael. It didn't matter. As long as Michael believed that playing along would further his goal, he wouldn't fuck up Bill's plans beyond repair.

Bill touched his dart gun, loaded with Evocane. He'd rather be with Jack perusing the building, but he didn't dare risk Peri killing Michael if their paths should cross. *Not yet, kiddo. Timing is everything.*

"Bill!" Jack shouted, his voice excited as it came over the live feed through his phone. "She's in the lunchroom!"

Tension jerked him straight, almost painful. His Peri was here. He'd known she'd come.

Michael rose, stretching to his full six-foot-four height. "About time."

"Sit," Bill barked, not caring whether Michael saw how excited he was. "Finish gathering the data. That's what you're here for. That knee of yours she stabbed makes you slow."

Silent, Michael eased himself back down, and Bill checked his Glock, shoving it into a holster and taking his dart gun in hand.

"You two, stay with him," Bill said, seeing Michael's dissatisfaction. "He doesn't move from this room until the data is uploaded," Bill added, and the remaining security reluctantly dropped back.

Eager, Bill slipped into the hall and jogged to the

kitchen, muscles moving easily and enjoying the rush. He liked the thrill of the field. Missed it. The thought to be Peri's anchor when this was settled crossed his mind, immediately dismissed with a smile. She was too much the queen bitch, and he couldn't imagine the two of them in the same apartment, much less the same bed. He'd much rather think of her as a daughter to be disciplined and shaped than as a lover to be discarded at will.

He turned the corner, twisting to a sliding halt at the burst of gunfire behind him at the CEO's office. *Damn it, Michael. What now?* Peri was on the other side of the building. Jack had said so. But then a feminine scream of anger split the dark hallway.

Peri, he thought, anger blinding him to everything else as he ran back down the hall to burst into the CEO's office. Two men in CIA combat gear were down, presumably dead in their blood-splattered puddles of red. Three more knelt with Glocks to their heads. Michael stood over a fourth, his knife at a long, feminine throat, his hand pulling her hair back to expose her neck.

Furious, he shoved Michael off her, only to find it wasn't Peri. Gagging, the African-American woman shouted, "Get out! Get out now!" into her radio before she was yanked back to a kneel with the rest of her team.

"You didn't take her radio?" Bill seethed, looking at the mess they were going to leave.

"It wasn't going to matter in five seconds," Michael said shortly as he snatched up the discarded radio and thumbed the channel open. "Peri. I'm going to kill your team. Then I'm coming for you."

"You are so damn melodramatic," Bill said impatiently, then jerked when Michael pulled his Glock, aiming it at the first man in line and pulling the trigger. The woman gasped as blood and hair made a fantastic pattern on the wall. Jerking, the man fell.

"Three left," Michael said into the radio, then threw it from him when he realized the connection was broken. Thin lips pressed together, Michael shifted his aim and twitched his finger. His Glock fired, and a second man died. This time the woman jumped, her lip bleeding where she bit it. Bill frowned, well aware the Glock would turn on him if he didn't give Michael enough freedom to feel in control. But every shot ate away at his bottom line, and it was frustrating.

"Has Peri been accelerated?" Michael said as he moved to the last man.

"You are making a bloody hell of a mess," Bill protested, seeing the sale of the carbon scrubber turn to nothing, but he was curious himself.

"I don't know what you're talking about," the CIA agent said. Arm extended, Michael coolly shot the back of his head.

Bill's breath slipped from him even as his

heart pounded. The pop of the handgun sounded ridiculously soft, and the man's brains hitting the floor made an ugly, sudden splat.

Stifling a cry of anger, the woman glared at them, her hands behind her head going white-knuckled. *Damn it,* Bill thought, frowning at the tissue and fluid staining the carpet. There was no way they could clean this up sufficiently fast enough; the information they'd come for was useless. Peri could always get information without the threat of death. She was an artist.

"Lies are temporary," Michael said as he checked his chamber. Blood speckled him, hardly seeming enough for the four men dead before him. "I always see through them, and it's vexing. You're not going to lie, are you?" he asked the woman kneeling before him.

The woman was pissed, even as she shook in shock. Michael shoved the man guarding her away, leaning over her so his face was inches from hers, the gun barrel just under her eye. "Is Peri Reed accelerated?" he asked again. "Tell me!" Michael shouted, and she jumped, jaw tight and eyes closed.

But Michael dropped back, brushing her hair from her eyes and studying her. "Loyalty," he said softly, but there was no gentleness in his expression. "It's misplaced. Harmony."

Her eyes flicked open, surprised, and Michael almost preened in the attention.

"Kill her or don't," Bill said grimly. "We're done here." He turned to go, but the woman gasped, and he hesitated; he'd just about had it with Michael's uncouth ham-handedness.

"I know your name, yes," Michael said, his thin lips inches from her ear, the Glock keeping her unmoving. "Your loyalty is misplaced. Your gut tells you not to trust her. You should listen to it. Peri has done ugly things. The White Plague, the first wave of Asian population decimation, the assassination of troublesome senators." He wiped a spot of blood from her with the muzzle of the Glock, and Harmony stiffened, pulling back from the warm metal. "She is not a nice woman. You don't like her. I can see it in your face. Is she accelerated? Is she waiting for her boyfriend to duplicate the Evocane first? How close is he?"

Bill hesitated, torn.

"Bring back my team, and maybe we'll talk," she said, voice cracking.

Michael smiled and inclined his head. "Too late. Even the best drafter can only manage ninety seconds."

"Good to know. But you can go to hell."

"Ladies first."

Bill saw the woman's death in Michael's eyes before the trigger moved. He heard the hammer click. He saw the puff of smoke as if in slow motion . . . and then the smoke shifted blue as time halted.

For an instant, sparkles cascaded over him as time reset, and then the world shifted.

Bill jumped as the gun fired, and he watched the last man die again.

They were in a draft, and Bill turned, finding himself again standing beside Michael instead of in the hall. Before them, the woman shook in shock and anger, unaware that they were reliving her nightmare.

"I didn't draft," Michael said, and Bill stiffened. Peri was on-site, and something had pushed her into drafting. *Damn it, I told them no live ammunition on her.*

"Time to die, soldier girl," Michael muttered, then ran out of the room, leaving the last CIA agent alive. The two men Bill had set to watch him followed.

"Michael, you stupid shit," Bill whispered, looking at the five dead men and the kneeling, empty-faced woman. "I don't suppose you'd stay if I asked," he said, then cold-cocked her.

The woman collapsed without a sound.

His hand hardly feeling it, Bill bolted into the hallway. He had to get there before Michael ruined everything.

CHAPTER ELEVEN

Her vision shifted blue. The pain in her chest vanished. Beside her, Allen groaned in relief. She exhaled sparkles, and they sucked up the blue until her vision was again crystal clear.

They were back behind the oven, and she stood, squeezing off a single shot at the approaching man without pity. He fell back, dead before he hit the floor. She turned to the next, finger twitching an instant before recoil. Sometimes forgetting was a blessing.

Grunts and pained cries sandwiched themselves between the rhythmic pops. Eyes wide open, she took the sting of gunpowder into her nose. She didn't use darts. She used slugs. Every one of them found their mark, witnessed and remembered from the previous timeline until the two timelines meshed and she forgot.

And then there was silence. The kitchen was empty. For the moment.

Bill is coming.

"We gotta go," she whispered, turning her weapon upward to fire a rapid circle into the ceiling tiles. Cool air spilled over them behind the chunks of ceiling falling on them.

Allen got up, choking on dust as he wrestled her gun from her and changed the magazine. "Thanks," he said, feeling his unmarked chest. "What the hell are they using? It went right through the Kevlar."

"I noticed." She ducked, shying sideways as a chunk of tile fell. Fear was a thin line icing her motion. She was going to forget. In about thirty seconds, she was going to forget everything past her last contact with Harmony. Bill was an anchor. If he was close enough to her when she snapped out of it, she might forget even more. "We have to get out of here."

"Reed?" Michael called, his long face hard with anticipation as he stormed into the lunchroom, two men behind him with unslung rifles. His Glock was in his hand, and he clearly wanted to use it. "Ah. There you are." A smile split his face as he took aim.

Beside her, Allen's weapon fired, numbing her ears and sending the men with Michael to cover. The recoil of her weapon thumped into her hand as she fired as well, but there were more men coming in, screaming at them to put their weapons up even as they ran for cover.

Face ugly, Michael hesitated, then, with a cry of outrage, pulled his aim from her.

Bill, she thought as she saw him come into the lunchroom, his brow furrowed at the haze and sudden silence. He knew they were in a rewrite—and he wouldn't forget. Halting, the heavy man smiled when he met Peri's eyes. "Get Michael out of here," he said softly, and Michael fell under an avalanche of men. "Sorry, kiddo," he said as he lifted his dart rifle.

"Move!" Allen shouted, shoving her, and she ducked, willing the draft to end. But she couldn't make time move faster, and with a puff of compressed air, a dart arrowed to her, the red fletch alive and boiling like lava. It hit her perfectly, thumping into her bicep with the sudden wedging pain of a monstrous bee. Breath held, she yanked it out, furious. He'd timed it perfectly, getting it into her in a draft where she couldn't rewrite the mistake out.

And then the world flashed red with the energy of twin timelines meshing.

"Peri! Get down!"

She gasped as Allen yanked her into cover. A red-fletched arrow was in her tight grip, and she stared at it, feeling a hard ache in her shoulder where it had hit, but not remembering it. Her head came up, and vertigo rose as she saw the dead men ringing them. More were shouting from cover, and one man screamed, his voice high in pain as Michael broke the man's wrist to gain his freedom. There was a ragged hole in the ceiling, and the Glock in her hand was warm.

I drafted, she thought, enormously relieved that

Allen was with her, his skinned shoulder bleeding slowly as he peeked over the oven and dropped back down.

"Someone shot us and you drafted," Allen whispered harshly. "Short version is Harmony can't help us. We have to get out on our own. Bill is here. He—"

"Set a trap for me. Yeah, I got that part," she finished, dart in her hand. It must have hit her as the draft was ending. It was in the last timeline, not the one she'd rubbed out. It was real and immutable. She couldn't jump with whatever antidrafting drug he'd hit her with.

"Time to move." Allen angled his weapon around the edge of the oven and fired off a few blind shots as more men spilled into the lunchroom. "We've used up our wishes and have to get out on bullets now."

Peri looked up at the ragged hole in the ceiling, then threw the dart away. "You first."

"Nah-uh." Allen dropped back down from looking over the edge of the counters, dust from the ceiling making his hair gray. "You're the lightest."

"Peri?" Jack shouted from the far end of the kitchen. "It doesn't have to be like this."

"Shit," Allen swore, and Peri eased forward, eyes narrowed as she shot at a shadow. It stumbled back, Jack's voice rising as he fell into a rack of pans. Satisfaction filled her. *Not the illusion-Jack, then.*

"Pull back. Give her some space," Bill said, but

she didn't trust the implied cease-fire, and she looked behind her for the men Bill had probably sent to circle them.

Allen squinted at the ceiling. "This is bad," he said, checking his ammo.

"It's over, Peri," Bill called authoritatively, and she sank deeper into the scant cover. "Weapons on the floor. Now! And that knife of yours, too."

As if.

"You go first," Allen said, looking at the ceiling.

Peri's gaze shifted from Allen's bullet graze to the hole above them. "I can't pull you up with a bum arm. I'm the better shot, anyway. I'll cover you."

"Fine," he muttered, gathering himself. "You got a new magazine in there?"

"Go!" She stood, firing at anything that moved. Men scattered, and her lips pulled back in an angry grimace when Bill dove for cover. *If I get shot again, Harmony will laugh her ass off for me not taking a vest.*

Allen fired six shots even as he levered himself up onto the counter. Grunting, he pulled himself into the ceiling. His legs dangled, jerking when a dart lodged, and then he was gone.

Anger pushed out why she was here. It didn't matter. There was only firing as many times as she could before someone got a good shot in.

"Hand!" Allen shouted, and she stood, continuing to shoot even as her palm smacked into Allen's and he lifted. She swung wildly, her bullets hitting nothing but keeping their heads down. Heart pounding, she felt the dusty, cold darkness take her.

"Damn, that hurts," Allen groaned, and she got a knee on the ceiling support and levered herself up and in. "I can see why you bitch about them."

"Can you move?" she asked, dragging him across the ceiling until they were over the walk-in fridge. As promised, it was one dark, open space. Bill would force the battle up here soon enough. "Allen! Can you move!" They wouldn't have hit him with an antidrafting drug, but Bill liked his sedation darts.

"Go ahead. I'll catch up."

Peri grimaced. He was slurring, but he had enough fortitude to slap her hand when she tried to see whether his eyes were dilated, impossible in the dark. Frustrated, she fired a few shots at the growing sound of men at the hole in the ceiling. "Can you move?"

His shadowed, pained eyes met hers. "Not fast enough."

Damn it! Peri's brow furrowed, and she wiped the cooling sweat from her forehead, chilled from the sudden cold in the ceiling. Adrenaline made her legs shake. It was her job to keep her anchor alive, and they were out of options. Grim, she reached to help him rise. "You'd better start moving because I'm not leaving you here."

Allen took her hand off his arm, eyes pained, but

from below came Bill's harsh demand, "Get up there before she's gone!"

Heart pounding, Peri gripped the Glock tighter, focus narrowed on the small patch of light from the kitchen, but not a single head showed. Apparently no one wanted to be first, and Peri's breath slipped out as the call for a high-Q drone rose. She scanned the dusky open area as her eyes adjusted. If they were calling for an eye in the sky, she had a precious few moments.

"Sedation darts only. You hear me?" Bill demanded. "I want her down, not dead or drafting. The accelerator has to be given intravenously within twenty-four hours, or this entire exercise means nothing!"

"Go," Allen slurred, head hanging. "I'll be right behind you."

Bullshit. Tucking the Glock away, Peri grabbed his arm. "Get up." But something Bill had said niggled at her. Why was he talking about accelerator? He knew she didn't have any Evocane in her system to buffer her sanity. *Twenty-four hours?*

She felt her expresson go slack as she remembered the discarded dart. That hadn't been a sedation dart, and it was looking less likely that it had been Amneoset, either. It had been Evocane.

Shit. Peri jerked at the hum of a drone, dropping Allen's arm in order to take a bead on it. She fired a single shot, and the drone fell back through the hole amid cries. “Well, at least we know one of them is still up there,” Bill said sourly. “Peri?”

Wire-tight, she backed away from the hole in the ceiling as the calls to position the ladder filtered in. Bill had always had more than one option to get his way. He’d gotten her hooked, and Silas had only a week’s supply. Less, maybe, because of what he’d been using to reconstruct it.

“Peri, you’re fine!” Allen said, his complexion sallow as he swung his head up. Clearly the dosage had been set for her. He wasn’t going down, but he couldn’t move.

“Bill darted me, didn’t he.” She couldn’t get enough air, and her finger shook as she pointed down. “Didn’t he!”

“You’re okay,” he said breathily. “You can still . . . draft safely. Nothing’s changed.”

She jumped at the metallic clunks of a ladder being set up. *Nothing changed? Bill said it was addictive!*

“Go,” he said, pushing weakly at her. “Get to Silas. Stay on the Evocane. He’ll make more.”

“I can’t leave you.” It wasn’t just that he was her anchor, her partner, her friend. It was that leaving him behind went against everything she believed.

Allen’s hand slipped from her cheek, his fingers fumbling to take his watch off and press it into her hand. “I thought you’d say that. Don’t trust Bill. Silas will figure it out in time.”

“Allen, what— No!” she exclaimed as he rolled

across the ceiling and down the same hole he'd pulled her into. "Allen!" She jerked back as men called out and the ladder fell. "Allen, you crazy bastard! What are you doing?"

"Go!" he shouted from below, and then he cried out when someone dragged him clear.

"This is unnecessary, Peri, even for you," Bill said, and then, louder, "Get up there."

Eyes wide, Peri grabbed the handgun and watch Allen had left behind, backing up until she found the oven's vent. Breath held, she checked her hoppers, then pointed. She'd take whomever she could for as long as she could.

"Reed!" came behind her, and she spun, almost shooting Harmony. She was dirty and disheveled, hunched from pain or the cold—hardly recognizable in the dark. "Let's go!"

"They have Allen," she blurted, her adrenaline burning. "If we drop down together—"

"Then we die together. Let's go. I called in air support but it won't wait."

Peri jerked her attention from the ragged circle of light and the masculine shouts filtering up. "Not without Allen."

Harmony crab-walked back. "You're the only one left, Reed. You were right. It was a trap. Michael is a sadist. We leave now, or I'll shoot you on sight next time I see you as one of Bill's brainwashed dolls."

"But . . ."

"Now!" The whites of Harmony's eyes were vivid, her determined anger held just in check. "We'll come back for Allen."

"Peri?" came Bill's oily voice in the sudden silence below them. "I've got Allen. If you want him dead, you just go ahead and shoot who I send up there for you. You want him alive, you drop your weapons down through the hole. I'm not mad at you, but it's time to come home. I won't let you need. I promise."

For three seconds she stared at Harmony. With a groan, Peri turned away, hunched as she darted around supports and sudden vents. Harmony was a dark shadow beside her, moving remarkably fast. Suddenly Peri realized there was blood splattered on her. *I don't even know whose it is.* "Are you okay?"

"I doubt it." Harmony halted at the shifted ceiling tile she'd probably gained access at. Behind them, the light was eclipsed as men cautiously poked their heads up through the ceiling. "It's a back office. Out the window. It's too hot for the airlift. We have to get at least three buildings over. You can run?"

Peri nodded. Her chest hurt. If she hadn't left, they would've killed him. They might kill him anyway, but there was the chance they'd keep him alive. Most drafters were sentimental about their anchors, and therefore they made good leverage. *I am a fool.*

"You first," Harmony said, looking at Allen's watch between Peri's palm and the butt of his weapon. There were men up here now. A dark shadow shifted where the light from the kitchen stabbed upward, and it jerked when Peri took a shot at it.

"Don't piss me off, Bill!" Peri shouted, and Harmony smacked her shoulder to be quiet and get through the opening. "If you hurt Allen, I'll kill you myself!" she added.

"Out. Go!" Harmony said, and Peri dropped through the ceiling and into the shadowed office below. Harmony was right behind her. Blinds fluttered before a broken window like a bird's shattered wing, and Harmony levered herself through it, not waiting for Peri as she ran across the icy lot and through the solar array to the adjacent building. Grim, Peri followed, not knowing how she could still move.

She'd lost Allen, but more than anger gnawed at her. She had wanted what Bill offered, wanted the power that remembering her drafts would give her. She wanted it even as Silas's warning that it was a poison echoed in her thoughts. But not like this, beholden to whoever held the keys to the lab.

As soon as WEFT knew she was hooked on it, they'd all start making their demands.

CHAPTER TWELVE

The ceiling of the off-site airport warehouse was lost in shadow, and the air was still and stale as Bill made his way past the organized shipments to the janitor room he had appropriated as a temporary holding cell. Michael was beside him, his steps meeting Bill's strike for strike despite the hint of a limp from where Peri had stabbed his knee. But Bill felt anything but unity with the tall, swarthy man still in his combat gear, the stink of his excitement at killing an entire team lifting off him like bad cologne.

Bill had taken the hour of downtime while everyone had pulled out to shower and change into a suit. That Michael hadn't—wanting to prolong the memory by continuing to wallow in another man's blood—seemed to Bill to be the capstone in what made Michael so unsuitable.

"I got what you wanted," Michael said, breaking the long silence, and Bill glanced sidelong at him as they wove past a cling-wrapped pallet of water purifiers.

"I told you to stay in the room."

"You said stay until I got the data. I got the data," Michael insisted, his calm, precise tone grating on Bill.

"And you still managed to make a travesty of it." Bill gave up trying to keep his polished veneer in place around Michael. "If I can't fix this, I'm going to have two major corporations thinking I'm playing them off on each other when what I'm trying to do is salvage something from *your* clusterfuck."

Michael frowned as they approached the man standing guard at a locked door, running his middle finger under the cut Peri had given him. "They were in my way."

Bill stopped, not wanting the guard waiting at the door to hear their argument. "I don't give a fly's dick about the CIA agents. I said no live ammunition, and you leave holes, casings, and brain tissue in the carpet."

"As I recall, it was your soldier girl who opened fire in the lunchroom," Michael said.

Bill leaned in, not liking that Michael was taller than him in his combat boots. "Everblue is going to know someone stole their information. They'd be fools not to go into production immediately. It's going to hit the market three years ahead of schedule. Their CEO will be *Time*'s Man of the Year. You pissed my new building and support staff away, Michael, and for what? Tormenting a woman for information she wasn't going to give? Information we were going to acquire anyway?"

"You wanted to know just as much as I did,"

Michael said, picking the blood out from under his nails. "This is not my problem, it's yours. Reed is still at large."

"She'll come in. She's halfway here already." There was blood on his ring, and Bill polished it off as he paced forward, eager for the endgame. Meeting the guard's eyes, he gestured for him to open the door.

Shoulders hunched in anger, Michael followed him into the barren room lit by a bare bulb in a protective cage. The janitorial cart, buckets, mops, and racks of cleaning supplies and poisons had been pushed into the shadows to leave a good-size ten-by-ten space. Bill's lip curled as he saw Jack hunched over Allen in the middle of it. The beaten and bloodied anchor was restrained in a folding chair, but both men looked as if they'd seen better days. As Michael and Bill stared at him in question, Jack slowly stood upright, his mood unclear.

The door shut behind them with a heavy click. Away from the guard's eyes, Bill turned, shoving Michael into a rack, pinning the lanky, taller man with his anger.

"I told you to stay in that office because I *knew* you'd try to kill her," Bill said, voice low and inches from his face. "Don't think I don't know your every thought. Leave her alone. She will slit your throat and walk away before you hit the ground if she decides you're a danger to those she cares about." *And a little threat to the ego never hurt.*

Michael's clenched fists slowly opened as Bill gave him a disparaging up-and-down look before returning to Allen and Jack. "She's not going to kill me," Michael promised in a dangerously soft voice.

Not as long as I can keep you away from her, anyway. "Jack," Bill said, his voice mockingly light. "How's our girl?"

A flicker of fear crossed Jack's face. "He said the dart was true. She's on the Evocane."

The rush of satisfaction was like white light through Bill. "Are you sure?" he said, unable to read the truth of it in Allen's hanging head.

Jack nodded, and Bill clapped Jack companionably across the shoulder and drew him from Allen. "Then we did well," he said. "Soon as she runs out, she'll come back." He looked at Michael. "And we have our final test subject," he added, knowing the man didn't believe it.

"She won't," Allen croaked, peering at them through a swollen, misshapen eye. "She won't." He almost breathed the words. "Denier will reverse-engineer it. She'll be gone in less than a week, and neither of you bloodsuckers will be using her again."

Expression ugly, Michael stepped forward, his arm raised to smack him. Tired of his ham-handed methods, Bill jerked him to an unexpected halt.

Michael needed to feel in control, but with too much freedom, he'd remember he could kill Bill, too. It was a balancing act, but Bill had a net and Michael didn't.

For a long moment they stared at each other, Michael off balance and unable to pull away until Bill shoved him stumbling back. Across the room, Jack waited, poised for anything. "Enough," Bill said. "You are *not* getting accelerated until I know it works. So you'd better hope we find her."

Anger made the scratch under Michael's eye stand out. "You have no intention of accelerating me. Admit it."

"I *own* you," Bill said, feeling his face warm. "I found you in that putrid, stinking mental hospital. I stopped the electroshock treatments. I dried you out from the drugs. I made your priors go away. I gave you everything you wanted."

"Except this."

"Don't make a mistake you won't walk away from. You need me, Kord," Bill intoned, pulling hard on his ugly past and hammering it against Michael's fear of making a mistake, a mistake that others could see and judge him a fool for. The anxiety was deep and ingrained, and the best way to manipulate the unpredictable man. "Peri will come home. What happens then is still open." He hesitated, backing off a step. "Understand?"

Michael's eyes dropped, and again in charge, Bill forced himself to his usual calm. From the corner, Jack exhaled. It had been chancy, but the altercation had bought him a few more days for Michael to stew before reaching his breaking point.

Satisfied, Bill leaned to look Allen eye to swollen eye, and the bound man jerked when Bill brushed a sweat-clumped strand of hair away. "You said she won't come back? Allen, we both know Denier is good, but he will need at least two years to reverse-engineer it, and that's assuming he can find the right equipment, which he won't. In a week, she'll be out of Evocane," Bill said softly. "Slavering on the floor and in the throes of withdrawal. A day later, if she doesn't die of dehydration or stroke, she'll begin to hallucinate. Really bad hallucinations, nothing pleasant or nice, like unicorns and rainbows. Shortly after that, you'll have to put her in a vulnerable, medically induced coma to keep her from trying to meet her maker from the thirty-fourth floor. I think she'll choose the alternative and come . . . see . . . me." He hesitated. "Our Peri is stubborn, not stupid."

Bill straightened to his full height, pleased to see Michael's anger soften at the reminder of what waited for an accelerated drafter caught without his Evocane. With repeated exposure, the painful withdrawal symptoms would turn into a death sentence. Allen said nothing, his breathing giving away his fear.

"Good morning, Allen," Bill said conversationally, relishing that he was taller than anyone in the room apart from Michael. "Did you really think we didn't know who you were all those years ago?" Turning to Jack, he inclined his head in invitation. "Save me the trouble of looking at the transcripts. What else has he told you?"

The rims of Jack's ears were red. "Just what you already know. She's aligned herself with WEFT in a bid for the labs to make Evocane. Headman is Steiner. No one there can draft or anchor. They think that's where the corruption started."

"That's a laugh," Michael said, sifting through the tray of drugs stacked atop the filthy Shop-Vac.

"Denier has full lab access," Jack said, clearly not liking Michael shuffling about with the vials and syringes. "He's not told me everything, but I've not forced it."

Syringe in hand, Michael turned, apparently eager to fix that.

Irritation filled Bill. "I'm doing this," he muttered as he took it away. "Back off."

Allen's jaw clenched, but he did little as Bill swabbed his inside elbow of his bound arm and injected it. A weird, thin-lipped, wild-eyed expression slipped over the captive man even as the drug took him, slowing his breathing and making his clenched hands ease.

"He's been conditioned to keep his mouth shut against that," Jack said flatly.

Michael jumped, startled when Bill's hand flashed out, slapping Allen's face with an unexpected crack. Shock crossed Allen, then hatred.

"That's why I use it in tandem with a secondary method," Bill said softly. "Michael, you're like a dog under the table. Back off before you fuck this up, too. There are ways to get people to talk other than assassinating their team."

Feet scuffing, Michael retreated.

"Now." Bill swung the room's only free chair around, straddling it so the back was between him and Allen. "What I really want to know—the reason you're here instead of a ditch to be found by an early-morning jogger—is why was *she* at Everblue?"

Allen glanced at Jack before fixing on Bill with his unswollen eye. "I don't know."

Bill hit him again, this time using a fist. Allen's head rocked back, and Bill reached out, yanking him forward before the chair could tip over, smacking him lightly to make sure he didn't pass out. "Hey. Hey! Over here, Allen. Focus now."

Allen twitched, shrugging to get Bill's hand off him. He spat out blood; the ugly sound of it meeting the cement floor was oddly familiar. "Hitting me won't make me talk," he rasped.

Bill's face was expressionless. "I'm not hitting you to make you talk. I'm hitting you because you thought I was stupid." Thick fingers moving with a slow precision, Bill took a bottled water from the tray. "What was Peri doing at Everblue?" he said as he dropped a straw into it and held it to Allen. "Did she demand to be there? Is she wanting to come home?"

Allen looked up from the straw, still too far away. "You don't think the half dozen of your hired men she left for dead are enough of a no?"

Bill held it so he could drink. "She's angry with me. She's expressing herself."

Licking his lips, Allen drew back from the water. "Peri will die before returning to Opti."

"Then it's a good thing she can reset time to make a better decision." It was closed and uncomfortable, and the silence grew. Bill set the water back on the tray. "Why was she there, Allen?"

Twitching impatiently, Michael stepped forward. Breath fast, he grabbed the expended syringe and used his weight to push Allen's head back. Jack's breath hissed in, but he didn't move as Bill was forced to rise and his chair was knocked over.

"Michael," Bill complained, willing to give Michael a little release as he leaned heavier into Allen, lips pulled into a grimace.

"Know what happens when you shove a needle into someone's frontal cortex?" Michael said, angling the syringe to Allen's nose. "You wiggle it around enough, and it mimics a lobotomy enough to pass inspection."

"He knows he's more useful alive, Michael," Bill said. "Knock it off."

"He doesn't need an eye to be alive." Michael shifted the angle of the needle. "How about it, Allen? You want to keep both of them?"

Swollen eye slitted in fear, Allen exclaimed, "Why do you care?"

Michael tightened his grip when Bill leaned in so close he could smell the drugs lifting off the man's skin. "You always did have a way with the anchors," Bill said to soothe the man's ego after the beating he'd given it. "Answer him," Bill said to Allen. "Why was she there?"

The man's fear was obvious, and Michael's hold became white-knuckled. Allen was fixated on the end of the needle, and when Michael moved it, he shouted, "She's after Michael!"

Bill made a knowing sound. Finding insult in it, Michael pressed down again. "Me?" he snarled, angling the syringe into Allen's nostril. "You think I'll believe that?"

"Enough!" Bill exclaimed. "If you give him a lobotomy, I swear I'll shoot you to get you to draft and bring you both back to usefulness. Back off, Michael."

Lip curled, Michael pushed off from Allen, throwing the syringe onto the tray where it slid into Allen's phone and wallet and stopped. Jack stood in a corner, grim-faced and silent.

"That's just odd enough to be true." Bill lifted Allen's good eyelid to gauge the level of drug in him. "Peri is nothing if not vindictive. Both her strength and weakness. Which is it, Allen? Pretend you're on our side again and you might live out the night."

Allen's eyes flicked to Michael, then back to Bill. "Steiner is mopping up, bringing in drafters in hiding. Michael is their biggest annoyance right now."

Bill rubbed his stubble to hide his smile as Michael's expression darkened. "And in exchange for her help," Bill guessed, "she gets lab access to reverse-engineer the Evocane that will make her their slave instead of my drafter?"

It had taken him five years to perfect Evocane. Denier picking it apart before Peri ran out was not going to happen. He had to convince her to come home. Five doses of Evocane would make it addictive enough that to go without might cause heart failure. But it was more than her risking death that bothered him. He'd promised her that he'd never let her need. He wanted her to come back because this was where she belonged, because of the thrill she got being who she was—not the need. Getting a larger stash of Evocane to her would prove his word was good and begin to rebuild her trust. She had trusted him once. She would again.

"She thinks she can bring me in?" Michael said, frowning when Bill chuckled.

"She doesn't care, but the CIA does, and that's who she's playing for right now." Bill inspected

Allen's phone and turned it on, sighing at the small icons he'd have to manage. "Peri is simply exploring the viability of a second source of Evocane." He frowned at the password prompt. "*That's* why she's helping the government. We can make that work for us. If she wants you, let's give her a shot at you. She'll show, even knowing it's a trap. Especially if Evocane and Allen are in the mix."

Michael's head was down, hiding his expression, but Bill could guess at it. Finding a stylus, Bill typed in 1997 for the password, which was denied. *Not your birth year, then.* "By tomorrow, we'll know if she's going to reject the Evocane, and if not, we move forward."

"Rejection?" Jack said. "There was nothing about rejection in the lab reports."

Bill tried again, this time using the last four digits of Allen's Social Security number, failing. "They vary from individual to individual," he said, trying a variant of Allen's birthday using the month and day, getting nowhere. "We've been tweaking to minimize them. Why do you think I'm trying to get her back?"

Allen pulled his head up, a new worry giving him strength. "What kind of rejection?"

Not wanting the phone to lock up, Bill gave it a rest. "Sometimes a sound or light sensitivity develops," he said, wanting Michael to have a doubt or two—seeing as the med wing full of comatose ex-Opti drafters wasn't enough. "It manifests as an avoidance of crowds or a lowered sensation limit. If it is too extensive, the agent has limited use. Occasionally Evocane will cause an increase in aggression, either sexually, which can be addressed, or more typically, as a short temper and inability to trust, even people he or she has in the past."

"Paranoia," Jack said, frowning.

"Sometimes there's an unusual salt craving," Bill added.

"Salt?" Allen echoed, clearly surprised.

Bill nodded, satisfied at Michael's attentive silence. "Upon occasion, Evocane causes an imbalance in the cellular ion exchange. They end up jerking uncontrollably, but we usually see the salt craving within the first few days. We can ask her the next time we see her." He smiled, suddenly realizing what Allen's password was, and punching in 2024, the year Allen and Peri had met. Sure enough, the phone lit up. "Why don't we do that now? She's probably in a van somewhere with nothing to do."

"You son of a bitch," Allen whispered, and Michael leaned closer, clearly trying to see the number. "She's better than a damn guinea pig, and you know it."

Of course he knew it. They all knew it. But Michael was getting too close to the truth for his liking. "Peri, Peri, Peri," Bill said softly as he scrolled through Allen's phone. "Ah, here she is. Let's give her a ring," he said, delighting when Allen's expression went from anger to fear.

The line clicked open. "Allen?" came her voice, and Bill beamed.

"Hi, kiddo," Bill said pleasantly as he put the phone on speaker. "No, don't hang up. Allen is here. Allen, say something so Peri knows I'm being honest."

Smiling, Bill held the phone to Allen, but he stayed predictably silent, eyes glaring past the swelling and bruises.

"Go on," Bill encouraged, and Michael ominously slid a syringe off the tray.

"Trust Silas, Peri," Allen rasped. "He won't let you go insane."

Peeved, Bill drew the phone away. "He won't mean to, I'm sure," he said to Peri. "But we all know Denier's track record. He won't make it in time, and it's going to hurt if you go without. It's more addictive than the high of running a task, and you've been fixed on that a long time. You don't know how to go without."

"If you hurt Allen—" came faintly, and Bill chuckled.

"You'll what?" Bill said flatly, humor gone. "Hunt me to the ends of the earth? I've hurt him. I'm going to hurt him some more if the mood strikes me. But there's an alternative. Are you alone? Are you listening?"

Allen's breathing was harsh in the sudden silence, and then her hesitant "Yes."

"Good," Bill said dryly, watching Michael for his reaction. "I'm willing to give you a vial of Evocane for your continued health. I'll even throw in Allen to prove my sincerity. You're going to need the Evocane to have any chance of keeping WEFT in the dark about your new addiction." He waited, letting that sink in. "I'll send Michael with them if that will make you feel more comfortable. You can be wired. You can even bring someone. I don't care. I simply want to impress you with the knowledge that your way home is already open."

"I don't believe you," Peri said, and Michael nodded, inching closer.

"I don't need to lie to you anymore." Bill pushed Michael away with a stiff finger. "You deserve to be your own anchor. I respect you. I always have. I wouldn't lie to you now even if it was to my benefit. You won't need an anchor, but someone to watch your back is prudent. Jack is here. Right next to me. You worked well together. He doesn't have to lie to you anymore, either." He hesitated. "Or you can spend the next week trying to hide from WEFT that you are a flight risk and liability. Tell me where and when. Michael will bring Allen and a vial of Evocane. Two vials."

"Detroit. Tomorrow, ten p.m. A casino. You choose which one," she said tersely.

Bill's smile widened, proud of his creation. Letting him decide the final destination was to stymie anyone who might be listening in at her end. "Then I choose the abandoned mall at the arena. Say . . . outside the old Waldenbooks? Three a.m."

Her scoff was laced with a hidden fear. "Midnight. *Before* I go into withdrawal," she demanded. With the time shift from St. Louis to Detroit, her withdrawal would set in at about one in the morning, EST, but Peri was never one to take a needless chance.

"Midnight it is," he agreed, not surprised.

The click as Peri ended the connection was obvious. Michael rocked back, his thoughts clear to Bill. Jack saw it, too, his blue eyes almost black in worry. *Not yet, Michael. I will keep you alive a little longer.*

"We're going to snag her, yes?" Michael asked, and Bill gave him a sidelong look.

"To do otherwise would rob us of our test subject," he lied, but by Jack's downcast expression, Bill knew Jack at least understood. He didn't have to *snag* her. Peri was already his. To treat her with anything other than dignity and respect would be counterproductive at this point. She'd come in when she was ready, and until then, he'd keep her in Evocane.

Michael eased back, his eyes on Allen's phone as Bill rolled it up around the stylus and tucked it back in his suit's inside pocket. "And you're sending me to bring her in?" Michael prompted, and Bill tugged the sleeves of his jacket straight, eager to get a very late supper.

"Because you're the one she wants." Bill knocked for the guard to open the door, gesturing for Michael to go first when the heavy steel creaked open. "You won't be carrying anything other than sugar water. Go take a shower. I'm not flying back to Detroit with you stinking like blood and piss."

No emotion on his face to give away his thoughts, Michael strode out of the makeshift cell, his steps quickly going faint. The limp, Bill realized, was almost gone.

Jack exhaled long and slow. He gave Allen a last glance before following Bill out. "That was fun," he said as the guard shut and locked the door behind them. "You do know he's going to try to kill her the next time he sees her."

The still air of the warehouse felt indescribably airy after the dead reek of the maintenance closet. "I'm counting on it," he said, attention rising to the flash of light and boom of sound as the outer door opened and closed as Michael left. "I wouldn't put him and Peri in the same building right now, much less give him access to Evocane. That's why you're going to take it to her, not Michael. If we're lucky, she'll chuck it all and come back with you right then and there." But he knew that was unlikely. Peri had trusted Jack once and had been betrayed. She wouldn't again.

Even so, Jack's posture eased, and Bill allowed himself a smile in the dark. He knew his people better than they knew themselves. "Thank you," Jack almost breathed.

"You're welcome," Bill said as he buttoned his jacket closed, but what he meant was, *I own you.*

CHAPTER THIRTEEN

The St. Louis med facility smelled like Opti, the air having an earthy, antiseptic, ozone-tainted breath about it. She was fairly certain she'd never been to the St. Louis branch, but the low ceiling and indirect light of the med room made it both familiar and foreboding. At four in the morning, it was all but empty, the argument between Harmony and Steiner in the next bay obvious as the lab tech cleaned a leg scrape she didn't remember getting. Her good right leg dangled over the edge as she held her left still. It was a good setup with the four bays for outpatient surgery and stabilizing trauma—sufficient to get a bullet out or stop massive bleeding without necessitating a hospital record.

Bill's "gift" of Evocane and Allen weighed

heavily on her. It was a trap, one she had every reason to sniff around but no intention to trigger. She didn't know how much Evocane Silas had left, much less how she was going to access it by tomorrow night without alerting WEFT she needed it. That withdrawal might give her away had her on edge. She had to get back to Detroit. Now.

"Ah, do you remember your last tetanus shot, Agent Reed?"

Distracted from her thoughts, she looked down as he finished hiding the ugly scrape under a white bandage. Her leg had been swabbed and cleaned, but the rest of her still sported the filth from their failed attempt to snag Michael and Bill, and she felt insufferably grungy.

"I get one on my birthday on the naught years," she said. "That would make it 2030?" It had been her mother's idea, the uptight woman trying to find ways for her daughter to hide her spotty memory, blissfully unaware that Peri had more doctors looking after her than the president of the United States. Guilt rose, and Peri quashed it, thinking karma was a bitch. *She wouldn't know or care if I was there wheeling her to breakfast anyway,* she thought.

"You're good, then." Standing, the tech handed her a packet of pills. "For the pain. We can refill it if you want."

"Thanks." Her eyebrows rose as she read the

package. They were heavy hitters, enough to down a horse, far more than she needed. *Someone wants me out for a while,* she thought, pocketing the pills with no intent to use them. She'd live with her scrapes and sore knee rather than risk drugging herself into a state where she couldn't draft.

Not yet having a plan to get home, she hadn't even texted Silas, and an unexpected fragile feeling dogged her, making her meek when she was usually bold, compliant when she'd usually question. She hadn't been accelerated, and her synapses were functioning as normally as they ever did, but doubt dogged her like a cur.

"Would you mind if I washed up before I leave?" she asked as the tech gathered his things, and he shrugged, looking at the tiny sink. "I don't have a room."

"Sure. Whatever."

"Thanks." Her intuition pinged as she caught his wary frown when he closed the curtain behind him. *Shoes are falling,* she thought, not knowing why or what it actually meant. Clearly it was a "Jack" thing. God help her, she'd been so stupid. Things might have gone differently if she hadn't assumed he'd been a hallucination. *Nice going, Peri.*

Peri slid from the exam table, dismissing her leg when it only made a dull throb. Her bag from the jet was on the chair, and she tweaked the curtain closed tighter before pulling her rank shirt over her head and dropping the expensive silk in the trash. Her black pants were ruined, and they went in on top of them. The tiny sink and paper towels were far away from the shower she wanted, but washing up was a good excuse to stay and listen to the evolving argument next door.

"Swift is not a recoverable asset," Steiner said, voice tight. "Reacquiring him will not further our goal."

"Sir, I already told Reed that we'd find him."

"You have no team, Agent Beam. It was all I could do to keep you from being suspended."

Surprise, surprise, she thought as she pulled a wad of towels to wash her arms, but Peri wasn't leaving Allen within Opti. Pretending to go along with Bill's offer might be her only chance to rescue him. But Bill knew all her strengths and weaknesses and wasn't averse to using them to his own ends. That he'd hooked her on Evocane and let her flee smacked of the beginning of a long-game ploy. She hadn't wanted this, and yet . . . now . . . even knowing Bill was manipulating her . . . she was tempted.

Her motions sponging her arms slowed as she thought of the syringe of accelerator, somewhere within Detroit's CIA facility. *Maybe I should accelerate myself and be done with it.* Warming, she continued to wash as she tried to figure out how she was going to get to Detroit when Steiner probably had them returning to Atlanta. It was Steiner's home office, after all.

But it was hard to stay focused. She'd lived for so long needing someone to fill in the blanks after a draft that the chance it might work and she'd be normal was unimaginable. The shock of suddenly not knowing where you were or how you got there or why people were shooting at you . . . she was tired of it.

Across the room, Harmony continued to build up Allen's importance in hushed, urgent tones. But it was a losing battle, and Peri could guess the end by the time she was dressed in her post-task black jeans and white top. She brushed her fingers along her empty boot sheath, feeling the lack. Her Glock and dart rifle were long gone, too. She looked up, startled, when Jack tweaked the curtain and came in.

"You gotta go, babe," he said, his stubble just the right amount and his tie loosened.

Pulse hammering, Peri forced down the urge to kick him unconscious just in case. It was her intuition, nothing more. "Duh?" she whispered, unnerved that the drape never really moved.

Jack peeked past the curtain into the main room. "I mean, you gotta go into the lion's den to get Allen and that Evocane. If you go into withdrawal, Steiner will know you're hooked and move you into your new cell to keep you from running back to Bill."

So I leave before they find out, she thought, that same flush of worry slipping through her. Zipping her leather jacket closed, Peri looked at herself in the tiny mirror, finger-combing her hair as she steadied herself. Jack slipped in behind her, and she closed her eyes, not wanting to see him standing there. He'd once been everything she'd wanted. He'd made her feel strong. It had been so good—until she realized they were lying to her. All of them."You aren't any different now from who you were a week ago," he whispered, and her eyes opened.

Maybe, but I didn't like who I was a week ago, either, she thought.

"We're done. You're dismissed," Steiner said stiffly, and Peri looked at the curtain. Harmony's shadow was a bare hint behind it, arms swinging as she stalked through the common area and through the med lab's door. Her limp was obvious, but she was moving fast. She wouldn't be that angry if she'd gotten her way, and Peri frowned, peeking past the curtain to watch Steiner follow her out, his two aides gibbering at his elbow, unsettlingly wide awake for four in the morning.

"At least she didn't lie to you intentionally," Jack said, and she let the drape fall, feeling the early hour all the way to her bones.

"But the end result was the same," Peri whispered as the lab tech yawned over his paperwork. Harmony had been genuinely upset, and it sat oddly with Peri. It had been a long time since anyone had felt outrage on her behalf.

Head down, she returned to her bag. It smelled like jet, and her nose wrinkled as she sorted through it to make sure her diary was still in there. An urgent need to read it came and went—that she might find a reason why her life was in the crapper if she did. *Three pairs of socks and underwear. Another top. Money,* she thought as she felt the bag's strap for the bump of folded bills tucked into the concealed pouch. "What . . ." she whispered when her fingers found a flat rise where it shouldn't be. "You little snake," she added, face warming when a closer inspection found the audio bug wedged into the pull tab of the zipper. They'd bugged her?

"Almost a disappointment if they hadn't," Jack said as Peri used her nail to pop it free. The tiny device skittered across the floor, and she stomped on it, hopefully blowing out the ears of anyone listening. The bag hadn't been anywhere near her when Bill had called, but concerned there might be a second bug somewhere in the bag, she dug deeper. Toothbrush, hairbrush. Tiny mirror for surveillance. *Everything looked clean.*

Zipping the satchel shut, she dropped it on the exam table. "This sucks," she whispered. Jack had vanished, meaning her intuition was as unsettled as she was. That Harmony had fought a losing battle for her held more meaning than it should, that she had sought Peri out to escape with meant more. But the need to get to Detroit was so strong she could hardly bear it. Bag hoisted, she pushed the curtain aside. She had few assets, but she could pick up more on the way.

The tech barely acknowledged her as she came out, and she gave him a bland "thanks" and went into the hall. Head down over her phone, she reserved a flight as she wove her way upstairs, copying Silas on the receipt so he'd know where she was. Once in Detroit, she'd call him about her needing what he had left of the Evocane. He couldn't have used it all in reverse-engineering it—could he?

Slowly the tiled nothing and long fluorescent lights gave way to fake wood doors and glass walls. The lettering on the hall signs was the same font that Opti used, and she followed the exit signs up the wide stairs, familiar with the layout. It was almost four in the morning, and she saw no one. She began to wonder whether they were really that stupid to leave their front door open.

Another stairway, this time carpeted, and she rose up, adrenaline making her steps fast. A quiet lobby lay beyond, and past that, St. Louis's night-abandoned towers and streets. Forty feet was all that separated them, then five. Jiggling her duffel, she fumbled for her building card and ran it, jerking to a halt when a pleasant ding chimed instead of the glass doors opening. *This is so bad for my asthma.*

"I'm sorry," the holographic image said as it wavered into existence above the sign-in, sign-out podium. "Your card has been temporarily disabled. Please see the receptionist."

"Well, at least they got their zipper up," Peri muttered, turning at the sound of someone clearing her throat.

"Hey, hi," Harmony said tiredly as she pushed herself away from the wall between the elevators, two coffees in her hand as she slowly approached. "Can we talk? It's decaf."

Peri glanced at the locked door, then the receptionist coming out from a back room, wiping his mouth on a napkin and tucking his white collared shirt into his slacks. "You don't happen to have a card that works, do you?" Peri asked, shifting her duffel to her other hand to gauge its weight. Not enough to knock Harmony down, but it'd give her an instant of distraction.

"Yes. Don't try for it, okay? I'm tired and Steiner already chapped my ass once today."

If that coffee hits me, I'm going to be ticked, Peri thought as Harmony halted right before her. The man at the lobby desk was now on the phone, probably calling for backup.

"I know I said we'd retrieve him, but will you listen to the options?" Dark eyes earnest, Harmony held out a coffee.

All the better to drug you with, my dear. Peri took it so as to lessen the chance of having it thrown at her. The impulse to lie was strong, but seeing Harmony, weight on one foot to ease her leg, hair dusty and still holding insulation fluff, she couldn't do it. "I'm done here," Peri said as surprise flickered across Harmony's face. "Michael knows he's a target. It's over."

"There's a bug in your bandage," the woman mouthed, and disgusted, Peri sighed. At least it wasn't in her phone. She'd grown fond of her latest and was tired of ditching them. *Why did she warn me our conversation is being monitored?*

The elevator dinged, and Harmony waved off the three suits-and-guns who got out. Peri evaluated their grace as they took up a distant position between her and the night, her eyes lingering on the glass doors and her freedom beyond. Opti glass tended to be bullet resistant—which could be made to work for her if handled correctly.

"Let me leave," Peri said as Harmony almost collapsed into one of the postmodern chairs set companionably around a low table. "I like you, and I don't want to mess up your hair. That must take hours."

Harmony gestured for her to join her. "It does, but I don't have to do it every day. We need your help. You need ours. Allen isn't lost, he's just misplaced for a day or two."

“A day or two. Do you have any idea how long a day or two is?” Peri dropped her duffel on the table but refused to sit even as fatigue pulled at her. “Steiner has nothing I want,” she lied. “I’m leaving. It’s over. End of story, put it on the shelf.”

Silent, Harmony sipped her coffee, her attention shifting past the glass doors and to the two cars that pulled up and parked, their headlights shining. Each one had four agents in it, clean, armed, and well rested, their suits looking classy in the bright glare of the headlamps. Seeing them, Peri shifted her weight to her other aching foot. “What are they doing? Waiting for God to say go?” Peri asked, and Harmony rubbed her forehead.

“I’m sorry, Peri. You aren’t leaving. Steiner finally understands that the chance of you being taken by Opti and wiped is too great.” She looked up, eyes pained. “I was hoping you’d just . . . accept that. We’ll get Allen back, but you won’t be there.”

“Don’t try to stop me. You’ve only got four beds down in the med facility.”

Fatigue showed in Harmony’s eyes. “Give me a chance to work the system, will you?”

“Yeah?”

“Yeah.” Gaze drifting, Harmony thought for a moment, then caught Peri’s eye and deliberately looked at her bandaged leg. “We’ll get Allen back,” she said deliberately, her gaze rising to

Peri's. "I'm not letting an old white man make me a liar."

Peri hesitated, getting mixed signals. "When?" she barked. "Tomorrow will be too late."

"Tomorrow we'll have intel and backing—"

"Tomorrow he might be dead," Peri protested, glad everyone was staying back, though she didn't appreciate the way the agents were circling them, some anxious, some eager. With an irate quickness, she put her foot on the table and rolled her pant leg up to rip her bandage off. Her lips curled upon seeing the bug sandwiched between the layers of gauze. Picking it free, she dropped it into her coffee.

A smile flickered over Harmony and was gone. Tired, Peri sat down and leaned forward with her elbows on her knees. It had been a long time since anyone had fought authority on her behalf. That it had come from someone who had made no bones about disliking her, someone who had survived Michael and come back for her, refusing to leave anyone behind . . .

Damn it, I'm a fool, she thought, but her gut said to trust her, and that was all she had anymore. "I got a call," she said, head down to hide her moving lips. If Harmony had a bug, she was screwed, but she didn't think she did. "I know where Michael will be tomorrow, midnight. I'm leaving. Right now. You want to come? I get Allen, you get Michael. Win, win."

Harmony's lips were parted when Peri looked up. "You'd still work with me? After I lost my entire team?" she whispered, then leaned back into the cushions, gaze going to the distant men when Peri nodded. "Don't make this harder than it needs to be," Harmony said loudly. "I don't want you in a cell. You can do more good out of it."

What is she playing at? Peri mused, fighting to keep the confusion off her face when Harmony shook her head.

"Maybe next time," Peri said as she stood and picked up her bag, not relishing the eight-hour drive ahead of her to Detroit. Maybe she could bum a ride with a trucker and get some sleep.

Calls rang out, and outside, the agents quickly arrayed themselves. Annoyed, Harmony stood.

"Back off! She's not going anywhere!" Harmony shouted, and Peri spun, fist set to hit flesh when the woman's hand landed on her shoulder. It never fell as Harmony had jerked back. Peri hesitated, poised on the balls of her feet as Harmony smiled wickedly—suddenly very much awake. "There're *different* ways to the same end," Harmony said, glancing up at the watching cameras. Then softer, "I want Michael, but I can't get you out of here until we go off high alert. That won't happen until you're in a cell. Make it convincing, okay?"

She wants to put me in a cell? Peri's breath came fast. "You back off," she threatened, no longer sure she knew what was going on. Was Harmony helping her or not? "Or I'm going to break your nose and *then* take your building pass."

Harmony nodded almost imperceptibly. "You know I can't do that."

"Well, I can." Peri threw her bag at her, following it up with a palm thrust.

Pulling her punch at the last moment, Peri stumbled when Harmony shifted sideways, blocking Peri's strike with one hand and punching out with the other.

The heel of Harmony's hand connecting with Peri's wrist was a quick shock, followed by a sharp blow of her second hand with Peri's middle. Air huffing out, Peri caught her balance and fell back, eyes watering as she struggled to breathe. "Nice," she wheezed.

"You sure you want to do this at four in the morning?" Harmony asked, her eyes bright.

Behind and around them, bets were being made as the watching agents gave them room. As Peri pulled herself up, her confusion strengthened. *It is a ploy, isn't it?* "Very," Peri said, then feigned a kick, shouting as she launched herself.

Peri's teeth clenched at the resounding thump of contact, but Harmony didn't go down. Instead, the woman spun to slam her elbow into Peri's ear. Head ringing, Peri dropped back, missing her follow-up strike. Harmony was still smiling. *Son of a bitch, that hurt,* Peri thought, her anger stirring.

Teeth clenched, Peri went at her again, in earnest this time: front kick, front kick, side, and crescent, backing the woman up to a thick pillar. Harmony blocked them all. Her arm had to be numb, and with a resounding cry, Peri kicked her coffee at Harmony, right off the table.

A brown rainbow flew in a beautiful arch. Peri followed it a half second behind, aiming for Harmony's bad leg. In the distraction, it would land.

But Harmony stepped into it, not back. The coffee splattered across her, and shock reverberated up Peri's leg as the woman blocked her with enough force to send her stinging back. Panicked, Peri thrust out, getting a softer blow to Harmony's side.

"Damn it!" Peri cried as brown fingers clamped onto her wrist and pulled her off her feet. Gut tensing, she went with it lest she get her wrist broken, and the watching agents cried out in approval as Harmony levered her over her shoulder and slammed Peri onto the tile.

What the fuck! Not breathing, Peri kicked up, forcing Harmony to let go. Harmony couldn't outfight her in hand-to-hand—not with her weight confined to one leg—but that was exactly what she was doing. Still on the floor, Peri rolled.

Harmony jumped to evade it, and Peri reversed, cutting her legs out from under her on the return. Swearing, Harmony fell right on top of her.

Harmony's elbow hit the stone tile instead of Peri, and Peri couldn't help her grin as she grabbed her by the cornrows and slammed her head down.

Groaning, Harmony brought her knee up, jamming into Peri's groin. Peri hesitated in shock, and in that moment of distraction, Harmony got a solid grip on Peri and spun her facedown onto the floor.

Pain lanced through Peri, so hard and fast she couldn't tell where it came from. Her face was on the cold tile. Blood slicked it, coming from her lip. Harmony had her knee on her back, and Peri's arm was wrenched behind her. Her breath came in with a gasping pain as Harmony let up, and she lay there, caught. *Damn, the woman is good.*

"Go ahead. Draft. I don't mind kicking your ass twice," Harmony said, leaning to put her lips inches from her ear. "Great, I think they'll believe it now," Harmony said around her whispering pants. "You're going into a cell—"

Peri bucked wildly at the sound of the metal cuffs. Harmony fell back, and Peri lurched upright, spinning to a crouch as the watching agents cheered them on. Coffee covered Harmony, and she looked ticked. The elevator dinged, and Harmony's expression shifted to annoyance when it opened to show Steiner and his aides. "I don't have time for a pissing contest," she muttered, then launched herself.

Peri's eyes widened. Screaming, Harmony

jumped onto the glass table, using it for momentum and speed as she flew right at her, feetfirst. They hit Peri square on, shoving her back into the pillar. Her head hit with a thunk and, dazed, Peri leaned against it, trying to remain upright. Before her, as if in a dream, Harmony hit the table as she fell, shattering it.

Peri could do nothing as the agents urged Harmony to finish it. A primitive fear struck her as Harmony dragged herself upright, shoving pieces of the table aside as she crawled forward. The urge, the need maybe, to jump was a faint tickle, and she shoved it away.

"I'll be down to get you in an hour, okay?" Harmony muttered, clearly in pain even as she pushed Peri over and yanked one, then the other of her arms behind her back. "Just sit tight."

Like I have a choice? Peri thought, shuddering at the feel of steel ratcheting about her wrists. "Get off," Peri wheezed, but Harmony had already pulled away, leaving Peri to sit up and lean against the same pillar she'd hit her head against. Her skull hurt, and she stared at Harmony as the woman got to her feet and tugged her coffee-splattered top straight. The agents ringing them had gone silent at Steiner's disapproving presence, but money was changing hands as they began vanishing.

"Make sure she doesn't have a concussion and put her in a cell," Steiner said.

"Don't touch me," Peri demanded, knowing that "helping hands" might hurt more than assist, and she staggered to her feet. Her breath came in slow, and the world stopped spinning. Harmony was good, exceptionally good, and a deeper respect sifted through her.

The lobby was emptying with a guilty quickness. Filthy and clearly hurting, Harmony retrieved Peri's bag before shoving Peri to the elevator.

Peri searched Harmony's face as she got in, ran her card, and punched a button, but there was nothing: no satisfaction from having bested her, no anticipation at the beginnings of an escape—just a pained tiredness. "You're a tough bitch," Harmony said as the elevator doors closed. "Did you black out?"

"No."

"Good." Harmony dropped her head, hiding her face from the camera. "I'll be back down in an hour to get you, and we can go. Nice and quiet out the back door. It takes that long just to free the pass codes after a lockdown." She glanced sidelong at her. "Thanks for taking it so easy on me."

"No problem." *That was easy?* Peri wiped away the blood from her lip with her shoulder.

"I just need to know one thing."

Pulling back, Peri eyed her. "What?"

"What did Heddles mean by 'I won't let you

need'? Don't lie to me. I have three younger sisters, and one dumb-ass older brother, and I can tell."

That Harmony hadn't asked where Michael was stuck in Peri's mind. It wasn't necessarily a sign of trust, but rather a signal of intent, an assurance that Harmony wouldn't take the information and go, leaving Peri behind. Her breath quickened, and she kept her head down and away from the cameras. The voice telling her to be honest with Harmony was only a shade louder than the one telling her to stick to her old ways and trust no one. "Bill darted me with Evocane at Everblue," she finally said, heart pounding. "Michael is bringing me a vial as a sign of goodwill. Allen is there to sanction it, but the reality is that it's probably a trap."

Harmony nodded, focus distant as the elevator's numbers counted down. "And you expect me to believe that bullshit? That you're not running back to Bill?"

Peri looked at Harmony past her sweat-clumped hair, shoulders hunched and tired. "I want out. That's all I ever wanted."

Harmony's grip on her arm tightened. "Why am I believing this?" she said. But it was obvious she did.

"You do know they're going to demote your ass if they don't outright fire you, right?" Peri asked as the doors slid open to show a familiar hallway, with thick glass doors at the end. It *was* an old Opti facility. No one built their containment like Bill. Her graduate thesis had been finding the holes and patching them.

"I won't be demoted if I come back with Michael," Harmony muttered, hand on Peri's shoulder as she escorted her down the hall. "Allen is your goal. Michael is mine. If you leave before Michael is in my custody, I will hunt you to the ends of the earth. If you're screwing with me and you're trying to get back to Bill, I'll not only hunt you down but kill you. Deal?"

Peri glanced sidelong at her, recalled Harmony's haggard expression and haunted eyes atop the kitchen in the ductwork. "What did Michael do to you?" she asked.

Harmony took a breath, emotion clogging her voice until she looked away, pain etching her brow. "There's usually a reason when chickens kill one of their own," she said when the elevator dinged.

Oka-a-a-ay. Midwestern farm trivia aside, this felt right. "Deal," she muttered as if she weren't in cuffs, her lip bleeding and cheek scuffed. "But I'm not paying for the gas. You've probably got some lard-ass SUV that eats gas stations for lunch. I'll get the snacks and water."

Harmony smiled, steeling her face as she ran her card and the man on the other side of the glass wall stood up. "Fine with me."

CHAPTER FOURTEEN

Diary propped up on her chest, Peri lay on the foam cot, her jacket wadded up under her head. The hum of 741 Hz vibrated her synapses and prevented her ability to draft, and she couldn't decide whether she was a trusting fool or just plain stupid. Sleep had been impossible, and now, after several hours of waiting for Harmony, even her diary was failing to distract her from the possibility that she'd fallen for a ruse designed solely to get her into the cell block. The other option, that Harmony herself had been found out and was in the next wing over, wasn't much better. Fortunately, she'd helped design the safeguards to escape; she knew the ways around them. But it rankled, having trusted someone only to have it betrayed before the sun came up.

"She'll show, babe," Jack said, but Peri was too pessimistic to trust even her intuition.

"One of these days, you're going to choke on your Pollyanna sandwich," she said, hearing her words bounce back from the pages inches from her face. A feeling of what might've been homesickness took her as she looked at Jack lounging on the narrow cot opposite hers. His head was thrown back and his feet were spread wide. A featureless black tie hung loosely about his neck, and the white shirt was unbuttoned at the top. She vaguely remembered seeing him like that once before . . . just not the particulars.

I can't wait any longer, she thought, squinting at her cramped handwriting. Steiner was a bastard. He might be grilling Harmony, keeping her stuck in an office somewhere.

Peri had gotten through almost an entire year of memories, and it was odd, seeing Allen as a frustrated suitor against the fabric of platonic partner she'd draped him in. In the pages, Silas's mood had improved, even if he still held himself at a discreet distance, enjoying her company mostly because Peri kept the other women away. Seeing her own infatuation bothered Peri, and it *was* infatuation. It was only love when it was returned.

> I can't believe I was so stupid today. Silas and I were sparring before regular class, just warming up. He got me laughing so hard I almost peed my pants, which he then used to take me down. He was so cocky I couldn't stand it, and like a dumbass, I kissed him. I don't even know why I did it, except that he looked happy for once. He just stared at me, this empty expression on his face. I tried to apologize, but he said forget it, grabbed his stuff, and

> walked out. He missed the entire class, hiding like an old cat gone somewhere to die.
>
> Allen saw the whole thing. He says Silas is still feeling guilty about Summer. She's been dead now for almost a year, and she's still in his mind. Maybe I should just let it go. It's not as if there's a real chance for us. He's one hell of an anchor, but they're going to move him fully into tech at the end of the year. It sucks, because he'd be good at this, too, and it's what he wants. But he's too smart to waste, even if a drafter will make him bulletproof. He knows it, and it makes him mad. Maybe Silas is the smarter of us, keeping his distance.

Peri turned the page to a new entry, her brow furrowed. She didn't remember it, but it might explain why Silas had always refused to spar with her.

> Good, good day, though I can't shake this feeling of waiting for the second shoe to drop. I don't know if I need to thank Allen or if Silas figured this out all on his own, but we're good. Better than good. Silas showed up at the range this morning, just as silent and broody as always, but before

I could get out my apology, he kisses me within an inch of me ripping his clothes off. It really wasn't a kiss as much as a mutual mauling. He wouldn't say I love you, and every time I tried to say it, he'd start kissing me again. I'm afraid to ask Allen what changed his mind, but I doubt Silas opened up to him about it. Frankly, I don't care. I feel safe with him. His silence is worth more than a hundred declarations of devotion. I watched him mourn Summer, and I know the guilt is still in him. I'm willing to wait for those three words, even if I forget.

"You need to stop reading that thing," Jack said sourly.

Peri used one of the pages that had fallen out as a bookmark and closed it. "That's not what Silas thinks."

Jack tilted his head and gave her an askance look. "I'm not Silas's intuition, I'm yours. It's going to bitch-slap you. You know there's nothing in the past except things that are no longer real. The only real thing is right now. And right now, you're screwed."

"Thank you, Jack. That's comforting to hear coming from you," she said, sure they didn't have any audio bugs down here with the 741 Hz going. At least with it being an old Opti cell, the antidrafting audio wasn't so loud that it was annoying.

Jack smiled impishly and straightened his tie. "Just trying to help."

Sitting up, she rubbed the ache from her neck. "Well, don't." Standing, she tossed her diary back onto the cot and stretched to keep her sore leg from stiffening. She was alone among the half-dozen cells, though she was sure there'd be a live guard in the detainment office. It was eight in the bloody morning, and she was so strung out that she was hallucinating.

I don't think she's coming, she thought as she extended her leg until the scab threatened to crack and bleed. She'd been captured by Harmony's alluded promises and outright lies, going meekly into her cell like a kid promised candy. If she had for one moment thought that Harmony would let her rot down here . . . But no-o-o-o. She trusted her, and now she was going to have to break out of here on her own. Not impossible, but Opti had a tendency to fill in their security holes when she pointed them out, and WEFT would likely be the same.

Jack shifted his feet to make a sliding sound that didn't really exist. "Maybe Steiner had her bugged and he heard the entire thing?" he suggested. "She might be in her own cell."

"Maybe." Taking her jacket, she stuffed her arms in the sleeves and zipped it up as if readying for a task. She couldn't risk missing her chance at Allen and a vial of Evocane, not to mention avoiding having to explain to Steiner why she was in withdrawal. *Sixteen hours.* She could evade a building of guns, but it would have been easier with a second set of eyes and something more than her fists and a bad mood.

Fidgety, Peri looked past the thick plastic to the heat-sensitive keypad by the door. Anticipation curled up through her like smoke. Breathing out the adrenaline, she tried to quash her excitement, her muscles still uncertain from their recent ordeal. She couldn't wait any longer.

Turning back to the cot, she ripped her pillow open, using a wad of the absorbent cotton to fill her ears and dilute the 741 Hz. More went into her mouth, and she chewed it to a stiff pulp.

Standing, she padded over in her spiffy keen prison slippers to one of the vent holes of her cell. The alarm pad glowed a dim green, and leaning against the plastic, she exhaled to steady herself as she spat a wad of warm cotton at the heat-sensitive door pad.

"Nice," Jack said as it fell off the pad, leaving a red three glowing on the screen. "They should've replaced Opti's old system, not recoded it," he added, coming to stand beside her.

"You think?" My God, she was even hallucinating his scent, masculine with just the right amount of sweat. One by one, she methodically punched in the code to open Opti's sub-diagnostics, then another to access the security systems and start a system check. In the upper corner, the glow from the security camera dimmed and went out. She smiled. *Halfway home.* The cell locks remained closed, of course, but with the system check running, she could go in through the diagnostics and do it manually—thanks to the fire codes.

Her smile widened when the door lock clicked open, a fleeting thought passing through her that Cavana would be proud of her. Tucking her diary into her jacket's pocket, she pushed the door open soundlessly before going to the pad and making sure the system check couldn't be shut down. She had ten minutes before anyone could access the higher functions in the cell block.

But her satisfaction vanished when the door to the central guard station beeped and hissed open. Peri spun, awkwardly jerking to a stop when she saw it was Harmony, her cornrows oiled and a new white bandage showing on her elbow. The woman stopped short, her lips parting in surprise as her eyes went to the empty cell, open door, then her. "How did you get out?" she exclaimed.

Relief spilled through her, surprising Peri at its depth. She hadn't been betrayed. "You took too long," she said, seeing a downed man behind Harmony in the guards' office. "I thought Steiner had incarcerated you."

"For beating you up? Not a chance." Harmony grinned as she held the door open. In the guards' office, an alarm began to buzz. "If anything, smacking you up got me points. You want anything from your cell?"

She looked back, seeing Jack beside the cot. Using her foot, she shut the door with a decisive kick. "No," she said tightly.

"Oh, that hurts, babe," Jack said, walking right through the barrier. "But I think I'm starting to like your new partner."

Peri's expression fell. "She's not my new partner."

Harmony eyed her, still standing in the threshold to keep the door open. "What's that?"

"Nothing." Anxious, Peri slipped past Harmony, almost tripping over the guard unconscious on the floor.

The light on the guard panel went out as Harmony let the door shut, and the faint alarm ceased. "Sorry about being late," she said as she cut the card key from the guard's belt. "Even with beating you up, Steiner was giving me grief. I got us a very clean three-minute window. It gets dicey after that. I managed to get you a knife, though. Here."

"Oh, hey. Thanks," Peri said as Harmony handed it to her, then shocked herself when she looked up from tucking it away to find Jack standing right next to Harmony, both of them slick and professional.

"Hell, I was impressed she got down here, but getting you a knife? Ballsy," Jack said approvingly. "I'm definitely starting to like this woman."

Me too, Peri thought. "You want to tie him up?" Peri asked, ignoring Jack as she opened drawers to search for plastic wrist ties.

Harmony checked her watch and peered past the door to the hall. "Don't bother. If we're not out in three minutes, it won't matter if he's tied or not. Stay three feet behind or right at my elbow. We're going to be on camera for eight seconds in the lobby, but I've got a little diversion."

Jack cracked his knuckles as a distant hooting began. On the guard panel, a light flashed.

"And there it is." Harmony swore softly. "It's early. Can you run?"

"Yep." Peri shoved a wad of wrist ties into her pocket, shut the drawer, and jogged after Harmony, the woman already in the outer hall. A smear of blood on the floor caught her eye, and she gave it a wide berth. "Is that going to be a problem?"

"No." It was curt, and Peri watched Harmony massage her hand in memory. "Up the stairs. Elevators are traps."

Peri was last into the stairwell, and Harmony grunted in impatience when Peri stopped to zip-strip the handle closed. They took the stairs fast, feet shushing on the tile. It felt good to be moving, and a faint, acidic scent tickled her nose.

"Why didn't you draft to get away? In the lobby," Harmony said, surprising her. "No one would have known you did. Or did you and I shut your ass down twice?"

Peri slowed, wary as Jack ran up the stairs ahead of them. "No, just once," she said, then jerked Harmony to a halt when Jack waved for them to stop and continued upstairs. "I don't like working alone, and you deserve the chance to bring in the bastard who killed your team." Peri looked at her, taking her eyes off the upper door leading to the lobby. "He did, didn't he. I'm sorry." She wouldn't say *I told you so,* but she had.

A myriad of emotions passed over Harmony's face until she forced her features to a blank nothing. "Thank you."

Peri turned away, seeing Jack at an upper door, peeking through the tiny window. "Besides, I don't trust anyone but you right now. Hang on. My spider sense is tingling," she said.

"Babe!" Jack hissed, gesturing for them to stay hidden as the screech of an opening door serrated the quiet.

Pulse fast, Peri pulled Harmony deeper into the shadows as a clatter of feet and masculine excitement spilled into the stairwell. They were going up, though, and Harmony's eyes widened.

"That's the lobby door. We would have been right there," the woman whispered, and Peri's shoulders drooped when Jack waved them forward. “How did you know they were going to be there?” Her eyes widened. “Are we in a draft? Are you going to forget? Should I tell you what just happened?”

“No. I, ah, must have heard them coming,” Peri said, not knowing what to make of Harmony’s innocent enthusiasm. Grimacing, she cautiously started up the stairs again. “You’re really good. Who taught you hand-to-hand?”

“No one special, but my brother taught me how to be smart in a fight, and that’s the most important thing. How about you?”

Peri couldn’t help her faint smile. “I got my basics from an old guy named Cavana. I was, like, twelve.”

Wary from the near miss, Harmony slipped up the stairs beside her. “Tall? Little goatee, liked to crack his knuckles?”

Peri looked askance at her. “You know him?”

Shaking her head, Harmony looked out into the lobby through a crack in the door. “I saw him do a demonstration once. You got to work with him? He’s good.”

“You’re better,” Peri said sourly, rubbing the back of her head.

Harmony shrugged. “Like I said, I had one dumb-ass older brother.”

“Oh, good God!” Jack complained. “Are you women done fluffing your respective egos? It’s like you’re shoe shopping or something.”

Peri frowned, that rank smell worsening as the propellant-tainted air tried to find escape through the stairwell. Harmony tensed, pointing as the guy at the front desk left his station, arms across his chest as he stood at the edge of his domain and watched the three men they'd seen on the stairs jog down the hall with two fire extinguishers. "You set a fire?"

"No. I overcooked a plastic plate in the break room microwave."

Jack snickered, and Harmony edged the door open. "Okay," she whispered, eyes alight as they found the door guard. "Black SUV at the curb. I'm driving. Key is on the dash."

Head beside Harmony's, Peri looked at the huge vehicle waiting in the early-morning light. It would be easy to spot and even easier to stop with the right computer. "How long has it been since you updated your car's antitheft software?"

"It's Steiner's. He had it modified," she said, beaming as she patted her sidearm, then handed her a building key. "I've got Steiner's building card as well. That's what took so long."

"Sweet!" Maybe they had a chance after all.

Behind her, Jack rolled his eyes. "After you," Peri said to cover her embarrassment, and the taller woman eased the door wider and slipped out, holding it until Peri edged through and quietly shut it. Peri's first anchor had been a woman. She'd forgotten how easy it was to work with someone who wasn't distracted by a body full of testosterone, the subliminal text of casual conversation easing the task at hand.

But her mouth dropped open when Harmony hesitated at the oblivious door guard, then signed the logbook, complete with date and time leaving.

"I like her style," Jack said.

"So do I," Peri admitted, light on her feet as she jogged to the podium and ran the card to open the door.

The guard turned when the podium wished the absent Mr. Steiner a good morning. "Hey!" he shouted, and Peri flipped him off before smacking the lockdown button and rolling under the quickly dropping fence behind Harmony.

"Whoo, that was tight!" Harmony exclaimed as suddenly three men were at the downed gate, trying to lift it. Someone took a shot at them and everyone hit the floor, cursing the idiot when it ricocheted off the bullet-resistant glass.

Harmony slid across the wide bench seat, starting the car and shifting into drive even before Peri had her door shut. "Go!" Peri shouted, feeling a pang when they took off, leaving Jack at the curb. He was a hallucination, but it still felt wrong.

"Where are we going?" the young woman asked, horn blaring and car swaying as she took a quick right and bounced through a busy intersection, cars honking and brakes squeaking in their wake.

"Detroit." Snapping her belt across her hips, Peri looked behind them at the chaos. They had three, maybe four minutes' head start. Doable, if Harmony had an exit strategy.

Harmony looked across the wide seat at her. "Are you kidding? You could have made some excuse about needing to see Dr. Denier and been there tomorrow!"

Peri's lips pressed together and she hung on as Harmony took a tight turn. "I don't have until tomorrow. I have twelve hours." She looked at the dash. "No, sixteen."

Harmony whistled. "Damn, girl. You like cutting it close."

"You *said* we were leaving in an *hour*."

Hand raised and wiggling to say she was sorry, Harmony navigated St. Louis's rush-hour, gathering traffic drones as she ran reds.

"How long did that take to plan?" Peri asked in admiration, then stiffened as Harmony wove through the slower vehicles and gunned it.

"An afternoon for the timing on the plastic in the microwave," she admitted, touching her hair to look embarrassed. "I did that last week. Then a few hours to get access to the vid room to see where the cameras were. Can you get the drones for me? I'd rather not be on the news."

"But you couldn't have known you were going to need a way out back then." Peri took Harmony's Glock when she handed it to her. She checked the magazine, shifting in her seat to roll the window down. Cool air blew in, pushing her hair into her eyes.

Harmony took a quick right; the drones followed, still trying to get close enough for a shot of the plates. "I thought it good to know." She hesitated. "Hold on," she warned, one hand on the wheel, the other beeping her horn as she ran a yellow.

Peri stuck her head out, squinting at the drones as they caught up. Two pops and they dropped into the street. More horns blew as they came crashing down, and grinning, Peri levered herself back in place, eyebrows raised in the question of whether Harmony minded if she kept it.

Harmony shrugged and Peri stuffed it in her pocket beside her diary. "Do you like the train?" Harmony asked, pace slower now that they'd lost their drone escort.

Our way to Detroit? she wondered. "Please tell me it's an express."

Head shaking, Harmony slowed even more, impatient as she leaned forward, looking past the slower traffic until she took a sharp left into a side alley amid the Dumpsters and stacked cardboard. "Nope. It stops in every town." Putting the car into park, Harmony studied the dash for a moment, then turned off the lights. Behind them, three black cars raced by. "But we're not taking the train," she added as she carefully backed up and returned the way they had come. “I changed Steiner’s plates with those belonging to a black SUV at the depot parking lot. They’ll be checking every stop, diluting their search. You’ve got a new ID under the seat. We’ll have to stop somewhere to get a pair of boots, though.” Her eyes went to Peri’s slippers. “Unless you like those.”

Which explained why she wasn’t worried about drones after Peri had taken down the two that had tagged them earlier. Curious, Peri stretched to find the ID, holding it awkwardly to catch the early-morning light to read AMY SMITH. It would do. It looked like her senior yearbook picture. “Okay. I’m impressed.”

Harmony grinned. “The IDs were the hardest part. I’m going to pay for that later. Where are we going, other than Detroit, I mean?”

The reality of what they were going to do came rushing back. “The arena,” Peri said.

“The arena?” Harmony echoed, eyes wide. “Why not a nice safe war zone?”

Peri put an elbow on the windowsill, her fist against her mouth and her focus blurring at the passing buildings. Even with Harmony’s help, the chance that she was actually going to walk away from this with Allen and Evocane was low.

Why not, indeed?

CHAPTER FIFTEEN

Bill's worry was a light thread through his mind as he traversed the short underground hall from the building's parking structure to his new office, the emotion not so much as troubling as a goad, urging him onto his next goal. The damage from Michael's . . . innovative interrogation techniques had unexpectedly been cleaned up by the CIA, and his information again had value. Which was fortunate, seeing as he'd already used funds he didn't quite have yet to take possession of the top floor of a small office building just outside Detroit. He could see ways to improve function and design, but he wasn't willing to spend the money to implement them. If all went well, he wouldn't be here long—and that was better than okay.

"Rodney," he said to the doorman in passing, pleased he remembered the man and getting a respectful nod in return. There'd been a time when everyone from the receptionist to the garage attendant had been an Opti agent waiting for advancement into active duty. Relying on rented personnel made internal security a living hell, but he was starting to appreciate the mobility it gave him.

The elevator was there and open, but he took the stairs, pleased his breathing was slow and even when he reached the fifth floor. “Hammon,” he said in greeting to the floor’s receptionist, smiling when the man scrambled to his phone, probably to alert his personal secretary he was on his way in.

Feet thumping on the faded carpet, he strode past the vacant offices and silent break room, empty since he took possession. It was just the highly skilled and irreplaceable who were left. He had fewer drafters since Peri had blown the whistle on the corruption in Opti and they had slipped like water through sand, but his fingers were on the pulse of the few who remained, and he knew them well enough that he thought up their schemes before they did. They might be gods, but he had made them and they were his to control.

“Margo,” he said pleasantly as he pushed the scarred door open and walked into his outer office. “When you’re done with your Danish, will you see if Helen is available to take my return call?”

“Yes, sir,” the older woman said as she threw her napkin away before reaching for her outdated but efficient Rolodex. He’d almost gone with a younger woman fresh out of college and the latest gadget on her hip only to be shocked to find that the effectiveness of shorthand and a cup of coffee on his desk in the morning more than made up for the lack of a pretty face. She'd known how to fix the outdated intercom that had come with the place, too.

Shutting his door behind him, Bill stood at the wall-size window overlooking the medical campus his temporary offices were situated on. The Detroit River was a sterile white ribbon cut with black at its center, where tankers kept it ice free. Solar arrays and surrounding buildings reflected the rising sun to give a feeling of light and purpose. Cars moved and drones flitted above them, but the green spaces were gray and dead in the bitter, dry cold, making Detroit look more like its original core of industrial steel, hard and unforgiving.

From here, with the ever-evolving skyline of Detroit as a backdrop, it was easy to pretend nothing had changed, but it had. The nine facilities bloated with government money were long gone. His backers had dwindled to one, and she was growing impatient even as she continued to invest heavily in his promise that he could take the anchor out of the equation and create a more productive drafter. And yet, with everything he lost, there was an undeniable excitement he hadn't felt since he first made the decision to divert funds, then agents, from their government tasks.

It had gotten too big and he'd somehow become an administrator. Small was better. Smaller would be even more so.

Maybe I should give some serious consideration to becoming Peri's anchor.

"Sir?" came Margo's voice from the ancient intercom. "Ms. Yeomon is on the line."

Adrenaline jumped. Turning from the icy vista, he strode to his empty desk. Everything he needed was in his laptop. "Helen!" he said cheerfully, careful to hide his Bronx accent as he picked up the land-based phone. "If I had known you were going to call this morning, I would have arranged to be available."

There was a click as Margo hung up, and he glanced at the tiny light on his state-of-the-art phone. The line was secure as a cell phone could never be.

"It's not a problem, Bill," Helen said, her low, mature voice laced with confidence. "Your time is spread as thin as mine. I've had a chance to go over Peri Reed's progress, and I have to say I'm excited your goal to bring her in is moving forward. She's been accelerated, yes?"

"Halfway, ma'am," Bill said pleasantly, beginning to pace. "She is currently AWOL from WEFT and on her way to Detroit to meet with one of my representatives. Though I was unable to accelerate her, there's no reason for her not to do it herself, seeing as she's hooked on Evocane."

"That you have her working again is encouraging," Helen continued. "Even if it's against us, for the moment."

His pace bobbled. “She will come back, ma’am. We made her.”

“As you say,” the woman agreed. “I called to find out if you’re comfortable with discontinuing the maintenance of the earlier live trials. A tidy house is a strong house.”

Discontinuing maintenance? She meant shredding five years of records and euthanizing an entire wing of people he’d kept near comatose for nearly as long. “Yes, ma’am,” he said evenly. “The faulty wiring has been seen, too. I was waiting for your approval.”

“Mmmm.”

He knew her reluctance wasn’t because of the lives in the balance. Striding to the wall, he waved the environment controls awake, turning the air-conditioning on as he loosened his tie.

“Has Reed drafted since she was on the Evocane?” the woman asked lightly, and he heard the sound of shifting pages.

“She has, ma’am, and Peri appears to be maintaining a stable mentality even with the additional stress.”

“Fine,” Helen said decisively, and Bill exhaled in relief. That wing made him uncomfortable. “Discontinue maintenance and destroy the records. I’ll look forward to your continued reports.”

Shit, she is going to hang up. “Ma’am, I’d like to broach the subject of Michael again,” he blurted, cringing when she exhaled. There was a soft rustle of papers, and a faint "Thank you, Chris. May I have some privacy, please?" He held his breath, feet still on the worn carpet.

Finally she came back. "You know I value your instincts, Bill. What are your concerns?"

He sighed in relief, not caring whether she heard it. "Michael has continued to show himself as inventive and tenacious, becoming an even more valuable asset."

"I'm glad to hear that."

Nervous, he began to pace again, trying to get that damned breathiness out of his voice. "His loyalty remains to himself, which I've begun to adjust accordingly," he rushed to say before she could interrupt again. "His innate recklessness, however, is an increasing issue. Bringing Peri back has brought it to a head and it needs to be addressed." He took a slow breath. It was time. It was more than time. "Decisively," he added.

"You've made me aware of his tendencies," Helen said, the clink of a teacup clear in the background. "You assured me they could be used."

"They can," he rushed, wiping his brow. His Opti ring caught his hair, sending a surprising jolt through him when it pulled free. "And this is why I'm bringing it to your attention. Dr. Denier is attempting to reverse-engineer the Evocane, a task that will take him at least two years and far more than the amount Peri escaped with. I can't risk her. Not now. I've already arranged to get her a new, clean supply to give her the time she needs to come back to us willingly."

The click of the teacup came again. "You think she will come back within the week?"

"Absolutely. We're in an excellent position. She's remembering herself, and once accelerated, she will eagerly stretch into a new, better skin. It was her reliance on an anchor she couldn't trust that held her back, and with that gone, the lure of her past will be irresistible."

"And you want me to . . . approve of your plan?" Helen questioned, and he almost panicked. The woman hated micromanaging. He'd only succeeded in making himself look weak.

"No, ma'am. My concern is Michael. He is the logical choice to get a new supply of Evocane to her without her suspicions rising. She wants to apprehend him for the CIA, and she will show just for that reason. My concern is that Michael might decide at the last moment to eliminate her."

"Remove Michael from the program," Helen said, and his eyes widened. "Find another way to get her Evocane to her."

"Snuff him?" he exclaimed, scrambling to fix this. He needed Michael. It wouldn't work without him. "Ma'am, there's no need to eliminate Michael. He only needs—"

"No." It was decisive, and Bill grimaced,

scrambling for a way to bring this back. "I'm not risking my investment on a drafter's jealous whims and paranoid delusions."

She had nailed it perfectly, but he had to have Michael for the rest to work. "Ma'am."

"Are you arguing with me, Bill?"

He wiped the sweat off his face, not liking it was there. "No, ma'am. But Michael has skills that Peri will never have and can't be introduced at this late stage. The very same traits that make him unreliable and difficult to work with are extremely valuable and will dovetail into what Peri will balk at. I'm confident he can be brought back into line if I can make him feel valued. He is, for all his faults, a drafter."

"Yet you don't approve of his acceleration," she stated, and he began breathing again.

"Not at this moment, no. If you could meet with him? He needs to be stroked, made to see what he's in risk of losing. He's exactly like Peri, obedient and willing. He just needs to see the benefits of playing within the rules."

Helen was silent. He was asking for a lot. She appreciated a discreet distance. But like every rich brat he'd met, she had an ego larger than her bank accounts, and to tell her that she could sway someone he couldn't might be enough.

"Ma'am, if you want to take him out of the program, I will do it myself this very afternoon, but I'd ask you to meet him first so you can see what I see. The boy has talent. He just needs someone he admires to look to. Someone he wants to please."

Bill held his breath, waiting. It hinged now on a woman's pride.

"Do you have an alternative way in place to get Peri her stopgap Evocane?" Helen asked, and Bill closed his eyes in relief.

"Yes. Her past anchor is willing to feign wanting asylum to get it to her."

"Jack?" she asked, voice rising in surprise. "The one she tried to kill? Why would he risk helping her? She'd never believe that. *I'd* never believe that, and Peri is a smart girl."

"She loved him, ma'am, to the point where she still talks to him when she's alone. If Jack shows up unexpectedly asking for sanctuary, she'll listen. Especially if he brings her current anchor with him to sanction it."

"Love," Helen said with a laugh. "But I like the idea of Jack back in her life. It will bring her past directly into her present, reminding her of what she had been."

"That was my thought, too," he said softly. Helen was going for it. He could smell the salt of the East Coast already.

"Fine. I will see Michael. I have time this afternoon. You still fly out of Detroit, yes?"

Breath fast, Bill turned to his desk, shocked to find there was no pencil, no paper. "Yes, ma'am."

She'd probably send her own jet, which meant he had a bare few hours.

"We'll get this sorted out. If they don't accept Jack, he can at least keep tabs on her from a distance."

"That was my intent."

"Good," Helen said. "I'll see you this afternoon."

"Yes, ma'am," he said, but she'd already hung up.

Exhaling loudly, Bill set the phone gently in its cradle. Smiling, he held his hands up to gauge them. "Not a tremor, not a shake," he whispered, then spun to his door.

"Margo!" he shouted, startling the woman. "Where is Michael right now?"

The wide-eyed woman touched her gray hair. "If he's holding to your schedule, he'll still be with his physical trainer, sir, working on his knee. But knowing him, he'll be in the pool doing laps."

"Pool, eh?" Bill said, then darted back into his office. Motions fast, he yanked open the bottom drawer, pushing aside the bottle of scotch to find the dart pistol underneath. His smile widened as he checked the expiration on the Amneoset it was loaded with. He'd get a tech and a sedation dart from medical. Calculating the dosage was tricky, and if Michael was in the water, he'd want some help.

First Peri, and now Michael. He hadn't brought

this many people down in a long time. Another pleasure regained in the pains of becoming small again.

"Clear my schedule for today," he said, dart pistol in his jacket pocket as he breezed through his outer office and down the empty hallway to the stairs, ignoring the older woman's bemused but uncaring response.

Michael was far more dangerous than he let Helen think, but killing him would be a tragedy and a waste. Peri was good—better than Michael would ever be—but Michael killed without remorse, and sometimes a throat that didn't deserve it needed to be slit.

CHAPTER SIXTEEN

Bill hardly noticed the soft bump as the chartered jet touched down. The hard brake the pilot was forced to make was substantial, though, and the med officer behind him gasped as they were nearly flung into the seats ahead of them. The runway was markedly short, originally built for private prop engines and still relying on Boston's tower for guidance. If they didn't leave before the approaching winter storm hit, he might have to take a commercial flight home.

Or wait until tomorrow, he thought as he

unbuckled his belt and began gathering his things. He'd been listening to the crew grumble about the possibility the entire way.

His frown deepened as he faced Michael, out cold in the chair across the aisle, his wrists bound to the armrests to keep them from flopping about. "Wake him," he said to the med officer, and the quiet man began rummaging in his little tackle box. Bill turned away at the sight of the needle, confident that Michael wouldn't make much of a stink. Guilt was a wonderful evener.

The jet was still moving, making its casual way to the single low building that housed the minimal security needed at the private landing strip that had once been *the* destination for Washington's up-and-coming who could afford the summer retreat. The med officer sat across from Michael and injected him with stimulant, and knowing he'd wake thirsty, Bill gestured for a bottled water before the pilot serving as their flight crew went back to tidy the toilet. "He'll need a few minutes," the med officer said as he moved to the back of the plane with his things.

Bill shifted to sit across from Michael, wiping off the moisture from the cold bottle on his slacks as he waited for Michael's breathing to increase. He had to get Michael to appease her, the little dick squirt. He could be unbelievably charming when he wanted to be, but he'd be a bastard if he thought it would make Bill's life harder.

He checked his watch, impatient as the jet stopped right beside a waiting black car. Men dressed inappropriately for the weather got out, one taking chucks from the trunk and wedging them behind and before the wheels. "I don't have a few minutes," Bill grumbled. His hand went back, and with a grunt of satisfaction, he sent it smacking across Michael's face.

Michael snorted awake, still groggy as he tried to lift his arms only to find them tied down. "You darted me," he slurred, and Bill quickly pulled the straps free, stuffing them in his suit's pocket and out of sight. From the back, the medical officer frowned.

"Mmmm." Bill handed him the bottled water. "You wouldn't have come if I had just asked. Don't worry, you'll be able to draft as soon as you can stand."

Eyes unfocused, Michael grasped for the water, unable to manage the top.

"Let me," Bill said, one thick hand covering Michael's thinner fingers, snapping the seal.

Michael slammed it, his breath sounding in come-and-go gasps. The door to the plane opened, and a flush of cold air spilled in. It drew Michael's attention, and his bobbing Adam's apple slowed. Hands shaking, he lowered the nearly empty bottle. "If you dart me again like that, I'll kill you."

"But then you'll have to draft to bring me back," Bill said, smiling as he forced Michael's head against the rest so he could watch his eyes dilate. Satisfied, he eased into his chair to give him time to find himself.

"Where are we?" Michael rasped, head hanging.

"Newport. Trying to keep you from being scrubbed," Bill said, the sour taste from his stomach becoming worse. "Do yourself a favor and play nice."

"Rhode Island?" Almost spilling his water, Michael fumbled for his phone to check the time. "Is this right?" he mumbled, words becoming clearer. "You," he said, snagging the copilot as she went by. "What day is it?"

"Tuesday," she said, taking his hand from her sleeve. "We need a three-hour prep time to go if we don't leave within the hour," she added, hoisting her daybag and heading to the bright rectangle of light.

Expresison sour, Michael plucked at the black-and-silver pin-striped shirt he'd had on when Bill had darted him in the locker room. "You pulled me off task. Why?" Michael asked, and Bill stifled his smile as the realization crashed over the younger man that he wasn't making the Evocane drop, and was thereby missing his chance to take Peri out. He could almost see his unspoken question: had Bill known he was going to kill her, or was it just happenstance?

Bill put his ankle on his knee. "I was this close to letting you meet with her, Michael," he said, enjoying the chance to see Michael sweat. "But you need to keep this gravy train going a few months more. Jack and Allen can handle getting Peri a stopgap supply of Evocane."

Silent, Michael drank his water, staring out the window at the black cars gathering a dusting of snow. Anxious to get moving, Bill stood. "Don't be sullen," he said as he grabbed Michael by the shoulder and yanked him out of his chair. "You have more important things to do than be a delivery boy." Submitting to his frustration, he gave Michael a little shove, pleased when he caught himself against the bulkhead. "It took me five years to get a bloody audience with Helen. You got one with me saying 'pretty please.' There's a suit in the lav. Put it on."

Ignoring him, Michael eyed his empty water bottle as he held on to the bulkhead and found his balance. Looking toward the back, he exclaimed, "Can I get another water here?"

Michael sounded peeved, not angry, and encouraged, Bill stood in the aisle and gestured for him to go put the suit on. "There's water in the car," he said, trying to hurry him along, but a crew member had come forward with a new bottle, and Michael grabbed it, wobbly as he brushed past Bill and took the stairs. He slipped on the last step, looking like nothing more than a wealthy drug addict coming off a high as he fell, legs splaying in the snow.

“You should have put on the suit,” Bill muttered as he followed him onto the stairs, squinting as the fresher air smelling of snow hit him. But he jerked to a stop when the world made a hiccup and he was back on the plane. Shocked, he looked out the window to see Michael carefully navigate the last step and stumble to the waiting car.

Lips parted, Bill stood where he was, astounded. Michael had skip-hopped. The man had actually skip-hopped. Bill hadn’t known he’d been practicing, having utterly refused to try it in front of anyone who might use the situation to wipe him. It both pleased and worried Bill. It was when drafters started experimenting on their own that he usually had to wipe them. Peri had been the worst of the lot, but it was that same experimenting that made her so versatile.

The plastic covering Michael’s suit rustled as Bill took it from the bathroom. His pace slow in thought, he stepped out into the cold again, grimacing at the bright light and the black line of clouds to the west. “Good God!” Bill heard faintly as he stomped down the stairs, gesturing for one of the drivers to open the trunk. “Why is it so cold?”

“It’s January,” someone answered, and Bill carefully laid the suit in the back. It whined shut of its own accord, and Bill slid in beside Michael, appreciating the warm, running car. He didn’t have to say a word. The driver knew where they were going better than he did.

Michael was still groggy, but his eyes were focusing again. Wanting to test his reflexes, Bill tossed a comb at him. Michael caught it, and the two men exchanged wary glances.

"We're going to see Helen Yeomon," Bill said, noting there was only one attendant at the airport entrance as the white bar rose up to let them leave. "She's the one making sure you have cookies in your jar and that Aston in your drive. Call her ma'am."

"Sure. Whatever."

It was breathy and disinterested, and Bill fought the urge to smack him again. "She likes you," he said. "Don't fuck this up."

Michael chuckled—probably because he'd gotten Bill to swear. "Then maybe you should tell me what I'm doing here."

Bill let his irritation show. It was the easiest way to manipulate Michael. "She's worried about her investment," he said, careful with his word choice since everything would end up in Helen's ears.

"She's worried about me?" Michael was oblivious to the homes becoming more expensive the closer to the coast they went: marble and stone, Victorian, French, and Italian Renaissance—all with a view of the Atlantic. Newport had once been the summer playground of young-America's rich, and one by one, the abandoned mansions were being reclaimed from the local preservation society as a new class of wealthy began to entertain once again on a large scale.

"I'm not the one being dragged back to your stable kicking and screaming," Michael complained, not impressed by the million-dollar palaces slumbering under the snow, waiting for the summer's party season. "You're the one she should be worried about, continuing to withhold an advancement that will widen my abilities." He glanced warily at Bill. "I'm not working with any more anchors. I saw what you did to Peri, and I won't let you wipe me."

Bill cleared his throat, not wanting to tell him that the investment Helen was worried about was Peri. "You need to trust a little, Michael. No one is going to wipe you. As you say, you're a team player. Peri . . . not so much. Think of this as your chance to impress the hell out of her so we can change the schedule."

Michael snorted, his motions more steady as he took a swig of his water and set it carefully in the cup holder. But Bill watched him the entirety of the short drive through Newport and back into the outskirts. As he had expected, Michael's expression evened out at the hint this might be the way to get what he wanted, and he stifled a smile when Michael pulled down the vanity mirror to check his hair.

Muttering something about the scratch under his eye, Michael smacked the mirror back up, his attention going to the manicured surroundings as they pulled into a gated double-lane drive. Security waved them through without hesitation, but Bill's eyes narrowed when a golf cart with two men followed them up the plowed and brushed road to a half-hidden white edifice at the edge of a dropoff. The extra security was new.

The house was sprawling, all of it one story and strikingly modern in comparison to the surrounding elegant three-story mansions they had passed on the way in. The snow looked as if it had been carefully removed from the private drive, not randomly piled out of the way, and Bill decided it had simply been melted by low-voltage heating units right in the pavement. The pristine evenness of the snow in the yard caught and scattered the sun even as the clouds threatened to overtake it.

"You sure you don't want the suit?" Bill asked, hiding a smile when Michael silently pushed the door open before the driver could get to it.

The flush of cold air pulled Bill out, and he sighed when Michael gave security a hard time when they searched him. Bill simply let them do their job, having known better than to bring anything that might be construed as a weapon.

"You didn't think they'd just let you walk in, did you?" Bill said when they got the okay to head up the shallow steps to the front door, where another man in security black waited. "Helen is the third-wealthiest woman after Oprah and Niks Sangdow."

"Sangdow?" Michael asked as he readjusted his shirt.

"Drug and flesh dealer in Asia," he said, nodding his thanks when the door security opened it and gestured them in. The air was markedly warmer and moist, and he coughed to clear his lungs, surprised when the expected echo was absent. Though appearing one story from the drive, the house was really three, the entrance on the uppermost floor and the rest dropping with the fall of the cliff it was built into. Most of the newly wealthy went for the safe bet of marble and cold spaces. Helen was no exception, her up-and-coming architect creating an environment perched on the edge of the Atlantic that somehow captured the power it looked out upon. Wide three-story windows faced them, twin staircases leading down to either side. Icy and dark, heaving water crashed on a rocky shore with no beach not a hundred feet away. Bill couldn't help feeling a slight foreboding. There was no dock. The ocean was too unforgiving here.

"This way," their escort prompted, and both he and Michael brought their gazes back from the icy, angry Atlantic and followed the slim man down the wide stairway and across the great hall to an opulent office overlooking the ocean. The cold harshness made an odd contrast with the girl kneeling at the coffee table, glue, crayons, and glitter strewn across the expensive wood and thick, warm rug. She was maybe six, and she never looked up as they were announced.

"Bill!" a mild voice exclaimed, spinning them both around. "Thank you for coming."

"It is always a pleasure, Helen," Bill said as Michael tugged his casual shirt to cover his worn belt. Helen set her pen down and stood from behind a small desk. There was a larger one on the other side of the room in the shadows, just as neat and precise as the woman herself. Her hair was short, the gray highlights lost among the original blond. Faint wrinkles about the corners of her eyes hinted at too much sun, but Bill was confident they were there because she wanted them. The rest of her face was tight enough to imply a youthful presence. Slim and well dressed in low heels and nylons, she came forward with a warm smile, dismissing the security with a small gesture.

Bill took her offered hand, erring on the side of too gentle as he shook it. Immediately he tried to make up for it with a professional almost-kiss on her cheek. Security wasn't really gone, settling in at the outskirts: not too far, not too close, just right.

Helen dropped back and looked appraisingly at Michael. "Nice flight?" she asked, eyes traveling over his mussed appearance. "Did they make you circle around the incoming storm?"

"I don't know," Michael said dryly. "I was drugged the entire way."

"Helen," Bill interrupted smoothly. "This is Michael Kord."

"Michael." She extended her hand, and Bill tensed as Michael took it. "It's good to meet you. I feel as if I know you already, seeing as I've been following your progress since you entered Opti. Thank you for coming to see me on such short notice."

Don't say it, Michael, Bill silently prayed as the dark man smiled charmingly.

"It was my pleasure—"

"No trouble at all," Bill interrupted, wary of the glint in the man's eye.

Michael put his hands behind his back. "Why am I here?"

Helen smiled. "Direct and right to it," she said as she escorted them deeper into the room and to the arrangement of couches and chairs before the windows where the little girl played. "Bill, your assessments are as precise as always. Would either of you gentlemen like some coffee?"

The little girl beamed at him, her fingers covered in glitter. Bill smiled back. "It looks as if we're having hot chocolate," he said, and she grinned to show a gap in her teeth.

"This is my niece, Annabelle," Helen said, a comforting hand on her head. "I have her for the week her parents are out of the country.

We're getting along famously, aren't we, Anna?"

"Yes, Aunt Helen," the little girl said, going back to her picture of glittery clouds. No, it was the haze on the rocks from the crashing waves, Bill realized.

"Anna," Helen said as she dropped down to crouch beside her. "Will you change into your swimsuit, please? It's almost time for our lesson."

Her eyes lighting up, the girl stood. "Can I jump from the big diving board today?"

"Of course." Rising, Helen gestured to the door. "Go on now. I'll be right along."

Leaving her glitter and glue behind, the little girl skipped to the door, a young woman in a dress suit waiting for her already.

"Water is fine," Michael said, and Bill sighed, not liking how this was starting.

"We can talk freely on the balcony." Taking a bottled water from the wet bar, Helen handed it to Michael. Bill hustled to the sliding doors, opening them with a flourish to find the entire area had been glassed in for the winter, moist and smelling like a garden as ice lay heavy on the surrounding rock and slumbering landscape. Helen smiled at him for the small courtesy, and he followed her and Michael into the expansive, seasonal greenhouse, where a steaming coffee set waited on a low table under a palm tree as tall as the house.

Helen looked even more stunning in the sun

edged by black clouds at the horizon, but Bill was sure they were out here because of security, not the orchids she was touching in passing as if they were fond friends. "Michael," Helen said, holding up two fingers to the woman beside the coffee set. "I asked Bill to bring you here so I might impress you with the thought that with a little more attention to your job, you might be ready for acceleration."

Michael brought his eyes back from the demure Asian woman now pouring coffee into two cups and arranging them on the low table. "I'm ready now."

Bill shifted foot to foot, not liking that there were weapons pointed in their direction, even if he couldn't see them. "We've talked about this."

Brow furrowed, Michael turned to him. "You have talked, and I have listened, but I've seen her," he said, pointing at nothing with his unopened bottled water. "Peri is handling the Evocane. The stabilizer works. Continuing to withhold it from me is counterproductive."

"Michael," he coaxed.

"Just a moment, Bill." Helen held up a restraining hand, and their motion to sit stopped. "I want to hear why he thinks he's ready."

Shoulders a little straighter, Michael calmed. But then, that's why he told Helen he wanted her to meet him. The reality was he wanted Michael to see the security—find the way in, where he could do the most damage.

"I'm as good at what I do as Peri, if not more," he said, glowering as if Bill would deny it. "Her mind is Swiss cheese, and I've never had to be scrubbed because I believe in what Opti is. I'm doing what I like."

Helen waved the coffee girl away, frowning as the woman's heels clicked noisily on the tile. "That's part of the problem," she said almost wistfully. "You're doing what you like, following your own ideas, not what Bill has set before you. I abhor bringing up the past, but what happened at Everblue is a good example."

Bill cringed as he helped Helen with her chair. "I've minimized the damage."

Motions graceful, Helen settled herself at the table under the palm, the fronds looking fantastically out of place as the sun vanished behind the encroaching cloud bank. "I'm not looking for an explanation," she said. "It's in the past. I only bring it up to show the repeating pattern. You do what you want, Michael, instead of what is best for Opti."

"You want a doll?" Michael sat down, his tone bordering on aggressive, and Bill caught a glimpse of movement from the shadows. They weren't alone. It just looked that way. "Dolls are toys," Michael continued. "And toys break. That's what Peri is, and your doll is ready to shatter."

"You're more right than you know." Primly arranging the napkin, she smiled at Michael without emotion. "If you were the one to break her, it would further your standing greatly."

Bill sat down. It was too warm out here, even with the snow beginning to hit the ceiling.

"I can understand your desire," Helen continued. "I can even applaud it. I wouldn't be here if I didn't break a few toys myself. Michael, be patient. Evocane isn't perfect yet."

"Peri is handling it," Michael said. "I can accomplish more in one afternoon than she can in a week because I like who I am and don't need to be tricked into doing it."

Helen looked at Bill, and Bill raised his hands, gesturing as if to say "See?"

"I need a reason," Michael said as he settled back. "Here I am. Convince me."

Helen sipped her coffee, the fine china clinking as she discreetly checked her watch. "You've done little to instill a feeling of comfort. Entertaining your desires to kill her for your benefit?" Her head inclined. "It is a good strategy, but it's not ours. You don't see everything. *You* need her alive and in Opti."

"And *you* are lying," Michael said calmly, and Bill cringed even as Helen smiled.

"Not this time," she said with a fond chuckle. "You will be accelerated, but it's not right yet. You're correct that your desire to work bests

Peri being manipulated into it, but we need a field test to ensure that the safety measures we've implemented are adequate. Peri is easier to control if there are issues. That's why she is first, not you."

It sounded more reasonable coming from her, and Michael sat back, his expression empty, as if he was finally starting to believe. That the safety measures she mentioned were to control drafters, not ensure their continued health, was not worth bringing to Michael's attention.

"We need to monitor Peri, see where we need to adjust the formula. It's too chancy with her in the wild the way she is. The way to make the acceleration viable and permanent is in her, but we need her alive to find out how to do that. Do you understand, Michael? We need her sacrifice to tell us how to make it safe for you."

Michael drummed his fingers, head cocked. "Rich people are good at lying."

Bill was horrified, but Helen laughed in appreciation. "True, but I'm not lying now. I like you, Michael. Bill was right to ask me to meet you. Scrubbing you would be a mistake."

Shit, he thought, wishing she hadn't said that. Michael was deathly afraid of being scrubbed, days or months of memories artificially removed to better manipulate him—so much so that he refused to jump unless his own life, or pride, apparently, was in danger.

Michael's thin smile had faded. Noticing, Helen stood, effectively getting them all to rise. "Leave her to us, Michael," she said as they returned inside, and the stabilizing air pressures blew her niece's artwork to the floor. "Peri is serving a function to benefit you, and until that task is over, she is to remain alive."

Michael's face showed the first hints of belief, and Bill began to relax.

"You are very good," Helen praised as she examined Annabelle's glittery haze. "One of a kind as Bill has promised me. Eager to act, unafraid of possible ill consequences, strong enough to see yourself through. Perhaps even more important, you get the job done, but you are splashy. Do you understand?"

"You want me to be more bland?" he questioned in disbelief.

"I want you to stop thinking you know all the options." Picture in hand, Helen went to the cork-board easel standing in the middle of the room. More artwork decorated it, and she searched for a thumbtack. "We want you around for a long time, and you're not being careful," she said as she stuck it in the place of most importance. "Like Annabelle's page, you're bright and sparkly, attractive to the point of distraction, but the goal was to make a memory of our trip to the zoo, and no matter how pretty this page is, it doesn't fulfill the goal and it won't go into my scrapbook." Head cocked, Helen eyed the glittery mess. "She has talent, for a six-year-old."

Michael was scowling again, but it vanished when Helen turned.

"It will come, Michael," she said, taking his hand. "Let Bill deal with this as he sees fit. It's his job. You will be accelerated when we know it works safely. In the meantime, impress us with your new understanding."

"Yes, ma'am. I'll keep the glitter off it," Michael said calmly, but Bill could see the threads of dangerous thought running through him, and his lip quirked to fight the smile. *Perfect.*

"Good." Satisfied, Helen dropped his hand and looked at her watch again. "Do you have time for a late lunch? The storm is likely hours away."

Bill let his smile show, eager for it. "Yes, ma'am. That would be appreciated."

"Wonderful." She gestured for her security, and Bill was satisfied when he saw Michael note where they came from. This was working better than he'd hoped. Lunch, followed by a short tour, perhaps? "My niece is waiting. Enjoy your meal. Gentlemen?"

Both Bill and Michael shook her hand, and without a backward glance, she walked out, heels clicking on the imported tile. A man came in after her, gesturing for them to follow him. To lunch, presumably.

"She's not going to eat with us?" Michael said, and Bill exhaled, relieved.

"No. We were lucky to get even this much of her time. And now that you've seen her, don't talk about it."

"Who would I tell," he said idly, but his eyes were scanning everything, finding the layout of the place and noting how security hung with her, not covering the entire premises.

Pleased, Bill clapped him across the shoulder. "Good choice in not wearing the suit."

CHAPTER SEVENTEEN

An almost-not-there heat radiated up from the thermal stone the commercial square was paved with. It was there to keep Lloyd Plaza clear of snow, but Detroit allowed the solar stones to free all their stored energy during festivals. It nearly felt warm as Silas tugged his winter coat close and waited for Peri at one of the outside tables.

People milled around him, taking up the tables or gathering beside the nearby small stage lit with neon and loud with preshow patter. The upscale clothing store Sim's Mules was behind him, the holographic simulations in the window getting a workout as they spiraled through a bewildering array of sparkles, colors, and styles, recognizing the clothing passing before their windows and mimicking them to lure patrons in. One of them had fixated on Silas's unmoving form, posing in the latest Armani suit as he beckoned to him. The complex algorithm had probably noticed his shoes and extrapolated his tastes from there.

Cars went past in the nearby street, and a burst of music rose and fell, echoing off the surrounding buildings. Silas hunched into himself, scanning the moving flow for anyone watching him. It had been early spring the last time he'd been to Lloyd Plaza. Peri had just realized that Bill had filled her memories with lies and had made her his queen in the very game she'd entered with the intent to shut down. She'd ultimately succeeded, but his gamble of giving Peri her diary to hopefully remind her of their love was looking slim at best.

Frustration, quickly smothered by guilt, pulled at him. It was up to Peri. It was always up to Peri.

Frowning, he turned from the shallow, engineered lake thick with ice-skaters and spun his empty coffee cup between his finger and thumb in a nervous circle. Peri's favorite coffee sat cooling next to him. The email of her flight reservation coming in at Detroit rather than returning to Atlanta hadn't surprised him, but her later text asking him to meet her here with any Evocane he could spare had. It was ugly stuff, growing worse as he picked it apart. WEFT had been in a tizzy when he left. No one was telling him anything. Actually, they were ignoring him. Being labeled a science geek had its perks.

Uneasy, he shifted on the bench, squinting up at the low-Q recording drones hovering over the stage, not comfortable with the thought of how easy it had been to slip out of Atlanta and make his way to Detroit with three injector pens full of what Evocane he had left. Sure, he'd gone through eighty percent of his field-agent training before abandoning it, and yes, mistakes happened when you pulled the best people from multiple organizations and various protocols mixed, but the door had been wide open.

That he might be leading Peri into a trap was a distinct possibility. That she'd left St. Louis without permission wasn't hard to figure out either. His first guess that she'd gone ghost seemed unlikely since what little WEFT gossip he'd heard was about Harmony and how pissed Steiner was at her. Peri had to be behind it.

Frowning, he crossed his ankles under the table and put his hands into his coat pockets to at least try to look relaxed. She wasn't late—yet. The cool shapes of the three Evocane pens met his fingers, worrying him more. He'd double-checked that it had been untampered with before he'd parceled it out and put a vial of tinted baby oil in its place. Peri had asked him, and he'd brought it, but he'd be damned before he let her get hooked on it—the lure of being able to remember her drafts or not.

Silas jerked upright when he recognized her silhouette among the throng, her petite form graceful and her boots giving her an extra inch. She looked good in her tight black pants, somehow making the utilitarian coat with the WEFT logo seem trendy and fitting in with the young crowd even with her intent expression. A ball cap covered her face, and she was watching the low-Q drones as she made her way over.

He gathered himself to rise, motion slowing when Harmony came up behind her. They were wearing the same coat, and Silas scanned the tops of the surrounding buildings for more than pigeons as the two women had a hushed, eye-darting conversation. Clearly not liking the situation, Harmony grimaced at him before settling herself against one of the snow-dead planters, where she could watch both them and the street behind her through the reflections. The CIA agent had the shadow of a bruise on her jaw and was moving with a pained stiffness that said she was feeling more than the extended travel to get here.

Silas's welcoming smile faltered as Peri got closer. She didn't look much better, her turned-up nose red with cold, her lip swollen, and a scrape on her cheek—rug burn, maybe? Eyes haunted past her long lashes, she looked too small to survive the crap her life heaped on her as she made her way through the gathered people. She'd cut her hair to its task-short severeness sometime between Atlanta and now, and she flicked it from her eyes when the wind gusted, meeting his gaze with a guilty swiftness. He couldn't help but feel a tinge of pride for her. She'd come a long way in regaining herself in the year she'd been out of Opti. They'd worked hard to instill in her an aversion to being alone, building on her natural fear of forgetting and lying to her that to not remember would lead to insanity. He'd have to remind her of that lie.

"How do you get so banged up in so little time?" he said, his hand going out to cup her cheek. People were watching them, but it was in question of what someone like him was doing with someone like her.

"You should see the other guy," she said, stiffening as his fingers touched her face. But it was guilt and heartache in her eyes, and he slid his other hand behind her back and drew her forward to sit.

Peri's eyes shot to his, the panic in them having nothing to do with Opti, WEFT, or the low-Q drones skating over the square. But he would not lose her again because of his own fear, and he pulled her into an embrace, needing to feel her against him to prove she was okay.

"I did, and she looks better than you," he whispered, his arm still around her and his head bowed to breathe in the scent of her hair. He felt her breath catch, and then, for an instant, surrounded by the happy chatter of people, her body relaxed into his, accepting him as her arms tentatively encircled him, so light they were almost not there.

And then she pulled away, still refusing to believe she deserved it.

Silas slumped as his hand dropped to his side. Harmony was staring at him. Worried, he gestured for Peri to sit. She wouldn't look at him as she settled herself exactly where he knew she would, able to see the skaters and the street busy with Sity bikes and commuter traffic. Behind her, the holographic mannequins began shifting into upscale leather and lace.

His heart ached at her heavy sigh as she reached for the coffee, her tension vanishing when most of the milling people were pulled to the stage with a guitar riff and enthusiastic cheer. "Thank you," she murmured, her words meaning more to him than they should.

Silas and Allen alone knew her past. Only Silas could guess her future. There were not, and never would be, any easy answers for her, and all he wanted was for her to be happy.

"Do you have it?" she asked around the rim of her cup.

His worry rushed back. "Yes, but I don't want you to take it. Peri—"

"Bill has Allen," she said, setting the cup down and putting a cold hand atop his.

Silas's breath caught. He didn't trust Allen, but he was his friend, and Bill wouldn't have a problem killing him. "No one told me. Is he okay?" he asked, and Peri's hand gave his a squeeze before slipping back into her coat pocket.

"For the moment," she said cryptically, wincing as she stretched her leg. "Bill is offering a trade. Allen and a vial of Evocane for a chance to snag me."

Trap, he thought, but she already knew that. "But you don't need Evocane."

Silent, she stared into the coffee he'd gotten for her.

"Peri?" he questioned, fear sliding cleanly through him when she wouldn't look up. "I know the lure to take the accelerator and remember has got to be incredible, but it's nasty stuff. You don't want to get hooked on it. The more I dig, the worse it gets. Some of these compounds are fighting each other, and I don't even know why they're in there. A sodium uptake inhibitor? Immune depressors? I know how much you want this, but they aren't balanced and there are going to be ugly side effects when the longer-lived compounds begin to build up."

"Then it's a good thing I don't need it," she said as she yanked the felt-tip pen from her pendant and scribbled on the napkin. He leaned forward, going cold when she wrote BILL DARTED ME WITH EVOCANE.

"How," he whispered, eyes widening as she wadded the napkin up into a tight ball. But the answer was obvious. Oh God. He only had three days to give her. She was running without a net and was rightfully scared. At least she hadn't been accelerated. The syringe holding the accelerator she'd taken from Bill was locked up in Steiner's office. *Had she?*

His lips parted to ask her, but Peri shook her head to stop his next words, pointedly letting the balled napkin drop between them. She thought one of them might be bugged, and with the ease he'd slipped WEFT, it was probably him. *Shit.*

"I expect that whatever Michael brings, it won't be Evocane. I'm just after Allen," she said lightly, but he could see the lie in the way she kept looking over his shoulder to the skaters, as if expecting Navy SEALs to come lurching up between them.

"This is a trap," he said, deathly worried as he handed the three Evocane pens to her under the table.

He watched, his heart breaking as she tucked them away. There was guilt in her eyes when they flicked up to find his—guilt and relief. "Of course it is," she said. She took a slow breath, gaze distant, as if she was feeling the paths of her life shift ninety degrees to a direction she didn't want. "That's why Harmony is with me. Trap or not, this is likely to be the only shot she'll get at Michael.

I think he killed her entire team in front of her for an object lesson. I help her get Michael, she helps me get Allen. You know I'm no good on my own."

She was, despite what she said, but the relief he'd seen when she took the injector pens made it clear that she was risking her life on chancy intel and limited resources for the hope that the Evocane Bill promised her would be real. *What if it isn't? Will she go back to Bill to stay sane? Would I tell her to go? Drive her there? Kiss her good-bye and walk away?*

"I've got to go," she said, rising as the crowd began singing along with the band. "I can't tell you how much this means to me. Thank you."

"Peri, about the Evocane," he said as he stood as well. "I'm getting close to figuring this out. A week maybe," he lied. But he'd given her only a few days' worth, and she knew it.

"I'll be fine," she said as she scanned the square, the thump of the bass beating into them. "Keep doing what you're doing. I'm seeing this through. I owe Harmony that much. Steiner was just getting in the way."

But she was dancing to Bill's tune, and they both knew it.

"Good," he rushed, not wanting to see her leave. He wished he could go with her, but the cold truth was he'd slow her down. His muscles were good for breaking heads, not speed records. "Don't let him accelerate you. Once you take it, there's no going back." *At least now, all she has to do is beat the withdrawal.*

From her distant bench, Harmony swore and stood. "They're here!" she said loudly, and Peri's focus blurred.

"They followed me," Silas said, but Peri shook her head even as she took a last gulp of her coffee and stuffed her crumpled napkin with her note on it in her pocket.

"No. They've been on us since we hit I-70. I'm sorry, Silas. Will you be our rabbit? If they follow us to the drop site, we won't have a chance. I'm sorry."

He could tell she was, and he nodded, not caring whether it made him into a chump. "Go," he said as he gave her a hug, eyes closing as her slight body relaxed against his. He could feel it even through his thick coat. She felt so small, he could hardly bear it. "Call me," he finished, refusing to let his throat close as she pulled away.

Nodding, she drifted back, her fingers lingering on his until the last moment. She hadn't pulled away first, and his heart ached.

Harmony had come forward and was tugging at Peri's elbow. "Now," she said tightly, and Peri looped her arm in hers, giving Silas a last look before turning and vanishing into the crowd.

Slowly Silas sat back down, calling himself a fool as he dropped his empty paper cup into hers. A couple pressed close, wanting his table, and he ignored them, jealous of their boring life, even if it came with cheap knockoff shoes and polyester suits. He'd lost her once. He'd do almost anything to keep her safe. Anything. And he'd just given her poison.

The couple inching closer protested as three men in identical suits pushed them back. Silas looked up, not surprised when three more flowed past him into Sim's Mules. Steiner was right behind them, his pale face spotted red with cold as he halted before Silas.

"Where is she?" Steiner demanded, eyes on the two cups.

The couple fled. Silas put the flats of his arms on the cold cement table and leaned in, casually playing with the two nested cups. She had a thirty-second head start. He could buy her a few minutes more. "Who?"

Steiner gestured, and Silas jerked when one of the agents grabbed his shoulder and yanked him to his feet. People scattered, but the band was loud enough that they were hardly getting noticed. "Hey! Watch it!" Silas complained, shaking the cold coffee from his hand as Steiner's face went red under his graying hair.

"I ask again, Denier," Steiner intoned, standing too close with his agents hemming Silas in from behind. "You left Atlanta. Came here to meet her. Where is she?"

Silas tried not to smirk. He didn't want to lose

his lab access, after all. "Probably her old apartment two blocks over on Wright Avenue, seeing as I gave her the key," he ad-libbed. "Harmony is with her of her free will. Neither one of them look fond of red tape. You might consider backing off and letting them do their job."

Motion brusque, Steiner motioned for someone to frisk him. "What's at her apartment?"

Arms out, Silas shook off the heavy hands, not liking the attention. "Besides memories?" he said as he fixed his coat. "Weapons, so be careful if you're going to follow her there."

"Then maybe we should put you at the front door."

Shrugging, Silas started into motion, heading for the nearby street and the two black cars parked illegally at the curb. He could slow things down while still being cooperative. "Sure. I've done that before. I want a vest," he said, knowing it would take some time to find one that fit him, and since he asked, they had to comply. Peri wouldn't mind his showing them the apartment, seeing as she hadn't lived in it for a year and it was likely occupied by someone else. Besides, the distraction of going through it might give her an entire day before they found her.

"Get him in the car," Steiner demanded, and someone shoved him.

Silas caught his balance, careful to keep his eyes down and not looking for Peri. She might be gone, or she might be on a roof watching them. He didn't want to give her away if it was the latter. He was confident the last place she'd be was her old apartment.

She'd left everything of her past behind, including him.

CHAPTER EIGHTEEN

"Peri? We're almost there."

Harmony's soft voice shocked through Peri. Her doze shredded with the jagged realization that she'd forgotten Harmony was driving the car—not Jack. That she'd nodded off at all was disturbing. But then again, she'd not had a chance to sleep for a while.

"Sorry," Harmony said, and Peri took her hand off her coat's pocket and the three pens of Evocane there. "Didn't mean to startle you."

"You didn't," Peri lied. "I forgot that it was you driving, not Jack."

Harmony's hands tightened on the wheel. The car still smelled like fast-food chicken, and with four empty coffee cups in the console, she wasn't surprised at the faint need to use the bathroom. The bright center of Detroit was behind them, leaving only the grittier outskirts where old city sprawl met decayed suburbs. Having sacrificed the edges to save the center, Detroit had left thousands to fend for themselves or move inward. It always surprised Peri how many chose the former, fearing they'd be taken advantage of or believing if they stuck it out, their property values would again rise.

Not likely, she thought as she wiggled her feet back into her new boots before pulling her WEFT-supplied jacket tighter about her shoulders. Detroit was currently balanced with high profit. The few areas left to themselves due to politicking and corruption lingered, attracting gangs and low-end drugs.

Get in. Find Michael and Allen. Kill Michael—not Allen. Get out. Easy peasy. But a slight, unusual tremor shook her hands. With it was a rising need to do something, an itch very akin to the sensation of adrenaline crawling along her synapses. The feeling was familiar—she tasted it every time she went out on task. This time, though, it hurt, the ache reaching to the pit of her belly and cutting like a knife. Nausea oozed in behind it, and her legs hurt, as if she'd had a fever. It was a warning: withdrawal.

Her heart gave a pound, and her fingers stretched, touching her pocket again as she recalled Silas's worry when he gave her the Evocane. His expression was nothing new. She'd seen it a hundred times before. But now, with the thoughts of their last year at Opti training ringing through her, that same look held new meaning. He'd loved her then. He loved her now. Seeing her younger self care for him, try to pull him from his depression and guilt . . . the lure to find some happiness with him was frighteningly strong.

A lump rose in her throat, and she fought it. He'd given her the Evocane knowing what it would do to her, he had let her walk away knowing her path would lead to more trouble, not less, and he stayed behind to muddle her trail, helping her the only way he could. And for what? So he would feel that ache and guilt again when her choice was utterly gone and she was dead or Bill's tool once more? She couldn't do this to him again. He felt too deeply, too long.

I never seem to have a choice, she thought as the pinch of need grew. She had two hours until she had to dose up, but unless she wanted to risk a full withdrawal while dealing with Michael, she'd have to shoot up now—in front of Harmony. It bothered her.

"You miss him," Harmony said softly, misreading her grimace.

"Silas?" Peri fumbled in her pocket, the click of the injector pen sounding loud as she uncapped it. "I hardly remember him," she said, trying to make light of it as she tugged her waistband down and jammed the tip into her thigh. The prick of the lance turned into a dull ache. "But he remembers me," she said, voice strained. She was good for another twenty-four hours.

Harmony was still looking at her when she glanced up, the woman's expression unreadable in the unlit, snow-caked streets of abandoned Detroit. "Not Silas. Jack," Harmony finally said. "You know . . . you thought he was driving the car?" she prompted.

Peri's lips parted, her first hot refusal dying. Apparently she did miss him—in a way. "You've never worked with anyone before, have you?" Peri said, feeling like a drug addict as she tossed the spent injector into the trash.

Harmony's expression became closed. "All the time. I've never been afforded the chance to work alone."

"I mean, worked so closely and for so long with someone that you know each other's moods, methods. How fast he can hot-wire a car or that it takes him thirty seconds to subdue someone expecting it, five if they aren't." *That he likes his coffee with four inches of ice when it's hot and he curses in Spanish when his cell phone craps out. That he knows where your shoulder cramps after a morning at the range, and to turn up the TV when that commercial with the goat comes on.*

"You still love him," Harmony said, looking angry—misled, maybe.

Peri stared across the car at her, wondering whether Harmony was having second thoughts and that Peri might run to Opti as Steiner had predicted. "Enough to kill him, sure," Peri said lightly. "And if I ever see him again, I'll do just that."

Harmony's shoulders eased. Silent, she took a side street, cutting across the snow-covered parking lot of a sporadically lit Wally World. It was almost empty, not with the hour but from neglect. Glancing behind them, Peri settled into the cushions. "I'm still trying to figure out why you're doing this."

Harmony shrugged as she parked under a light that was in view of one of the security cams. "You know that glass ceiling that doesn't exist anymore? I hit it two years ago."

Peri took in her guilt, but not knowing what it was there for. "No," she said. "I want to know why. Right now. You don't throw your career away trying to save it."

Harmony turned the engine off. Hands landing back on the wheel, she stared out the front window. "He butchered my team with less thought than he'd give slapping a mosquito. He did it because they didn't have the information he wanted. That doesn't deserve to walk around."

Peri's thoughts sifted through the cracks in her fragmented mind, catching on emotions without faces attached to them. This, she understood. "I figured it was something like that."

"Those were good people," Harmony said, her

grip on the wheel white-knuckle tight. "He took everything from them, everything they had, everything they *would* have: days, years, births, promotions. I survived because I was a woman and that bastard saved me for last. Like dessert."

"Fair enough," Peri said, wishing she'd stop talking. Too many emotions were trying to surface, making her ill with fractured memories.

"Besides, with me losing my team, my glass ceiling just turned into cement. Steiner might forget about it if I come back with Michael." Harmony reached for her purse, clearly not sure she believed it herself. "I don't care if you forget. People forget battle trauma all the time."

Peri didn't know what to think about that, so she muttered a soft "Thanks. You need to run in for ammo?" Her gaze went to the big-box store, wondering whether that's why they'd parked there, but Harmony chuckled and unlocked her door.

"I'm not taking my car into the arena. We walk from here."

Walk? Through the arena? At night when there's a perfectly good car? But then again, taking a car into what was supposed to be an abandoned area would get them noticed, too. Not liking either option, Peri looked out the front window across the weed-choked railroad tracks to the low cluster of boarded-up commercial buildings. Behind them was even more dilapidated, unlit, and condemned low-rent temporary housing originally built to get the homeless and displaced off Detroit's streets before reconstruction had begun. None of it had been intended to last more than a decade, but not everyone had left when new housing had been built.

Calling it the arena had been the cops' idea. The concept was good, but it hadn't gone well, and the mostly deserted area had become a haven for drugs, prostitution, and gangs. Every electoral year there was a push to get it cleaned up, but the way the cops figured it, if all the bad apples were in one basket, it was easier to catch those trying to sample the fruit. Cops seldom came into the area, and never at night unless they were in well-armed packs with high-Q drones and riot gear.

"It's bad enough leaving Steiner's car here," Harmony muttered, brow furrowed as she took her wallet and phone out of her purse before shoving it under the seat. Peri couldn't help but notice there were three missed calls, all of them from Steiner. "Hand me up the duffel, will you?"

"Sure," Peri said, reaching into the back for it.

Harmony unzipped it, making a small sound of satisfaction as she took out her Glock and tucked it into her shoulder holster under her open coat. "What do you think?" she asked. "Big enough to be seen and envied, but not so much that it looks as if I'm looking for a fight?"

"I'll stick with my knife if you don't mind." It

was doubtful the car would be entirely intact when they returned, so Peri stuffed her pockets and belt pack with everything she wanted to keep. Her diary was going to be a problem, new pages leaking out every time she opened it.

"I do," Harmony insisted. "Be a woman. Take the Glock. That's why I brought it."

Nodding, Peri took the semiautomatic pistol with a quick-change ammo clip. "Guns aren't my go-to," she said as she zipped it into her belt pack, snuggling it at the small of her back. "They have a tendency to kill me, and then I have to draft and fix it," she added, smoothing her journal out before dropping it into her coat pocket. It was lumpy, but leaving it in the car wasn't an option.

Harmony tucked a second ammo clip behind her shirt, shuddering when the cold hit her. "I'd do anything for a reset button. So I'd forget. Some things, I don't *want* to remember."

Mulling that over, Peri shifted her belt pack until the extra weight felt natural. "You sure you want to do this with me?"

"The arena?" Harmony opened her door, the cold night slipping in as she got out. "Two women? After dark?" Looking at the abandoned buildings, she adjusted her holster to make sure it was visible past her coat. "Bring it on."

Peri's faint smile grew as the unusual feeling of kinship drifted through her. Stretching the stiff hours from her, Peri got out as well, carefully shutting her door so the sound wouldn't carry. The cold woke her up fast. Two inches of new snow crunched underfoot, but it would likely be gone by noon.

Peri fell into place beside Harmony, thinking they should've left the car unlocked so the thieves wouldn't have to break a window to get in. "You don't have another set of keys, do you?" she asked as they cut across the parking lot, their path obvious in the snow.

"No. Why?"

They slowed as they hit the shadows, waiting for their eyes to adjust. "I, ah, usually have a set," she said, sorry now she'd brought it up. "Never mind."

"No, I should have thought of it," Harmony said. "Sorry. You want to carry them?"

"Good God, no," Peri rushed, glad the darkness hid her face. Their twined voices echoed off the empty shop fronts, reminding her of the women in Africa who walk unafraid through lion-infested brush, talking loudly to warn the huge carnivores away. It worked only because the cats had been conditioned to be afraid. *Here, though,* she thought as they passed the broken windows, *the lions aren't afraid.*

"You've done something like this before," Peri said, making it more of a statement.

"Something like it."

Her voice had become distant. Clearly Harmony

didn't want to talk about it. But the sound of their boots in the unplowed street was giving Peri the creeps. She kept scanning the rooftops for silhouettes, but nothing broke the cold sterility except solar arrays and outdated satellite dishes. "That was impressive how you got us out of the St. Louis facility. But why spend that much effort on being stealthy when you're so good at offense?"

Harmony's teeth caught the light as she smiled. "The best offense is not being there to take the hit." Her smile faded. "And *I* don't have a golden parachute to get me around one."

The woman's annoyance was obvious, and Peri frowned. "Why are you mad at me about that? It would be like me being angry because you're black and can dance better than me."

"Excuse me?" Harmony blurted.

"Sorry," Peri said immediately. "That was supposed to be funny."

Mollified, Harmony resumed her pace. "I can, you know," Harmony said softly.

"Can what?"

"Dance better than you."

Peri smiled, her feeling of kinship growing, but she jerked when a sharp clang echoed. The sound stiffened her spine, but neither woman altered her pace. It had been a signal, a warning, and they kept moving forward—ignoring it.

"You should have brought bigger guns," Peri whispered as she unzipped her belt pack.

“You think?” Harmony frowned. “We can’t sit and wait. If Michael isn’t at the mall, we keep walking. Okay?”

“No problem.” Peri slipped the Glock into her coat pocket. Her phone was cold against her fingertips and she took it out, quickly turning the glow down when it threatened to ruin her night vision. Scrolling to Allen’s number, she hit send. The connection went through, and faint in the nearby distance, a phone began to ring. They weren’t anywhere near the mall. *Son of a bitch.*

Exhaling, Harmony stopped right in the middle of the street. “I don’t think that’s necessarily a good thing.”

“Allen?” Peri called loudly, ending the call and tucking the phone away.

But it wasn’t Allen who scuffed out from the shadows. It wasn’t Michael, either.

“Hello, ladies,” a heavy man in a ragged coat said, sauntering confidently from between two buildings with five of his thugs behind him, each one looking more thin and disheveled than the last. *Casino trash. Great.* “Where are you two fine crotch-riders going tonight? Lookin’ for something? Me and my boys got more than enough.”

Laughing, his buddies grabbed their privates suggestively as they circled them. Peri focused on the one who hadn’t. He was shorter than all of them, Asian, and his clothes, while just as mismatched and tatty, were clean. His coat was leather, and his fingers weren't stained from drugs or nic caps. A lit phone glowed from his pocket. *Boss,* she realized, thinking he was smart to have the big man do the talking. He was also the only one who didn't have a pistol jammed into his waistband.

Harmony shifted to put her back to Peri's. "We aren't looking for anything you got. Back off. Let us by, and no one gets hurt."

That got the expected chuckle, but safeties were clicking off. It was the phone Peri was interested in. "That's my friend's phone," Peri said when the light on it went out. "Where is he?"

Surprise flickered over the big man's face, but the short guy smiled, his thin lips pressed together as he took in Peri's swollen cheek. "It's mine now," he said, and Peri readjusted her opinion from Asian to American Indian. "Did he do that to you?"

He was looking at her bruise, and Peri grimaced. "No, she did," she said, nodding to Harmony, and the man's eyebrows rose in question.

"LB," the big man protested when the smaller man pushed his way to the front, smacking the larger man in the chest to be quiet. The light hit LB, showing the stylized tattoos of bears, eagles, and little fish decorating his neck. Peri was betting they continued over his chest and back. His confidence was absolute as he stood before them with his arms crossed, more men slipping out of the shadows with clinks and sliding thumps to circle them. Soon as they had enough, they'd try for the guns. And then whatever else they wanted, probably.

"You give us the guns, we might let you walk out of here," LB said as his men sniggered.

Doubtful. Fingers shifting, Peri popped the clip out and threw the weapon at him. The men surrounding them reacted slow, falling back and swearing, but LB caught it. "Have it."

"What are you doing!" Harmony hissed, appalled as her aim shifted from man to man.

"What?" Peri complained as she dropped the clip into her coat pocket. "I want my hands free. Besides, he can't shoot it without bullets."

The men laughed as LB took out a clip from his pocket and snapped it in.

"Unless he carries his own," Peri grumbled, shifting to find her balance. Her knife was a half second from her hand, another half second from the neck of whoever touched her first. She didn't like buying respect that way, but they weren't listening.

The circle was closing, moving around the smaller man like water moves around a rock. Peri's pulse quickened, her eyes never leaving him. He was small to have commanded this much control over them, and she wanted to know why.

Harmony eased closer, the scent of sweat growing strong. "You see that Ford truck?" she said, chin shifting to point it out. "I'm going right."

Yeah, we should probably try to escape. "I'll go left," Peri said, finding her balance. Six men circled them. One looked stoned, another just bored. Three firearms, two pipes. Say . . . ten people watching from the shadows, with maybe two willing to shoot? One that might actually be good at it? The odds were better than at first glance.

"Gun?" the big man said, face ugly as he grinned. "Give it to me now, Cornrows!"

Harmony started, her tension tinged with anger. "Did you just call me Cornrows?"

Peri eyed the dark, broken windows above them. She'd have five seconds until surprise wore off and they began shooting. Fat Man would be her shield.

"Drop it!" Fat Man bellowed, and Harmony shook her head, jaw clenched.

"You can have my gun—"

"When I pry it out of your cold, dead hand," LB said in a tired tone. "That gets so old."

"No," Harmony said grimly. "After I shove it up your ass!" Screaming, Harmony darted to the right, planting her foot into the gut of the man in her way. He doubled over, but she was already gone, sprinting for the dubious protection of the abandoned vehicle.

Peri jumped at the pop of a gun, darting left to

catch one man and dislocate his arm as she swung him. He shrieked in pain, then bellowed when a bullet hit his beefy shoulder. Grunting, Peri pushed him into the rest and ran for the truck. He'd be fine.

Three, two, one . . . she counted down as the man screamed, "Pop it out! Oh, God! Someone, pop my shoulder back out!" She shifted to the left, almost falling on ice when a spray of concrete peppered her legs. More weapons fired until LB shouted for them to knock it off. The gunfire might bring the cops, but not until sunup.

"It's me!" she called, hoping the dark shadow by the car was Harmony.

"You hit?" Harmony asked as she skidded to a crouched halt. Peri looked at the empty windows. It would take time to get up there, but not forever. She and Harmony would have to be gone by then. Finding Allen or Michael was looking slim. "I said, are you okay!"

Peri brought her gaze back down and inched closer to the truck. "Sorry. Yes," she said as LB barked orders. He was pretty good. He'd have to be either really smart or have good drug connections to keep a leash on these bad boys.

"Do you think they have Allen and Michael?" Harmony asked, and Peri snorted, not believing the woman was still wanting a play for them.

"Maybe." Tugging Harmony's elbow, she began to inch her way backward and tuck into the deeper shadows. "They don't strike me as having been hammered on already tonight. I'm betting Michael gave them Allen's phone and arranged for them to take care of us for him." *Damn it. Where am I going to get more Evocane?*

The *pop-ping* of a bullet made Harmony jump. "The profiler said Michael would be here. He wants you dead, and he's got a deep-seated urge to do it himself."

"And you didn't think to tell me that?" Irate, she watched the empty street. "Can I borrow your weapon?" Peri asked, grabbing it when Harmony stared blankly.

"Hey!" the woman exclaimed, but Peri had stood, rattling a battery of bullets into one of the empty buildings.

"Move!" Peri shouted, tossing the pistol back and jogging up the street, deeper into the arena. They couldn't go back. The only way out was through. Besides, Michael might be up there somewhere, gloating as he watched through night binoculars.

Harmony's footsteps were loud as she came even, and they picked up the pace, dodging piles of snow and stumbling on hidden potholes. "You had to be a smart-ass and give him your gun," she complained.

Peri gasped, instinct jerking her back as the pavement sprayed up right in front of her. "Harmony, no!" she cried, but the woman had darted into an alley. Teeth clenched, Peri stood firm as another bullet went *ping-whap* into the pavement. They were driving them into a tighter trap, and Harmony had fallen for it. "Harmony!" she shouted, torn.

Shouts and gunfire rang out from the black mouth of the alley, and swearing, Peri ran into the dark after her.

Knife to a gunfight, she thought, pounding along until skidding to a halt at the edge of the light. Two men were getting up off the filthy, slush-coated pavement between the buildings, but Harmony was caught in the grip of a third, his bearded face nasty as it pressed up against hers, her head thrown back with his arm tight around her neck and a small handgun shoved into her side. The glare from a flashlight made sharp, ugly shadows.

"Let her go," Peri demanded, then slumped when the cold feel of a pistol muzzle pressed the back of her neck. Sighing, she realized it was the one she'd given LB.

"Hello again," he said softly. "Don't move, or your girlfriend will get it."

Lip curled, she stiffened as he amateurishly frisked her, taking everything from the wadded-up napkin from that afternoon to her clip, pen pendant, and knife. "This is a mistake," she said when he tossed her belt pack to one of the arriving men, panting and out of breath.

"Yeah?" LB said, the pistol firmly against her skull. "I'm about to make the same mistake twice. I don't care who you are. You shouldn't be here. That's Detroit's first rule. Stay where you belong, little girl."

Peri's eyes darted to Harmony, almost on tiptoe with that big man's arm around her neck. *Same mistake twice?* "You've got Allen and Michael?"

Silent, LB jammed the muzzle harder to get her to shut up. "What's she carrying?"

There were three men now clustered about her stuff, and Peri stiffened when one depressed the plunger of one of the spent injection pens and sniffed the tiny drop. He tasted it and shrugged. "Same stuff, maybe," he said. "It's not recreational. Sedative, maybe?"

"It's mine," Peri said, pulse quickening. They had Michael, or at least run into him.

"And it appears to be addictive," LB mused aloud, mistaking her anger for fear. "This is one fucking crazy night. Take them to the pit and shoot them. Did anyone bring a zip-strip?"

Shoot them? Hooking her foot behind his, Peri jerked, her elbow going back into the man's solar plexus at the same time. The gun went off, deafening her, but it shot wild. Men scattered, and, ears ringing, Peri spun, following LB down and flipping him face-first to the snowy pavement. Kneeling on his back, she wrenched his arm up, putting pressure on his wrist until he dropped the gun. *No blood in the snow this time. Keep it clean, Peri.*

"Holy shit!" someone exclaimed. "She downed LB!"

It hadn't been hard, making Peri think it had to be money or drugs that kept him on top of the shit heap.

"Nice try," LB wheezed, almost laughing as she pulled his wrist higher, forcing obedience. "But they don't call me Lucky Bastard because the girls like me."

"Yeah?" Peri said, pulling higher to make him grunt, but she gasped when the thin light from the dropped flashlight went blue. Her mind hiccuped, and the world turned inside out. Vertigo spilled through her, and her muscles went slack as an indigo flood pushed through her thoughts, blanking her vision. He was drafting. It wasn't her. The little prick was drafting!

And then the world flicked back on, and she was standing with her own gun pointed at her head.

Her pulse pounded as the disconnection ricocheted through her memories of a time that hadn't happened yet. *We're in a rewrite,* she thought, the shock firming through her. *I still have my knife,* she realized a half second later, and she smiled. LB didn't know he was doing it. If he had, he wouldn't have taken them back this far to where she still had a weapon.

"That explains a few things," Peri said as he took a breath to tell her to stay still. Her foot went back behind his again, and she took him down. This time, her knife went to his throat and, her knee on his back, she pulled his head up by his scalp. That fast, it was over.

Men shouted and weapons pointed at her, but she had a blade at his neck, and they were afraid. "Everyone back!" she demanded, pulling his head up so they could see his fear and that he was unhurt—so far. "If you shoot me or my partner, I'll slit his throat. Got it?"

To them, the knife was a more of a danger than a bullet, and as they retreated, she put her face right next to LB's. "Hi, sugar. We need to talk. Too bad we're both going to forget this conversation in about fifteen seconds."

"H-how . . ." LB stammered, confused. "How do you know I black out?"

Peri flicked a glance at Harmony, still caught and on tiptoe in some thug's grip.

"I can redraft time, too." Her gaze darted back to Harmony. "I said back off, or he's breathing through another hole!" Pulse fast, she whispered, "You are a god, LB, and you don't even know it. I can tell you how to work it. Give Harmony a trust word."

"Let him go! Get off him, bitch!" echoed between the buildings, and she wrenched LB's head up until he grunted in pain.

"Give it to her!" Peri demanded, running out of time. "I know you all have them. We're both going to forget in about six seconds, you little shit. Give me a safe word, and I'll tell you everything!"

"My mother's name was Rose." LB gasped, and they both shuddered as time caught up and meshed.

Peri's breath came in a quick heave. She was kneeling on LB, her knife at his throat and her fingers twined in his dark, dark hair. She had drafted—jumped and forgotten.

"Let him go!" the men bellowed, guns pointed. "Now!"

"Peri, let him up!" Harmony shouted, her eyes wide as the man holding her had her almost on tiptoe in his grip. "You promised you'd let him go!"

The man under her shuddered, almost as confused as she was. She'd promised to let him up? Was she nuts? Damn it, she needed an anchor, and her grip on her knife tightened. Something bad must have happened or she never would have drafted.

"He's like you," Harmony said. "You said he was going to forget. You promised to let him go and tell him what's going on. His mother's name is Rose, damn it! Let him go!"

He can draft?

Shocked, she let go of LB. Peri lurched to her

feet, dropping her knife and backing away with her hands up. A sudden pulse of agony cascaded through her, buckling her knees, and she caught herself when someone yanked her up. Pain flashed, but she'd had worse.

"You said you'd help him!" Harmony was shouting, even as they muscled her down into the cold, wet pavement. "He agreed to it. You all heard him!"

"Babe," Jack said, and she spun, her hand reaching for her fallen knife.

"Get her fucking knife!" Fat Man bellowed, and she hit the pavement hard, spitting the hair out of her eyes as she tried not to lose sight of Jack. Jack shifted and danced, trying to stay out of everyone's way. No one looked at him.

"Are you real?" she wheezed, and the hallucination shook his head, grinning.

"Sit her up," LB was saying, and someone yanked her upright, guns pointed at her head from all angles. She watched him, familiar with his confusion, anger, and frustration. Fat Man was at his shoulder, whispering something that made LB grimace. The man had drafted, but it was growing more obvious that he didn't know he was doing it, and she was calm as they frisked her again. Nearby, Harmony spat curses and threats.

"Want to know why you blacked out?" she said, then reeled when a man smacked her in the head. Stumbling, her knee went into the filthy snow—and then someone yanked her up again.

"Babe, don't do it," Jack warned her. Damn it, she could even smell his aftershave. "You can't tell him. They won't believe you."

But he'd have a chance, at least. "I've got the same thing you do," she said, ignoring Jack and the man pinching her shoulder. "I can help. I know how to work it, give you ways to cope. Hide it."

LB's face went ashen in the dim glow from the flashlight. "I don't need any help." Gesturing wildly, he began to walk away. "Shoot them. Take them to the pit and shoot them."

"Get your hands off me!" Harmony shouted. "You gave her a safe word! You said your mother's name was Rose, you son of a bitch!"

LB stopped dead in his tracks, and Peri kneed the man holding her.

Sneering, the man backhanded her. Stars exploded. Dizzy, she punched out, hearing them swear and dance back. Men were shouting, but it wasn't until three shots echoed that everyone backed off and she could make sense of the world.

Peri wiped the blood from her nose, flicking her hand to send it splattering against the snow. "You told me your mother's name was Rose," she said, panting. She didn't remember, but she trusted Harmony. "You told me so you'd listen when you came out of it. LB, what I can tell you will turn you into a god."

LB hesitated, his fingers tracing the mouse

tattoo on his wrist as he thought about that. “Let her go,” he said softly, and a protest rose. “I said let her go!” he shouted. “Both of them.”

Peri jerked out of the man’s grip. Beside her, Harmony pulled her shirt straight, muttering about goddamned animals. “You okay?” Peri asked.

“Yeah. Is he really a drafter?”

“Yep.” Peri’s eyes fixed on LB. “He’s a feral drafter. I’ve never found one before. I don’t know what to do.”

“You’re not going to tell him, are you?” Harmony asked, voice hushed.“He’s a—”

“I’m a what?” LB said as he shoved Fat Man out from between them.

At the top of the alley, Jack sniffed, flicking a piece of dirt off his sleeve, untouched and perfect in the snow. “Even she knows it’s a bad idea, babe.”

Jaw clenched, Peri looked at LB’s gang, imagining the trouble he could cause if he was aware of his abilities. Then she remembered the horrible dissociation, the confusion and shame she’d grown up with until Cavana had found her. She wasn’t insane. The blackouts had not been a weakness. She was skilled, not a basket case. “You’re a drafter,” she said. “Same as me.”

“You ain’t gonna bring them in the house!” Fat Man said, and Peri frowned at Jack until he threw his hands in the air and walked away.

“I lost three years once,” she said loudly. “I killed the man who did it to me,” she said, glancing at Jack's back. "I don't forget that much anymore."

LB patted Fat Man on his shoulder. "Maybe if I kill you, I won't forget, either."

She smiled. "It's science, LB, not magic. But I know the rules. I can help."

"LB don't need help. He's got us, and we got him!" someone shouted.

But LB was looking at his hand and the faded note inked there. Slowly he made a fist, his eyes rising to her eyes. "Where's that napkin you took from her," he said, his gaze never leaving hers.

"Shit, man, I threw it away," one of them said, scooping it up and handing it to him.

Peri's pulse pounded as LB carefully smoothed it open, her chin lifting when he read the words BILL DARTED ME WITH EVOCANE. She hadn't written it in case she might forget, but he didn't know that.

LB wadded it up and threw it back into the shadows. His eyes held a new question. "The cops might drive through. You want to come in?"

"LB," Fat Man protested, hunched in distress, but she smiled—until someone pushed her from behind and she stumbled into motion

"I want to talk to her," LB said, escorting her and Harmony to the end of the alley and into a burned-out shell of a building. Jack hustled forward, staying at the edges so no one would walk through him. The men trailed behind, cell phones turned into flashlights and talking loudly as they crossed the broken floor.

LB stopped at a huge chest freezer, dented and too heavy to move. "Ladies first," he said as he tugged the door open.

"Damn," Harmony swore when thumping music echoed out with the bright light of electricity and the sweaty warmth of bodies. A hand-hewn tunnel went down, probably to the basement of the building next door. LB gestured, and when neither of them moved, he went first, his sneakers clumping down the rickety staircase hard enough to shake it.

"You do realize he's going to kill you when he gets what he wants," Jack said, and Peri ignored him. The deeper she went, the warmer it was. Calls rang out ahead of her, and she blinked when she came out into the light.

It was like a giant living room, with worn couches and mismatched tables. Bags of chips, beer, nic caps, and drugs were scattered everywhere. Women wearing more guns than the men played a car game on their phones. A big-screen TV tuned to cartoons blared, and someone turned it down when Fat Man shouted.

"Oh my God," Harmony whispered, and Peri followed her gaze to two figures tied to chairs set in front of the TV. Allen was in one, and beside him was Jack. The real Jack.

Peri stared, heart pounding.

"That's me," her hallucination said, amazed, and he vanished in a pop of blue sparkles.

Eye swollen shut, Jack turned to her, trying to smile. "Hi, babe. I can explain."

Furious, Peri shoved her escort into the men behind her, spinning to grab a rifle. Breath held, she swung it up to her shoulder and reached for the trigger.

Something heavy slammed into her. The gun went off as she fell. A woman screamed, then laughed as Peri hit the floor, Fat Man on top of her.

"Let me up!" she demanded, wheezing, the men ringing her more amused than alarmed. "I'll kill the son of a bitch. Let me up!"

LB leaned down, and she squirmed, breathless under Fat Man as LB brushed the hair out of her eyes. "Hey. Hey!" he shouted, and she tore her gaze from Jack. "Looks like you know everyone, huh? You going to be nice, Peri Reed? Or do I have to tie you up, too?"

She thought for all of three seconds, an eternity for her. "I'll be nice," she rasped, having to spit the hair out of her mouth.

LB straightened, hands on his hips as he considered it. "Sit. Right there," he finally said, and Peri took a huge breath of air as Fat Man got off her. "I want to talk to your friend first," he said, gesturing for Harmony to go before him. "Hell of a night," he added, calling for a beer even as someone yanked her up and he walked away.

CHAPTER NINETEEN

The couch had lost its springs years ago, and Peri sat gingerly on it, still in her coat despite the warmth of LB's underground lair. Who knew what kind of bugs might be in it? That LB had her Evocane held her more firmly than any guns or straps, and she pushed herself up to sit on the very front of the couch, elbows on her knees as she wondered how she was going to get out of here with it without killing everyone.

Someone had brought in pizza, and the smell of it made her stomach growl despite it being near midnight. Allen and Jack were still tied to their chairs set mockingly in front of the big TV, but they'd managed to shift them somewhat before LB had sent a second man to watch them. Harmony was at the other end of the large room where LB and Fat Man had a semi-private area of couches around a low table. LB was constantly checking his state-of-the-art glass phone, making Peri wonder what Harmony was telling them. It had been at least a good half hour.

"I wish you hadn't come," Allen said, glancing at the nearby man more interested in the TV than watching them.

Her neck hurt, and she tried to stretch it out. "I missed you, too."

Allen winced at her sarcasm. Blood still clung to his face where something had hit him, and his clothes were filthy, the same ones he'd had on when he'd been abducted. "I wanted you to escape, not get caught up again."

Her lips pressed together, and she glanced up at a loud shout at the card table. "I don't leave anyone behind, remember?" she said, then turned to Jack. "Except maybe him."

Jack's head came up. "Same old Peri," he said, trying to smile around a swollen face.

"Shut up." Peri rubbed her forehead, wondering why he was here instead of Michael. LB had confiscated both their supplies of Evocane, and it stuck in her craw that a part of her felt a sliver of gratitude to Bill for trying to get her some even as she despised the man.

"You should just accelerate yourself," Jack said, and her teeth ground together. "If you're hooked on it, you may as well get the benefit of it. It makes good sense."

"Shut up!" she shouted, blowing off steam and garnering laughs from the card table.

A high-Q drone with a government shield was hovering at the ceiling, clearly hijacked and reduced to a toy. Peri stared at it when it dropped down to hover annoyingly before them, its red eye winking as it focused in on her chest. From across the room, LB shouted, "Quit sending me that shit, Hinks! Get your ass upstairs!"

Catcalls rose, and the drone flew to a corner of the room, where it landed. A burly man in a ragged jeans coat picked it up, a controller in his grip as he headed for the stairs. Two more men followed him, each with their own flyer. At the table, LB leaned over his phone and frowned at Harmony. LB's gang was clearly tech savvy, and Peri would bet her panties that all the information was being funneled into LB's phone. It reminded her of how the space missions that once took a room of monitors could now be run by one man at a single station.

Impatient, she turned to Allen. She could see his pity past his swollen eye, and she hated it. "Bill said Michael was going to make the drop."

"Bill nixed it. He was afraid Michael was going to snuff you. The man is certifiable," Allen said, and Jack bobbed his head, wincing as something hurt. "I don't know how anyone can anchor him. Bill and Jack are playing him like a badly tuned guitar, but they are playing him." Allen sighed. "He will kill you, Peri."

"Jack?" she blurted, almost laughing.

His eye was nearly swollen shut, and Allen hesitated as he pulled his first words back. "I meant Michael, but yes. I think Jack will kill you, too. Only a little slower is all."

Jack stiffened. "I'm not going to kill Peri. I want

out. You think I'd risk being caught with you and enough Evocane to keep you safe if I didn't?"

"I said *shut up!*" Jack's story of wanting asylum from Opti was weak at best. No one believed it. Especially her.

"Bill is betting that once you can work without depending on anyone, you'll come back," Allen said, eyes pinched from his hurts. "That's why he let Jack leave with the Evocane."

"No one let me go. I left on my own," Jack said.

Peri stretched a foot out, grunting as she shoved his chair over.

"What? Hey!" Jack exclaimed, hitting the floor hard. LB glanced up as a laugh rose, but no one moved to set him upright again. "What is *wrong* with you, Peri Reed!" Jack said, his face red with anger as he lay on the floor and struggled, still tied to his chair.

Ignoring him, Peri looked at her chipped nails, wondering whether they would ever be clean again. "I'm not going back to Opti," she said, but it was soft and unconvincing. She wasn't going back, even if she'd almost been a goddess, able to flaunt the law with impunity, live the way she wanted. But if she was hooked on Evocane, what she wanted might not enter into her choice.

"I know," Allen said as Jack began to wiggle in earnest. "But as long as you aren't accelerated, you might be able to get yourself off the Evocane." He hesitated. "Ah, have you been craving salt lately?"

Her head came up, fear sliding through her as she remembered Silas mentioning a sodium uptake inhibitor. “No. Why?”

“Possible side effect,” Jack said breathily from the floor. “You’re not the only drafter Bill’s tried this on.”

“Shut up,” she said softly, “or I’m getting up out of this ugly couch and pounding you.” She looked away from Jack, eyes tracking the fast-moving man who’d come in. He was making a beeline for LB and Fat Man. *Bad news?* she wondered, taking in his stilted pace.

“How about uncontrolled tremors?” Allen said, bringing her attention back. “Sensitivity to light? More angry than usual?”

“Just at Jack,” she said, not liking it when Fat Man whistled for some of his people.

“Good.” Allen’s smile was relieved. “You’re metabolizing the Evocane okay then.”

Peri’s eyes closed in a long blink. *Hurray for me.* Steiner would have a cow if he knew the flight risk she was. Probably lock her up in a cell—for good reason. Worried, she looked across the room at Harmony, wondering how long her decision to not tell him would hold.

“You’re okay, Peri,” Allen said, misunderstanding her expression. “If you weren’t, Bill would’ve never let Jack go to get the stopgap serum to you. You don’t need me anymore,” he said, voice softening. “You don’t need anyone. You never did.”

On the floor, Jack squirmed. "Hey! Some help here, maybe? Come on, Peri . . ."

Peri couldn't meet Allen's eyes. LB got along just fine with no anchor and no training, but her confusion not one hour ago when she forgot that LB had drafted was all too real. Her gaze lifted to find that people were leaving—some with pizza, but all with weapons. Even as she watched, Fat Man took Harmony's shoulder and led her away. Harmony looked back, her expression saying nothing. She seemed bone-tired, ready to drop—but not afraid.

LB was on his way over, and Peri stood. Something was happening. Everyone was moving, darting out the door even as they checked their ammo clips. She stayed silent as LB scuffed to a halt before her, his still-wet sneakers torn at the toe. Still on the floor, Jack looked up, pleading for some help.

"You're a drafter," LB said as he tucked his phone away. "And they are anchors who can recall both timelines and tell you what happened when everyone else only remembers the last?"

Clearly Harmony had been giving him the basics, and Peri nodded. "They've been trained to recognize and destroy the first timeline in my mind so I can safely remember the correct one." She looked at Jack, her jaw clenching. "Usually."

LB turned to look at Harmony, now sitting at the abandoned card table. Fat Man was beside her, arms over his chest. "She says you hallucinate Jack."

"Hey, can you stand me up?" Jack said, and was ignored. "Hello-o-o-o-o . . ."

Peri frowned. She hadn't realized that Harmony had known that. "That's not normal," she said, embarrassed. "It's a lingering scar from when I was forced to remember two timelines at once. It was either that or die of paranoia. That's kind of why we forget them."

LB moved closer, sitting on the edge of the couch across from her. "And when I black out, I'm rewriting time?" Smirking, he took one of her injector pens from his pocket and undid the cap. "This must be some good shit. That's one hell of a story. Maybe I should try it."

"Don't," she said when he made motions to inject it, and he paused, his expression telling her he'd only done it to get a rise out of her. "It's the kind of story that makes a king into a pig herder, or vice versa," she said, and he put the cap back on.

"It's true," Allen said, voice rough. "There's lots of you out there."

"But those not found and trained are usually in a medical facility," Peri added, her intuition pinging when LB stiffened. *He's been in one,* she thought, wondering whether that would work for or against her.

LB fiddled with the pen, watching her watch it

like an addict. "And this will help me remember my blackouts?"

"Not on its own, no." Peri shifted her weight, not liking that the place was emptying out. "I said I can tell you what's going on," she continued. "Help you control it. Tell you ways to keep from looking stupid." Something was happening. *Michael?* she wondered, exchanging a worried glance with Allen as more people left. "Are we going to talk, or are you just going to let me sit here watching cartoons?" she finally asked.

"Don't do anything stupid," LB said, gesturing for her to walk before him.

Nodding, she started forward. "Can I have my injection pens back?"

"Doubt it. What's in them?" LB took her arm and angled her to his little table. "Drafter to drafter," he said softly, leaning in toward her to whisper it.

He believed, she thought, elated. And not only that, but he had already found a sense of worth in it. She'd tell him the truth—inasmuch as she could.

"The pens hold a maintenance drug called Evocane," she said, hoping he hadn't already wasted one. "Forgetting a draft is natural, but you can destroy the part of the brain that causes that to happen. Only problem is we can't handle both timelines. We go crazy. It gets really bad, really fast. Evocane stops that," she said, sitting down when LB indicated for her to.

LB confidently slumped into the chair across from her. "And lets you remember."

Peri shook her head. "No, the accelerator does that. Evocane enables you to survive remembering. You can't regrow brain tissue, and once your body's natural defense is destroyed, you're on Evocane the rest of your life." Her lip curled, remembering the shame of shooting up in Harmony's car. Every twenty-four hours. She was going to kill Bill for that.

Eyes narrowed, LB thought about that. "I know people who get themselves addicted to all kinds of shit just to feel good for a few hours. Being able to remember . . . It might be worth it."

"Yeah. Okay. Whoever controls the Evocane controls you." Peri frowned, then forced herself to let it go. "It's not as if you can pick it up on any street corner."

"That's just a matter of lab time." LB idly checked his phone. She'd been right. He was looking at a view of the city being piped in from one of the drones. There were lights coming up the expressway, too many for the early hour.

Concerned, Peri watched Fat Man take Harmony to the couch, leaving her there to amble back to them. Jack was still on the floor, swearing and demanding someone stand him up."You've known him long?" she asked, indicating the large man, comfortable in his own skin.

“LB is my brother,” Fat Man said as he sat down with them, clearly having heard her.

Peri’s eyebrows rose. LB was American Indian, and Fat Man was . . . Germanic?

“Blood brother,” LB said as he slid his phone to Fat Man to continue monitoring.

“He’s your anchor,” Peri guessed. “He tells you what happened when you black out. Hides from everyone that you do. Covers for your lapses.”

Fat Man stiffened, and LB’s eye twitched. “Something like that.”

“Well, you’re doing a great job. Most untrained drafters are in a medical asylum.”

Fat Man’s thick lips cracked into a smile. “Where do you think I found the little shit?”

“Shut up!” LB exclaimed, smacking his shoulder, and Fat Man slumped.

“We were both in there, LB. It’s no big deal. They got good drugs.”

Peri hid a smile. “Really. You’ve been doing a good job. Can I have my stuff back?” It wasn’t just the Evocane. They had her diary. She’d known better than to put anything security related in there, but hell, it was her *diary*.

“No.” It was flat, but she could tell he’d only said it because he wasn’t ready to talk about it yet. “I looked up Opti on the Net. It just says a government special task force.”

Her eyebrows rose. He’d looked up Opti? Steiner would be here within half an hour. Maybe sooner, if those lights meant anything. "Nothing about the ability to rewrite small chunks of time, eh?" Chuckling, she reached for a piece of pizza, hesitating until LB nodded. "Yeah," she said around a cold mouthful. "That'd go over really well. You don't believe it, and you're doing it. They find us, train us if we're not too far gone thanks to well-meaning health providers, bribe us with gobs of money into doing what they want. We get paid extremely well, but it's a tenth of what our bosses get."

LB and Fat Man exchanged a knowing look. "And Jack?" LB questioned.

The pizza soured in her mouth, and she swallowed. "What about him? LB, you have to be careful. A trained anchor can wipe years of your memory right after a jump when the brain is trying to readjust, and if they find you, that's exactly what will happen."

LB brought his gaze back from Jack, now struggling violently to sit up. "He wiped your memory? No wonder you want to cack him."

"Every time I started to figure out where the corruption started. Allen is very good at it."

"But you don't want to kill him." LB leaned back, gaze flicking to and away from whatever Fat Man was showing him on his phone.

Feigning indifference, Peri picked off a piece of pepperoni and ate it. "Allen and I were moles in Opti, trying to shut down the corruption. I was young and idealistic. Thought I could make a difference. Allen wiped my memory so I'd have the plausible deniability to successfully infiltrate. Jack became my anchor, and with careful wipes and misinformation, I became part of the corruption instead."

LB smiled knowingly. "It happens."

"I didn't do it intentionally," she said hotly. "And when I found out, I brought them down. But Bill only went deeper. Hell, I think he enjoyed that I cleaned his house. He wants me back. That's what the Evocane is about. You going to give it to me yet?"

"No."

Peri dropped the half-eaten piece of pizza in the box, watching LB fiddle with the injector pen, messing with her. She gave him a moot look, and he stopped, nodding to Fat Man. His bulk shifting like rocks, Fat Man dug out two vials from his pocket and set them on the table.

"And you trust that that's what's really in them?" LB asked.

There was at least two weeks' worth there, maybe more, and Peri forced her eyes off the vials. "Not until I get it checked out. Look. I just want my Evocane, Allen, Harmony, and Jack so I can beat his ass at my leisure. We'll get out of your hair, and you'll never see us again."

"I find that hard to believe." LB took his phone back, angling it so she couldn't see.

"I'm a simple girl," she said, then realized it had become quiet. Everyone had left but for the two men watching Harmony, Jack, and Allen. Something was clearly going on.

"LB," she said, feeling the need to move. "You're right. Drafters are rare. Drafters like you who have found a way to deal with it on their own are even rarer. Last year, I would've lied to you, walked out of here, then headed the task to pull you in, get you wiped and working. A year ago I thought Opti was Camelot. A year ago I didn't think a drafter could survive without an anchor. A year ago I was a Barbie doll with a license to kill."

Her voice had risen, and she caught her anger. "I have little left now except the killing part. You've got a good thing here. Keep your nose clean and I won't be back to bother you."

Fat Man looked affronted, but LB was thinking even as he scrolled through the incoming texts. "Say I let you walk out of here. You said you could help me control it."

Peri nodded. "There's a man named Silas Denier. Doctor. Psychologist. He's good at bringing drafters back from the brink when things get confusing. You can trust him to do what he thinks is right for you, not himself or anyone else. He won't turn you in—especially if you drop my name. You got a pen? I'll give you his number."

"And what assurance do I have that he won't sanitize me?"

"It's called wiping, and he won't. He hates Opti more than I do. Call him if you start to hallucinate," she said, taking her own pen pendant that LB slid across to her and writing his number on the pizza box. "Don't wait. It's a signal you're trying to remember something, and if you do, you won't come back from it."

She hung her pen around her neck, feeling more like herself. Fat Man growled something inaudible, sullen and angry.

"Silas can tell you what's going on, why you remember until the timelines mesh, and why you forget after they do. Oh, and trust Fat Man, especially if you start to hallucinate. It's the only occasion your intuition will lead you astray."

LB's brow furrowed. "Fat Man?"

Peri warmed as she looked at the big man. "Sorry. That's what I've been calling you."

"No, I like it," Fat Man said, preening almost.

"And your intuition?" Peri said, eyeing the drugs on the table. "As long as you're not hallucinating, trust your gut. You never forget anything, you just can't recall it. The emotions never go away." Her thoughts went to Silas, remembering the feel of his hand on her face, the heartache in his eyes when she pulled back from him, the longing for her to remember, the wish in herself to remember . . . maybe.

"What if my gut is telling me to shoot you and dump you in Lake St. Clair?" LB asked as he closed his phone down and tucked it away.

Perhaps the danger is past. "If you were going to do that, you would've done it by now. There's no profit in it, which is exactly why I'm not going to tell anyone about you." She refused to look at the vials again, but it was getting harder. There was a thump in the distance, and dust shifted down from the ceiling. "Unless you start drawing attention to yourself," she added, looking up. *Perhaps not.*

"LB," Fat Man warned, and Peri shrugged.

"Hey, it's what I do. You want me to lie about it?"

LB lifted his chin to indicate Allen, Harmony, and Jack. "Okay, I believe you. But what about them? Can they keep their mouths shut?"

Peri fiddled with her pen. "Harmony will, sure. Jack and Allen weren't there, so they don't know. You could always come in and be trained. Not Opti, but Harmony's group. Bring Fat Man with you as your anchor. It will take longer, but they'd probably wet themselves to get someone with your background."

Head cocked, LB looked over her shoulder to Harmony and Allen. "Is that what you would do? If you could start over?"

"Hell no. I'd do exactly what you're doing. Minus the illegal stuff—of course."

LB smiled, taking one of the vials and tucking it in his pocket as he stood. One vial remained on the table with her injector pens; Peri's smile vanished. "I don't have the accelerator. It's not going to do you any good."

"It still looks rare to me."

His eyes were bright in challenge, and she shrugged. Half was better than none, unless he got himself hooked. And it might not be bad having a potential source outside of her pocket. "Okay. Half." Fingers shaking, she slid her injector pens and the last vial to herself. It was still warm from Fat Man's pocket. Her shoulders slumped, and she took her first real breath in what seemed like hours. She had time now.

Fat Man dropped her belt pack and phone and diary on the table, and she put everything back on, starting to feel normal again. "What about my knife?" she asked as she tucked the loose pages back behind the cover of the journal, and LB grinned.

"It looks kind of rare to me, too," he said, gesturing for her to join Allen, Harmony, and Jack, now freed apart from Jack's hands still being cuffed.

"LB, don't take this the wrong way," she said as they merged into one group. "But I'm proud of you."

Fat Man snorted, and LB gave her a sideways smile. "It's not you," he admitted. "It's the government choppers going overhead and the old white guy with the bullhorn. You're hot goods, lady, and I want you off my island."

"Steiner?" Harmony blurted. "He's here? I thought we lost him."

"LB did a search on Opti." Peri zipped her belt pouch closed. "It probably pinged."

"Tall, creepy man with gray hair?" LB said, and Harmony nodded. "That's him. We either hand you over or they're coming in to get you. Keep him out, okay?"

Steiner. They headed for the stairway, Peri's head beginning to hurt. Her expression screwed up in distaste and frustration as she touched the vial LB had returned to her through her belt pack. Steiner was going to search her, find it, take it away, maybe start wondering why it had been included in the deal to get Allen. Steiner would be an idiot not to realize she was hooked on Evocane. "Move it, Jack," she muttered, giving him a shove. "I've got a cell with your name on it."

Jack turned to look at her over his shoulder, his stubble thick and his suit grimy. "Babe, I just wanted to be with you," he pleaded.

It meant nothing. Her heart was cold. "Out," she said as she pushed him into the stairwell. Jack caught his balance, his expression hurt as Harmony took control of him as the ranking agent. They hadn't come away with Michael, and her bid for Evocane had backfired.

Someone opened the freezer door at the top of the stairway, and the sound of choppers and a bullhorn drifted down with the scent of snow. Yep, that sounded like Steiner. Her thoughts went to her diary. *Son of a bitch . . . He'll take that, too.*

"Peri."

It was LB, and she paused as Fat Man pushed past her, leaving her and LB alone. His eyes still held the wonder that she'd given him. "You're not going to give me my knife back, are you?" she joked.

"You should have let me kill him," he said, eyes finding Jack at the top of the stairway as he smacked the hilt of her knife into her hand.

She smiled at the weight of it, then leaned to slide it away. "I know. He's really bad for my asthma. Will you do something for me?"

Hip cocked, LB eyed her. "Seriously?"

Her heart seemed to flutter as she handed him her journal. "I don't want Steiner to have it, and he's going to strip me to my skivvies. It's my diary," she said, face warming as he took it, expression puzzled at its torn and scuffed state. "Don't read it. Just . . . hang on to it for me." *God, I feel as if I'm thirteen.*

"You want me to hold your diary?" he said quizzically.

"There's nothing important in it," she said, fidgeting when Harmony shouted down for her to hurry up. "I don't want Steiner to have it. I'd let you keep that second vial of Evocane for me, as well, but Jack is bound to tell Steiner he came in with two. Steiner might believe that you broke one, but not two, and if he thinks I left them here, he'll tear your place apart for them."

"Not to mention Steiner's drug cabinet is going to be closer than mine." LB tapped her diary against his palm. His brow furrowed as if he knew it wasn't a diary but a piece of herself. "Sure. You're coming back for it, right?"

Her eyes dropped to the pocket where he'd put that second vial of Evocane, then rose to find his. "I'll be back for both. Count on it."

CHAPTER TWENTY

The operations van had Opti's symbol on the steering wheel, making Peri think they were headed for Detroit's old Opti complex. The vehicle's acceleration was impressive for being electric, the quiet nothing of their swift passage pleasant. Even so, Peri thought a little engine noise might be preferable to the tense, one-sided conversation of Steiner standing in the middle of the van's aisle, reaming out Harmony. Cold, Peri drew her coat closer, thinking it ironic that it had the WEFT logo on it, with her since the fiasco in

St. Louis. *God help me, I don't even know when I lost my wool Reuso.*

The man had started in even before they'd cleared the lines that WEFT had strung at the outskirts of the arena, questioning Harmony's motives and loyalty both. As expected, everything on Harmony had been confiscated. They'd cleared Peri out as well, making her glad she'd left her diary with LB. It didn't sit well that all her Evocane, right down to the two remaining pens, was in the van in front of them. That she was hooked on a drug that did nothing for her was worse. She didn't think Jack would say anything to Steiner about there being two vials, but she wasn't going to risk losing them both.

Harmony had been silent so far about her new addiction, but by the looks of it, Steiner was close to figuring it out, picking up on the slight hesitation in Harmony's voice as she lied to her boss. The man hadn't let up, making Harmony repeat her story a handful of times in the hope of finding an inconsistency, but seeing as Harmony was telling the truth—mostly—there'd been none.

A stone-faced man sat beside Harmony, facing both Peri and Allen. It would be absurdly easy to knock him out, take his holstered pistol, kill everyone, and flee. But she didn't. It wasn't who she wanted to be. Besides, Allen wasn't in any shape to help, huddled in a CIA coat with an ice bag on his face and grimacing every time they went over a railroad trestle or hit a pothole.

"You *removed* Reed from her cell," Steiner said flatly, and Peri frowned, her focus out the front window blurring to make Detroit's midnight lights a kaleidoscope of sliding color as they headed to the repurposed Opti complex. "Transported her across state lines and into a high-risk area. Did it occur to you that she might be trying to return to Opti?"

"That was a very low probability, sir," Harmony said, her voice having lost its respect about ten miles back. "Her goal was to retrieve her partner, not return to Opti."

Steiner's frown was obvious in the passing lights as he swayed with the van's motion. Her gaze slid to the guard's weapon, wanting it. She missed her Glock. She missed her knife. She missed everything they'd taken from her thirty seconds after crossing into WEFT jurisdiction, including much of her confidence.

"Peri isn't a flight risk," Harmony insisted. "We need Michael, and I wasn't going to compromise anyone else again. Not after last time." She hesitated. "We had a better chance with two."

"We don't work by chance," Steiner said. "And without authorization, you were lucky no one was injured or killed. I wouldn't have been able to protect you."

Allen pushed his glasses back up his nose. "*I* was injured," he muttered, but it was obvious Steiner meant protection from the law.

"I promised Reed we wouldn't leave Allen Swift behind," Harmony said.

"Congratulations," Steiner said dryly. "Your honor is intact. Your ID, please."

"Sir?"

Peri winced at Harmony's shocked alarm. Harmony had trusted her, and in return, Peri had flushed the woman's career straight down WEFT's toilet.

"Your badge?" Steiner repeated, reaching for the van's wall as they wove through the slow turns of the technological park.

"But she didn't run. We recovered Allen." The light glinted on the holographic image as Harmony removed her badge from around her neck and handed it over. "And Jack. Peri is here. Right here!" she said, gesturing. "She could have run at any time, and she didn't."

"Which only means she hadn't gotten what she wanted yet," Steiner said, her ID in hand. "You took a flight risk out of custody. That woman is *hooked* on Evocane, and if we hadn't gotten to you first, she would have left you dead in the arena and returned with her old partner to Bill Heddles. She used you, Beam."

"You don't know that," Harmony whispered, and Steiner grimaced.

"That vial of Evocane we confiscated says otherwise."

Peri stared at Steiner, the blood draining from her face. Across from her, Harmony choked back her next words, her sudden doubt cutting Peri to the quick. But what had sent Peri's pulse racing was that Steiner knew. He was going to withhold the Evocane to prove his dominance, to force her to do what he wanted, when he wanted. *Bill would never be this crass.* He was an artist when it came to manipulation, so skilled that you didn't even mind. Most of the time.

Peri looked at her hands, free for the moment, then Allen, his eyes suddenly bright, wide awake but clearly hurting from two days of beatings. Everything had changed. She couldn't wait to see whether Silas could reproduce the Evocane. She wasn't going to return to Opti, but she wasn't going to dance to Steiner's tune either. All she wanted was to be left alone, but the temptation of remembering her drafts had bitch-slapped her. *Damn it, I'm hooked on Evocane, and everyone knows it. I have to get out of here.*

"I disagree," Harmony whispered, but it lacked conviction, hurting Peri more.

"With what?" Standing in the aisle, Steiner swayed with the motion of the van. "That she would return to Heddles? Or that she would leave you for dead?"

Determination pulled Harmony's brow tight.

"Both. With all due respect, sir. You're full of shit."

Lips quirked in amusement, Steiner turned to Peri. "Come see me when you feel the desire to talk about your loyalties, Ms. Reed. I'm guessing you're going to need your next fix in about . . . twenty hours?"

"Son of a bitch," Allen swore softly, and a wave of heat took her. She could escape, right now, but if she had to draft to do it, she'd likely wipe out hearing Steiner say he knew she was hooked. Peri's palms grew moist. She had to wait, play along until the realization and the knowledge of what she had to do was deep enough in her past that she wouldn't forget it. But they were close to WEFT's gates. It was going to be tight.

Finding confidence in her silence, Steiner tapped Harmony's ID against his long hand and tucked it away. "You let yourself be used, Agent Beam. You are officially done."

"Are you *firing* me?" Harmony said, aghast.

"That depends how well I can spin this to my superiors." Still standing, Steiner turned to look out the front window at the back gate a quarter mile ahead, his expression sharp in the white light that bathed the area. "As of now, you're off task. Take a few weeks' vacation."

Allen leaned into her, his ice pack in his hand ready to throw. "Peri . . ." he whispered, knowing she had to go, knowing her dilemma of not wanting to draft herself into ignorance.

“Tell Harmony this was not my intention,” she whispered, her eyes on the feet of the guard across from her. Her breath came fast as she held her need to move.

Eluding the CIA was primary. She couldn’t allow herself to be taken. The hole she used to escape her cell would be plugged by now, and the CIA had only had a week of Evocane. LB had that much, and she could use that week to kill Bill, because whereas with a little effort she could evade the CIA for as long as she liked, Bill would be a problem. Bill would never give up on her. He had to die or she’d never be free.

Peri’s pulse quickened as they passed the last of the autonomous light-manufacturing plants. The road dead-ended just ahead; a new WEFT sign had been glued over the old Opti logo. Kill Bill? She didn’t know whether she could do it. It was more than their shared past. He was an anchor. If she made one mistake, he would force her to draft and artificially wipe her back where she’d do whatever he wanted and think it was her idea. But what if she could get someone else to do it?

“Peri,” Allen whispered. “You have to go. Now! Before you get behind the gate.”

A smile quirked her lips as she looked past Steiner to the back entrance, brightly lit to look like noon. True. But she got second chances, and she nodded, wanting to move but waiting.

Michael wasn't that far from the neurotic, paranoid man Bill had pulled from the psych ward, mistrustful and easy to manipulate. If he thought Bill betrayed him, Michael would kill him before coming to find her, and then she'd only have to kill Michael. All *she* had to do was tell Michael the truth, that Bill never intended to accelerate him. And with Bill dead, she could vanish. As long as she remained unaccelerated, she could kick the Evocane. She'd only had two doses. How bad could it be?

"Peri," Allen muttered, anxious and ready to help. Bringing him with her would be impossible, and she fought the urge to give him a chaste kiss good-bye.

"Thank you," she said instead, voice throaty as the need to be gone warred with the knowledge she might never see him again—and that even knowing that, he would do everything he could to help her disappear.

"Whoa, look at that," the driver said, and Peri's head came up as he slowed in response to the van swerving ahead of them. It righted itself before slowing at the reinforced gated lock across the road, making her wonder whether Jack had tried something last-ditch that hadn't worked. The driver's radio crackled to life, laughter and the sound of Jack's pained grunts spilling out before Steiner smiled and relaxed.

Her eyes on the self-satisfied man, Peri gave

Allen's cold hand a squeeze, seeing his good-bye in his eyes. "Give me a count of forty-five," she whispered, and Allen casually leaned back, his hand slipping away as he looked over the van. In forty-five seconds, she would draft. It would put her on the right side of the gate, her plan to manipulate Michael into killing Bill still in her mind even if she lost the time between. Anything after this point, though, would likely be lost.

One: Peri carefully watched the guard across from them, feeling in her imagination the smoothness of the Glock's butt in her grip, how it would feel to fire it, kicking back with the scent of spent gunpowder. The van eased to a halt under the lights. Voices grew loud, and the clatter of the opening gate was harsh as Steiner cleared them. She felt powerful and broken at the same time, knowing she could get out of this, but without an anchor to bring it back, that she'd never remember how she'd done it.

Ten: She stifled a shudder when the scanner went over them, front to back, and everyone's badge briefly lit at the ping. Her foot would take out the guard, and her fist would bring down Steiner. The driver and second guard would be shot, but not fatally. Harmony . . .

Oh, God. She'll think I'm betraying her.

"I want them both in ankle cuffs the instant we hit the yard," Steiner said as they inched forward and the security gate slid shut behind them. They were within WEFT's fences, and she smirked when Steiner relaxed, clearly thinking there was no way out.

"Sir," Harmony protested as the van pulled to a wide security door and stopped. Six men in snow-camo coats waited under the harsh security light. Five went to the van where Jack was, a loud commotion rising when the van's wide back door swung open. Beside her, Allen quietly hyperventilated, guessing how this was going to go down and bulking his oxygen up.

Thirty: She sat unmoving when their side door rattled open and Steiner swung out onto the pavement. She could hear shouted demands for Jack to get moving. "Sir!" Harmony launched herself out of the van after Steiner, her loud protests echoing off Opti's thick walls.

"Out. Now," the guard across from her said, and she stood, remembering where he had been sitting and how it would feel when she launched herself at him in about fifteen seconds. She held a hand to Allen, and he eyed her from under a low, pained brow.

"For what it's worth, thank you for coming for me," he said, his voice soft with guilt.

"Thanks for saving my ass in St. Louis," she said, and he smiled, fitting his hand into hers, cold from the ice pack and knobby. He groaned when she pulled him up and they made their way to the opening. Moving slow and careful, Allen held on to the van as he lurched to the salt-stained asphalt.

"Five seconds," he whispered, and her pulse quickened.

She looked across the fenced-in yard to where Jack was being manhandled out of the van. Counting the original four guards in the van, there were now nine men circling him to her one, and she laughed at how badly they misjudged her. Cool steel glinted in the security light, and she looked up, her breath obscuring the few stars that made it through Detroit's light pollution.

"Not another word, Beam!" Steiner exclaimed, his implacable calm finally cracking.

Ticked, Harmony stalked to the wide door being held by another agent, an irritating whine of an alarm obvious. She vanished inside, and a knot of worry tightened. *Three seconds?*

"You don't have to push!" Jack complained, and Peri's eyes flicked up. She froze as their eyes met and Jack, his hands cuffed before him, made a "well?" gesture. Peri froze. *Does he think I'm going to save him, too?*

"Detroit!" Steiner shouted, clearly cold as he stomped toward the doors in his light WEFT jacket."If I wanted to work at the North Pole, I would have signed up to be one of *Santa's helpers!* My God! Why is it so cold? Who knows where my office is?"

"Now, Peri." Allen took her hand. "I'm going to miss you."

But she couldn't look away from Jack, hating his crafty, knowing look.

"Tell Harmony I'm after Michael," she whispered, his hand slipping from hers when the guard behind them gave her a shove. "And to not find me. And Silas that . . . I'm sorry."

"Go," Allen whispered. "Or you're going to miss your window!"

As if somehow knowing, Steiner turned, his face suddenly slack as he stood in the doorway. But it was too late, and giving in, she flipped him off, smiling as he bellowed for someone to down her. He had forgotten drafting worked backward, and it was going to cost him everything.

Reaching out with her mind, she found a still-point of distraction, forty-five seconds in the past. Her breath came in, and she used it to expand her reach, wrapping her psyche around a three-block area. She could go wider, but she didn't need to. Eyes opening, she watched the light spilling from the hot flood lamps drop an inky blue to hit the ground and billow up until it dissipated through the world and everything stopped.

For a scintillating instant, she saw the world: Allen's grief and worry, Steiner's anger and frustration, the guards' confusion . . . and Jack's confident pleasure that she was going to save his ass again.

This is not for you, she thought, and then the blue sparkles flashed, obliterating everything.

CHAPTER TWENTY-ONE

"Whoa, look at that," the driver said, and Peri lurched, catching her balance as the van holding Jack swerved. They were back outside WEFT. The only people who would know they were rewriting time were she, Allen, and Jack. Her pulse hammered as her plan held firm. She was going to manipulate Michael into killing Bill. She had a week to do it if she could slip WEFT and reach LB.

Her eyes went to Allen, his hand still in hers, cold from that ice pack. "Take care of yourself," he said, and then he bellowed, throwing himself at Steiner standing in the aisle.

The man cried out in shock as he went down, falling in between the two front seats.

She moved, her foot slamming into the rising guard to send him flailing back to smack his head against the wall of the van. Peri lurched into him, using her elbow to send him crashing back again, this time falling unconscious.

"Peri!" Harmony exclaimed, wide-eyed as she tried to stand, falling when the van swerved wildly.

Peri's hand was already on the guard's Glock, and she ripped it from his slack fingers.

"Steiner knows. If I go behind those walls, I'm never coming out."

"We're in a draft?" Harmony said, and then she became angry. "It wasn't me. I didn't tell him."

"Look out!" the driver shouted, and Peri fell as the van swerved to avoid crashing into the vehicle ahead of them. Pain lanced through her knee as she hit the floor, and she ignored it. Her grip tightened on the Glock, refusing to let go even as the van lurched to a stop. Eyes wide, she watched out the front window as Jack's van careened into one of the trees strategically placed to line the drive to the gate. Muted gunfire sounded from inside it, and their driver reached for his sidearm.

"Firefight!" the driver said, reaching for the door even as he turned to look behind him for permission to leave, his eyes widening as he saw the guard out cold and Steiner down under Allen. He scrambled to bring his weapon to bear, then froze as his buddy in the front seat already had, Peri's Glock pointed at his head.

"Not happening," Peri said, still on the floor, and she shot them both in the arm.

The twin pops and kicks jolted her. Adrenaline was a sweet drug, and she rolled, knee throbbing, to the sliding side door. As the men in the front howled, she opened the door and slid to the ground. Guards were coming out of the nearby gatehouse, and they all had weapons.

"Peri!"

She turned at Allen's demanding call, and he threw a phone at her. She caught it, feeling the warmth of the guard he'd taken it from.

"Call me," he mouthed, pantomiming a phone with his thumb and pinky, and then he went down under the two guards she'd shot in the arm. "Go!"

Grimacing, she ran for the surrounding trees, her knee throbbing as she fired into the air to keep everyone where they were. She was free and moving. For the moment. Not a sound came from Jack's van as she passed it, and she wondered whether she wished he was dead.

"Someone get her! Beam!" Steiner bellowed from inside the van, and Peri dodged behind the trees lining the road, headed for the nearest industrial building and the cars in the lot, praying the men in the guardhouse were not good shots. It was a good half mile. *Not fast enough,* she mused. A gun fired, muffled from the van, and she hesitated. *Allen.*

But then she heard him screaming obscenities, and relief spurred her on. "Go! Run!" Allen shouted as he stumbled out of the van and was downed by the first guard to reach him. Steiner lurched into the van's door, his face ugly in anger. "Shoot her! Bring her down!"

Peri zigzagged into the thicker cover of the trees, hearing branches break from bullets.

"Peri!" a familiar voice called, and she stumbled, her heart seeming to stop as she turned, arm shaking as she pointed her Glock.

It was Jack.

He was free, a rifle beside him as he knelt behind a tree and used a paper clip to unlock his cuffs. She froze, the sound of men organizing behind her meaning nothing. And then he tossed his hair out of his eyes, smiling up at her as his cuffs came free and he stood, rifle in hand.

Emotion plinked through her, anger at his betrayal, anger that she'd loved him, anger that not all of those feelings were dead. That he was not a hallucination left her unexpectedly scrambling. He was real, from his torn and dirt-smeared suit to his too-thick stubble, and she was suddenly scared. *I don't love him. You can't love someone you don't trust.*

"I wouldn't have shot you in the back if you hadn't turned it on me," she whispered, her arm holding the Glock falling, and his smile became quirky as he ran his eyes up and down her in assessment.

"Isn't that the truth. Are you hit? Can you run?" he asked, his attention lingering on her knee, now sporting a bright red as something bled out. Even so, she nodded, almost in shock as his fingers circled her wrist and he pulled her into motion, headed for the nearest manufacturing building. Behind them, the sound of men grew loud. “Thanks for the draft. It was exactly what I needed, when I needed it. Damn! I miss working with you. Right like clockwork, almost as if we’d planned it.”

This is so bad for my asthma, she thought. “I didn’t draft to help you,” she said, but her gaze went to the two vans as more gunshots rang out. Allen was fighting, buying her time.

“That’s what you say, but you did what you did.”

Jack tugged her into a run, aiming for thicker trees. “I can help. I know things. Where you stash your car, the safe house that you made and probably don’t remember.”

“You stay away from my Mantis,” she said, making it a threat. The beautiful thing could change color by altering the current running through the solar-panel paint that charged the batteries that ran it. They were illegal outside of Detroit because of the color-changing ability, but most cops didn’t know that.

But Jack only laughed, his pace slowing as they found deeper cover. “You might not need me, Peri, but I have things you do need.”

“No!” She jerked her wrist from his grip and halted. “I’m not going back to Bill. Not with you, not ever.”

“Good God, woman, I’m trying to get you out of here,” he said, but she wasn’t buying it. She could feel time beginning to mesh, the first tendrils of thought and action starting to echo within each other in her mind like two radios a millisecond apart.

"Stay out of my head," she threatened, bringing her Glock up to bear on him, and he dropped back, hands up. "I mean it!" she screamed, frantic that she was going to lose everything—again. "I should just shoot you right now! You stay out of my head!"

"I'm not going to wipe you!" Jack exclaimed, his expression more angry than scared. "God, woman. I'm not here for Bill. I'm here for me."

Her arm holding the Glock shook, and then time meshed, mended itself with the quiet hush of feathers falling.

Peri looked up, panic icing through her as the faint light from the distant gate flashed an old-blood red and then cleared. She was on the right side of the gate, her back against an old street tree. It was dark, cold, and she was pointing the guard's Glock at Jack.

"I didn't touch your mind," Jack said impatiently, and she knew he was real, not her imagination. "I'm here for you, not Bill." His eyes pleaded as he held out a hand. "You drafted to get us free of WEFT. I can explain, but I'd rather get out of here first."

She lowered the Glock. "I didn't draft to save your ass," she said, and he grinned.

"See? I didn't touch your mind," he said, and a

flash of memory came and went, too fast to be identified outside of a sensation of having done something extraordinary and daring. Her pulse slowed. He hadn't touched her mind.

Her shoulders eased, and with a sudden realization, everything up to the gate came back with a painful clarity. Steiner knew she was hooked on Evocane. Michael had to kill Bill for her or she'd never be free of him. How she ended up with Jack was lost, but Michael would believe Jack before trusting her. "I need your help," she whispered, hating herself as much as it was true.

"Damn right you do. Let's go."

She was still herself, and the relief of that made her pliant as she fell into old patterns and let him angle them to the bright lights of the nearby manufacturing plant. The sound of a chopper warming up drowned out the calls of men. She had done it. She'd gotten free. With Jack?

She looked behind them. Both vans were before the open gate, one smashed into a tree. "Did you kill everyone in the van?"

"Yep."

She hated his matter-of-fact attitude. Something told her it was a long-held complaint, even if it had probably saved her life—again. "What about Allen?"

Jack turned to her. "If you wanted Allen dead, you should have shot him yourself."

"Did you kill him?" she exclaimed, and Jack's

expression soured as he understood her thinking. "Is he alive?"

"I don't know. I didn't stick around to find out."

Her pulse slowed. They hadn't escaped together, then, and she found strength in that. *Damn it, I can't go on not knowing like this.* "I want you to make a call." Her knee was starting to throb, the dissipating adrenaline leaving behind an ache that was growing harder to ignore.

Jack slowed as she fell behind. "You said you weren't shot."

"How would I know if I was shot or not, Jack," she said bitterly, stopping to pull her pant leg up. Together they looked at it in the dim light, a frown growing at the swollen mess that was slowly but surely leaking. *Another scar I won't remember getting.*

Motions fast, Jack ripped a strip of cloth from his already tattered shirt. The sound of a chopper warming up was growing. It wouldn't be long before they started walking the area with dart guns and flashlights.

"What. Now?" she said as he crouched down and jerked her pant leg up higher.

"You want to bleed all the way to the parking lot?" he said tightly. "We can be out of here in five minutes, across the border in a few hours, and from there, wherever you want."

It was tempting, more than he knew, but even

if Jack was telling the truth, Bill would never let her go. "I want you to call Michael," she said, thinking his fingers felt familiar as he probed her skin to see whether there was a bullet in there. "You're going to tell him that after Bill got me hooked on Evocane, I accelerated myself. I want you to tell him Silas can't duplicate the Evocane, and I'll be defecting to Bill when it runs out. And I want you to tell Michael that Bill used him and that he never had any intention of moving him forward in the program."

Jack looked up, his confusion obvious in the faint light. "Why would I do that?"

"You owe me." Her knee hurt as he tied the strip of cloth around it, but it was swelling too much to have a bullet in it.

"I owe you?" he said, but then he squinted up at her, his lips parting. "Shit, you're serious. Babe, what's the goal here? To piss Michael off?" His expression cleared. "To turn him against Bill?" He stood, the motion achingly familiar as he tucked his torn shirt in. Even disheveled and in need of a shower, he was gorgeous, beautiful, capable . . . and angry. "Why am I making a rift between Michael and Bill?" he asked. "You think he's going to kill Bill for you? Bill's the only reason Michael hasn't offed you already. The man is nuts."

Disturbed, Peri checked her Glock. "Let's go. You can call him in the car," she said, beginning to limp forward.

"Or are you trying to kill Michael?" Jack guessed, tight beside her. "You think Michael is Bill's new boy and you need to reclaim your spot? You don't have to go through all this bullshit. If this is what you want, I can have a chopper pick us up in two hours, though to be honest, I'd rather run and keep running."

Liar. There was no running. The only way out was through it. "I am not going back," she said, but her face was cold and she couldn't look at him. It would be so easy. *He is not my partner, and this is not what I want,* she told herself. "I'm not job hunting. I'm just hunting. Michael wants me dead. You know it. I know it. But if he kills Bill first, then all the better."

"Oh my God," Jack whispered. "Once Michael is done with Bill, he's going to come after you. Babe, this is a stupid plan."

"Stop calling me that," she threatened as she stumbled. Jack caught her arm, and she jerked away. The nearest building was just ahead, a few late-model cars parked outside.

"Sorry." He hesitated. "It's just that we're good together. You deserve more than some pathetic government task force that doesn't even know what to do with you."

"No, *you* were good," she whispered, thinking she could hear voices behind them. "*I* was your doll. Yours and Bill's." She stopped at the edge of the parking lot, frowning at him in the new light.

"I'm smelling what you're stepping in, so shut up."

He made a huff of exasperation. "You don't remember it, but I *wanted* you to run. Almost a year ago," he added bitterly. "Away from Opti with me. *I* wanted to go, but you wanted to prove there was corruption."

Her eyes squinted; she didn't remember it. They probably hadn't run because the same things that made her good at her job made her easy to find. But that wasn't so anymore. *Shelve it, Peri. Deal with it later.*

But he was right. They had been good—had to have been with the amount of confidence that was sifting through her along with her anger. She might not remember it, but it was there, undeniable and heady. He knew her. She knew him—trusted his limitations or lack thereof, maybe. And as she looked back at the distant WEFT gate, she realized the danger of this wasn't getting caught by WEFT, but rather not getting caught. Jack was bringing everything back that she was trying to forget, and it was . . . uplifting.

That's why Bill sent him. Mother-sucking Bill.

"Pick a car. Let's go," Jack finally said, and she sent her eyes to the outskirts.

"Brown Gremlin," she said, and he started, looking at the Firebird at the back of the lot.

But then his eyed darted to hers, his coming complaint vanishing. "I hear voices!" he hissed.

"I know the feeling," she muttered, scrunching

deeper behind the tree. "Gremlin, or I'm not going." *Damn it all to hell. Why am I trusting Jack? He's just another perfect mistake.*

"Son of a bitch . . ." Jack whispered, hunched down, his useless rifle in his hand as the chopper rose up, spotlight playing over the building beside them, the winter-dead grass sharp in the harsh light. "We're not getting out of here."

"Yes we are," she insisted, and then she gasped, stifling her shout of affront when he picked her up and boldly strode into the lot. She froze as a memory surfaced, of them together in the depth of the night. "Put me down," she said, not liking how right his hands felt around her.

"You've got the Glock. Keep them off us," he said, walking fast. "You can't run."

"Neither can you while you're carrying me," she insisted. "Put me down!"

"No. Deal with it."

"Gremlin," she insisted as he angled to the Firebird, and sighing, he shifted direction. His breathing had taken on a harsh rhythm that was both familiar and somehow intimate. His arms around her were the only spot of warmth in the January night, and she hated that she relished it. The scent of two-day-old sweat tickled her memory, and it was gone.

The jarring became harsher as he picked up the pace. Behind them, shouts rose up. Peri turned, firing six shots at nothing over his shoulder.

More voices rose in alarm. “We’re not going to make it,” Jack huffed.

“Put me down,” she demanded. “Run ahead and start it. I’ll catch up.”

He didn’t argue, and Peri gasped in pain when her feet hit the stony pavement and he raced ahead. He never looked back, but nowhere in Peri was there the thought that he wouldn’t wait for her. *Where is this trust coming from?* she wondered as she limped after him, Glock in one hand and leaving bloody prints on the cars with the other. But she knew it wasn’t him she trusted, but his abilities. No one was better. Angry, she quashed the feeling.

The chopper swung close, and when the spot-light hit her, she stopped, hair whipping into her eyes as she shot at it. Immediately it angled away, but not before she took out its light.

The puttering roar of the Gremlin never sounded so good, and Peri limped faster, fumbling for the door and almost getting it in her face when Jack leaned across the seat and shoved it open. “Let’s go!” he shouted, and she lurched into the brittle-cold vinyl, her knee flashing into agony.

The door hit her calf on the bounce, and then she made it, glad it hadn’t crushed her foot as she settled into her seat, fumbling for the seat belt while Jack wove in and around the parked cars for the exit. She braced herself as he took a corner fast and they found the road.

"Interstate," she breathed, pointing it out, and her eyes closed against the pain as he skidded around the corner. The car roared ahead, the jostling finally easing as they found a street.

Her eyes cracked in the new smoothness, and she took a careful breath. Jack sat beside her, hands gripping the wheel tight as he wove the ugly car through the few vehicles on the road at this hour as if they were standing still. Opti was going small behind them, and she began to wonder whether they just might have done it. *For the moment,* she thought as she turned in the seat to look behind them.

"A Gremlin?" Jack said. "You wanted a *Gremlin?*"

She looked at the gearshift, deciding she'd chosen poorly. "Firebirds are shit on ice," she said, feeling her pockets for the guard's phone. It was humming, and she looked to see it was Steiner. Allen was caught, then, and had told them she had the man's phone. *But he's alive.*

"Okay. I'll give you that. But I'm picking the next car," he said, clearly curious when she set the phone on the seat, screen side down. "Border?"

"Downtown," she said, not liking having to show him her comic-book apartment. It had been her safe spot since she was eighteen and had bought the entire building for five hundred dollars and a promise to renovate. But in hindsight, she'd probably already shown it to him, and she slumped when she turned the car's heat on and it only blew cold air.

Clearly not liking her choice of destinations, Jack inched the speed up to a hundred, pushing for more but hardly getting the needle to move. He zipped around the night-driving semis as if he were playing a racing game. “You going to answer that phone?” he asked when it buzzed again.

“What’s it to you?” Blood was soaking through her pant leg, and she looked over the car for something else to wrap it in, finding nothing.

“Will you cut me some slack!” he exclaimed, fingers tightening on the wheel. “I’m trying to make it up to you. If you would just let me render something back, I—”

Let him render something back? “You could what?” she interrupted, the pain from her knee fueling her anger. “You honestly think I’m going to let you into my mind? Ever again?”

“I can’t pretend those three years didn’t happen,” he said. “They did. I’m sorry.”

“Sorry?” She was angry, and it was all she could do to not shoot him right then and there, but he *was* driving. “You erased my memory,” she said bitterly, not believing he was bringing this up here and now. “Years of it. To keep me oblivious and dumb. You touch my mind again, and I will open your throat and walk away. Got it? I have one thing I want you to do, and we’re done.”

Jack looked at her. His face, lit from the glow of the dash, was hard to read. “Your complaint is valid,” he finally said.

"*Don't* try to make me laugh." Her foot was cold, and she tugged her pant leg down again to deal with later. "I'm not going back to Bill. We get out of here clean, you make the call, you go your way, I go mine. Actually, there's no reason you can't make the call right now."

"This is stupid," Jack said. "We could be over the border and gone in an hour."

It was an overly generous estimation with her knee bleeding like this. "Drive," she said. "I'll hold the phone to your ear."

"Now?" Jack stared at her. "You're serious about this? Peri, Bill doesn't even like Michael. He's going to retire him the same hour you come back. I promise you."

Promise. She doubted he even knew what that meant beyond a way to convince people to do what he wanted. And she doubted that Bill would permanently "retire" Michael. He'd always be a threat, stuffed away in some cell in case Bill ever needed his talents again.

"*You* promise *me?*" she said as she held the phone for him to punch in Michael's cell. "I'm not coming back," she added as it rang. "If he's this side of the sod, I'm forever looking over my shoulder. Tell Michael I'm hooked and accelerated. That as soon as I run out of Evocane I'm coming in, and that Bill never intended to accelerate him. Make it convincing so he comes after me."

"Babe."

“Call me that one more time, I’ll break your kneecap.”

He snuck a glance at her, lowering his speed as she held the phone to his ear. She heard the connection click open, and she put her free hand on her Glock, sitting on her lap. Jack’s eyes pinched at the corners as he remembered something. Probably her shooting him in the back. Yeah, she’d pull the trigger, and he knew it.

“Michael,” he said when someone said hello. “Can you talk?”

Shit, my hands are shaking, Peri thought, not liking that it made the phone jerk against Jack’s face.

“Yes. Where are you?”

Jack looked at Peri for confirmation, and she nodded. “You’re not going to believe this,” he said. “I’m in Detroit. Peri took me out of WEFT. She’s accelerated herself. Silas doesn’t have a prayer to reverse-engineer it in time and she knows it. Soon as she runs out of Evocane, she’s coming in.”

Her grip on the pistol tightened.

“That wasn’t the plan,” Michael said bitterly, and Jack stiffened.

“Me taking your place in Detroit was Bill’s idea. I didn’t have a choice. Look. I’m going to wipe her the first chance I get, then bring her in as Bill told me. But Michael?” Peri’s finger tightened on the handgun, and Jack stared at her, eyes virulent. “I don’t think Bill had any intention of accelerating you. Remember who told you that when you need someone to watch your back."

Peri's finger eased up, and a drop of sweat trickled down Jack's neck.

Michael laughed. "You tricky bastard! Where are you?"

"No. I can't risk Bill thinking I'm screwing with him."

"Jack—"

Peri took the phone from his ear and hung up. Her fingers were still shaking as she rolled her window down. The wind whipped in, and she flung the phone out, the assault on her hair slowly vanishing as she cranked the window back up. *I'm so cold I could pee ice cubes.*

"I wouldn't wipe you, Peri. I only said that to give us some space to think."

She fiddled with the heater controls, giving the dash a smack when nothing changed. Sucking on the fatty part of her hand, she glared at him. She didn't believe him, but she wanted to. "There is no us, Jack," she said softly, but memories were creeping back.

Jack stared straight ahead, his hands tight on the wheel. "He's going to kill you."

"Not if I kill him first." But Jack was right. If Michael went for Bill first—and survived—he'd come for her next.

"Tell me you know what you're doing."

She turned in her seat, surprised that she was

comfortable with him doing a hundred down a night-black highway where deer were known to cross. "I know what I'm doing."

But as she searched the glove box for a flashlight to look at her knee, her doubt crept out, black and ugly. She was with Jack and a part of her felt at peace. The pain of being lied to, used, and scrubbed like an Etch A Sketch was being layered over by a calm relaxation that she hadn't felt for over a year. It was more than the peace instilled by a successful task. She hated it even as she basked in it. It didn't matter whether it was Opti conditioning or not, it was real. She'd enjoyed breaking out, doing something no one else could. Besting Steiner before his own men. It felt good, and not much had in a long time.

Maybe this was who she was after all.

CHAPTER TWENTY-TWO

Silas leaned back from his calculation, rubbing his aching eyes before reaching for an open reference book. He'd gotten the first chemical assay back on the Evocane, and it was like trying to balance an octogenarian's pharmacy list to make sure the multiple compounds weren't coming together into a lethal combination. He still didn't know why half of what was in there was in there, but he had a suspicion that most of it was to make it criminally addictive.

Four sixteen, he thought, looking at his clock and feeling tired. He was never much of a night owl, but rumor had it Steiner had gone out after Peri, and he couldn't sleep.

Thumbing to the index, he looked up the compound in question.

But then a curious, inside-out feeling ripped through him, and he blinked as the light pooling from his desk lamp shifted blue, and then flashed clear. *Someone just drafted.*

Silas stiffened. The book he'd been referencing was back where it started, out of his reach on a pile with the rest. He set his pencil down, his gaze going to his clock. It was four fifteen, clicking over even as he watched. Standing, he pushed his rolling chair back.

He had been under loose house arrest since Steiner had found Peri's old Opti apartment empty. Rumor had it a ping from a search engine had pulled the distasteful man out from behind WEFT's walls, but that had been hours ago. By the sound of it, he'd found her.

Pace fast enough to furl his lab coat, Silas strode out of his temporary office. The familiar scent of electronics and floor cleaner wafted up, and he followed the sound of men shouting. His brow furrowed in worry. If Steiner had figured out she was hooked on Evocane, she'd do anything to keep from going into a cell.

The rolling sound of a gurney pushed him to the edge of the hallway, and he slowed, his expression vanishing as three bodies rolled by, their slow pace saying they were going to the morgue, not the emergency medical floor. The men were covered, but they were in combat suits, blood seeping past the drapes.

Jesus, Peri, he thought, looking for her lithe frame among the bulky bodies and not seeing her. Relieved, he broke into a jog, following the commotion to the back door. Leaving bodies was not Peri's style. It was too noisy, too drastic. Bodies smacked of Allen.

His fast pace slowed as a man ran down the hall toward him. "Where is Agent Reed?" Silas asked, but the man never saw him, heavy in his combat boots and a demand for the chopper to get in the air coming over his radio.

Silas hesitated, torn, until he heard Steiner yelling. His expression hardened. Hands fisted, he ran forward. He didn't like how he always felt helpless when it came to Peri. She was so capable and inventive. But she got herself into trouble trying to be delicate when a quick bullet would be more efficient. Even so, he wouldn't want her to change.

The air suddenly went chill, and Silas slowed as he came around the corner. The wide back door was open, spilling the heat of the complex into the January night. Two men in combat gear were sitting propped up against the wall, ignored as they tried to stanch their shoulder wounds while around them agents buzzed like angry hornets over tablets spewing data.

"Doc!" one of the downed men shouted, gesturing at him with his good hand, and Silas stared until he realized he was still in his lab coat.

He didn't see Steiner or Peri, and, pulse fast, he went to the two wounded men, checking the younger one first as he tried to stay unnoticed. "You're going to be fine," he said as he moved to the other, looking under the makeshift bandage to the torn fabric and bleeding tissue. "In and out. Just apply pressure, and you'll be back on the range in two weeks." *Peri did this.*

He stood, wanting to go out, wanting to find her, afraid it would be too late.

"Doc."

The man grabbed his sleeve, and Silas paused. "You'll be fine," he repeated, then realized there was powder residue on the man. The shot had been close, really close. "Did Reed do this?" he asked, dropping back down to crouch before the man. "Did she kill those men?"

The man grimaced, clearly in pain. "Reed shot both of us, yeah, but Twill was the one who killed everyone in the other van. It was so fast they didn't have a chance. The bastard."

Silas stood, his mind shifting into a new worry. *Jack? Here?* He looked down. "Where is she? Is she hurt?"

"Hurt? No." The man took a peek under his soaked pad. "She's gone."

And then with a curious flip of sensation, time caught up and merged with hardly a whisper of disturbance. Silas took a breath, estimating the length of it. Forty-five seconds or so. It had been his Peri. She was running. Steiner had found her, captured her, and tried to bring her in. And Peri had balked, right at the gate by the looks of it.

Head shaking, Silas started for the open doorway and the pavers bathed in the stark white of electric lights. Steiner had made the mistake of not darting her to keep her from drafting. It was hard to fault him for it. Most people would make the same assumption that reliving a minute of time would change nothing, but knowing how someone was going to react gave her an immense advantage. Couple that with her training to evade . . . Steiner wouldn't make the same mistake twice.

"It was perfectly executed," the man was saying. "Like they planned it."

"Shut your mouth, Taylor!" Steiner shouted as he came in, clothes scuffed, bloodied, and filthy from melted snow. "I want a locator cuff on this man. Now!"

Silas pulled himself to his full height. "Why? I've been here all night."

Steiner halted right before him, the anger in his cold expression easy to read. "It's either that or a cell. I should put you in a cell anyway."

Feet spread wide, Silas crossed his arms over his chest. "I'm doing exactly what you told me to do," he said, but he lost his aggressive stance when Allen was dragged in between two men. Old bruises between new swellings decorated his face, and there was a cuff on his ankle already. Their eyes met, and Allen smiled, giving him a thumbs-up as he was dumped unceremoniously beside the two wounded agents.

"Now," Steiner demanded, and Silas grimaced when a man he had once trained came over, an open cuff in his hand.

"Sorry, Dr. Denier."

Knowing it wouldn't fit, Silas obediently pulled his pant leg up, smug when the band wouldn't clasp shut. "Ah, sir?" the technician called out, helpless.

Angry, Steiner snagged a passing man with an unfired rifle in his hand. "You. Watch him," Steiner said. "If he tries to leave, shoot him in the foot."

"Yes, sir!" the man barked.

Silas looked his new babysitter up and down, assessing the threat at a low three.

Apparently satisfied, Steiner started down the hallway, trailing a half-dozen aides. "I want to know how she got so far so fast. And why we can't find her. She's in a car, isn't she?"

"She is, sir," the man at his elbow said. "But it's

an old model and doesn't have a computer. A Gremlin, we think."

"You want me to put out an APB on a Gremlin?" Steiner rubbed his forehead, then said, "Do it. I want the borders shut and the river patrolled. No one crosses without an eyeball check."

"She's not going over the border," Silas said, and Steiner stopped short, his entourage scrambled to get out of his way as he turned.

"And how do you know that?"

"That's not where Michael is," he said, and Allen nodded, his head down in exhaustion.

Steiner pushed his aides aside. "You expect me to believe this is so she can go after Michael?"

"And Bill." Silas looked at his watch, wondering how far she'd gotten. "And when they are dead, she is going to vanish, and you will never find her."

Steiner walked slowly back. "I don't think so, Dr. Denier," he said, holding up a vial. "She needs this. She either comes in, or I will kill her. No more darts, no more second chances. I will kill her. Tell her that if she contacts you." Turning, he walked away again, his aides following.

"Not if she finds Bill first," Silas said loudly.

Steiner kept walking. "Swift, get yourself looked at," he said over his shoulder. "I want you in my office in an hour. Armand, where are the lockers? Are there executive showers in this facility?"

"This way, sir," someone said, and the entire group quickly strode down the hall.

"Yes, sir," Allen said sarcastically, still on the floor. "Right away, sir. I don't remember you signing my paycheck—ass hat." He looked at the two wounded men beside him, giving them a weak wave as the incoming medical people smothered them. "Hey, no hard feelings, okay?" Wincing, he held a hand up to Silas. "Get me out of here, will you?"

Weight on his back foot, Silas extended a hand and hauled him up. "Where's Peri?"

"Yes, I did get shot and beat up by both Bill *and* a Detroit gang," Allen said loudly. "Thanks for asking."

Silas jerked him off balance. "Where is Peri?" he intoned.

Pulling out of his grip, Allen rubbed his wrist. "The Detroit Astoria?" he said, knowing as did Silas that any conversation in the hall would likely be monitored. "I don't know. Steiner figured out she's hooked on Evocane and she freaked out. I don't think she meant to leave with Jack, but you know her."

"She doesn't like to work alone." Silas felt a new worry slip in behind the old. *Jack* . . .

Allen started down the hallway, slow and awkward. "Do you think she'll return to Opti?"

"No." Silas looked at his watch, estimating her next dose to be around midnight. She'd likely try to tough it out, and when that failed . . . He didn't want it to be Bill she looked to, but Steiner was worse. He had to get out of here. Take her what Evocane he could find. Give her the time she needed to gather her thoughts, weigh her options. But that would take planning, and he was sure his office was bugged. Steiner was oblivious, not a fool.

"You don't think the CIA got rid of the twenty-four-hour kitchen when they took over, do you?" Silas said, affecting a false lightness. "I'm starving." The table under the air conditioner would be open at this time of night. If it was running, any listening devices would be useless.

Allen's eyes were bright among the bruises. "Maybe they still have that guy who cooks eggs to order." He reached for a wall for balance and left a dirty handprint. "I liked him. He always got my yolks runny."

"Let's find out," Silas said, his thoughts on the Opti-initiated technological fence he was going to have to get through, because he was not going to let Peri run back to Bill. He glanced at their escort. His weapon would be handy. His security card would be helpful, too. "Are you going to be with me twenty-four/seven?" he asked, beginning to think about gathering resources.

"Yes, sir."

Silas's eyebrows rose. "If you try to sit at the cool kids' table, I'm going to tip your tray."

"Yes, sir."

He couldn't help his sarcastic smile as he looked up at the ceiling camera before taking Allen in a more secure hold and helping him down the hallway. The lights were dimmed because of the late hour, and it felt like old times at Opti, beaten and bruised as they limped down the hall at the speed of "ow."

"I haven't slept in like two days. I just want to eat and go to bed. Steiner can make it with a goat if he thinks I'm going to show up in his office in an hour." Then he leaned toward Silas. "You still have the code for the climate control, right?" he asked softly.

"Why would they change that?" The lunchroom was predictably empty, and Silas stifled a sigh as he took in the low-ceilinged, whitewashed bland-ness of tables in rows and cafeteria-style food. He hated cafeterias. It was one thing he and Peri shared.

Resigned, he put a damp tray on the bars, disliking the sound of plastic on metal. Behind him, Allen hit the disinfectant stand with a tired vengeance. His hands still glistening, he slapped a tray onto the bars, clearly not happy that their babysitter was following.

Leaning in, Silas put three milky-plastic cups on his tray. "What was *Jack* doing there?"

Allen looked at their guard picking through the silverware. "Complicating things." Expression brightening, he smiled at the night chef, who had come forward to flick on the griddle. "Four?" he asked. "Scrambled?" he added as Silas took his tray to the oatmeal station. *May as well make it breakfast.*

Allen loaded his tray with something full of fat and grease, then limped after him. Silas looked at the cameras in the corners, recording everything. Shifting to put his back to their guard, Silas filled a bowl with oatmeal. “Why did Bill send Jack instead of Michael?”

“Bill says you can’t reverse-engineer the Evocane in time.” Allen’s eyes roved over the empty tables. “He sent Jack more as a goodwill gesture, trying to convince her to return rather than force her. He’s that certain that she’ll come back once she sees what he’s giving her.”

“A lifetime of addiction?” Silas said bitterly, and Allen’s expression became grim.

“The freedom to remember her drafts, the assurance that no one could use her again.”

But it came with a steep price. Silas ached that she might be willing to pay it because the more Steiner pushed her, the more she would be pulled to Bill.

“Damn, I’m tired. Where do you want to sit?” Allen asked, seeing that the table under the air conditioner was missing.

Agitated, Silas filled his three cups with chocolate milk. Tray in one hand, he indicated one of the tables near the air vent.

“My eggs aren’t done yet,” Allen said. “I’ll be right there.”

Silas took his tray over and set it down. Eyeing the nearby vent, he grabbed the table and pulled it, scraping and screeching, to sit directly under it. The unit wasn't running, but he could fix that. "Don't even try," he said as their babysitter hustled forward, Allen limping close behind.

"Steiner said watch us." Allen pointed at a second table. "Watch from over there."

The guard's eyes narrowed, and Silas crossed his arms over his chest, making his biceps bulge. "Don't," he said, and after a tense moment, the guard took his tray and sat down twenty feet off and out of earshot.

"Dumb-ass," Allen muttered, sighing heavily as he slumped onto the bench.

Silas took his phone from his pocket before he settled himself as well, using his pinky to handle the tiny icons as he logged into Opti's climate control. Above them, the fans began to whirl. Cold air spilled down over them. The guard frowned, but he made no move to join them.

Silas resettled in a huff of satisfaction, but it faded when he looked from his bowl of oatmeal to Allen's heaped tray of bacon, eggs, sweet pastry, and sausage. Resolved, he poured chocolate milk over his oats. "She's going to go into withdrawal by midnight tomorrow." He hesitated, his hand propping up his chin and milk dripping from the spoon to land on the brown sugar and melt it into the chocolate milk. "I'm not letting that happen."

Allen snorted as he dug in, the steam rising from his eggs to mist his glasses. “She might be able to tough it out.”

“Maybe, but this stuff is ugly. It was bad forty years ago, and Bill has made it not just hard to quit but impossible.” Guilt swam up, and he hunched over his bowl, not hungry. “I’m weeks away from even knowing how it works, longer if they don’t give me a decent lab.” He couldn’t leave her to suffer withdrawal alone. Steiner had two vials now, and the accelerator.

“So what do you want to do?” Allen slumped deeper onto his bench. “I’m all escaped out,” he added, tapping his ankle bracelet against the table supports.

Silas’s brow furrowed. He wasn’t useless. That they thought him a lab geek had worked well for him so far. But there was a reason he hadn’t gone all the way to be a field agent. He was too big to be evasive. “I need to talk to Steiner,” he said, and Allen chuckled. “Maybe encourage him to free up a sample or two for me to work with, then slip out the front door.”

“Yeah, you do that.” Allen hunched over his food as if he were in prison. “They’re watching you a lot closer now since your little walkabout from Atlanta to Detroit.”

Uneasy, Silas tucked his phone back in his pocket.

“She’ll be okay,” Allen said. “I bet she’s planning her way back in right now to get her

Evocane out of Steiner's office. Frankly, I'm more worried about Jack."

His chest clenched. "She isn't going to stay with Jack," Silas muttered, but she might—if she forgot who she wanted to be.

"He might wipe her," Allen said, and Silas looked up, hating how easy that came out of Allen's mouth. "He has before," he muttered as he shoveled eggs and sausage into himself with an eerie focus.

Silas put his spoon down with a clatter. "You're a real dick, you know that?"

As if only now hearing how he sounded, Allen looked up. "I gave her a phone," he said, swallowing his latest mouthful. "She'll call us if and when she needs us."

Silas stared at him. "You really think she's going to call you? I know where she'll go. To catch her breath, anyway." He had to get out of here, but it was going to take more than just him. He needed help. Allen, though, was in bad shape, half-starved and resources tapped out. He'd be good for a distraction, but not much else.

Silas jumped when Harmony stiff-armed one of the glass doors to the cafeteria open, hitting it so hard it nearly smacked into the wall. The woman stopped dead in her tracks when she saw them, the thought to turn around and walk back out obvious on her face. But with a slow intake of breath, her fire washed out of her. Slumping, she took a tray and pushed it along the silver bars.

"I don't trust her," Silas said, his lip twitching when Allen chuckled.

"Peri does." Allen was smiling, seeming to enjoy Harmony's bad mood. "She knew Peri was hooked on Evocane even before she left St. Louis and didn't tell Steiner."

She trusts Harmony . . . Pensive, he leaned across the table to Allen under the excuse of reaching for the salt, whispering, "Do you think she might help me get out of here?"

Allen's eyes shifted to watch Harmony push her tray past the steaming sausage and bacon, taking nothing but a bowl of Jell-O and a yogurt. "Maybe," he said. "Steiner is pissed at her if that ankle bracelet on her foot is any indication. She could chuck what's left of her career to help you, or chuck you to Steiner to save what's left of her career."

That didn't help at all, and Silas stiffened when Harmony plopped herself down across from him. Still silent, she put a spoon in her Jell-O, then pushed her tray to the center of the table and hid her head in the cradle her arms made. "I'm changing my name to Phillips, I'm so screwed," she said, voice muffled. Her head came up, and she took in Silas and Allen, one in a lab coat, the other still in the down-filled WEFT coat he'd gotten in the van. "Good God. Why is the air on? It's freezing in here."

"It keeps out the bugs." Allen pointed up, and

Harmony's expression shifted from wonder to anger to a deep-set fatigue and resignation.

"Of course it does." She pulled her Jell-O closer. "Steiner is a dick."

"And baby makes three," Allen said, eyes alight as he started in on a sticky bun.

Watching them eat made Silas's stomach hurt. Time was moving, and he had so little to spare. He had to get out of here. He had to tell Peri how bad the Evocane was before she shot up with a third dose. The stuff was not just highly addictive, but after enough exposure, it would kill you if you quit cold turkey, such was Bill's zeal to keep his drafters.

Allen shoved a fold of bacon into his mouth, a happy *mmmm* making both Silas and Harmony look at him in envy before dropping to their respective bowls of oatmeal and Jell-O. "I can't believe you didn't tell Steiner she was addicted," Allen said around his full mouth. "It might have gotten you out of the doghouse. If he finds out you knew before Atlanta, you're really up crap creek."

"Then he'd better not find out." Harmony eyed his bacon-strewn plate. "Besides, they can't fire me twice."

"They fired you?" Silas exclaimed, and Harmony held up two fingers spaced an inch apart.

"This close. Are you going to eat that bacon?"

Allen started. "Ah, yeah."

"Thanks." She took a long piece, her eyes

closing in bliss as she chewed. "I just flushed my career saving your ass. You can float me some bacon. You're welcome, by the way," she added with zero sincerity.

Silas snorted as Allen fidgeted. "Thanks."

"My dad would be pissed," Harmony said. "Everything wasted. I don't know if it would have made any difference if Michael had been there and we had brought him in. Damn it, this sucks. I can't believe I'm eating *bacon!*"

Silas sat unmoving, his need to find Peri growing stronger. If he wasn't there to remind her of who she wanted to be, she *would* turn to Bill when she ran out of options. In the meantime, Jack would be filling her head with lies, luring her not only with the chance to remember her drafts, but also with some of her past that had been erased.

He looked at Allen and Harmony, knowing his assets lay there, thin as they were. Allen was eager to give a little back if Bill was the end goal, but so bruised and beaten that he'd be little help. Harmony wasn't a team player—unless the team was doing what she wanted. He'd have to rely on chancy intel and even more chancy follow-through. It would take all of them—and put more than Harmony's career at risk.

Silas took a deep breath and slowly exhaled; limited options or not, he had only action. "I have to get out of here," he said softly, and Harmony looked up from her yogurt. "I have to get to Peri before she goes into withdrawal and contacts Bill."

"Like they're going to let you anywhere near the door." Allen licked the pastry frosting from his fingers. "You don't even know where she is."

Harmony glanced at their guard and leaned over the table. "You're kidding, right? Steiner has the Evocane locked up tighter than his daughter's virginity."

He stiffened, not liking their disbelief. It was too close to his own estimations. "I have a pretty good idea of where she might be. You going to help or not?"

Harmony flung a hand in the air, letting it fall heavily on the table in disbelief. "Peri Reed just busted Steiner up. Killed three men. My career is over; I'm not killing it twice."

"Jack killed those three men, not Peri," Silas said quickly. "She shot two men in the shoulder and ran. That's all she wants. To be left alone. That was all she ever wanted."

"Until she met up with Jack and they took off together." Allen shook his head. "She's gone, Silas."

Silas forced his hands flat on the table so they wouldn't turn into fists. Allen always was one to give up on her. "She's gone, but she's not gone back to Bill. And she won't if she has half a choice," he added when Allen cleared his throat. "Steiner put her on a kill list because of me," he said, the guilt bringing his eyes down. "Because I couldn't figure this out fast enough and she had no choice but to run or be put in his cell, knowing there was only one week between her and dying from withdrawal. This is my fault."

Harmony was silent. Beside her, Allen shifted uneasily, clearly still hurting. "I told you, I can't get to the Evocane," Harmony finally said. "The accelerator, maybe, but not Evocane."

"I don't need it," Silas said, scrambling to find a justification for them to risk their lives to help him get back to Peri. "Bill was right. I can't duplicate the Evocane, but the more I dig into it, the more I think I don't have to. She hasn't been accelerated, so all I have to do is create something that addresses the addictive properties, a substitute to handle the withdrawal. She has no choice. Don't you see that? Let me give her one."

"She can have any choice, as long as it's the one you want?" Allen said bitterly. "Let her go, Silas. Maybe this is who she is."

Something very close to hatred trickled through Silas. "I'm not turning my back on her again. Evocane or no Evocane, I'm getting out of here. I'm going to find her, and I'm going to keep her alive. Are you going to help me or not?"

"Fine. But I want you to take the accelerator, too," Allen said as he wiped his fingers on his napkin.

Silas's lip curled. "To give to Peri? No. It's poison."

Allen tossed his wadded-up napkin aside. "So much for choice."

"The accelerator isn't a choice, it's madness," Silas said.

"And forgetting isn't?" Allen leaned forward, hunched over his plate. "That hallucination you put in her to cover up your mistake isn't madness?"

Silas exhaled, putting his hands under the table to hide them.

"You know, if you have it, Steiner can't force it on the next drafter he finds," Harmony said, and Silas eased back. He could do that, and it might even be helpful in creating an Evocane substitute.

"Fine. I'll take the accelerator," he said softly. "How long until you can get it?"

The two men looked expectantly at her, and Harmony hesitated. "Ahhh, what the hell," she finally whispered. "A few hours, maybe?"

Elation filled him, and his eyes closed in a long blink of relief. He wouldn't let her be forced into something because he failed. He would find her, keep her from suffering through withdrawal. But what scared him most was Jack, filling her head with the memory of when she was strong, bulletproof, and more vulnerable to manipulation than a two-year-old child.

He would risk everything for her. All Peri needed was time.

CHAPTER TWENTY-THREE

The smooth, lithe arm lying over Bill's moved fitfully, pulling up and away as Susanne turned over. Bill's eyes opened at the flush of cooler air on his backside. A faint glow had lit the bedroom, and an accompanying hum came from the bedside table.

"Bill, get your phone," the woman complained. "I have to be up in an hour."

Groggy, he rolled to the edge of his bed, dragging the covers with him. She pulled them back when he squinted at the phone to read the name in a faint, holographic print. *Jack?* he thought, surprised the anchor had gotten himself to a phone already. He hadn't expected to hear from him for at least a week. Maybe WEFT had believed him and given him some freedom. *Idiots.*

Eyes closed, he flopped back onto the pillow and thumbed the connection open. "Jack?" he breathed. "It's five in the morning."

"I'm with Peri," came faintly through the line, the sound of water running in the background telling Bill that Jack wasn't on a secure line. "She pulled me out of WEFT custody."

"You escaped together?" His eyes flicked open as Susanne flung the covers aside and stomped to the bathroom, her black negligee showing off her pale limbs in the dim light. "Fabulous. Wipe her and get back here. You need funds? Assets?" he asked, watching the light coming in under the bathroom door.

"No, we're in Detroit. She left without any Evocane, meaning she's got a source outside WEFT's walls. Soon as she gets it, she's coming for you."

"You say that like it's a bad thing." Peri had a right to be pissed, but kill him? She was his girl. Swinging his feet to the floor, Bill tugged the sheet to cover himself and turned on the light. "Denier?" he asked, not believing he'd cracked the biologic.

"The arena's pissant," Jack said, his sarcasm heavy. "Peri left half with him, gave half to Steiner so he wouldn't know there was a second vial and tear the arena apart looking for it. Listen, she made me tell Michael—"

Bill tensed as Jack's words cut off. He stood, sending his hand under the covers in search of his boxers and dragging them out from the foot of the bed. "Jack?"

"Just a sec," Jack said, and Bill heard the sound of the phone being set down.

Impatient, Bill tugged his boxers on. Fully awake, he went into the living room, shutting the bedroom door carefully behind him. Detroit spread out below him past the newly renovated window walls. The city lights looked bright even under the light-pollution reduction bulbs that Detroit had put in ten years ago. Habit kept him from going closer to the window for a better view, and he stood in the kitchen, impatient.

"Okay, I'm back," Jack said. "I wanted to make sure she was in the shower."

"You told Michael what?" Bill asked, not liking this.

"She had a gun to my gut," Jack said, and Bill's brow furrowed, not knowing what was going to come out of Jack's mouth. "She made me tell him that she had accelerated herself and was on her way home. That you were never going to accelerate him. Bill, she's on the warpath. Looking for a head on a pole. She doesn't care if it's yours or Michael's. Either way, she gets a win."

Bill leaned against the glass counter, the entire surface lighting up with the home's security system, TV schedule, email accounts, and kitchen stores. *I'm out of wine,* he noted absently, then waved the surface off, head down as he thought through the ramifications. "That sounds like something my Peri would do," he said, proud of her even as it wreaked havoc with his plans. She was angry and wasn't going to let anyone walk over her. "Okay." He'd worked miracles with less. "She's showering, eh? Get her to draft, and when she jumps, scrub her and get her back here."

"No."

"No?" It wasn't the first time he'd heard it, but the last occasion Jack had told him no, his world had gone to hell.

Bill's head snapped up as the counter lit up again, the security frame a bright red. From beside the door, the locking panel began flashing. In his hand, his phone began to glow as a security text came in. It was the silent alarm, and his frown deepened. "Oh, good," he said sarcastically, wishing he was wearing something more than boxers. "I think Michael's here. Get Peri back to Opti, or I'm coming for you myself, Jack. Understand?"

"Bill," Jack began to protest, and he hung up. The counter dutifully recorded the phone call, then went dark.

"That's my girl," Bill muttered as he yanked the dishwasher out from under the counter. Fingers fumbling, he found the handgun taped to the underside of it and checked the clip. "Keep 'em reacting and disoriented."

Adrenaline jerked through him as the door exploded inward. Bill dropped at the crack of a rifle, the shrapnel from the granite counter cutting his face.

"Stand up, you son of a bitch!" Michael shouted, and Bill sighed.

"Bill?" Susanne's voice was clear, and Bill stood when she shrieked, just in time to see her flee back into the bedroom and slam the door.

Michael's attention swung back to him,

steadying as he saw the pistol pointed at him. The ambient glow of the city lit them, and Michael chuckled. Bill calmly took the safety off. "She's lying," he said simply.

"Like hell she is." Michael's voice was just as calm, and it unsettled Bill. "Jack said you had no intention of accelerating me."

Pushing Michael into a corner would make the man more unpredictable. The pad by the door had stopped flashing, meaning a response was coming. A bead of sweat ran down Bill's back, and with a deliberate motion, he set the pistol within his reach. It was doubtful that Michael would draft and risk Bill wiping his memory right down to the day of his birth.

"I've never lied to you, Michael. Think about it."

"You're lying to me right now." Michael eased deeper into the living room, dangerous—like a lion. "Jack called me. He took her out of WEFT, you son of a bitch. You don't need me anymore."

"He called me, too." Damn, even his feet were sweating, sticking to the tile floor. "Jack didn't take Peri. Peri took Jack. She's running rabbit, and she forced him to make that call in exchange for helping him. She's trying to kill you," he said, then hesitated in thought. "Or me. She doesn't really care. Be smart about this, Michael."

"Bullshit!" Michael shouted.

Not even looking at the rifle pointed at him, Bill

showed his hands in a gesture of bewilderment. "Think it through, Michael. I have been transparent about the research. You've seen the med wing. Hell, you've brought in the retired drafters we experimented it on. Once accelerated, a draft will cause a psychotic episode unless you buffer it with Evocane. That's it. She is trying to kill you," he said, his disgust thick in his voice. "And you believe her?"

The boom of gunfire jolted both of them. For an instant, Bill thought Michael had shot him, but it was Michael who fell, hands clasped about his knee. Bill's gaze shot to the front door. A man thick with Kevlar garments rocked in, shouting. It was Bill's men, not the police, and anger furrowed his brow.

"I won't forget this," Michael moaned, teeth clenched.

Furious, Bill strode from the kitchen, arms waving. "Did I tell you to shoot him?" he shouted at the armed men, feeling his face become red. "What the hell are you doing!"

"Sir." The man fumbled, lights flashing on the walls from the cars outside. "He had a semiautomatic."

"Get out!" Bill exclaimed, and then he staggered back when Michael's rifle went off, the solid boom of it rocking the windows. The Kevlar-coated man was flung back, his head hitting the stone wall with a resounding thud. He fell to the floor, out cold but probably alive. The shouts outside became more demanding.

Flat on the floor, Michael grimaced, panting as he pointed the rifle at Bill. One hand clutched at his knee, the other shook on the trigger. "You lied . . . to me," he gasped.

It was falling apart, and that pissed Bill off. "I said, stay out!" he shouted at the team clustered around the door. "If Michael wanted to kill me, he would have already!"

At least that's what he told himself as he shoved the fear down and strode brusquely to Michael. Kneeling, he yanked the rifle from Michael's grasp, tossing it to the blood-splattered couch. He wrapped a kitchen towel around Michael's knee and sat him up. "I never lied to you," he muttered as he tried to be as gentle as he could, thinking it was odd—tending to Michael as if he were a baby when the man had just pointed a rifle at him. "I told you she would try to kill you if you threatened her. This is her way of doing it."

"Accelerate me," Michael said, panting as he listed sideways. "Now."

Blood coated his hands, and Bill levered himself up and back to sit on the edge of the cushy chair. A weary chuckle slipped from him, and he waved the guards away with a red-stained hand. "You're not going to draft to fix this, are you?" he said, thinking it had to be getting close to Michael's ninety-second ceiling. "It's your lack of trust that holds you back.

And now you're going to let fear keep you out of the game of bringing her down. Michael, this is why I wanted to accelerate her first, not you."

"I wouldn't be weak if you accelerated me!" he shouted, so pale Bill wondered how he wasn't passing out.

"No, you'd be dead," he said, reaching out to push Michael upright again.

Michael lurched forward, falling into Bill and sending them both to the floor. Bill took a breath to laugh at Michael's obstinate temper tantrum, but it exploded from him in a wash of pain. White-hot agony ran down his side, and he hit the floor, staring at the ceiling as his hands clutching his neck were suddenly slippery and warm.

The bastard slit my throat! he thought, not even having felt it happen.

Flat on his back, Bill stared at the ceiling.Panic, new and unreal, washed through him in time with his pulse as his blood ran out and his brain began to falter.

Michael stood grim and bloody above him, blotting out the light as the rifle exploded again and again. The scent of gunpowder threatened to make him cough, and the cries of his men filled his ears. And through it all, Michael fired with an ease that belied his pale face.

Goddamn it, he's shooting up my entire house.

And then it was silent except for Bill's pained gasps. He jerked when a heavy hand gripped his throat, stopping the outflow. His sight grayed when Michael leaned over him, his eyes hard. "Now, old man," Michael breathed heavily, "tell me the truth."

The fucking cretin was insane. But he'd known that. "I-I did," he rasped, sucking in air as if he were drowning.

"Are you sure?"

Bill spasmed as Michael eased his grip and a soft warmth flooded over their hands pressed to his neck. "Draft!" he choked out.

An ugly smile crossed Michael's face, and he pressed down, ending the flow. "The truth."

He wouldn't remember anything when the draft ended, but if Michael wasn't satisfied, he wouldn't draft at all. "I have," Bill said. "She's trying to kill you!"

Michael leaned back and the light struck him. "I think she's trying to kill you," he said. With a sideways smirk, he let go.

Bill shuddered, gasping for air as his body thought he was drowning. *He killed me. The son of a bitch killed me,* he thought, and then the pain vanished with a sideways twist of déjà vu.

Michael had drafted, and Bill's oxygen-starved brain floundered as it tried to cope until, with the sensation of breaking ice, everything flooded back with a crystalline certainty.

Bill groaned as time reset. He staggered, finding himself again behind the counter. His pistol was before him. His hand flashed to his neck, not the weapon, and his attention jerked to the door. "Don't shoot!" he bellowed before his men could come in, his arms raised. "Goddamn it, the first person who shoots Michael is going to get my foot up their ass! Get out. Get out!" he shouted, and Michael, who would remember both timelines until they meshed, smiled.

Still resonating with the fear from his narrow miss, Bill held a hand over his neck. Michael had drafted over his ninety-second ceiling. Twice as far as Peri had ever managed. "How long have you been able to do this?" he whispered, still shaking.

Michael smiled like the devil himself. "Ask them to leave."

Bill left the handgun where it was. "You heard him. Get out!"

The door was busted, but they backed off. Michael sat on the pristine couch, cradling his rifle, and Bill came closer, anger pushing out the fear. The little prick had tried to kill him.

"So what are we doing, Michael?" he said, feeling vulnerable in his boxers.

Michael took a pen from the coffee table and wrote on his palm. Leaning back, he took his rifle in his hands. His smile said he thought he was in charge. "There's a way to keep you from scrubbing me when I snap out of this."

Bill sat across from him. The absolute

whiteness of his hands after the bloody gore of them was riveting. "Yeah?" he said, tired.

"Yeah."

Bill looked up at Michael's swift motion, not even getting a cry out before the butt of the rifle hit him square on the temple.

He woke up flat on the floor, his face pressed up against the thick pile carpet. It was silent except for a soft, feminine whimper, and he levered himself up, wiping the drool from himself.

Dead men ringed his living room, blood radiating from each one like broken flower petals. Michael was sitting pretty in the middle of it, the scent of gunpowder choking. Susanne was tied to a dining room chair, her eyes red but looking unharmed. It had to be very like what a drafter experienced after a jump, and he wondered how long he'd been unconscious. He'd be damned if he'd ask. Judging by the tears on Susanne's face, at least ten minutes. By the dead men, not much more than that. *And my house is shot to hell again.*

"You had to kill them all?" Bill complained, and Michael shifted his posture.

"They didn't trust me."

Bill levered himself up onto a chair, ignoring Susanne's muffled but increasingly loud demands for help. "Why should I?" he asked, rubbing a tired hand over his head.

"Because I knocked you out instead of killing

you." Still holding his rifle, he showed Bill his palm. KILL PERI, NOT BILL was scrawled across it. "You want to fill in the blanks?"

Bill stood. Shuffling to Susanne, he untied the knots on her wrists. "You want to quit taking out my hired help, maybe?"

Susanne yanked the sock from her mouth. "Bill, you suck. Don't call me again. Got it?" She stood, pushing Bill out of the way as she stormed over the downed agents and out the broken door. She was still in that black negligee.

Michael smiled, and as the electronic whine of Suzanne's car went faint, Bill strode to the bookshelf and poured himself a shot. He downed it in one go, feeling it burn his throat and give him distance from what had happened. But the memory of his blood warm on his fingers wouldn't go away, and he looked at Michael, the cold hatred in his eyes hanging heavy in him. The man was certifiable, dangerous—and exactly what he needed to get this done. But for the first time, Bill wondered whether he'd survive it.

The door pad was a neutral green, but someone would eventually come investigate the noise of six men dying in gunfire. Tired, Bill set the bottle back among the books and gathered his thoughts. If Peri was on the warpath, he should take the fight to where he wanted it. Michael, though, would never agree to what would sound like retreat, not the careful plan it was.

"Jack tells me she's rabbiting," he said, wanting to stick as close to the truth as he could. "This story of her coming in was a ploy to get you reacting. Get you to kill me for her." He looked at Michael from under his lowered brow. "Which you obliged her."

Michael brushed the gunpowder off his rifle. "What are you griping for, old man? I brought you back."

The memory of gasping his life out on the carpet shuddered through him, and he hid it behind a last swallow. *You are a wild boar, Michael, and you will be culled.* "As you say." Resolute, Bill reluctantly set his empty glass down, feeling as if he'd failed Michael in some way. "Peri won't leave ends this time."

Eyebrows high, Michael waited. "And?" he prompted.

It was looser than he liked. There were too many variables. But Michael was still the best option he had. "I think we need to talk to Helen. See about taking Peri out of the program and putting you in her place."

Michael chuckled. "It's about fucking time."

And *that* would get him to Newport. Peri would follow. Tension trickled through him, a warm wash that rebounded at his toes and settled in his groin. "Are you hungry? Have you had breakfast? It will take the flight crew at least four hours to get themselves in order."

"Breakfast sounds good." Michael snickered. "You want to get dressed first?"

Bill stopped short and looked down. "Indeed."

"I'll pull my car around," Michael said as he walked to the door, treading around the fallen men as if they didn't matter.

But in the grand scheme of things, Bill thought as he strode to his bedroom, *they don't.*

CHAPTER TWENTY-FOUR

The scent of eggs and sausage tickled the edge of her awareness. Concentrating on the softly glowing screen, Peri ignored it, even as her stomach rumbled. Feet on the worn coffee table, she propped the screen against the rise of her knees, her fingers moving rapidly over the icons and keyboard as she searched for evidence of Bill. She'd borrowed the tablet from the guys downstairs, and she couldn't help but wonder whether she wasn't charging enough rent. It was this year's model, but even that was frustratingly slow compared to her old Opti tablet.

Waiting for the search to finish, Peri carefully rubbed her sore knee through her torn slacks, skirting the ragged, bloodied edges. She hadn't been keen on the idea of showing Jack her safe house, but the way Jack was maneuvering about her kitchen making breakfast led her to believe he'd been here before, and if Jack knew about it, it was a good bet Bill did. She couldn't stay here. As soon as she got a bead on Bill, she was gone.

The aroma of sausage became stronger, and she flicked a glance at Jack standing before the small efficiency stove, his hair damp from a shower, the sleeves of his once-white shirt rolled up, and his filthy suit coat carefully folded over the back of the kitchen chair. Under the musty staleness of the couch was the faint hint of someone familiar. Not Jack, but a man nevertheless.

Finally the page to her financial house loaded, and she typed in her password. It was the same thing she did to check every well-lined patron who came into her coffeehouse. This time, though, she was going to go a step further outside the law to use it to infiltrate Bill's financial house. From there, she could track him—see where he had been spending money. Impatient, she put in Bill's phone number. If he was using his p-cash, she'd find him.

The domestic sounds of breakfast cooking were incredibly soothing. "Where did you get the food?" she said softly as the program searched. It would take some time.

All smiles, Jack turned halfway around. "The sausage was in the freezer next to some crusty black-cherry ice cream and five boxes of Thin

Mint cookies. The eggs were in the fridge. They're good for a year if they're kept right. And they were. No coffee, though. Sorry."

He looked good there, comfortable, and not liking that fact, Peri prodded her knee to estimate the damage. She hadn't taken any of the meds she'd found in the tiny bathroom cabinet lest she medicate herself into a nondrafting state. Her knee was sore, but all it needed was a hot bath and some stretching. A shower would be a good second, but leaving Jack alone again wasn't an option. That she had fallen asleep for a few hours was bad enough.

I can't believe I fell asleep. Eyes rising from her knee, she looked over the small one-room apartment in the light of day. The blinds were closed and the room was shadowed, her shelves of treasures dark. The furnishings were comfortable, worn, and mismatched. The rug, too, was old, doing little to cover the scratched floorboards. A forgotten project bag with yarn and a half-unraveled scarf was tucked in a corner.

Don't I ever finish anything? she wondered, even as a weird peace was growing in her, far greater than the coming breakfast warranted. She couldn't tell whether it was from Jack, that she was free of authority again, or just that she wasn't alone.

The page dinged for her attention. Leaning over it, she felt a quiver of excitement. There was a charge on Bill's security system early this morning. He'd had a ping and dismissed it. Even better, there had been an enormous influx of funds last week. Most had been parceled out, but it was enough to fund a small country for a year. *Everblue?* she wondered. *His backer?*

Nothing had been spent at an airport, though, and she frowned until she saw the Your Skies payment. The jet-for-hire service had been put on retainer at opening of business today. Peri's eyebrows rose. Private jets were the best way to move around when you were covered in gunpowder residue. He was alive.

Not knowing how she felt about that, she closed out the financial records and opened Detroit International Airport. Everything in a fifty-mile radius from Detroit used the same tower whether it was a glider at Parkway or a crop duster at Ypsilanti. Stomach rumbling, she reached for her pendant pen, jerking it open and writing NEWPORT on her palm when she found a match.

Peri recapped the pen, focus distant as she thought. She had a direction, but it had been too easy—an invitation to find him, almost.

The sound of silverware clinking pulled her attention, but seeing Jack still fussing over the bacon, she returned to her tablet, closing everything out and wiping the search memory. A timer popped up, and not wanting to shut it down until it was finished, she glanced at

Jack's back and typed in an address by memory.

An uncomfortable unease seeped into her. Fidgeting, Peri tugged the tablet closer as her mother's facility loaded. A few more taps and she had access to all the cameras, little slices of life in three-by-eight rectangles. Her brow furrowed as she leaned in, her knee throbbing as she searched the grainy black-and-white displays for her mother. Guilt rose as she saw the wrinkled faces and fading hair. Some were vacant, some angry, some eerily happy as they watched old movies as they sat in rows of wheelchairs and scooters. It was too cold to be outside, and she searched the nature room, where goldfinches and cardinals made a living display. Her mother liked birds, though Peri could never remember a time they'd had a feeder. She had always told Peri that birds were filthy.

"Breakfast is ready," Jack said cheerfully, and she snapped the tablet off. Standing above her, Jack hesitated, two plates of food in his hands. "You're going to eat it, right?" he said as he set one on the table and collapsed into the overstuffed chair across from her with the other. Plate on his lap, Jack looked mildly hurt. "If I'd wanted to turn you over to Bill, I would have already. It's your usual. At least, it was the last time I got you breakfast."

"I don't remember." Setting her tablet aside, she picked up the fork.

Jack lowered his head over his food. "I do."

Her eyes narrowed. In sudden mistrust, she pushed her food across the table to him and took his plate right off his lap. Jack chuckled, continuing to eat her eggs instead without pause. Emboldened, she took a bite. Salt and protein hit the sides of her mouth, waking up her appetite. She began eating in earnest. Jack was clearly pleased, and she muttered, "This doesn't mean anything except I'm hungry."

His expression didn't dim at all. "I know it's going to take time."

She stopped chewing, then swallowed fast. "There's not enough time in the world, *Jack.*"

"I'm sorry I lied to you," he said, his brow furrowed. "I'm sorry I tricked you into believing you were one thing when you were something else. If I could draft back to the beginning, I'd do it differently." She snorted, and he added, "What can I do to prove myself?"

Pushing her eggs around, she chuckled and said, "You can kill Bill for me."

"Peri, I lied because I loved you. And you loved me."

She pulled her head up, ticked. "You lied because you loved me. Seriously?" He didn't love her. He loved what she gave him. *And it was such a nice breakfast, too,* she thought as she set her plate down. "Three years, Jack. You made me a corrupt agent, the very thing I was supposed to be fighting."

"You put yourself there, not me," Jack said. "I didn't make you into anything you didn't want to be. If you don't want to go back to Opti, fine, but don't go back to WEFT."

"If Opti can't have me, no one can? God, tell me it is more than that," she said bitterly.

"You're better than this!" he exploded, arm waving dramatically, and she had a fleeting memory of seeing him like this before at some forgotten task. "If you try to bring in Michael with that lousy excuse of an anchor Allen Swift, a desked CIA agent, and a . . . a . . . *psychologist,* you're going to get killed."

"Then it's a good thing I can get around that."

"You aren't listening!" he said, his anger somehow comforting. It was real when not much right now was.

"No, you aren't listening to me," she said, not backing down. "We are *done*."

Jaw clenched, he pointed his fork at her. "You need me," he said softly, adamantly.

"It's not about need."

"Sure it is." He returned to eating, stabbing his eggs with angry jabs. "If you're serious about taking Michael down, you need me there to render your drafts back if nothing else."

"Excuse me?"

Jack lifted one shoulder, easing back into the musty chair in an obvious attempt to look harmless. "You think I wouldn't notice you aren't remembering? That you haven't been accelerated? I *know* you. I know you better than you know yourself, babe."

"Don't call me that."

"I'll call you whatever I want. You're not accelerated, but you *are* hooked on Evocane," he said, and it was all she could do to not smack his insufferably confident face. "You need my help to get that secondary source of Evocane. Steiner has one vial. Where is the other? Did that punk in the arena keep one?" he said, the light in his eyes shifting. "I thought so."

"You don't know me at all."

Jack leaned across the table and grabbed her wrist. "I helped make you."

Her lips pressed together. "If you want your hand to keep functioning in the next ten seconds, you will let go of me." She tried to jerk away, but he tightened his grip, his eyes determined.

Peri stiffened to pop him one, but her anger vanished when a second Jack was suddenly standing at the door in a clean suit and tie, listening at the crack. "Babe, someone is coming," the illusion said, and she froze, shocked at seeing them both together like this.

Jack, the real one, saw her sudden fear and he let go. "What?" he asked, staring at the door, obviously not seeing his twin.

"Someone is on the stairs," she whispered. "You called Bill, you bastard!"

"I didn't." The real Jack rose, motions furtive as he padded silently to the door, ready to act. "You still have weapons here, right?"

Her gaze shot to the ceiling, but the faint creaking had ceased and a decisive knock at the door shocked through them, bringing Peri to her feet, pulse fast.

"Peri? Are you in there? I brought an overnight bag."

Silas? Her mouth fell open, and she lurched forward, knee protesting. He found her?

"For God's sake," the hallucination complained. "Another boyfriend. Why do I bother?"

"Denier?" Equally disgusted, Jack rocked back from the door. "You must be bugged."

"I am *not* bugged." Peri walked through the fake Jack, forcing it to vanish. "If anyone is bugged, it's you."

"Babe, if I was bugged, it wouldn't be Denier in the hall."

"I said," she said, angry as she worked the last lock, *"don't call me that!"* Flustered, she opened the door.

"Silas," she said around a whisper, relieved in more than a few different ways. He was there, looking good in his long cashmere coat, a tweed scarf about his neck and his shoes still damp from yesterday's snow. There was a satchel with a WEFT logo in his hands. "How did you find me?"

His eyes rose from her torn and bloodied knee, his expression becoming even more stilted when his attention flicked behind her to Jack. “I’ve been here before,” he said as she took his arm and dragged him in.

Unthinking, she gave in to her impulse and hugged him, needing to go on tiptoe to do it since she didn’t have her boots on. She felt him start, but then his arms went around her, first tentative, then more sure, as if he wasn’t convinced. Cold air puffed up between them as his coat compressed, and her breath caught, but not before she smelled lab cleaner and aftershave. Her thoughts went to her diary and the scant few pages that remained. A need to read them gnawed at her, but she could guess at what remained, and she closed her eyes when a real memory hit her, of her and Silas at a lab bench, the ridiculous safety glasses that she’d decorated with pipe cleaner butterflies rakishly perched on his nose.

He cleared his throat and she let go, uncomfortable knowing Jack was watching.

“Going back to Opti, then?” Silas said, his eyes on Jack as the man took his plate to the kitchen to rinse it. “Seems I owe Harmony a chunk of change.”

“I’m not going to Opti.” Flustered, Peri put space between them.

Jack washed his plate as if nothing was wrong.

"At least you'd be free with Bill," he said, standing sideways so his back wasn't to them. "Steiner is going to put you in a cell. That's why you ran in the first place. Or am I wrong about that, too?"

Silas dropped the bag. It hit with a soft thud that said clothes, not weapons. "There's always option three," he said. "Tie up Jack in a bus station for Steiner and go ghost."

Jack stiffened, his wet hand dripping as he turned. "Like hell you are."

Peri raised a hand in placation, her thoughts more on the chance for a new pair of underwear than their argument. "Hey, hey, hey! Both of you. Silas?" She waited until he looked from Jack to her. "I'm not going back to Opti. I'm not going to WEFT, either. But I can't leave Bill and Michael as a loose end." Her shoulders slumped. "Not this time."

"Besides, killing them would prove she's a good little WEFT agent," Jack said bitingly.

"Shut up!" both Peri and Silas said, and he leaned casually against the sink, ankles crossed as he dried his hands.

Head dropping, Silas hesitated. "Do you mind if I make some coffee?" he finally asked.

She nodded, glad Silas was here but not sure how she was going to handle this new wrinkle. "Go ahead. I don't think there is any, though." Silas went into the kitchen, and she scooped up the bag and took it to the couch to see what he'd brought. *Please, may there be socks.*

Silas scuffed to a halt in the kitchen, facing Jack belligerently until the smaller but far more dangerous man moved aside so Silas could open a cupboard and bring out a teakettle. Jack vacillated for a moment, then sat down at the tiny laminated table as Peri looked through the bag to find a new pair of black jeans and a forest-green V-neck cashmere sweater. Under it was a black turtleneck and yes, three pairs of socks. *He broke out of WEFT to bring me a new set of clothes?* "How mad is Harmony at me?" she asked. "Did Allen tell her this wasn't my idea?"

Silas turned, a fuzzy knitted cover for the teapot in his hand. *Okay, maybe I did manage to finish a project.* "Steiner thinks you're headed back for Opti with Jack. Harmony helped me get out, so it's a fair assumption she still trusts you." Silas pulled open a drawer and set a diffuser on the electric burner to insulate the glass kettle. "She's not very happy, though. Steiner put her on unpaid leave." Mood casual, he opened a cupboard and brought down two mugs. "I wouldn't want to be her tae kwon do partner tomorrow."

Peri watched him, every move precise and deliberate. He knew where everything was, even the instant coffee both she and Jack had missed. Clearly he'd been here more than once, but she didn't remember it. She was tired of forgetting.

Peri glanced at the couch, now recognizing it was his scent in the cushions. *More than a few times, it seemed.* "She helped you escape?" she asked as water chattered into the kettle.

"I find that hard to believe," Jack said as he stretched his legs out under the kitchen table. "They just let you *walk* out the front door?"

Silas dropped the kettle on the burner with a clatter. "That's exactly what happened," he said tightly, his expression easing when he turned to Peri. "I wasn't going to let you run alone, Peri. Not this time. Allen would have been the better choice, but he's beat up, and they watch Harmony too closely." Silas shifted his shoulders as if he was uncomfortable. "Besides, I was the only one without an ankle cuff. So Allen blew up the parking garage. Started a fire in one of the electrical runs. I wanted to bring you Steiner's stash of Evocane, but it's locked down too tight."

Brow furrowed, Silas touched his coat to unconsciously indicate his inner breast pocket, and Peri wondered what was in it if not Evocane. Maybe he was lying for Jack's benefit.

"And yes, I just walked out along with the rest of the firemen," Silas finished, his hand in his pants pocket now. "Allen is probably in a cell, but he can't run with that busted knee."

"It never really healed, did it," she said softly as she dug deeper to the bottom of the satchel past bottles of over-the-counter meds to find the smooth feel of her phone. “Thank you,” she added, relieved that Harmony wasn’t angry with her. “For everything.” She wiggled her phone in explanation before tucking it away in a pocket. Cam had called again.

“It’s clean,” Silas said as if Jack might argue.

From the table, Jack grumbled, “You’re going to bring them right to her.”

“He is not.” Peri’s gaze shifted between the two men, seeing more than casual trouble brewing when Silas lifted a shoulder and let it drop, anger in the slant of his eyes.

“I can get you through the withdrawal,” Silas said. “You’ve only had two doses.”

Jack scoffed, picking at a flake of laminate on the table. “You really think she’d leave without a source of Evocane already in place?”

“She is not going back to Bill,” Silas said firmly.

“Not Bill,” Peri said, wondering whether there was time for another shower now that Silas could watch Jack. “LB.”

“Who is LB?” Silas asked warily.

“The punk who owns the arena,” Jack said, He touched his forehead with a finger, then pointed it at Peri as if they were thinking the same thoughts. “I thought you might leave him one. Good thinking, Peri.”

Like I had a choice? Peri stifled a frown, not wanting to talk about LB in front of Jack. But then again, he’d probably figure it out on his own when she dumped Jack there on the way out. "He's a feral drafter," Peri said softly, and both Silas and Jack jerked.

"He's a what?" Jack exclaimed, his shock too real to be faked.

"A feral drafter," Silas said clearly excited. "In Detroit? Like five minutes from here? Does he know? Does *Steiner* know?"

Peri couldn't help her smile as she shook her head. "I gave LB the down-and-dirty of it. I gave him your number, too. He might call when his curiosity gets the better of him. I told him the Evocane is worthless without the accelerator to make it all work, but he'll probably shoot up with it and get himself hooked anyway."

Silas's expression suddenly dimmed. "You don't need me at all."

Jack chuckled. "No, we don't, little professor."

"Shut up, Jack," Peri said, wishing she didn't have to deal with this right now. Seeing Silas standing before her, still in his coat and scarf, that same broken look on his face she had read about in her diary, gave her a headache, as if something was trying to come back. Disjointed memories that Allen had burned to ash flickered at the edges of her soul, filling her with a need to respond, but not answering why. Within her mind, there was Silas, and her, and a growing feeling that she was being remiss, intentionally keeping herself blind so she could remain safe and alone. But she didn't want to be alone anymore.

Throat closing, she turned away, her focus blurring on the satchel he'd brought. It wasn't just clothes and her phone, but his desire to help her made real. And here she was, not only having voluntarily erased the memories of their love but intentionally keeping herself oblivious to any chance of recall. *Had it been worth it?* She didn't think so anymore.

Taking a resolute breath, Peri touched the clothes, knowing he'd brought them in the belief that he was useless. "I'm glad you're here," she said, voice low so it wouldn't break. "I don't want to go through withdrawal alone. Thank you."

Silas's hands relaxed and his shoulders eased. He glanced at the warming water and then came forward. "You're limping."

Immediately she put her foot up on the low table and pulled the torn slacks up over it.

"I looked at it last night," Jack said from the kitchen. "It's fine."

The couch slid her into Silas when he sat beside her, and she stayed where she was, feeling his warmth against her, trying to recall why it felt so right—but there was nothing.

"When did you get shot?" he asked, brows furrowing.

"I didn't. At least I don't think I did. There's no bullet," she said, then caught her breath when Silas carefully lifted the tape and it pulled. "Ow?"

"Have you put anything on it?" His eyes flicked up, his worry obvious.

"Just an antibiotic. It's not warm, so it's probably not infected."

"I told you I looked at it last night," Jack said, ignored.

Silas pulled the bandage back into place, using the old tape to fix it back down. "I brought some stuff, but nothing for infection. We can stop at a pharmacy. I need to pick up a few things, anyway." His tone caught her intuition, and her eyes jerked to his. Shrugging, he added, "I want to try weaning you off it. Tonight. The more you take, the harder it is."

Peri glanced at the atomic clock on the shelf, understanding. "We can stop on the way to LB's," she said, her ire flashing into existence when Jack cleared his throat in protest. "I want to pick up his vial of Evocane." Fear tightened her gut, fear she might not be able to kick it. "It would probably be easier to wean me off it if you had some."

"You're not ditching me, Peri," Jack threatened as he tugged his sleeves down and fastened the cuffs. "You're going to need someone experienced to bring in Michael. Denier is a couch warrior, a bloody psychologist, and you are his latest pet project."

Silas stood, slipping out from under Peri's soothing hand. "If you don't shut up, I will pop you in the mouth, Twill."

"Try it, big man," Jack taunted. "You will only get her dead." Jack stood from the kitchen table, his motion smooth as he put his suit coat on. It made him look more polished, even if it was dirty and torn. "I bet you can't run a mile without puking."

Peri rubbed her temple. No wonder her head hurt.

Silas ran a hand over his hair and turned to her. "Why is he still alive?"

"He made me breakfast. I was waiting to kill him until he finished the dishes."

The water was boiling, and Jack flicked the burner off. "Very funny. Ha-ha. You need me if for nothing more than to get close to Michael. Admit it. Once you get your Evocane, you're going after him. I'm your ticket in."

Silas eased into the kitchen to stand aggressively before Jack until he moved. "Is he for real?" he asked as he tore open two packets of coffee and filled the mugs with steaming water.

Peri shrugged, thinking the brewed coffee smelled old. "How much cash do you have? Everything I left under the silverware drawer is gone." She took the mug as he handed it to her, grateful even as she felt guilty that he'd risked his life to find her—again. And she was going to ask for more.

"Few thousand, but it's on my phone." Silas's nose wrinkled. "I'm not drinking this."

"Caffeine is caffeine," she said, wondering why Jack was standing before her bookshelves. "What are you doing? Hey!" she exclaimed when he reached for the photo of her on a Harley. That she didn't remember it being taken bothered her, but not enough to throw it away.

"You need money, right?" he said as he took the back off and bills fluttered down to land on the faded braided rug. *Great, he'll never let me forget this,* she thought as he gave it another shake before setting the picture down and crouching to collect the money.

"You've been tucking it away for years," Jack said, his demeanor mild as he extended the bills to her. "A little every time you visited, depending on how fed up you were with Bill at the moment. You said when you got enough, you were going to quit and drive away, but you don't remember that anymore."

Setting down her coffee, she took the bills and made a rough count. "There's enough here for two bikes," she said, shocked, and Jack's lips pressed together tightly.

"You noticed that, huh?" he said stiffly. "I'm going to do right by you, Peri. I promise."

I was going to ride away with him, she thought, not liking that at all. But it did make one thing very clear. Her safe house wasn't safe. Everyone, apparently, knew about it.

"We need to go," she said, deciding her shower would have to wait. "Silas, you remember where I stashed the weapons, right?"

Mug almost lost in his big hands, Silas looked at the ceiling. “We bugging out then?”

“Yep. Soon as I change.” She looked at the coffee mug. “And maybe put that in a paper cup from downstairs.”

“Good.” Silas set his coffee on the counter and dragged the kitchen chair to sit right under the ceiling fan. “You want noisy or quiet?” he asked as he stood on it and carefully lifted a ceiling tile.

“Quiet.” Her knee was throbbing, but she ignored it as she gathered her clothes and headed for the bathroom.

“Noisy,” Jack added.

“You aren’t getting any,” she said, suddenly reluctant to enter the tiny bathroom. It still smelled like Jack’s aftershave, and in a surge of pique, she stalked to the yarn bag, dropping the half-knitted thing into the trash, needles and all. It was an Opti-sanctioned calming technique, and she was done with it. Done with Jack, done with knitting, done with it all.

Silas pulled his head out of the ceiling at the noise, and he and Jack exchanged odd, wondering looks. “If I’m coming with you, I should be armed,” Jack said hesitantly.

“You’re not coming with us,” Silas said, his voice muffled as he stuck his head back into the ceiling. “We’re going to tie you up and leave you here for Steiner.”

"You need me, Peri. You are not leaving me here!" Jack said, louder.

Half in and half out of the bathroom, Peri sighed. "No," she said reluctantly. "We're not."

"Peri . . ." Silas complained as he came back down off the chair, putting two knives, a Glock, several magazines, clips, tactical sound bombs, and a handful of small-radius EMP grenades into her satchel and giving it a shake to settle it all.

Smug, Jack took a dollar out of his wallet and tucked it behind the frame as if it was seed money. "Suck it up, couch warrior. I'm more useful than you."

But that wasn't it. She might not be able to dump Jack in the trash like a ball of yarn and walk away, but she was not letting him back in her life. Not now, not ever. "No weapons," she said, and Jack grinned as if he didn't care. "No phone. If we feel like tying you up or locking you in a closet, you go without complaint. Got it?"

"Sure." Jack flopped onto the couch to wait.

She retreated into the bathroom, unable to tolerate being in the bloody, filthy clothes a second longer if she had clean ones. Silas caught the door as it shut, clearly wanting a private word. "Don't start," she said, knowing just by the slant of his brow where his thoughts were.

"You're going to leave him in the arena, right?" he said softly, his feelings of helplessness almost palpable.

Her eyebrows high, Peri slipped her hand behind his coat, watching him start when she took out the capped syringe. It was the accelerant, and her first flush of disappointment that it wasn't Evocane was lost under a sudden desire to use it—become what she could be, something other than this broken thing that could be used. "Silas," she choked, torn.

He covered her hand, glancing at Jack before angling himself deeper into the bathroom. "I didn't bring it for you. I took it so Steiner can't use it. It might help me create an Evocane substitute. It's poison. You know it."

She nodded, not liking the ugly feeling of want as he took it out of her hand and hid it away again. "You mind if I carry it?" she asked.

He resettled his coat about his shoulders. "I do, actually. Look, I know I'm not the best agent, but I can do more than bring you a new set of clothes and your phone."

His belief that he was not fast or nimble enough to keep up cut her to her soul. "*I* don't need his help. *We* need his help," she said, cupping his face with his hand and drawing his eyes to her. Emotion plinked through her, and feeling uneasy, she looked over his shoulder to where Jack played with the remote. "At least for the moment."

Silas let go, grimacing. "And the second we don't, we leave him behind."

"Absolutely," she said, believing it to her core.

CHAPTER TWENTY-FIVE

The cracked lime-green vinyl seats of the Pinto, which was currently parked outside a fuel station, smelled like crayons. Peri's lip curled as she tried to decide whether she wanted to touch the vent to angle the warm air from the running engine to her, or just live with the damp chill that gripped Detroit despite the afternoon sun. Jack's sigh was heavy from the cramped back, and her eyes shifted from the refueling station's twin glass doors to him. He'd wanted to jack a BMW using her phone and an app that connected him to the owner's security company, but she'd nixed it, wanting the less obtrusive, no-computer Pinto instead—even if it was a POS.

Silas was inside, changing her Harley fund into p-cash connected to a new, neutral phone. She'd pulled into the upscale hydrogen station under the excuse that there would be little traffic, but the reality was that she'd wanted to get a closer look at the new Jaguar parked under the refueling kiosk, the pack panel open as the black expended cylinders were exchanged for shiny new white ones.

It hadn't taken her long to realize how badly she'd chosen when the government drones began to drop in and take off from the quick charge on the roof. Apparently Detroit had given the Feds a place to recharge their surveillance drones in exchange for subsidizing the expensive hydrogen stations, technology still so new that stations couldn't survive on their own. She was making mistakes, either from fatigue or worry, and she didn't like it.

A woman with two kids came out of the associated convenience store, squinting at the sudden light and cold. Fumbling for their hands, she headed for the nearby rail stop. The wind gusted, billowing her coat and drawing Peri's attention to the nearby fallow green space where last year's faded banners flapped, put there to discourage the local deer population that made their home amid the skyscrapers and light commerce. A new species was evolving, smaller, less sensitive to noise and dogs, and having the occasional white coat. They kept the environment students at Detroit University busy charting their slow, steady domestication.

A whining hiss gave her warning, and Peri lowered her head as another drone dropped in.

"He's taking too long," Jack said, and her thoughts went to the smut stick she'd found at her apartment. Adding a little facial-recognition deterrent would only get her noticed, though.

"I'll go in and see if he needs some help," Jack added.

Peri smoothly slipped Silas's Glock from the satchel and angled it toward him, the flat finish glinting dully in the sun. "Stay in the car."

Eyebrows high in challenge, he reached for the door, never dropping her gaze.

"Please, continue. It will make my life so much easier," she said, smiling painfully. She wanted a memory that would only hurt her. Had she and Jack really been squirreling money to buy bikes? Her bank account had once held more than enough. The money behind the frame had been a promise, not a gathering of funds.

Jack hesitated, then eased back into the seat. "You are such a bitch when you don't get your sleep," he said, and satisfied, Peri tucked the Glock away as two late teens got into the Jag and drove off. They were laughing at her Pinto, and Peri scowled. She didn't do anything without a reason—even if she didn't know what it was, exactly.

Her phone, on the dash in case Silas called, lit up. She scrambled for it, her adrenaline falling when she saw it was Cam. "I'm taking this," she said, thoughts shifting to her cat. "Keep your mouth shut."

"I would've brought you back your favorite candy bar," Jack grumped, falling into an untidy mess in the back.

"You don't know my favorite candy bar," she muttered, hitting the accept key. But the truth was, she didn't know what it was, either; her memory of it being a Three Musketeers bar when she had been ten was probably out-of-date. "Hi, Cam. Everything okay?"

"Peri!" Cam's voice was warm and concerned, making her feel guilty. She'd forgotten all about him. "I half expected your voicemail. I was calling to ask you the same thing."

Jack opened his mouth, and she jiggled her grip on the phone so she could aim the Glock at him. Grimacing, he changed his mind. The shot would be awkward with one hand, but at this range, even a miss would hurt. "Could be better," she said. *Hurry up, Silas.* "How's Carnac?"

"Fine. Do you have a better idea of when you'll be picking him up?"

She could hear the soft patter of a news program and the whirr of a can opener. He was working from home, then. "Uh, no. Sorry." Jack was laughing at her, and her face flamed. "Hey, this actually isn't a good time," she said when Jack draped his arm over the back of the seat so he could hear better.

"You've got a strange man cat sitting for us?" Jack asked loudly.

"There is no us," she whispered harshly, phone to her shoulder to block her voice. Then to Cam, "Can I call you back?"

"Sure, no problem." He sounded embarrassed. "You are coming back. Right?"

Peri half turned away to hide her flush from Jack. "Right." But even as she said it, she knew she was never going to return to the coffeehouse again—apart from clearing out the weapon's stash, maybe. The peace she'd found there was gone. Bill had stolen it, and she had let him.

"You're not coming back," Cam said flatly, and Jack, hearing everything, smiled cattily.

"Cam," she pleaded, hating Jack for seeing this. "I want to."

"No, I got it," Cam said, his tone almost hiding the hurt. "Don't worry about Carnac. He's a good cat. I'll take care of him."

"Cam— Hey!" she exclaimed when Jack yanked the phone from her.

"God, Cam," Jack said, laughing as he fended her off. "Give the woman a break. She's got a lot on her mind right now."

"Knock it off!" Smacking Jack smartly, she got the phone and settled into the front seat. "Cam?" But he was gone, and she hit the end icon in disgust. "Did he hear you?"

Still smiling, Jack shrugged. "He sounds as if he's got money. Is he nice?"

Her head was pounding, and she glanced at the convenience store and the flickering e-board ads as she considered calling him back. But what would be the point? "Let's play the quiet game, okay?" she said as she put her phone away.

Jack's smile grew wider. "Why are we in this

piece of crap?" he asked, kicking the back of the seat. "I think someone threw up back here."

"Because I normally wouldn't touch it, and the less I am of myself, the longer I'll survive," she said sarcastically as she tucked the Glock away. If he left now, she'd let him get halfway across the parking lot before she shot him in the back—the government's high-Q drones dropping in and out be damned.

The satchel was beside her, and she moved it to the floor out of Jack's easy reach. It shouldn't take this long to turn bills to p-cash, and worry tightened her shoulders. "Why did you agree to take Michael's place at the arena?" she finally asked.

"Ahh, thinking at last, eh?" he said, eyeing her from under his lowered brow.

"Never mind," she muttered, turning her back on him.

"Aww, come on, Peri," he coaxed as he leaned over the seat again. "Don't you get it? I'm not here for Bill. I'm here for you. After you get your Evocane from LB, why don't we just run?"

"Run?" she said bitterly as she fingered her coat's zipper. The familiar scent of Jack's aftershave plinked through her, triggering half memories that lingered to feed her doubt. They'd been good together. It was in the way he knew just what to say; she had sensed it when they had escaped. She could feel it in her soul as clearly as she could feel Silas's longing for her to remember.

"Why not?" he said, sounding reasonable. "Just put the car in drive, go to the arena, get the Evocane. And . . . leave." He hesitated. "With me," he finished softly. Vulnerably.

He made it sound easy. That's all she wanted. Peace.

Hearing cracks in her resolve within the silence, he edged closer. She dropped her head into her hand, pushing at her temples as her head throbbed. "I can get you through the next twenty-four hours," he urged. "If you want, I can bring it all back. Or we can just start from where we are now. How about it? We'd be free. We could do what we want. Stay off the grid."

It hurt so bad, she had to close her eyes.

"It will be better than before," he coaxed. "Just the two of us. And Carnac. We can pick him up on the way out. Wherever you want to go."

She jerked, her eyes clamped shut when his hesitant touch landed on her shoulder. Emboldened, his fingers searched, moving until they found the trigger point in her shoulder, and he gently pressed, relaxing her. Her eyes began to jerk, wanting to slip into REM.

"I know you better than anyone, Peri," he whispered. "We had a good life. We can start over with just the good stuff in it this time, none of the bad. No WEFT. No Opti. Just us. Remember how good it was?"

She didn't, but her body did, and her throat closed at the chance to find a peace that never existed. Her eyes opened, and with her focus blurry with regret, she whispered, "I'm going crazy."

"Not with me around," Jack said, lips inches from her ear and his whispered words sending her thoughts in a new direction as he'd done a hundred times before.

She stiffened.

Jack's hands sprang away and he flung himself to the back of the car as she turned, her swinging backhand just missing him. "Don't touch me," she demanded.

"If that's what you want," he said casually from the back, but it didn't feel like a win.

His eyes flicked past her to the store, and she turned, relieved when Silas's heavy but trim form jogged across the lot, dodging the incoming Nightwing, the car as sleek and powerful as old Detroit. "It is," she said, starting the Pinto and putting it into drive.

"He's not your magic bag of rocks, babe. I am."

"Leaving you dead in this car is still an option." Leaning, she unlocked Silas's door.

Jack sprawled over the seat, putting his face inches from hers. "I know you. You fight it, thinking it makes you a better person. But you are who you are. And the sooner you accept that, the happier you'll be. What the hell is wrong with being happy? You don't owe anyone anything."

He retreated as Silas opened the door, leaving her alone with her thoughts as he slid in.

"Sorry it took so long," Silas said, and she hit the accelerator. Drawn by the noise, the old couple getting out of the Nightwing looked up from their phones. "LB called, and I wanted to take it," he added as he lurched for the swinging door, finally getting it shut as she hit a bump. "Are we in a hurry?"

"Too many cameras," she said as she looked both ways and bounced onto the street as if no one else was on it. The tiny engine puttered, hardly moving as it spewed a blue smoke. *God, I miss my Mantis.*

"You kept your phone, too?" Jack said from the back, the click of his belt obvious. "We are so caught."

Silas gave him a dry look. "I'm beginning to understand why you're upset at me for making him the focus of your hallucinations," he said, then louder, "Allen checked it out before I left. Cleaned it. I'm not stupid."

"No, but Allen is," Jack smart-mouthed. "If Michael doesn't kill you, Peri, Denier will."

Peri's grip tightened on the wheel; she wanted to weave through traffic but was hardly able to keep up. *Why did I want this POS? Am I punishing myself?*

"I'm not going to kill Peri," Silas said, looking cramped in the front seat of the tiny car.

"You can't help it," Jack said. He appeared marginally more comfortable in the backseat. "She'll trust you, and you won't be up for the task, and *you* will get her killed."

The upcoming light changed to yellow, but the thought of sitting unmoving was unbearable. Jerking the wheel sharply, she wove around the slowing car ahead of her to make the light, glancing back to see whether a traffic drone was chasing her down for a shot of her license plate. It wasn't, and she exhaled, settling into the tired, worn vinyl. "I'm tired of pulling myself off the grid every time we need to stop for munchies," she muttered.

Not liking her weave-and-accelerate, Silas put his belt on. "Better that than waking up tomorrow thinking you're Suzy Homemaker."

"I'm not going to scrub her," Jack said, his words going right to her core and twisting.

"Will both of you shut up? I can't remember if the arena is up or down from here," Peri said.

Silas gave Jack a look, clearly thinking he'd won something. "Down, but keep going uptown," he said, and she shifted lanes erratically to take the next right. "We aren't going to the arena. Thank God."

"Why not?"

"LB doesn't want you down there." Silas

gripped the door handle, clearly uncomfortable with how close she was to the bumper of the car ahead of her.

"He used it all?" she said in disbelief, but Silas was shaking his head.

"He doesn't want you near his people. He's waiting for us at Roosevelt Park."

Peri exhaled in relief, not caring that Jack was learning just how freaked out she was about needing that Evocane. "Fine," she said, thinking it was a good spot. Lots of ways out, lots of ways in. He'd find her.

But even as Peri drove crosstown, doubt began to trickle through her, born from a lack of intel. The interstate would be faster, but the entrance ramps had cameras. They'd sat too long in that parking lot. As much as she wanted to trust Allen, she knew that if someone was going to bug you, they'd find a way.

Rosa Parks Boulevard was busy, and no one would let her over, the dilapidated state of the Pinto doing her no favors. "I hate Detroit traffic!" she shouted, leaning on the horn. "We should have just taken the necklace. We would have been there by now!"

"You mind if I drive?" Silas offered, and Peri scoffed, shifting gears as if it was a race car. "No, really," he said again, pale. "There's a station right there."

Jack spun to look out the back window. "No,

don't!" he exclaimed, tense as he looked the way they'd come. "I know that guy."

Sweet adrenaline poured into her, banishing her worry like the extravagant luxury it was. Eyes bright, she looked behind her at the black car, meeting Jack's gaze in the rearview mirror. The sly anticipation in his expression was familiar, kindling a long-muted desire to outlast the odds until they shifted to their favor. "Go. Now. Fast," he said, and she quivered, the silver sensation born from a thousand forgotten tasks. It felt like home.

She couldn't get into the right lane, but she could cross the boulevard to the other side. Teeth clenched, she jerked the wheel.

"Peri!" Silas shouted as she jumped the curb, tearing up the frozen landscape as she bounced into the eastbound lane, horns honking and tires squealing behind her. "God bless it. This was just what I was trying to avoid!"

"They echoed!" Jack exclaimed, and she hit the gas, the car hardly moving. "I told you we should have taken the BMW. This thing can't run worth crap!"

"I *didn't* want the fricking *BMW!*" Peri leaned on the horn, and people began to move. But it only made it easier for the guy behind them. They caught up fast, but she began to smile, her pulse fast and easy.

Silas braced himself against the dash. "Don't

antagonize them," he said, seeing the gleam in her eye. "Please?"

"But that's the best part, Silas," she said slyly. The truth was, though, if she didn't shake them in forty seconds, the cops would be on them as well. *Which might not be a bad idea, actually.*

"Stairs!" Jack pointed out, and Silas gasped when she jumped the curb and took the wide, shallow steps down into a new downtown commerce court. The smaller car might make it where the bigger car following them wouldn't.

"Are they still with us?" she stammered in time with the steps, her breath coming in a heave when they hit the end with a scrape. She accelerated, people jumping out of the way and staring. A high-Q traffic drone swung in behind them, its stabilizers screaming louder than the siren. "Jack! Are they with us!"

Jack looked out the back window, ducking at the squeal of brakes and pop of weapons. "Dude, they're serious. Can you squeeze out a few more miles per hour?"

"No." Her hands were sweating, and it felt wonderful.

"Ahh, it's a pedestrian mall," Silas said, voice thick with panic as he realized where they were. "There's no way out. Peri? Peri!"

"Then we make one. Coming about!" she exclaimed, jerking the wheel to the right to the new construction, blocked off with a temporary chain-link fence.

"Peri!" Silas shouted, and she locked her arms as they rammed it, hitting the gas to make the snow spurt up behind them as the gate flipped and swung. Bouncing over the ruts, they rocked through the construction site and back onto the service road behind it. The drone came even, and Peri waved when it got a good image of them and dropped back.

"They're still there," Silas said, slumping in his seat as they sped past Dumpsters and parked employee cars. "That didn't slow them down at all. We need the interstate."

"This car can't run for shit," Jack said in disgust. "The interstate is a death trap."

"Which is exactly what we want." Peri smiled as she recognized where she was. Roosevelt Park was a few miles up the road. Perfect. "We need to get rid of WEFT. Jack, full moon tonight?"

"Wha-a-at?" he stammered as she revved the engine hard, horn blowing as she skidded to a halt in front of a café, window rolled down as she screamed obscenities and waved a finger in the air at the cop car parked outside.

"Peri, you promised," Silas complained as a second traffic drone joined the first, the human voice projecting from it demanding they stop and wait for Detroit personnel.

"No, I didn't." She was breathless, and the tires

squealed as she took off in the other direction, headed for the interstate. They'd follow.

"That did it," Jack said, arms braced as she swerved through traffic. "You got 'em."

"You got them?" Silas exclaimed, his face pale. "You want the cops on our ass?"

"For the moment," she said, grinning wildly. "Jack?"

He looked behind them, eyes bright. "Find some space. They won't act if it's crowded."

"Expressway on the right."

Silas's expression brightened. "You're going to have the cops get rid of WEFT?"

Her head bobbed and she milked a few miles per hour out of the puttering engine. Grinning, she waited until the last moment to turn onto the expressway, skidding to cut off a gold Cadillac. It lay on the horn, but she floored it, feeling the WEFT car creeping up behind her as the traffic drones fell behind, unable to keep up. Far behind were sirens, but they had radios, and once she was committed to one direction, they'd take steps.

"Would it help if I got out and pushed?" Jack asked, his arms draped over the seat.

"Maybe," she said, but her smile never dimmed even as Silas's face paled.

"Well, they'd better hustle," Jack complained. "This car doesn't have enough power. We should have taken the BMW."

"Will you get off my case about the BMW!"

Peri jerked the wheel to give the WEFT car pulling up beside them a little love tap. The five men in it looked affronted, and she hit them again when one of them pulled a weapon. *Don't you dare shoot at me.*

"Peri?" Silas warned, but the cops had finally caught up and people were pulling their cars to the side, making it easier to maneuver.

"Wait for it. Wait for it . . ." she muttered, smacking the wheel in success when the WEFT car chasing them began to quickly decelerate. "There they go!" she exclaimed, trying to coax a few more miles per hour from the choking Pinto as the WEFT car stalled, a victim of technology. If Jack had an app to steal it, it was a good bet the cops had one to bring it down.

Exhilarated, she looked behind them and the four cop cars swarming over the WEFT vehicle. Two more followed her, the unchanging distance between them saying they had something to slow her down, something more mundane than remotely shutting off the car's computer.

"Okay," Jack said moodily. "You were right. The BMW was a bad idea."

"Man, I hope I remember this," she whispered, wondering just how far they'd get before the TV helicopter showed.

"Park coming up," she said, spotting the sign. "Silas, grab what you want to keep."

"We're going to outrun them on foot?" he

questioned as he felt his pockets. His eyes were wide, and she felt a pang through her.

"Oh, look," Jack pointed out casually. "Two cops on the exit ramp and one on the overpass."

"Not using the exit ramp," she said, alive as she sent tendrils of thought out into the universe, reading the currents of time, nestling a hole in it that she could use. "Ready?"

"Oh. Shit," Silas whispered, hands braced on the dash. "She's going to do it again."

"Spike strip!" Jack shouted as it slid out from behind the overpass. Hands clenched, she swerved.

"Too tight!" Jack called out. "Too tight!"

"I can see that!" she exclaimed, losing control as one wheel hit the spike strip and they skidded, the back end sliding majestically into a pylon.

They rocked to a halt, and Peri looked up, heart pounding. Outside, the cops screeched to a halt, weapons pointed and the men screaming at them to get out. Her nose wrinkled. *Gas?*

"This is one of the retrofitted Pintos, right?" Jack asked.

And then the back end exploded.

Instinct jerked into play. Peri's vision shifted blue, and she cried out, a stab of pain slicing through her forehead. And then . . . she drafted.

CHAPTER TWENTY-SIX

The Pinto's engine sputtered, exhilaration filling her as they sped down the expressway, headed for the overpass and the unseen spike strip.

"Let's steal the Pinto," Jack said mockingly as the WEFT vehicle was left behind, swarmed by the cops like ants on a caterpillar. "I love a car that explodes when you hit it."

Face white, Silas watched the chaos go distant through the rearview mirror. "Watch for the spike strip," he said as he braced his arms. "Right side. If you slow down at the exact moment, it will pass in front of you."

She'd put them five, maybe six seconds back, not wanting to lose chunks of time. But with Jack in the car, it might not matter. The spike strip was the least of her worries, and her sweat went cold. She couldn't jump without opening her mind, making it vulnerable.

"I swear, Jack, if you scrub me, I will kill you," she threatened, and Silas's eyes widened, echoing her new fear. "You hear me!" she exclaimed. "Silas is an anchor, and he'll know! If you touch my mind, I will kill you twice!"

"Spike strip!" Silas reminded them, pointing.

"Screw it!" she yelled, jerking the wheel again as the strip slid out.

"Yeee-haa!" Jack shouted as the tires skipped, narrowly keeping them on the road as they sped around it. His exuberant cry seemed to bounce against the dash and explode into red sparkles. She breathed them in, hands clenched in fear. *If he touches me, I'll kill him,* she thought.

And then she exhaled, and forgot.

Her head seemed to split apart, and she gasped as the world snapped back into place.

"I didn't touch your mind!" Jack exclaimed, one arm clamped over the seat to put his face next to hers. "You swerved to avoid a spike strip, hit the wall, and drafted."

Dizziness swam up from the sound of the racing engine, and she looked at Silas, who nodded. She glanced behind them, seeing the cop car hit the strip instead. The car behind it swerved to miss him, overcompensated, and hit the wall. *Two down.*

Jack retreated into the backseat, content for the moment. "Damn!" he whispered, clearly happy. "I missed you, Peri. We have *got* to get off this road, though."

Three high-powered Fed drones swung into place overhead, their stronger charge maintaining the eighty miles an hour the Pinto could manage. They were passing the park, but two more cars had filed in behind, closing the gap. They had maybe seconds between them, no more. "We're ditching the car. Hold on," she muttered as she yanked the car off the road, bouncing over a ditch, through a wire fence.

Pain thundered in her head and neck, and she realized she'd hit her head on the ceiling. Dizzy, she aimed for the parking lot. Dead grass and icy clods of mud spurted up behind them. LB would be there. He had to be.

"There!" One hand on the ceiling, Jack pointed between them out the front window. "LB's trident!"

Her head still hurt, and she blinked fast to focus. Suddenly she realized she was going to pass out.

"Peri!" Silas shouted as her body went slack. "Take your foot off the gas! Take it off!"

Eyes closed, she distantly heard the Pinto's engine race. Jack swore, and then her head swung forward as they hit something. Arms limp, she let go of the wheel. The engine choked and died. "Ow," she whispered, squinting at the sudden flush of cold air.

"Shit, woman. You know how to make an entrance." Someone smelling of pot and old cigarettes leaned close, and she struggled to focus. It was LB, and as Silas fumbled at her belt, LB stood over them, his hands on his hips. She could hear kids in the background, and the pop of a gun followed by a cheer.

"Thank God you're here," she slurred, slapping Silas's hands away. "I can do it myself," she said, but her fingers wouldn't work. "Where's my bag?" She blinked, relieved when Silas pushed it into her hand.

LB fidgeted at her open door, impatient. "I got my boys out here on the excuse to shoot down some payloads," the scrawny man said. "There's a droneway that passes over the park. It's off our turf, but letting them take potshots at them got enough of them out here that any local cops will think twice." His gaze went to the horizon. "There they are."

She could hear sirens, and the sudden bang and cheer when someone took out a drone. Peri blinked fast, her grip on her bag easing as her vision settled. "I thought Roosevelt belonged to the Scraps."

"Okay, she's good," Silas said from beside her, and LB grabbed her arm.

"There haven't been any Scraps since the early two thousands," LB said as he pulled her out. "Me and the boys are Detroit's last gang."

Somehow she thought that was a real shame as she found her feet, swaying until Silas came around the car and took her elbow. By the frozen pond, six people looking like *Mad Max* extras were taking turns shooting at drones, three Detroit muscle cars behind them looking used and aggressive. Several families with kids watched at the outskirts—not afraid. "Jack? Where's Jack?" she said, then threw herself to the ground when a drone flying overhead exploded.

LB and Silas ducked, but it was Jack who yanked her up, frowning at LB's boys, laughing at the drone pinwheeling dramatically to crash and skid on the ice. "That was a Fed," Jack said as he pushed Peri to the nearby van, brown with flaking paint and rust. "Only the Feds put self-destructs on their bees. Get her out of here. I'll draw them off."

"Hey, wait!" Peri protested, but things were happening fast, and LB whistled three sharp notes in quick succession, turning heads.

"Back on the boats!" LB shouted, and people moved, gathering downed payloads and running for the cars.

"Jack is not running rabbit," Peri said, frowning at the flashing lights of the incoming cops. Only now did the watching families scatter, which she thought was telling.

"Get in the car," LB demanded, then turned to Jack. "Take the Charger. It can handle a hit. Ed will get you clear, then you run. None of my boys are taking the rap for this."

"No," Peri said, all but ignored. "Jack comes with me. I want him in LB jail."

"I'll drive the Charger," Silas demanded, then yelped when three big men pushed him into the back of a brown '67 Pontiac GTO. His protests became violent until LB shoved her in with him, her short-job bag landing atop them both. The seat flipped back, trapping them, and Silas glowered as LB and another man got in front. "Don't let Jack go. It's a mistake!" he exclaimed as the angry engine rumbled to life, the road joined by the Dodge Charger and Oldsmobile.

"A big, beautiful mistake," Peri whispered, numb as Jack in the Charger took off, leaving them and the Oldsmobile to go the other way. Jack was going to give the cops something to chase while they got away. And in turn, he'd be gone as well. *Effin' fantabulous.*

Silas was rummaging in the satchel, his motions becoming more and more frantic. "What is your problem?" she finally asked, and he looked up, grabbing the seat as they jostled off the parking lot and onto the grass.

"I'm not used to being the smallest man in the room," he muttered, hesitating with a Glock in his hand until seeing LB's guy riding shotgun, using a rifle to take out the drones following them. "God bless it, I think Jack took it!"

Peri held on to the door with one hand and propped herself up with the other. "Took what?"

Silas kept looking, shoving everything from one side to the other. "The accelerator. He only touched the bag for like three seconds to hand it to me, and he took it!"

Immediately she relaxed. "No, he didn't. It's in my sock." Guilt flickered through her, not for having lifted it earlier, but for the remembered flash of desire when she'd stuffed it away.

Silas's eyes went from her foot to her face, his fear fighting with his obvious relief that she hadn't used it. "What's it doing there?"

"Not getting stolen by Jack," she said, the lure to inject herself even stronger after having drafted to escape both WEFT and Detroit's finest. Forcing a smile, she zipped the satchel closed. As long as she wasn't accelerated, she could still walk away from this and disappear. *Maybe.* "LB, where did you get these righteous cars?" she asked as they bounced and lurched over the grass, clods of frozen ground spurting up behind them.

Behind the wheel, LB grinned, turning where he sat to see them. "When everyone left, the cars stayed behind. As long as there's no computer, my guys can get them running; eBay does the rest." His eyebrows rose in question. "Dr. Denier? You're the reason I'm here. I want to talk to you."

"Sure," Silas said guardedly. His attention alternated between LB and the front window as they careened over the park lawn, headed for a distant street. "Don't you think you should be looking where you're driving?"

But there were no lines to stay within, much less a road, and LB laughed. "Shit, girl, you look like you haven't slept in days. There're easier ways to make a pickup than bringing the entire Detroit police force with you."

Her pulse leapt. "You have the Evocane," she said, an unreasonable need rising from everywhere, crushing the faint vertigo. "Right now? With you?" With a final bounce, they found the road. Behind them, his guys were taking potshots at the drones that had followed them. Most were going the other way. Jack had bought her a way out. What it might cost her would probably be more than she wanted to pay.

LB turned back to the front, weaving between the slower cars. "Yep."

"Give it to me. Now," she demanded, and LB met her eyes in the rearview mirror. With a casual slowness, he took a vial from his shirt pocket and tossed it to her.

It hit her palm, and she spun the warm glass to read the label, a flicker of mistrust dying at the thought he might have put anything in it. If it wasn't Evocane, she'd bring him down. "Thank you," she said softly as she dropped it into the satchel and zipped it closed.

"Don't thank me," LB said, his expression empty. "Nothing is free."

Silas stiffened, and she raised her hand, telling him she'd handle it. "Yeah? Be nice, or I'll shove it down your throat," she threatened.

"How do you know I haven't sampled it already?" LB said slyly, and she relaxed.

"Because if you had, you'd die before giving it to me." Satisfied it was Evocane, she settled back, thinking it was odd that she was safe in the back of a drug lord's GTO. "You shouldn't have let

Jack run rabbit." Damn it, she had been hoping LB would hold him for her, and the man just let him walk.

Thoughtful, LB followed the finger of the man riding shotgun to an upcoming exit. "Relax. The cops will get him. And if not, we will."

"Yeah? Good luck with that," she said, then went silent, feeling her fatigue all the way to her bones. Despite what LB had said, she knew Jack was gone until he wanted to show. Worse, she didn't know how she felt about that. She didn't remember her draft, but she'd seen his eyes afterward. He hadn't touched her mind—and even with Silas there, it had been the perfect time to scrub her.

He was there for her, not Bill, and that changed everything . . . and nothing at all.

CHAPTER TWENTY-SEVEN

The Packard's main mall lacked the comfortable, familiar feel the repurposed automotive manufacturing plant usually did. It rankled Jack that it was probably because Peri wasn't beside him, her slim, attractive figure drawing envious, appreciative glances, a reminder of how good they looked together. He got noticed on his own, but with Peri, the stares were envious.

His attention drifted from the high support beams—repaired or replaced and acid etched to look old—down to his drink. The heavy paper straw he was using to stir his caramel banana smoothie had bent, and he grimaced. His hand ached, strained somewhere on Peri's mad dash to Roosevelt Park, and he wished he'd gotten a frozen drink instead of the room-temperature fruit blend. Evading the local cops, and then LB's gang after that, hadn't been difficult. He'd been lucky that Peri had been knocked on the head and dazed; otherwise she'd never have let him drive off, the gang's need for a rabbit or not. The only crime he regretted was having to dump the classic muscle car in the river.

The mall was busy, the cinema having just let out its largest theater and sending almost seven hundred pumped-up moviegoers back into the upscale shops that lined the three-block social sink Detroit had created for their new population to spend their money and time.

The Packard plant had been abandoned in the late fifties after having helped supply marine and aircraft engines for WWII. Almost vanishing from neglect, it was revitalized when it was realized that the distance between I-94 and Detroit's rebuilt center was perfect. The derelict complex had been turned into a shopping experience like no other, where you could do everything from train your dog to publish your self-help video to enjoy a gourmet meal at one of the themed cafeterias or bars, before sleeping it off in one of the tiny hotel rooms affectionately named coffins. The complex was so large and sprawling that self-propelled vintage autos ran an assembly-line track right down the middle and through the more affluent shops: a loving nod to Detroit's history.

But old cars on tracks were less than useless to Jack, and giving up on his smoothie, he squinted up to the second-story level, where Harmony was burning off some steam in one of the athletic centers. The front of the dojo was glass, and the mixed class sparred over oblivious shoppers, their thumps and shouts muffled but audible over the surrounding chatter and the young-man band from Australia, in town and mixing up their rhythms with old black men who'd never left Detroit and lived the beat their entire rich lives.

Even as he watched, the class ended. Jack didn't move as Harmony chatted with a few of her friends before vanishing out of his line of sight and presumably downstairs. Uneasy, Jack resettled himself against the maple tree growing smack-dab in the middle of the walkway. According to urban legend, the tree had been growing out of the abandoned building when the developers had moved in. It had been allowed to remain, stretching to the distant glass ceiling as a reminder of how fragile man's works were. It was Peri's favorite spot in the mall—he had no clue why. An unexpected flash of angst lit through him at the reminder of her.

Perhaps Peri wasn't the only one conditioned to never be alone, he thought, then threw his half-empty cup away in disgust, deciding to blame his unease on his lack of a weapon. Outwitting TSA was a hell of a lot easier than bypassing the mall's subtly integrated but efficient weapons detectors. Fortunately not all the toys in his pockets went *bang.*

There was a soft chime and the receptacle beside him shifted from white to black. It was full, and with a slow movement, it began to move to the nearest reception niche for cleaning. Jack watched it go, his mood lifting when it stopped short, stymied by two boys messing with its obstacle recognition software until their mother jerked them out of its way.

The crowd at the end of the hall cheered at the rising, complex rhythms coming faster from the freestyle concert. The memory of his and Peri's last vacation flitted through him, the way she had found common ground with people so far from her. He didn't understand how she could do that and still not love him. He hadn't lied to her about his feelings; she had just extrapolated far beyond what they actually were.

Eyes going to the dojo's first-floor door, Jack straightened his newly purchased tie, glad he knew people here, people who would float him a suit without question, three years of healthy tips keeping their mouths shut about his ever having been in. A faint smile crossed Jack's face. Detroit wasn't his city, but he knew his way around her underskirts almost as well as Peri did. He chuckled when a memory intruded, of him and Peri at the big billiard hall over where the executive offices had once been. They'd capped the evening off with drinks and dancing in the members-only club. The view of Detroit always turned her soft and compliant—daring.

Jack's smile faltered. He had to get Peri back. He had no intention of retiring, and he'd become too accustomed to being bulletproof.

Good mood broken, he sat down on the ironworks bench, his knees spread wide as he waited. He didn't need Harmony; he wanted her was all. The woman was a source of information, a buffer for when he found Peri, and cannon fodder in case there was trouble. This doubt that gnawed at him was becoming tiresome.

He hadn't lied when he told Bill he thought he could flip her back to Opti, but now he wasn't so sure. The lure of remembering wasn't as strong as Bill thought it would be. She didn't need them. Didn't need him. And that was more than dangerous, it was potentially deadly.

He was nothing without Peri, an easily replaced cog. Only with her could everything return to as it had been. He might have romanced an understanding between them by promising to go ghost with her, but neither one of them would be able to stand such a mundane life. He just needed to get her away from Denier long enough for her to remember how good they had been. If that failed, he'd scrub her. She'd thank him in the end. And if she wanted Bill dead, he would keep that option open, too. Maybe then she'd believe him.

Finally Harmony came out of the dojo, hesitating with her friends before the door. Jack's eyes narrowed in concern, watching from under the drape of his bangs, but the thin woman in her colorful leggings said good-bye and went the other direction, a heavy tote bag over her shoulder and a sassy sway to her hips as she wove through the shoppers.

Sucking his teeth, Jack rose and fell into step behind her, careful to keep her red cap just in sight. He was glad to have had the chance to see Harmony in action. Peri had taught him a healthy respect for what a woman could do, and he was used to maintaining a delicate balance of restraint without injury when dealing with them. He had Harmony on weight if nothing else.

He almost lost her as he fended off two saleswomen trying to lure him into sampling a fragrance. The slight pause in motion triggered a trio of holographic mannequins from the upscale clothier, and they shifted to match his day-old stubble and tailored suit, trying to lure him in. It jerked the passing bevy of ogling girls to a stop, slowing him even more.

Peeved, he pushed past them, leaving giggles and requests for his number in his wake.

His breath quickened as he hustled to catch up. Adrenaline trickled through him, and he sent his eyes to the droneway high at the ceiling, the stream of low-Q drones and their payloads looking like Hogwarts owls. Just below them, the fixed cameras recorded a four-hour loop of happy shoppers before they began to rewrite over themselves. As long as he was quiet, all evidence of his presence would be erased by midnight.

Still, his pulse was faster than the small task warranted, as if failure here would translate into failure everywhere. His anger slowly grew as justifications began flitting through him. He didn't need Harmony's help, but he wasn't used to working alone, either. A second pair of eyes, the comfort found from two predators as opposed to the solitary hunter—both would be helpful. She'd be the easily sacrificed tail of the team so he might survive.

He almost missed it when the woman strode confidently into a narrow hallway, a highly monitored, underground shortcut to one of the other buildings and the elevated rail. It might be empty, the break in the weather drawing most people into the skyway and the view of Detroit.

His pace quickened, his head down to avoid

being lured into looking at the main camera when the TV under it blared an attention-getting cartoon.

Who doesn't like Tom and Jerry? he thought wryly, taking a tiny EMP button from his pocket and readying it. Peri hadn't noticed him lifting it, whereas she would have missed the Glock he would have rather taken. The tactical blast would short out anything transmitting within a thirty-foot radius, cameras included, and he checked to make sure his phone was off.

Her heels clicked smartly, her voice pleasant as she said hi to the woman with two kids in a stroller passing her. Jack slid to the side and nodded, waiting until the kids' voices vanished before looking up again. There was no guilt in him for using Harmony. If she was after Michael, she was dead anyway, and where Michael and Bill were, Peri was sure to follow.

Motion confident, Harmony reached for one of the double glass doors that led to the stairway. Jack's hair shifted in the equalizing pressure, and he jogged to catch up as it swung closed. Her feet were vanishing up the curve of the stairway. Eager, he hit the EMP button and raced up the stairs.

Instinct screamed, and he ducked as he spun onto the next landing, turning it into a controlled fall as he hit the cement. A stick of wood rapped smartly on the worn iron railing above him.

"You picked the wrong woman to jump, candy ass," Harmony said, and he scuttled backward to the cement block wall as she made ready to swing at him again.

"Wait—" he managed, and then her eyes widened in surprise.

"You," she whispered, stepping forward, the whoosh of air from her martial arts baton making him slip down a few stairs. It was padded, but it would still hurt.

"I'm looking for Peri," he said, then used his arm to block a kick, retreating a few steps more.

"Aren't we all." Harmony pulled back, her frown deepening when she noticed the little red light was out on the camera in the corner. Lips pressed together, she slipped her bag from her shoulder and gracefully iced down two steps, body balanced and ready to smack his head as if it were a softball on a tee. "Funny us running into each other. Steiner will never believe it. I sure as hell don't."

Jack put his hands up in placation. "She didn't betray you. She was running. I was running. We didn't plan it."

"I don't care. You're coming with me." With a howl, she lashed out with a front kick.

Jack lurched back, narrowly avoiding it. "God, woman. Will you just listen?" he complained, all the way down to the first landing. "I need *your* help, not WEFT's. Peri wants to kill Bill. Michael will be with him." Harmony's anger shifted, tainted with the bitterness of betrayal. "You want Michael?" he said, forcing his shoulders to relax. "I sure as hell don't."

Harmony's baton drooped. "Steiner didn't like you escaping," she said, gaze flicking to the dead camera. "Killing his men. He wants you bad. Maybe enough to put me back on active duty if I bring you in."

The hard part was over, and a flash of tension zinged to his groin. He always did like manipulation. "Steiner doesn't want me." He risked looking down and away as if unhappy. "I'm just a link to Michael and Bill." Tossing the hair from his eyes, he glanced up. He couldn't have planned this better, with her standing over him, justified in her confident strength. "Peri needs my help to finish Bill. She doesn't want to admit it, but it's true."

Squinting mistrustfully, she looked at the defunct camera again. Slowly the baton rose.

"You want to spar some more?" he said flippantly. "Can we go back to your dojo and do it on the mats? My back is killing me."

That brought a wry smile to her face, and warning him with her eyes to be still, she came down a step, her martial arts stick lowered. "Why would you help Peri?"

Jack glanced sidelong through the double glass doors, but no one was coming down the long hall.

He had time. “She was my partner for three years, and I don’t want to see her dead. Once Bill is gone, she can vanish. She wants out. She deserves it.” Yes, she deserved it, but she was not going to get it.

“Thanks for the info,” she said, motioning for him to go up the stairway ahead of him, presumably to her car. “You won’t mind repeating that for Steiner, will you?”

He hesitated as if thinking it over, but he already knew what he was going to do, and, head bowed as if in capitulation, he scuffed his way back up the steps.

“Smart man.” Harmony reached for him, hand twisted to snap a restraining hold on him with the help of the baton.

Jack’s hand flashed out, shoving her into the wall. She hit hard, her head thumping into the cement. But it was the breath being knocked out of her that bought him a precious three seconds.

Smiling, still smiling, he jammed his arm under her chin, forcing her head back. His other hand was on her bicep, pinching a nerve to numb her arm. If he bore down hard enough, it would take days to come back, if ever.

“Knock it off,” he said, giving a squeeze, and he saw her anger flash into pain as the baton dropped, clattering on the step. “You’re not that dumb. Bringing me in won’t get you anything. You’ve been sidelined by your own people. *You* took Peri out of custody. *You're* why she's free. You need the entire pie, not the crust. But that's not why you're going to help me."

"Help you?" she said, strained, eyes flicking from the baton to him. "No way in hell."

With a fast motion he let go, retreating to the far end of the step before she could act. Harmony stayed where she was, hand over her arm. He had her. All that was left was deciding whose car to take. "It's a matter of pride," he said. "Your pride, your future. Soon as Peri finishes cleaning house, she's going ghost. I'm going with her. She might have to kill Michael, too, unless you take him into custody first, but Bill . . ." He lifted a shoulder and let it fall. "She won't let that go."

Untrusting, Harmony hesitantly scooped up her baton and tote. Jack turned away and headed up the stairs. "I just want Peri," he said when she followed. "If that means Bill dies, I don't care. I want her to be free to live her life. I want to be there with her." He didn't say he loved her. He couldn't say it anymore and sound convincing. "I could use your help."

Why couldn't Peri have just let everything alone? Everything had been perfect.

Steps slow and methodical, they rose up the stairway, into the brighter light, side by side, together but apart. He watched her eyes flick to the functional camera, then down to the age-gray cement steps. "I'm starving," she said, and the tension in him evaporated. "You like Asian?"

"Love it," he said, lurching to reach the door before her and open it, forcing her to pass within inches of him. She smelled like sweet-woman sweat, and his smile widened. It was obvious by her grimace that she didn't trust him, but he didn't need her to for this to work.

"I've just got one question," she said. "What's in this for you?"

He squinted in the bright light, feeing the chill wind scour him to his soul. "Peri asked me to," he said, remembering her flippant words in her apartment. "Maybe then she'll believe I love her."

Harmony made a rude noise, then looked over him to the horizon. "You don't love her."

Hands in his pockets, he shrugged and pushed himself into motion, sure she'd follow. *She doesn't know that.*

CHAPTER TWENTY-EIGHT

Feeling muzzy and slow from her headache, Peri slid the clock on the tiny armchair table toward her, squinting at it in the dim light of a scarf-draped lamp. It was the only spot of femininity in the entire room—apart from her. "Almost midnight," she breathed as she pushed it back, realizing where her sudden disquiet was coming from. Withdrawal. It had been only five minutes since Silas had left to get some tea. It had seemed like five times that.

She stood, wavering until she found her balance and shuffled to the industrial-looking three-piece bathroom that LB's conjugal closet came with. The small suite had probably once been a janitor break room, and between the bed, couch, and the huge TV screen, there wasn't much floor space.

"I told you to turn that off," she said, jerking the TV's cord out of the wall on her way to the sink as she passed Jack—the hallucination, not the real one. The TV flickered, then held firm; the game show was an illusion as well.

"You didn't say please." His head down, Jack continued to synch his phone to the TV. She knew the flat-screen wasn't really on. She knew the man in his thief-black suit wasn't really there. But by God, it sure looked real. She'd begun hallucinating him right about the time Silas had started pushing that herbal tea on her, the delusion voicing the darker side of her psyche as Silas steadfastly adhered to the sunny side of drug addiction.

Peri splashed lukewarm water on her face, not looking at herself in the cracked mirror as she dried herself and shuffled back out. LB's digs had been a noisy blur when she and Silas had come down the freezer staircase earlier today. The little hidey-hole just off the big playroom had been a little slice of heaven when LB had shown it to her, telling her she looked like shit and to take a nap while he and Silas talked. After she had assured Silas she'd never blacked out from hitting her head on the Pinto's roof, he had left so she could collapse on the overstuffed couch.

That had been hours ago, and instead of waking refreshed, she'd been pulled from sleep by a migraine-like pressure in her skull. The clock said it was withdrawal, not a concussion, and it had swiftly been joined by the twin feelings of nausea and debilitating hunger. She'd gone through drug hangovers before in the course of duty, but this was an unending misery.

Pulse racing, she collapsed onto the couch, elbows on her knees and head in her hands. "Will you *please* stop fiddling with that," she whispered.

"You didn't say with sugar on top." Jack chuckled. His attention went to the steel door that led into the big communal room, and she wasn't surprised when a light knock sounded, shortly followed by Silas's voice.

"Peri? I found some more tea."

Great. Her expression scrunched up. "Come on in." She tried to pull herself together as the door opened, a flush of noise coming in with Silas. He had a thermos in one hand, a bag with a pharmacy logo on it in the other.

"Here you go, Peri." The wide-shouldered man

closed the door with his foot, pace fast as he came to refill the ridiculous teacup already on the tiny table. “Nice and hot.”

She sighed, but the deep breath spun in her gut and made her that much more ill. “I don’t care if it keeps me hydrated, it tastes like Chernobyl cardboard,” she said.

His eyes flicked up, then back down. “I’ll just put it over here.” He hesitated, finally setting the thermos on the bedside table before gingerly sitting on the couch with her. “How are you doing?”

Jack raised one eyebrow and tossed his phone to the bed. “How are you doing? He asks you how you’re doing?” The game show blared from the unplugged unit. Her mind had even added a glint of light from the bedside lamp, and she marveled that her imagination could invent such detail. “Take the Evocane and get on with your life. You can’t kill Bill if you’re dead, and this is going to finish you.”

With only two doses? Peri rubbed her pounding head. “I’m fine,” she whispered. Her hand shook as she reached for the cup, and she pulled it back, curling her fingers under to hide it. With a start, she realized the host of the game show was Steiner. *Shit, I’m going crazy.* “Just fine,” she added as her stomach cramped. *Not again . . .*

Peri flashed hot, then cold. Miserable, she pulled the afghan up and around her. It felt as if she had the flu, and she was sure it would get worse before it got better. "I've not been accelerated. I can stop taking it if I want," she whispered, feeling the pain of that broken promise to her bones.

"I'll get you through it," Silas said, and she huddled into herself, feeling the couch shift as he scooted closer, that plastic bag he'd brought in crackling. "I have some stuff that might help take the edge off. Get you over the hump."

"Hump? It feels like a mountain," she said, her hope crashing as he pulled a box from the bag. *Nicotine patches? Is he serious?*

Jack ambled out of the bathroom and pointedly set the wastebasket next to her. "Like that's going to help."

Peri's gaze flicked from the trash can that really wasn't there to Silas. "At least he's trying," she said aloud, then flushed. Silas knew about Jack—hell, Silas had been the one who put the illusion in her mind—but it was still embarrassing. But there was only interest in Silas's eyes when she met his wondering expression.

"Jack is here?"

" 'Fraid so," she muttered, closing her eyes and holding herself together as her arms began to tremble. She was glad Silas was with her. She didn't want to do this alone. By morning she'd either be dead or through the worst of it. The need to do something was growing, making her fidget even as her muscles began to twitch in earnest. She couldn't think, couldn't breathe.

"I guess that means your higher functions are still okay," Silas said, finally getting the box open and peeling the back off a patch.

Peri pushed her sleeve up. The plastic felt alien against her, and she tugged her sleeve down to hide it. "Maybe I should chew it. What else you got in that bag?" she prompted as a cold sweat broke out on her.

"Something better than nicotine patches, I hope," Jack muttered.

"You can just shut up, *Jack!*" she exclaimed, pulling her knees to her chest to try to hold in the ache. *God, it's like being pregnant,* she thought, then wondered whether she had been once and had forgotten. "I'm okay," she insisted when Silas leaned to look into her eyes, but when she tried to unclench herself, a new wave of vertigo hit her, and her sight grayed. Her head felt as if it were splitting. Jack's game show had gone into sudden death, and the colors and spinning lights were making her ill.

"Will you turn that TV off before I throw you into it?" she moaned, her stomach roiling.

Suddenly everything cycled down to one point in her gut. "Oh, no. I'm going to puke." Surging to her feet, she ran to the tiny bathroom. Muscles rebelling, her stomach heaved. "Get out," she demanded between the harsh gags, and Silas reluctantly left her alone. She was shaking even worse when she finally looked up, hunched under her afghan in a cold sweat. Silas was talking to someone.

LB. Embarrassed, she flushed the toilet and rinsed her mouth out. The water hurt both her ears and her hands. It was warm against her but made her fingers ache.

"How long has she been like this?" LB asked, his voice clear over the chattering water.

"It didn't get bad until an hour or so. It comes and goes in waves. Each one is worse."

Their voices serrated over her nerves, but she was more afraid of the silence, and she started when she pulled her face out of the sink and found Jack behind her, cool and collected. He was beautiful, but her eyes were red and her face slack. She looked a hundred years old, and she turned away, unable to believe there would be a tomorrow. She wasn't going back to Bill. Evocane was a leash.

"Babe, why are you putting yourself through this?" Jack said. "What does it matter if someone is telling you who you can and can't go after? You're still doing what you love."

"Go away," she muttered, pushing past the hallucination to shuffle back out, not meeting either man's eyes as she listlessly sat down. She hadn't wanted LB to see her like this, but he probably knew the hell she was going through better than she did. “Welcome to the party,” she rasped, needing two hands to bring that cup of Silas’s tea to her mouth. It still tasted like crap, but she needed something, and she almost spilled it as she gulped it down, her hands were shaking so badly.

“You look like run-over shit,” LB said, making tears of self-pity prick at her eyes. “Hey, ah, I thought you’d want this back,” he added, setting her tattered diary on the foot of the bed.

“Thank you.” Miserable, she couldn’t even bring herself to wonder whether he’d snuck a peek in it or not. Her gaze went past him to Jack, anger giving her strength. “Jack, if you don’t turn off that TV, I’m going to kick you in the balls.”

Peeved, Jack clicked the TV off and sat at the foot of the indulgent bed and sulked. But the shakes had abated enough that she could sit up. It was a breather, nothing more. The next wave was going to be the tipping point—and she didn’t know whether she could take it.

Confused, LB turned to the TV. “She told me she hallucinates,” LB said.

“That’s not the withdrawal,” Silas said, his head down over the open bag.

“No, I’m schizophrenic,” she said. “But Silas says the voices in my head are real.”

“You are not schizophrenic.” Silas dug in his bag. “I have something stronger. You want it now?”

"Why not," she said, and LB frowned, clearly thinking it was a mistake.

"It might knock you out," Silas said, and her eyes slid to him, drawn by the rattle of pills as he wrangled the safety seal off.

"Nicotine and now barbiturates?" LB asked. "Why didn't you just get some nicotine caps and let her shoot up with them?"

"I've got my reasons," Silas said, head down as he jiggled two into his palm.

Head aching, Peri grabbed the bottle instead of the two pills, shaking them into her mouth like candy.

"That's why," Silas said when she handed the half-empty bottle back and he dropped the original two pills back into it. "That's too many," he added, voice resigned.

Peri tugged her afghan closer. "You got anything to wash it down with?"

"Well . . ." Silas hedged, a bottle of what looked like cough syrup in his hand. He started to put it back in the bag, and Peri snatched it out of his grip. Her stomach clenched, and she gritted her teeth as the *click-click* of the seal breaking seemed to hurt her skull. It was getting harder to focus, and a lethargic, hot sensation was coursing through her muscles, making them feel as if they weren't her own.

"You're going to kill yourself taking it all at once like that," Silas said, but that he was even saying it meant she hadn't crossed the line—yet.

"Then at least it will be over." Ignoring LB's worried frown, she tilted her head back and the sweet, syrupy alcohol slipped down. It burned, tripping her gag reflex. She coughed, fending off Silas's help as her eyes watered.

"She shouldn't be mixing those," LB said, and Silas patted her back.

"I know, but she's going to throw up in about fifteen minutes," he predicted. "What gets into her system between now and then isn't going to kill her. Probably."

Her foot began to shake. At this point, she wasn't sure whether it was the withdrawal or the meds. Frankly, she didn't care. Vertigo hit her, and she reached for the stability of the couch's arm. "It's not working," she panted as her gut twisted. "Give me another patch."

"No. That's all you get," Silas said.

"Give me another patch, damn it! It's not working!" she shouted, tears springing up unbidden. She knew it was from the drugs, but nothing felt real anymore.

"Peri, I'm sorry! This is what I have," Silas said. "It's going to get better. I promise."

Peri pulled her eyes from the bag, knowing there was nothing in it that could help her. "I've only had two doses. Why is it this bad?" she whispered. Her heart hammered and she looked at the ceiling, feeling the room spin. "It shouldn't be this bad."

"I'm sorry, Peri. I'd do this for you if I could."

His eyes held an unexpected vulnerability, and she quashed her emotion as the bolts in her life slid to a new, locked position. She was not going to kick this, and she was not going to give in. Adrenaline pushed into her, and her stomach clenched. "It's not working, Silas," she moaned. "I can't do this again. I can't!"

"It will be okay," he soothed, pulling her back to his front, holding her to keep her from shaking. From the corner of the room, Jack watched, hearing the lie as well. "I promise."

But she wasn't going to make it. Her hands were sweating, and she looked at them, shocked. They had gone pale. The adrenaline wasn't mixing well with whatever was in that cough syrup. Her stomach cramped, and she held her breath. Her pulse was too fast, and she suddenly realized she was going to pass out.

"Peri!" Silas shouted as her body went slack.

Eyes closed, she distantly heard LB swear, and then her head swung forward. Arms limp, she felt herself shifted to the couch, the musty cushions pillowing her—almost like clouds.

"Shit, that was fast. She's going," someone said.

"Going? Going where?" another voice said, frantic.

"Under the ground, you idiot." It was LB, but she couldn't open her eyes. "Pick her up. Keep her awake. Slap her if you have to. How much does she usually get?"

"A half cc. No, she's got this!" Silas exclaimed as she felt herself picked up, and the cloud cushions became arms, thick and warm, holding her as if she would break. But she had broken already, feeling her skin crack and fall away, the pieces slipping to the floor, one by one. She could hear them hit and shatter like ice.

"I don't know what this shit is, but she can't quit cold. Look at her. I'm giving her the Evocane. Now."

Evocane? "Silas?" Shaking violently, she cracked her eyes. She wasn't in pieces. Her skin was still whole. Silas was holding her, his expression twisted in fear for her. "You have Evocane," she said, the need rising from everywhere, crushing the shakes and fatigue.

LB was standing over them, his eyes wide in surprise. "My God. I thought she was gone."

"She's tougher than you think," Silas said, and she grunted when he shifted her in his arms, and pins and needles stabbed her.

In LB's hand was a vial.

Her breath came in harsh, and her heart stuttered. "You have Evocane!" she exclaimed in an ugly rasp. She tried to sit up, get out of Silas's arms. But her muscles failed her, and all she managed was to spill out of his arms and hit the floor. Pain shot from her hip to her skull, clearing her mind for a half second. He had what she needed, and with a mindless drive, she sprang at him.

"Peri!" Silas exclaimed, lunging after her. His thick arm wrapped around her waist as she lurched for LB, and she and Silas fell back, hard against the cement floor.

"Give it to me!" she screamed, trying to claw her way out from under him. "I can smell it! Give me the fucking Evocane!"

LB watched, wide-eyed, what she needed in his hand. "Okay. Right. Calm down."

Silas grunted as her elbow hit his face. She struggled to be free, but he wrapped his legs around her in a wrestler hold, shifting his grip and forcing her to be still. "Do it," he grunted.

"Give it to me!" she raged, the need unbearable. But she couldn't move, bound by Silas's arms and legs, and she began to cry in frustration. "You little bastard! Give it to me!"

LB crouched down in front of her, a wary distance between them. "Promise to hold still, and I'll give it to you."

She forced herself to stop. She was whimpering, hating it as she watched LB push her sleeve up. "Please hurry," she begged, vertigo fighting with the shakes to see which could kill her first. If she could ever see straight again, she was going to kill Bill.

"Shit, man. I don't think I've ever seen anyone

so white and still be alive." With a casual expertise, LB filled a syringe and jabbed her. "You tell me if you're going to blow, okay?"

With three beats of her heart, peace flooded into her. Immediately she relaxed, and Silas's arms went from confining to comforting. "Oh, God," she slurred as he felt the difference and he sat up, pulling her into his lap and rocking her, right there on the floor. Her eyes closed at the relief of no pain. And then she started to cry.

"No . . . I didn't want this," she said, head down to hide her heartache and guilt. "I was this close! Damn it, Silas, I was right there . . ."

"You were there all right." LB stood, looking at the vial with a new respect. "You were this close to dying. Damn, this is some wicked dragon shit."

Her head jerked up, and a cool certainty filled her, pushing out her misery. "That's mine," she said, voice utterly devoid of anything but a hard intent.

Silas slowly let go of her, and she sat herself up, her hand out until LB dropped the vial into her grip. It was cool in her fingers, and she hated how she couldn't let go of it.

"That's not euphoria," Silas said as he stood up, leaving her there alone on the floor. "It's just the absence of pain. Peri. I'm sorry. I don't care what it takes. You're not doing that again. I'll pick the addictive parts out and wean you off, but you're not doing that again."

LB snapped the needle and threw it away. "All that grief, and it doesn't do anything?"

She shook her head, her throat tight as she scooted to put her back against the front of the couch and just breathe for a moment. Jack was gone. Hopefully for good. But she was never that lucky. She was right back at square one, and there was no way she could ever move past it. She was hooked. The Evocane was warming in her grip, but she couldn't let go of it. By her estimation, there was only five more days' worth in it—five more days until she had to decide who was going to hold her leash. *Damn you, Bill.* "Where's the rest?"

"Ahhh . . ."

Her focus sharpened. "You didn't try it, did you?"

"No," LB reassured her, but the vial wasn't full.

"Where is the rest?" she demanded. "There should be more."

Silas stood, giving her shoulder a squeeze. "We've been trying to duplicate it."

"You're wasting it?" Peri asked, suddenly concerned.

LB shrugged. "It's not a waste if we can duplicate it."

"But Bill said it was too complicated." She was feeling better remarkably fast, and she levered herself up onto the couch as LB sat on the corner of the bed.

"We've got five days," Silas soothed. "By that time, I will have made up a modified version that will address the withdrawal. I'm sure some of the addictive additives were a safety measure to be sure you never let yourself go without it and accidentally MEP from a routine draft, but Bill made it a hundred times worse to ensure you never left him. And he's right. I can't duplicate it, but I don't need to. You haven't been accelerated, so all you *need* is the addictive stuff. I can do that. It's going to be okay." He winced, clearly not entirely happy.

Need, she thought, thinking it was an ugly word. She hadn't even known what it meant until now. Hope that she could be as she once was, even if that had been flawed and forgetful, seeped out of the cracks of agony, somehow making her feel worse.

The pain was gone, but her hands were still shaking, not in withdrawal but shock. She was hooked. She couldn't fight this, and slow, silent tears slipped from her. She let them fall, not caring whether they saw them. She was no longer in control. She no longer mattered.

Silas's attention sharpened on her. "I'll crack this, Peri. I can do it."

But that wasn't why she was crying. She wanted to remember her drafts. She wanted to be free of being forced to trust by necessity, not desire. And if she couldn't have that, she wanted to have the ability to just walk away. But what she had was a horrifying need pushing her into more and more desperate acts. "Maybe I should just take the accelerator. At least then I'd have value," she whispered.

"Don't." Silas sat beside her, his weight making her slip into him. "We can get around this. I should have told you before, but I didn't think it was going to be this bad."

"Bad?" she said hotly. "You think that was just . . . bad?"

His head cocked and he jerked her into him, his relief making his mood soft. "Don't get mad at me for my word choice," he said as he coddled her, protesting, into his arms. "You haven't been accelerated, so all you need is the addictive stuff. I can do that."

"Yes?" A glimmer of hope sparked, wavered, and threatened to go out.

"Promise," he said, his arms around her becoming more sure, more grateful, almost. "I should have told you earlier, but I wanted to get LB's opinion on it first."

"Thank you," she whispered, eyes closing as she gave in and felt herself melt against him, his warmth finally easing the last of the shakes. She felt loved, her emotions paper thin. Something tickled the back of her brain. His arms around her felt familiar, like home. *From the year Allen had erased,* she thought, swallowing hard. Why had she been so stupid? Opti was officially ended, and she was still fighting the same war.

"You make it really hard to love you, you know that, don't you?" Silas whispered as LB left, closing the door behind him.

CHAPTER TWENTY-NINE

LB's back room seemed a lot nicer when she wasn't half-delusional with withdrawal, and Peri sat on the edge of the bed in a borrowed T-shirt and dried her hair as she waited for Silas to come back with her clean clothes and maybe some of that pasta she could smell. The soft conversation from the big playroom had long vanished, replaced by what sounded like a Disney movie. It was surprisingly soothing. LB had something unique here. It wasn't a family. It was bigger than that. A community, maybe?

But even as she thought it, her contentment slowly shifted to an uncomfortable unease. Stretching, she reached for her phone on the bedside table, and the flexible glass lit up at her touch. She had only twenty-four hours before withdrawal hit her again. Twenty-four hours, and way too much to do.

Tossing the towel to the couch, she finger-combed her hair, wondering whether getting Bill hooked on the stuff might be a suitable revenge—the son of a mother-sucking ass-wipe bastard.

She felt as if she'd been beaten up, making it hard to tell what was symptomatic of trying to fight her addiction, and what was from the bumpy car chase. She wanted to go out and find Silas, but not dressed only in a T-shirt, so she settled back to wait. Her diary still lay at the foot of the bed, and after a moment she pulled it close, wondering whether LB had succumbed to reading it in her absence when more pages slipped free, needing to be jammed back in place like her forgotten memories in her mind.

Settling back against the headboard, she turned to the last unread pages.

> Silas and I spent the weekend together, sort of a retreat before the last push and the team is chosen. It's what I've been working my entire adult life for, and I've never been more confident in the people I'd be working with. I trust Silas and Allen. But now I'm having doubts, not about the mission, but what it is going to do to Silas. For the first time, I'm seeing him without the shadow of Summer on him, and I don't know if I can do this to him. Not again. He was happy yesterday, and I realize that sounds simple, but for three entire days, there was not a shadow

of guilt or regret on him. It made me feel more than good that I might have had some small part in him finding that. And it wasn't just the sex, which is never just sex for him but almost a holy commitment. It was the way he sheltered his happiness, as if he knew it wasn't going to last and he would be lost and alone again.

Allen will be inserted into Opti with me, but Silas, especially now, with the emotional ties we've been making, will be relegated to the background. I don't know if I can ask him to bear the burden of remembering when I forget.

But it's too late now. I can't back out, and certainly not because I might love someone. I'm going to give this journal to Silas so he can look back at it and know that what we had was real even if I don't remember it. I hope it helps him understand so he won't wall himself off from love as he did when Summer died. Silas should have these thoughts, my thoughts, because he is, and forever will be, my anchor, the only one who I trust to remind me of who I want to be when there is nothing left.

Please, don't give up on me.

Peri swallowed. She should've walked away from the task. She should have let someone else do it. But pride had stopped her, and it had ruined too many lives, most of all Silas's. And here she was, poised to do it again. *How much pain can a soul survive?*

A soft knock jerked her head up. "Peri? You decent?" Silas said, and she flushed, jamming the diary under her pillow.

"Come on in," she said, and the door opened, bringing in the noise from the TV. "Mmmm, smells good," she added, and Silas padded closer in his bare feet, his face stubbled, dressed in jeans and a raggedy borrowed T-shirt with a plate of takeout food on a Mickey Mouse platter in one hand. Their cleaned clothes were tucked under an arm, and seeing his quiet contentment, her guilt grew deeper. It hurt seeing him there, his lumpy feet poking out from under his borrowed, frayed jeans and nothing but worry in his tired eyes. He loved her, always had, and she only now was ready to believe that she deserved it, now when she had nothing but trouble to offer him.

She forced the thought from her, making her smile brighter. "You haven't slept at all, have you," she said, and he dropped their clothes on the couch before sitting down beside her.

"Ah, not really," he said. "Hungry?"

She nodded. The warmth of his shoulder against hers was heady, and the soft sounds of the silverware as he shifted to arrange the plate of food on his lap pulled her eyes down in guilt.

“Thank you,” she whispered, knowing she didn’t deserve it. Not after what she’d done to him, what she was going to do.

Silas’s motions stilled. “Guilt?” he said incredulously. “For what? None of this is your fault. And it’s not like I cooked it. Just put it on a plate.”

“But you got it for me,” she said, eyes down. She’d hurt him beyond forgiveness. She’d willingly forgot the year they’d fallen in love for the chance to bring Opti down. She’d selfishly killed their love for a chance at glory. “I’m so sorry,” she whispered, throat closing. “I can’t believe how stupid I was.”

“Peri.” He set the plate aside and took her in an awkward hug. “This isn’t your fault.”

“That’s not what I’m talking about,” she said into his shirt, muffled. His scent rose around and through her, and she breathed it in, willing her memory to return. Why hadn’t she made any memory knot of him? Not one?

“Oh. That.” His chest moved as he took a deep breath. “I always figured it was my fault you asked Allen to destroy that year.”

Eyes wet, she looked up at him, seeing the love in his eyes. “Your fault?”

“I could have stopped the whole thing. Maybe if I had been honest with you, you wouldn’t have done it in the first place.”

“You?” This wasn’t anything in her diary.

His gaze dropped, the twitch in his eye pinging

on her intuition. Something had happened between them, something that hadn't gotten into the pages, had not even been hinted at. She took a slow breath, not willing to delve into it right now. "So here we are." Hesitating, she smiled up at him as his arms slipped away. "Where exactly are we?"

"In a better place than you might think." Clearly glad for the shift in topics, he resettled their dinner on his lap. "I checked out LB's lab. It's so far out of OSHA standards it's scary, but making up more withdrawal preventative isn't going to be a problem. Two days, maybe? It won't be Evocane, but it will tamp down the withdrawal this time. I promise."

"Thank God." She eagerly took the fork he handed her, stabbing one of the ravioli and angling it in. The tart, acidic taste hit the sides of her mouth, and her hunger hit.

"There's still nothing on Jack in the news," he said as he unrolled one of the foil-wrapped breads. "But WEFT probably asked the cops to keep it out of the news."

Her empty stomach growled, and she slowed. Eating spicy tomato sauce so fast might not be prudent. "They didn't have much of a choice after I tangled them up on the interstate."

Silas grunted in agreement, handing her the bread before unwrapping the other. She could smack LB for letting Jack go. He was an ass, but what he'd done was almost noble. They never would've evaded WEFT and the cops without Jack's help. If she'd landed in custody, it might have been hours before WEFT gained jurisdiction and she got her Evocane fix—assuming they gave it to her. Jack had given her freedom and the chance to act.

Seeing her brooding, Silas leaned over their shared plate. "He did it," he said as if reading her mind, "so you wouldn't make LB lock him up. That's it. Nothing more."

"I suppose." Peri stabbed her ravioli. "He didn't scrub me, though."

Silas's frown deepened. "Don't do this. Jack is in it for himself. He didn't scrub you because he wasn't sure he'd be around to sell you his song and dance." He pointed his fork at her. "What does your *intuition* say about him?"

"You mean my *hallucination?*" she mocked, still not pleased Silas had put Jack there. "He hasn't weighed in on it." She ate half a ravioli. "He's more interested in making Steiner the host of a game show than helping me figure anything out."

Silas's smile became odd. "Game show, eh?" he said as if that explained something. "LB put his chemists—and I use the term loosely—on the Evocane substitute. He thinks it would be better to wean you off it compound by compound instead of going cold turkey." Silas hesitated at her fierce look, then added, “You scared a drug lord, Peri. If he thinks it’s unsafe, then it’s unsafe.”

Mollified, she returned to eating. “And you trust them to get the substitute right?”

There were only three ravioli left, and Silas set his fork down. “LB supplies the I-75 corridor. His crew stinks, farts, smokes, and has a shocking disregard for authority, but they know their product and what they’re doing. Any one of his chemists could work at one of Detroit’s research facilities but they have, ah, issues,” he finished uncomfortably. “Other than the stink, fart, smoke . . . thing.”

“That an East Coast drug lord is cooking my fix makes me *so-o-o-o* much more comfortable,” she said sourly, but there was a kernel of truth to it. She didn’t want the last three ravioli either, and she set the plate aside, leaning back against the headboard and tugging the afghan over her. “We head out tomorrow, then? Where do you want to go?” A solid day’s sleep might be possible in the depths of a drug lord’s den. Funny how that worked.

Silas scooted to the end of the bed, and her first complaint turned into a moan of pleasure when he pulled one of her legs out from under the knitted blanket and began to rub her foot. “I’m thinking Arizona,” Silas said, and her eyes closed in bliss. She’d forgotten that the Opti requirements for their psychologists included sixteen credit hours of massage therapy. “A ranch close to the border where it never gets cold,” he said as he found a trigger point and released her back. “You could raise quail.”

She opened one eye to find him half-serious. But she liked people too much to become a hermit. Slowly her smile faded. She was going to miss Detroit, the way the city had found a new greatness—an independent confidence, maybe—after being abandoned to those who were too poor or stubborn to move—like she was.

“Still holding your tension in your lower back, I see,” he said, running a firm thumb to the outside of her arch.

“Oh, God. Don’t stop,” she moaned as the pain evolved into relief—and then guilt. He knew how to make her feel good, and she’d done nothing for him but abandon him and ignore that he loved her. Being scared was not an excuse.

She must have stiffened because he sighed and let go of her foot. Her eyelids cracked, and she closed them again as he moved to the head of the bed, expression pained. “Move over,” he said gruffly, but it wasn’t as if she had a choice as he pushed her to the center of the bed, his bulk moving her slight frame easily. Jaw clenched, she scrunched down under the blanket. She could feel his warmth, soaking into her, and she avoided his eyes.

“Why are you so hung up on me doing anything nice for you?” he finally said.

“I’m not.”

He cocked an eyebrow at her. “Is it because you think it’s the Opti conditioning? That they made you into a deadly but dependent princess who expected to be waited on all the time?” She looked away, and he made a knowing sound. “Peri, you broke that a long time ago. Well, most of it,” he added, and she grimaced at his chuckle. “You don’t need anyone. But that doesn’t mean I don’t need you.”

God, why is this so hard? “Silas . . .”

“No.” He put a finger to her lips, shifting to lie sideways beside her, propped up on an elbow. “You read your diary, right? The one I gave you?”

She nodded, thinking of it stuffed under the pillow. The love she’d had for him was obvious in the pages, and still, she’d destroyed it—for a chance at glory. “I did,” she said softly.

“Then why?”

“Because I don’t remember it. Every time you look at me, I feel as if I’m broken.”

He brushed the hair from her forehead and kissed it. “So?”

“So I don’t like feeling broken.”

“Everyone is broken.”

“But my pieces don’t fit together anymore.” Unable to face him, she rolled away. Her chest hurt when he snuggled tight behind her. His arm draped over her, a taunting familiarness wisping about the edges of memory. Her eyes welled up, but she refused to cry.

"You're the strongest person I have ever known," he whispered in her ear. "Do you remember how we met?"

"I don't want to do a recall," she said petulantly, and he chuckled.

"You were with Allen at the time. Just friends, but it was obvious that anyone hanging with you had ulterior motives."

"Allen?" Interested, she rolled back, wondering at the weird, pained smile on him.

"He'd hijacked a drone, and you were trying to fly it into Opti's armory to get a look at the weapons you'd be up against in one of yourfinals. One of the stabilizers went out. It crashed into the med hall auditorium right during an exam. Knocked me a good one." His smile became fond and he pushed back a lock of hair from his forehead. "Look, you can still see the scar."

She touched it, finding it by feel. "How come I never wrote *that* down?"

"You vaulted through the broken window after it. Bold as brass, you picked up the drone, changed one of the answers on my test, and walked out."

She chuckled, imagining it. "I'm surprised I didn't get expelled."

"You would have if you hadn't been wearing smut to throw off the recognition software.

You were new. No one recognized you. Yet."

His fingers ran a delicious trace of sensation over her shoulder, following a line of muscle, and she shivered. "I ran into you a few days later, pissed because my entire exam was thrown out because of you. It was at Overdraft, actually. I recognized the limp you got by kicking the professor into a wall when he tried to detain you."

"Huh." Settled back in the pillows, she played with the hair about his ears. "That might explain one of my grades."

Silas's expression shifted abruptly. "I'm sorry you don't remember, but I do."

"Silas," she protested.

"Just . . . shut up, will you?" he said, leaning over and soundly kissing her.

Her flash of startlement vanished in an inrush of air. His lips were warm and soft . . . familiar. Her fingers tightened in his hair, and she wouldn't let him pull away until a slip of his tongue surprised her and he drew back. The sound of their lips parting echoed through her memory, the scent of his skin against hers sparking flashes of vision.

Silas's eyes were wary. "This isn't—" he started, and she laced her hands behind his neck to keep him from pulling away.

"What?" she asked. "Smart? Not what you had planned on doing, coming in here wearing raggedy jeans and a Van Halen T-shirt?" Gently she pulled him back over her, her fingers aggressive as they raked through his hair and down his back. "You kissed me first."

"I shouldn't have. Peri, you're feeling very vulnerable right now."

She shoved him just enough to get the afghan between them free, and lifting it in invitation, she smiled when he looked. He hadn't moved, and she flicked the blanket half over him. "That's just the psychologist in you talking," she said, pulling him back to her. She could tell the instant he gave up, and her lips left his to hop-skip down his neck as she slipped a leg between Silas's. His skin held a hint of salt, and she tugged gently on the soft part of his throat. "I'm not feeing at all vulnerable. Trust me."

He chuckled, and she shut him up with another long, soul-stealing kiss.

His weight shifted, covering her with a heavy security, and she sent her hands down his chest, fumbling for his zipper. The cold slipped under the afghan as he moved, and she shivered.

Silas's hand was warm and rough as he slipped her shirt over her head, finding the small of her back and easing her deeper onto the bed with a sensation that was both domineering and gentle. His head lowered, and she buried her fingers in his hair, arching upward when he found her breast with his lips. She moaned, her grip tightening as he grew rougher, his hands at her waist keeping her pinned to the bed.

She gasped when he pinched too hard, and immediately he eased. “S’okay,” she whispered, wishing he’d do it again, fingers fumbling for his zipper.

But he didn’t, and she groaned when she finally got that damned zipper down and reached past it to find him. Again his touch became deliciously rough as she moved up and down his length, finding his neck with her lips, his ear with her teeth, his back with her nails—tracing a one-finger path up the center of his spine to feel him shiver and goad him into a more demanding touch. *He wanted to leave with me. Forever.*

Her breath came in with disappointment when he leaned out of her reach, but he was only wiggling out of his jeans, and then he was back, his gaze holding a questioning familiarity as he pinned her hands beside her ear. Their breath was fast, and his smile turned devilish when he saw the desire in her eyes and she lunged to find his mouth, imprisoned but not.

Wrapping her legs around him, she pulled him close. *Maybe vanishing is a good idea.*

Warmth overflowed as Silas bent close, holding her unmoving as he kissed her neck. She slipped one hand free to find him, caressing, guiding, arching up and teasing before falling back. Sensation plinked through her as they fell into a rhythm. Giving in to her own desires, she guided him in, exalting in the slow rise of how he felt both above and in her. Loved. Desired. And he was willing to give everything up to hide with her. Be with her.

Her breath caught as their rhythm shifted and he pressed deep, staying within her even as he found her breast. The twin sensations arced through her, almost unbearable. Wild with desire, she arched into him, demanding more, urging him, feeling the need quicken in him.

The slightest widening of rhythm warned her, and she gave herself to sensation, moaning as a wave of ecstasy rose, hesitated, and crashed over her. It hit Silas and he stiffened, groaning as he climaxed as well. Eyes shut, she lingered, afraid to move and end it. Their breathing twined together, the heavy sound of it finally pulling her eyes open as he shifted to get his weight off her.

"You're not too heavy," she whispered, and their eyes met.

"Yeah?"

"Yeah," she echoed, playing with the hair about his ears as he settled back. She could feel the sweat between them, the pleasant exhaustion. *Forever?* Maybe. It was worth struggling for. It finally felt as if she was doing something right, here in a drug lord's playroom.

But he was still smiling down at her, and she arched her eyebrows at him when he took a breath to speak. "Think carefully about what is going to come out of your mouth," she said, liking the way the dim light glistened on his skin to show the muscles underneath. "You didn't take advantage of me, and it wasn't the first time we've done this." It wasn't just that he knew exactly what button to push and when, but that there had been no awkwardness.

"No, but it's the first time you remember it."

She sighed as he lifted from her, exhaling in happiness as he fell to the bed beside her. It had been fast, almost too fast, but only because it was comfortable with the patterns of familiarity. There would be time for lingering and exploration later.

Rolling, she snuggled in beside him. First time she remembered? Yes. Hopefully not the last. *Damn, how could I just willingly forget this?* Stretching, she nibbled on his earlobe, tasting its texture between her teeth and letting go when he grunted and rolled off the bed.

"You want a washcloth or the shower?"

She stared at the ceiling, feeling good for the first time since who knew when. Why had she waited so long? "Shower," she said as she sat up. "Mind if I go first? I honestly don't think it will hold both of us."

"Not at all." With a happy sigh, he collapsed among the pillows.

Her knee, forgotten until now, slowed her shuffle to the bathroom. The water was hot almost immediately, and feeling like a different person, she got in. Water cascaded where his fingertips had traced, and she looked down at herself, smiling at the thought of having him with her always as she reached for the soap.

"We can have a year's supply of substitute Evocane in a few days," Silas called out.

"A few days?" she shouted back, not believing it.

"You haven't seen his labs," Silas answered. "By then, things will have cooled off to move safely. I was serious about Arizona. My uncle works at one of the parks out there, and they're always open to selling property off. Nice and quiet."

The ardor sluiced from her as if stripped by the water, and she looked over the shampoo selection, wondering whether she should have worn flip-flops. Nice and quiet sounded perfect. The wide Arizona horizons even better; and the aches drained away with the bubbles. Water dripping, she leaned to check out her knee. It was healing cleanly, but she grimaced at the coming scar. *Like I don't already have enough,* she thought, running a hand down first one, then the other arm, cataloging the soft marks.

"Don't remember this one," she whispered upon finding a ragged mark on her thigh, not recalling where she got it but that Jack had been with her. He'd held the bowling towel they'd found in the trunk against her the entire ride back to Opti.

She didn't remember what they did with the dead man who had cut her, though.

Solemn, she turned off the shower, motions slow as she reached for a towel, counting the scars as she dried herself. Most had a reason she could point to, but there were enough that didn't to cause her worry. "What am I doing?" she whispered, suddenly seeing beyond her dream that she could just walk away from who she had been. Her head started to hurt, but she refused to give up. She wanted what Silas offered, wanted it with everything in her soul. But like her scars, Bill would always be there. The only way to get what she wanted would be to face Bill and end it. Running away would only make him chase her harder.

The worst part? She would survive. It would be Silas who would suffer.

Towel wrapped around her, she padded into the bedroom. "Silas?"

She stopped, seeing him asleep, vulnerable with the blanket half over him. His hair was mussed, making her want to arrange it. The half-light was beautiful on him, the shadows and glints inviting her to trace her fingers. He hadn't slept at all since they'd joined LB, watching over her and making sure she was okay. He loved her—and it was going to get him killed.

"I can't do this yet," she whispered. He wouldn't let her walk out of here alone, and she couldn't wait two days for the Evocane substitute, but she didn't need to.

The towel fell about her ankles, and she got dressed with a frugal quickness of motion. Hesitating instead of kissing him good-bye, she dropped the vial of Evocane into her short-job bag on top of her unworn clothes, then the syringe of accelerator he had hidden in his coat. Her diary was out of reach under the pillow, and she reluctantly left it.

Grabbing her boots, she slipped out, easing the door shut behind her. The main room was quiet, and she leaned her forehead against the door, hoping he'd understand when he woke and found her gone. "I'm sorry, Silas. I'll be back," she whispered.

"I wouldn't have pegged you as a one-night stand," LB said, and she spun, finding him sitting alone at a table.

He lifted a beer in salute and, flustered, she leaned against the wall, arms crossed over her to hold her bag to her middle. The large room was empty but for him, the movie about the kick-butt princess playing to an absent audience. "I need some clean syringes," she said, the drips from her hair trailing down her back to make her shiver.

Silent, he looked at the ceiling as he took a handful from a nearby plastic bag and pushed them across the table. "You've only got five days of fix. What are you going to do?"

One day out, one day back, two to get things done, and a spare in case something goes wrong. "I'm going to the East Coast to kill Bill," she said.

He nodded, not passing judgment. "Don't forget your katana," he joked, then his expression grew serious. "I can't help but think this is a mistake. That is some dragon-shit stuff."

You scared a drug lord, Peri, resounded through her, and she pushed the fear down. She tucked syringes in her bag, and the cool glass of the vial as it brushed against her fingertips felt like the devil's smile itself. Newport was twelve hours away. She could be there by dusk if she didn't stop to sleep. *Sleep . . .*

"You're not weak, Reed, for needing it."

Her breath caught as the remembered ache filled her. "You're right. And this is a mistake. Every time I take it, it makes it harder to quit, but it's all I've got." Angry, she sat down to put on her boots.

LB watched. "What do you want me to tell him?"

She looked at the door, then thunked her heel into her boot. Her knee gave a twinge, easily ignored. "Tell him I'll be back."

"Yeah. That's what my dad said."

Her head snapped up. "I'm. Not. Leaving. Him."

LB raised a hand. "Swell. You're going to come back."

Her face was warm, and she hated that it made her look as if she was lying. "If Silas is with me,

Bill will use it against me. I can't . . ." Her breath caught. "I'll give Bill anything he wants if he threatens Silas. Keep him here, okay? Tell him you need his help with the Evocane substitute or something."

Eyes empty of emotion, LB nodded. "That's the truth, but he's going to be pissed."

Peri laughed bitterly. "Why do you think I'm leaving like this? I am such a coward." She stood, wiggling her foot into her second boot. "Thank you. For everything."

LB stood as well, his head bowed. "Thank you for showing me I'm not crazy."

A smile spilled over her. Maybe she'd done one thing right. "We are, you know. Crazy?"

He chuckled, his hand falling to her shoulder as he escorted her to the open archway door and the night beyond. "I can get you off it, Reed, but not at once. Call me when you're ready."

She took a breath to tell him he hadn't given her his number, spinning to look behind her when Silas's muffled voice called her name with equal amounts of panic and anger. "Shit. He's up."

"Here." LB pushed a hanging curtain of beads aside. A rough-hewn opening lay beyond, the light failing after only a few feet. "It goes to the surface, but it's too tight for Lorenzo, so we never use it."

"Lorenzo?" she questioned as she slipped past him, her bag pressed against her.

"Fat Man," he said, digging into his pocket and handing her a wad of bills and a rail pass. "Be careful. They haven't found Jack yet." And then he was gone, the curtain swinging slowly to settle between them.

"Peri?" Silas called, and she shrank back, afraid to move in the dark. "Peri?" he called again, and then he swore softly. "She's gone, isn't she," he said, anger thick in his voice. "And you let her walk out of here?"

"Yep." The broken shadow of LB sat down in front of the TV with his beer. "I didn't get to be king of this rodeo by being stupid."

"Damn it, she shouldn't be alone!" Silas exclaimed, and Peri froze. "Where are my shoes? Where are my blasted shoes? Did she hide them again?"

Again? she wondered, seeing a glimpse of their shared past.

"Slow down, Tex," LB said as he clicked through the channels to settle on a nineties sitcom. "She has itchy feet is all, and an hour's head start. She's only got a day's worth of Evocane, and she went looking for Jack. She'll be back tomorrow."

He lied for me? Peri thought, not liking how easy and convincingly it had come out of him.

"God bless it." His hands in fists, Silas stared at the ceiling. He exhaled, abruptly losing his anger and collapsing on the couch beside LB, his head cradled in his hands. "I can't believe I fell asleep," he whispered, his gaze haunted as he lifted his head. "She took the accelerator with her. Don't lie to me, Leon. I'm a psychologist. How much Evocane does she have?"

His real name is Leon?

LB sighed. "All five days," he admitted, and Silas groaned. "Enough to take care of Bill. She'll be back."

Silas bowed his head, his fingertips pressing into his forehead hard. "If she remembers me," he whispered.

Breath held, she carefully turned and headed for the surface. She'd be back, she vowed.

If I remember him.

CHAPTER THIRTY

The screwdriver slipped from the panel's cover, gouging the fatty part of Peri's thumb. Hissing, she sucked on it, fighting the urge to throw the tool into the predawn dark as she crouched beside the security panel behind her coffeehouse. It didn't help that she'd snuffed the safety light with a well-placed rock. It also didn't help that her coffeehouse had originally been a satellite cop shop with thick walls, bullet-resistant windows, and a built-in security system like few others. She'd already disabled the alarm, but getting through the magnetic lock was proving difficult.

She needed money, her secondary ID, a vehicle, and the peace of mind a few armaments would provide. Her coffee shop held all that. Her key, long gone, was not the only way in. If she could get the panel open, she could hard-code her password in.

Squinting at her hand, she rubbed the blood away and wedged the screwdriver under the panel again. *Jack usually did this,* she thought out of nowhere, then quashed it.

"This is a first for me" came out of the dark, and she spun, rising to her feet, screwdriver held to gouge as she scanned the tiny private parking lot.

"Cam?" she questioned incredulously, recognizing his silhouette in the thin street light. "What are you doing here?"

"Breaking my rule about not chasing a woman." He picked his way closer between the frozen rocks and weeds, his breath steaming. "Lose your key?"

Flustered, she shifted the angle of the screwdriver to something less agressive. "You shouldn't be here."

"Don't I know it," he said faintly. Hands in the pockets of his short leather jacket, he halted on the small cement pad. His attitude shifted from a sour acceptance to a questioning scrutiny. "Are you okay?"

Peri licked her lips, feeling self-conscious in her

tight black jeans and soft boots. She looked like a thief, but it was her store. "Seriously. Why are you here?"

Cam looked at the shop as if able to see the street beyond. "Your place is on my way to work. I saw the security light was out, and for some stupid reason, I felt responsible."

Slumping, Peri turned back to the panel. "It's five in the morning. You go to work at five in the morning?"

"I get more work done when I'm alone."

"Me too," she muttered, and the screwdriver slipped again.

Cam shifted from foot to foot, his expensive dress shoes looking wrong in the dirt and weeds. "So . . . you're back?"

The hint of ulterior interest in his voice didn't go unnoticed, and Peri glanced up. "No," she said carefully. "I'm here to pick up a few things is all." Cam's brow furrowed, and blowing the hair out of her eyes, she added, "Thank you for watching my cat. He means the world to me."

"He's not been any trouble."

Peri picked away at the panel, trying to figure out what she'd done to encourage him.

"I knew you were different, but this?" He gestured to her sleek form crouching in the dark trying to break in with a screwdriver. "Who are you? The good guy, or the bad guy?"

"Uh . . ." She looked up. A glint of light over his

shoulder shocked through her. Standing, she yanked Cam behind her. Her hand slapped at her side, reaching for her nonexistent weapon, and Cam cried out, startled as his dress shoes ground against the grit and he caught his balance.

"She's the good guy," Silas said from the dark, and Peri's adrenaline crashed, shifting to anger.

"Silas?" she blurted out. "How . . ." Her voice trailed off as he stomped forward into the dim light looking betrayed, angry, and threatening even in his long wool coat that cost more than most people's rent. *I should've just knocked over a 7-Eleven,* she thought. Cam edged out from behind her, and she sighed, looking for strength. "Silas, this is Cam. Cam, Silas."

Neither man moved to shake hands, and in the awkward silence she realized how menacing Silas was. He only felt small in her mind because he was a big soft teddy bear. *One who could bend iron rods and scare gang members. Damn LB anyway.*

"You're the man watching our cat?" Silas said, and Peri frowned.

"Carnac is not your cat. If he's anyone's, he's mine and Jack's," she said, crouching back over the panel and wishing they'd both leave.

Cam inched away from her as Silas came forward. "I suppose I am, yes."

"Think you can watch him for a few weeks more?" Silas said.

Peri sat back on her heels and stared up at them both. "You're not coming with me."

Silas hunched, losing every ounce of threat he ever had. "You need me. Admit it."

Eyes on the panel, she angled the screwdriver a little higher and pushed. "I do. But you're not coming. Bill will use you to hurt me, which means you will be dead." The screwdriver slipped, narrowly missing her hand again. "Silas, I can't deal with this right now!"

"You're going to have to," he said, taking a large step onto the cement pad. Cam backed up fast, and Peri did nothing as the bigger man took the screwdriver out of her hand and pushed her out of the way. "You're not leaving me behind this time."

Peri watched him wedge the screwdriver between the metal plates and twist, his extra muscle making it easy. "Yes, I am."

The front of the panel box snapped off with a sharp ping. "Look, I'm a help already."

"Peri, I told you if you need help, I have the means," Cam said.

Silas straightened, giving Cam a tired look before handing her the screwdriver still warm from his fingers. "Manipulating Michael into taking care of Bill might have been a mistake. He knows you're out for his head. His only chance is to bring this to his playground, and you're going right along with it. I'm coming with you. You can't stop me."

"My God. It's like a soap opera," Cam said, clearly trying to be funny. "Can I get the earlier episodes on my phone?"

Peri breathed in the cold night, feeling it soak to her bones as she thought over what Bill was capable of, what Cam was hearing. *This is not who I wanted to be.* Frustrated, she looked at her coffeehouse, seeing it as the hopeful lie it was. She could never be what she wanted to be. As she turned, her gaze fell on Cam as he stood behind Silas, both dressed well, attractive, and smart. Another lie, another wish. *Another mistake.*

"I'm sorry, Peri," Silas said, his regret so honest it hurt. "Bill is going to take everything you care about until you snap."

"Which is exactly why I want you to stay here," she said, eyeing Cam as he crouched beside the opened panel and used his phone as a flashlight.

"Wow, is this a Catch-Twenty-Two? If you tamper with this baby without the password, it explodes," he said in envy.

Cold, Peri held her arms to herself. "That's why I bought it."

Silas cocked his head in thought. "Peri is the same way. How do you know what it is?"

Silent, Cam rose, obvious he thought he'd said too much. His phone went out, putting him back into darkness. "I've, ah, got one at home."

"Cam's net worth is eight million," Peri said as

Silas dropped down to take Cam's place. "When the market is up, that is."

"How—" Cam stammered, and Silas chuckled.

"My baby don't hang with trash," Silas muttered under his breath, and Peri frowned. *My baby? Had he really said "My baby"?*

"I looked you up," she said. Then seeing Silas stiffen, she added, "Anyone who comes into my store more than once gets looked up. Don't think it means I'm interested or anything."

"You're an espionage agent?" Cam guessed, and Silas snorted, his thick finger deftly wedging open the access panel behind a curtain of wires. "For who? CIA? FBI?"

"No," she said flatly, and the lock beeped.

Silas made a low hum of discontent. "You change your password?" he questioned.

Peri's attention shifted down. Things were getting out of control fast. "How would you know my password?"

"Because you always use the same one." He hesitated, then sighed. "What is it?"

It bothered her he knew, but most drafters used the same password as a matter of convenience. "Twenty, five, one," she said. "And now I have to kill you both."

Silas gave Cam a disparaging glance when he laughed nervously. "That's what I put in."

Fidgeting, she leaned over to look. "Twenty. Enter. Five. Enter. And then one."

Grunting, Silas tried again, and Cam whistled, his phone angled to light the maze of wires and circuits. "You sprung for the three-digit model? What are you afraid of, woman?"

"Just herself," Silas said as the panel beeped, and with a solid click, the magnetic lock thunked open. "It's a large part of her charm."

"Thank you for that assessment, Doctor." Peri reached for the door and yanked it open. She had been planning on catching a few winks before heading to Newport, but that wasn't going to happen now.

"You're a doctor?" Cam was asking as she strode in. "Doctor of what?"

Silas grumbled something back. She wished they'd stay out, but they followed her past the unused back offices and out to the remodeled front. She left the lights off, knowing the way and not wanting to advertise her presence. She felt safe in the dark. "No lights," she said when one of them bumped into a chair, and she frowned at the thought of the dirty snowmelt they were tracking in.

"Peri, listen to me," Silas said as he caught up. "I know you think you have this under control, but Bill is playing you. You're doing everything he wants you to."

There was a whisper-thin layer of dust on everything. Outside, the street was empty and silent, but in a few hours, it would be busy with life that never touched her, even when it walked in her door. *Maybe it wasn't a sanctuary,* she thought as she looked at her knitting stuffed behind the register counter. *Maybe it was a prison.*

Opening a low drawer, she found the spare fob to her car. "Don't touch anything," she said as she slipped the thin metal plaque into a pocket. Her secondary passport and ID were right beside it, and she tucked them away as well.

Silas came up behind her, and she pushed his hand off the counter. "I'm not saying you shouldn't go after him, but you're going to need my help," he said as she wiped his prints away.

Grabbing her knitting, she threw it in the trash.

"Hey," he said, brow furrowed as he pulled the yarn back out and set it where it had been. "You need to slow down."

"Don't make me put you in the holding cell," she threatened as she opened the register and took every last folding piece, shutting the drawer with a cheerful *ting*.

The familiar sound cut through her like a bullet. Throat tight, she pushed past Silas. The man wasn't taking no for an answer. Cam, at least, had accepted the situation if his glum look and slumped shoulders were any indication.

"I'll drive the car, then," Silas insisted. "Give you a chance to sleep. Help you plan it out. Stay where you tell me. When you tell me. I'll never even *see* Bill."

Like that's a promise he has any control over, she thought as she tugged the microwave out from its built-in cupboard. It was heavy, and Silas lurched forward to catch it, easily manhandling the heavy appliance to the counter.

"Sorry about the prints," he said, using his coat to try to wipe them clean.

But she'd given up on leaving a pristine site, and she went on tiptoe to reach the three Glocks and extra clips hidden behind the microwave. "When have you ever done anything I've ever told you?" she said as she put one in her boot and another in her pocket. The third she hesitated over until Silas put his hand out, and then she tucked it at the small of her back, hating how it felt.

"Huh," Cam whispered, his shadowy self shifting from foot to foot. "Boy, do I feel silly. I keep my guns in a locked cabinet."

Shit, Cam. He shouldn't be seeing this, but she was fairly confident he wouldn't say anything to the authorities.

Silas took her elbow and turned her away from Cam. "You need an anchor. I need to be there if something goes wrong."

"Peri, are you sick?" Cam asked, his tone suddenly wary as he came a step closer.

"Yes." Peri wedged Silas's hand off her elbow and moved around him.

"No," Silas shot back, his shoulders hunched.

"There's nothing wrong with her. She's perfect. Don't ask me to stay behind. I know I'm a lousy partner, but I can help."

Standing in the middle of the room, Peri pushed her hair up off her forehead as she weighed the trouble of going upstairs to get a new set of clothes against them following her up there. "Silas, I need to know you're safe. It's easier for me to do what I have to do if I know you're safe." *There to catch me if I fall.*

Seeing her softening, Silas pressed close. "In two days, LB will have enough Evocane substitute for a few months," he said softly, but it was obvious Cam heard. "By then, things should be settled and I can start getting you off the addictive stuff piece by piece."

Cam's expression shifted, losing the rich-boy besotted lightness and taking on a wary, walk-away-now look. *Fine. It's better that way.*

"Please." Silas touched her face, bringing her back to him. "I can't keep up if you don't let me, but if you walk away from me now, I'll never find you again."

Even in the dark she could see his love. Blinking fast, she looked over the empty tables to the hazy lights beyond as she remembered the peace she'd made here. It hadn't been a lie, but even if she could settle with Bill and return, WEFT would hound her forever. *There is no peace but what you make.*

But why did her past keep destroying it?

"I'm done. Everyone out," she said, pulling away from Silas until his hands fell away.

His head down, Cam headed for the door. Silas stomped after him, his thick arms swinging. She knew that attitude. He wasn't taking no for an answer, and it scared her. Fingers shaking, she took the spare key from the register, carefully leaving an obvious print on the dusty counter. Alone, she listened to the silence, letting it soak in and make a memory knot, tying it to the scent of dust, the chill of an empty room, and the sharp edges of the key pinching her fingers. She didn't want to forget this place, ever.

Pulling herself up, she dragged her knitting across the counter and threw it away again. Breath held against the hurt, she walked quickly to the back door and shut it behind her.

The sound of distant morning traffic filled the silence of two men standing awkwardly before her. "I'm going to keep following you," Silas said, the security system at his feet already reset. "I'll make a mess of things. It would be safer if I was with you."

But she'd already come to that conclusion, and she aimed the fob at the ramshackle shed at the edge of the tiny parking lot that had once held police barricades. An aggressive *baruum* of a growl exploded from the garage as the warming engine engaged, and she strode forward, feeling a surge of sexual satisfaction. Yep, it was that kind of a car. She'd been born in Detroit, and the need for power went to her bones.

Both Cam and Silas turned in surprise, the latter laughing in disbelief. "You keep your Mantis here?" Silas asked.

"Yep," she said saucily, feeling better as she hit the entrance code and the rickety-looking door swung up with the precision of modern electronics behind it. Hips swaying, she strode to the wide gate that led to the alley. Unlocking it, she pushed the heavy wood to the side. Beyond it, Detroit waited in the predawn chill.

"Damn!" Cam swore, his back to her as he stood at the open garage, staring. "Is that a Mantis?" Silas cleared his throat when he reached to touch it, and Cam drew back. "It's got a six-point-two L, V8, right?" he said, eyes glinting in the sudden light from the headlamps. "Zero to sixty in three-point-eight seconds. The only thing that can outrun it is a Lamborghini. Damn, it's the premier year, before they took all the illegal stuff off it."

"And maybe an Aston Martin," Peri said, coming to a satisfied halt before it. Silas was hiding a smile, but Peri didn't care. It was a nice car, and she didn't have much of a chance to show it off.

"I'm on a list, but I haven't had a Detroit address long enough. Does it really change color?" Cam asked, and Peri went around to the driver's side.

"As you say, that would be illegal," she said as

she lifted the latch. The car recognized her print, not the fob in her pocket, and unlocked. She slid in, and as the car enfolded her with the scent of leather and suede, she flicked through the onboard screen and toggled the color from its energy-saving white to black with a surge of extra electrons.

"That is the sexiest thing I've ever seen," Cam said, his voice breathy.

"It gets me there." Relishing his appreciation, she shut her door, eyes closing briefly in bliss at the soft thump that said money. God, she'd missed this. But it wasn't the kind of car she could go to the store in for cat food.

Silas intentionally bumped Cam as he went between him and the front. "Pick your jaw up before she runs it over," he said as he reached for the handle.

Peri hit the lock button, but she must have cleared him in the past because it recognized his print and opened. He got in with a hasty lurch—as if she might bolt out of the garage with him half in it. Secure in his seat, he looked across the surprisingly wide expanse, his eyes glinting in challenge.

"You'll have to shoot me," he said breathlessly. "I'll get blood all over your seats."

Frowning, she hit the start button. "At least if *I* shoot you, you'll wake up in the morning."

Cam's tall shadow was flitting in front of the car

as if not knowing what to do. Peri revved the engine to get him to move, and he darted to her side. Silas put his belt on, adjusted the vent, and turned on the seat warmer. Clearly he'd been in it before, if the lock being primed to him wasn't enough of an indication. Nodding, he hit a dismiss key on the lighted touch screen. *Maybe he'd helped me set it up.*

"We going or not?"

Sighing, she twisted in her seat and handed him the Glock from the small of her back. "Fine," she muttered. "You can come. But you already knew that. Damn psychologist."

"Just a matter of hitting the right buttons," he said, clearly relieved. "God, I love this car. Hey, my station is still in the queue," he added as the car found the satellite and slow jazz lifted from the speakers.

My gut feels good about this, she realized as she pulled slowly forward, the power and ability coiled up in the engine spilling into her through the wheel and gas pedal.

"Peri!" Cam tapped on the window, and she lowered it so he wouldn't touch it again.

"We have to go," Silas prompted, and she obstinately put the car in park.

"What?" she asked Cam, ignoring Silas.

Cam pulled his eyes from the lighted dash, his brow suddenly furrowing. "You're not coming back, are you."

"Yes I am."

"No," he insisted. "You're not."

Knowing he was probably right, she dropped her head and dug in her belt pack for the key. "Do what you want with the store," she said, pressing it into his hand.

"Peri," Silas protested, but the peace she'd found here was spoiled.

"Sell it," she added, refusing to take it back. "Use the money for Carnac's vet bills. Whatever. I don't care. You saw the security code, right? Twenty, five—"

"One," Cam finished softly. "Peri—"

"If I can take care of this, you'll be fine," she interrupted. "If I can't, then Bill won't have any reason to bother you."

"Either way, you're not coming back," Cam said—and it hurt.

"I'm sorry." The car rumbled under her, the embodiment of her wish to be gone.

"Don't worry about it." Cam tucked the key away and glanced at Silas. "I knew there was no real chance. My psychologist says I only go after the women I can't have, and I thought I might have broken that, but I guess not."

"I'm trying to fix this," Peri said, not liking his sad smile. "Once Bill is gone, I have a chance at something normal."

"But not with me," he said, his eyes going back to Silas. "I know when a woman is in love."

She flushed, her grip on the wheel tightening. Beside her, Silas cleared his throat. “It’s going to be light soon,” he muttered.

“Cam,” she said, not wanting to leave it like this, but he was backing up.

“Do me a favor,” the tall man said, his eyes on the lights of Detroit. “If you come back for Carnac, leave me a note so I don’t waste my time looking for him, okay?”

“Cam!”

He was walking away. “I’ll get the gate for you.”

“Jesus,” she swore, and Silas smirked. “Why is he laying this guilt trip on me? It isn’t as if we did anything together.”

“He seems nice,” Silas said dryly, and she inched forward.

“Not another word,” she warned.

“I was just going to say—”

“Stop,” she demanded, trying to catch Cam’s eye as she carefully drove out of the gate and angled into the alley. But he wouldn’t look at her.

This wasn’t what she had intended, but as Silas settled into his seat as if it were his lounger in front of his TV, shut his eyes, and went to sleep, she realized that it was the calmest, most relaxed she’d been in months.

Maybe, she thought, looking at him.

Maybe not.

CHAPTER THIRTY-ONE

"There is no police report because I didn't report it," Bill said, his voice even but temper fraying as he argued with the disaster recovery company. "Get someone out to look at it. Give me a quote so I can write a check. Fix it. What is the difficulty?"

"I'm sorry, sir, but we are required by law to report gun damage."

Bill pressed his fingertips into his forehead, fighting the urge to pace the floor of the East Coast office that Helen had insisted he use while he was here. He wanted to go home to a house that had no reminders of Michael or his lifeblood spilling from him, but that was looking less and less likely. "Guns didn't make the holes in my walls. Bullets did. Are you required by law to report bullet damage?"

"You're talking semantics, sir."

"Semantics? Someone learn a new word today?" Bill said snidely, then hung up.

"Margo!" he shouted, then remembered Margo was eight hundred miles away. "Sean!" he shouted instead, and the man poked his head in.

"Another coffee, sir?"

Bill eyed the man's lavender polo shirt and Dockers, imaging the impression the clean-cut man would make if he was in a suit. Sean had been with him for years, able to put five shots in a silver dollar, but not everyone was comfortable with the uglier side of Opti. "No," he said, looking at the untouched sugar bomb he'd found on his desk this morning. "Get me the handyman you recommended on the phone. I should have listened to you in the first place."

"Yes, sir."

He didn't mind the smugness in Sean's voice, seeing as he deserved it. "And double what he's asking if he can be in and out in twenty-four hours!" he added as the door closed.

"Yes, sir" came through the intercom, and then, "Sir, Michael is here to see you."

Michael? Bill's gaze shot to the drawer where his Glock was. "Send him in," he said, unlocking it even as Michael pushed open the door.

"Hello, Bill."

Bill's expression froze. Irritation melted into a wary alertness at the self-satisfied tone and insufferable cockiness as Michael rocked to a halt in the center of the room. Wanting to keep the upper hand, Bill checked his motion to rise, pointing to a chair instead. "Just who I wanted to see," he said, his entire attitude realigning. Something had changed. The little snot thought he had something on him.

Michael grinned to show his teeth. "Liar." Eyebrows high, he passed the chairs to look out the window at the city's quaint "skyline" instead. His back was to Bill—another not-so-subtle show of dominance.

Little boy wants to play? he thought, remembering the feel of Michael's knife slitting his throat. Silent, he waited. It was an old tactic, but effective nonetheless.

"Have you set up a meeting with Helen yet?" Michael asked, his nail rubbing a nonexistent spot on the window.

Bill's eyes narrowed when their gazes met through their reflections. "She abhors me calling her. She knows we're here. If she doesn't call by noon, I'll leave a message." He leaned back and laced his hands across his middle. "Why?"

Michael turned. "Harmony is ten minutes from here at a drive-up motel."

"What?" He checked his motion to rise, cursing himself when Michael's grin widened. Son of a bitch, there was a hole in his intel. How had Michael found out first?

"Helen." Michael said the word as if it were a piece of chocolate to be savored.

Bill's anger shifted to a slow burn, and he settled back. The contriving bitch had gone around him. If he complained, she'd say it was to endear Michael to her, but the reality was she was probably testing the viability of cutting out the middle man and dealing directly with Michael. *Too soon. Too fast.*

Full of himself, Michael went to the wet bar and decanted a shot of scotch. "You want to come with me to get her?" Michael said as he downed it, hesitating as it burned. "I should have an anchor to back me up. Bus leaves in thirty minutes."

He had to slow this down. Bill stood and tucked his phone in his pocket. "Listen to me, you little pissant—"

"Or what?" Michael set the shot glass on the bar with an aggressive thump.

Motions holding a deliberate slowness, Bill came around the desk, shoving Michael back to reach the scotch and cap it. "I'm leaving in ten minutes," he said, running through his to-do list as the adrenaline spilled into him. "Or do you need more time to put your big-boy panties on?"

Chuckling, Michael walked out the door. "Ten minutes," he called over his shoulder, leaving the door open. "Nice shirt," he said to Sean, his dress shoes clicking on the imported tile.

Bill's thick hands clenched, and then he forced himself to relax. He had only a short staff, but they were all available. Ten minutes was just enough, and it might bring Michael down a notch.

Returning to his desk, he tucked his Glock into his ankle holster. "Sean!" he called, and the man was there, phone at the ready. "Walk with me."

"Yes, sir."

He liked that this facility was all on one level,

and he headed for the armory. It was right off the motor pool. "David is on call, is he not?"

"Ah, yes. Do you want him on-site? I have the address already."

Nice. Bill cleared the armory lock, then yanked open the door so hard it swung into the wall. "No. Traffic. Distraction. Make it a bridge at least seven minutes from the take site. Nothing fatal, but heavy on involvement. Harmony might be messy, and we'll need a few extra minutes to clean things up." He reached for a vest. Sean took his suit coat's jacket as he checked the size and slipped it on.

"Who do you want there, sir?"

He put his jacket back on, deciding it was a little tight with the Kevlar underneath, but not bad. "Smith is in a car. Put her on distant surveillance until we arrive. If Harmony moves, she follows. Tell her we'll be there in ten."

"Got it. Driver?"

"Anyone who doesn't know Michael," he said sourly as he kicked off his desk shoes and reached for a pair of boots, checking the size before slipping them on. "Same for the rest. I want one for front, one for back, and you as my gofer."

"Me!"

Bill grinned as he stomped into his boots and tugged his cuffs free. "Relax, Sean. You're the wild card. Go where you want, even if you never leave the van. Follow your instincts. Shoot at someone if you want. Have some fun. You'd make a hell of a field agent if you'd learn to trust yourself. Get a vest. And some boots."

"Yes, sir!"

Bill grabbed an energy bar from the bin next to the clips and turned away. Leaving Sean to gather the team and find a vest and a pair of boots, he stiff-armed the door and headed into the garage. The cold air smelled like gas, metal, and a low tidal pool, and he breathed it in, feeling it all the way to his toes. God! He missed this. Maybe he should send Helen a thank-you bouquet for getting him out from behind a desk.

The no-window panel van was obvious, and he smiled as a woman in overalls ran from a distant door, keys jingling. She slid behind the wheel, making her their driver. He closed the gap between them, holding up a hand for the extra fob.

"Where is the little shit?" he mused aloud as it thumped into his palm and he pocketed it. Checking his watch, he vowed they'd leave without him if he didn't show in time. The van's side and back doors automatically opened, both moving with a heavy slowness that said bullet resistant. Two benches lined the sides, leaving lots of room in the center for equipment or casualties.

Sean hustled out of the armory, bright-eyed and dangerously excited in his vest and new boots, a Glock on his hip. Two slick-looking men were behind him, elbowing each other at Sean's wide-eyed excitement. Michael was last, his steps fast and frowning as the team assembled in the dank shadows of the parking structure. *Suck it up, Mickie. You should have thought this through if you wanted your people with you instead of mine.*

"Glad you made it," he said to Michael as the others gave him a respectful nod. "Load up!" he called louder, feeling himself regaining control. "We get there in five. Small target, small team. Everyone works alone." He looked at Michael. "Except for you. You're my bullet buddy today. Get in."

The door to the garage was sliding open, and Bill hung back and watched his team settle into the van with a calm preparedness. It was good to work with professionals, and the tension eased into that delicious hum that was just shy of pleasure. He was last into the van, motioning for their driver to head out as he settled himself across from Michael and threw the energy bar at him to get his attention.

"Brought you a snack," he said as Michael caught it with one hand.

Peeved, Michael tucked it away. "You had this all prepped? You surprise me, old man."

"You don't surprise me." The van hit a bump as they exited, and Bill moved in the sudden flash of sun. Lunging, he slammed his arm under Michael's chin, pinning him to the wall. Sean cried out, but the rest of his team didn't move apart from their initial jerk. Glock nestled at the man's gut, Bill leaned in, lips curled back from his teeth. For anyone else, it would be a killing shot. He'd have to shoot Michael in the head or he'd just draft to fix it.

"Don't ever go around me again. Understand?" he said quietly.

Still not getting it, Michael began to laugh.

Leaning in until inches separated their eyes, Bill laughed as well, and the eerie sound of their twined voices stifled Michael's. The driver flicked nervous glances into the back. Sean scrunched into the corner, eyes wide and hand on his Glock, but his team watched with a wary caution as they continued their prep.

"A woman gives you a piece of information, and you think that elevates you to take me on? You almost deserve what's coming."

"You can't kill me with a gut shot," Michael said, unable to push Bill off him.

"Who says I'm trying? Go ahead. Draft," Bill taunted. "I don't mind telling you twice." Michael stiffened, and Bill jammed the Glock harder. "Helen is playing a game, and you did *exactly* what she wanted you to do." Confident he'd made his point, he pushed off him. "Don't screw this up. I've got plans for you. Just be patient."

Michael pulled himself out of his slouch and tugged his jacket into place. The tall man wasn't even wearing a vest. It wasn't over yet, but it was a good start, and pleased, Bill maneuvered to the front, leaning to the driver and whispering, "Where are we going?"

The woman glanced at him, clearly unnerved—though not as much as Sean, whispering to the man next to him. "Ah, just another mile up. The Crab Shack. It's on the right."

"I know it," he lied, giving her shoulder a squeeze before slipping back to his seat. "Intel?" he questioned, finding his phone. Sean should have sent it by now. Sure enough, it was in his inbox, and he scrolled through it as Sean nervously went over the layout of the two-story drive-up motel.

"Unless she's moved, she's in room twenty-six, second floor, right at the top of the stairs," Sean said, hesitating as the rest of the team checked their phones and followed along. "Street is a one-way and narrow. She's got a blue rental car," Sean continued, beginning to relax in the familiar. "Parking is in front, and Smith is on scene. She says Harmony just came back with doughnuts. There's four other renters, all of them out except a woman on the far end. She works at night and will probably be asleep."

"Man on the scene?" Michael questioned, and Bill put his phone on VIP mode and tucked it away.

"It's been ten minutes," Bill said as they pulled

in and parked at the outskirts of the motel. "You don't think I'd send an entire team out without a vanguard, do you? That's how people get killed." *Doughnuts? It's a little late for breakfast,* he thought, wondering whether he should have brought a larger team. He'd have his hands full making sure Michael didn't do anything stupid. "Tom, you have stairs. Dan, cover the back. Jillian, sit tight and be ready to roll. Sean, go where your nose takes you."

"Sir."

Excitement tightened as the back door whined upward and the damp scent of cool cement and the sound of traffic slipped in with the crying gulls, urging him to do something—anything. "We're playing it loose here. Stand back and give Michael room to work. It's his show; let him demonstrate what he's good at."

Michael stood, hunched from the tight confines of the van, his attitude back in place as the January cold shifted his hair about his darkly brooding eyes.

"Stay out of his way unless he loses her," Bill added, pleased at the flash of anger that crossed Michael. Anger was good. Cockiness wasn't.

"I'm not going to lose her," Michael said as he pushed out past Bill.

Sean was quick behind him, followed by Tom and Dan. The two men walked calmly to the outdoor stair and elevated walkway, heads together as they compared notes. Bumping fists, they parted. Tom eased into the shadows under the salted walkway, but Dan held up a hand to show thirty before vanishing around the back.

God, he'd missed this. "Thirty seconds until Dan is in place," he said softly, still not seeing Smith, already on-site. "It's all yours, Michael. Impress me."

Sniffing, Michael headed for the stairs. He almost wished Harmony would put Michael out of Bill's misery, but as insufferably irritating as Michael was, he had earned the right to be that way. He was good, infuriatingly so. *And he'd lied about how far he could draft. What else hasn't he told me?*

"I don't need you backing me up," Michael said as Bill fell into place beside him.

"I know that, Michael, but as you're so fond of pointing out, I need you."

Michael went up the stairs, and from the top, Bill finally spotted their on-siteman and motioned her to the front desk. It was unlikely that shots would be fired, but if they were, keeping witnesses blind would be an asset.

It was a beautiful morning, the air dry and cold. From the second floor, the wind lifted through his hair, and Bill breathed it in deep, relishing the way it tickled his neck where his shave had gone too close. Steps quiet, they settled before her door. The curtains were drawn, and there was no noise from the room as Michael took up position to the side where the wall would be the thickest. Glock in hand, he knocked.

"Shit," came a feminine whisper, but no gunshots—meaning she was going for her weapon, not aiming it.

Michael jerked into motion. With one kick, the door was knocked off its hinges. Michael followed it in, Bill proud of him as he went without fear, without hesitation. "Don't move!" Michael shouted, his loud voice brooking no disobedience.

He loved watching Michael work. Bill confidently entered the small, dumpy hotel room. Smiling, he moved out of the window and to the corner. Harmony stood as if frozen beside the made bed, powdered sugar on her front and fingers. There were two cups of coffee on the dresser, both of them steaming. Bill's smile fell.

"Bathroom!" he hissed as he pulled his weapon. "Check the bathroom!"

But he almost choked when Jack rolled out, his weapon pulled.

"Jack!" Michael exclaimed, starting to laugh. "This just keeps getting better."

Bill's aim never wavered from the lanky man in his rumpled suit. Jack had said no to him too many times. He was here on his own agenda, not Bill's. Knowing death crouched behind the mattress, Bill didn't move, staying where he was in the open, and said the only thing that would keep Jack thinking he was safe, the only thing that would keep Jack from firing at him. Michael might not bring him back.

"Very good, Jack, but you brought me the wrong girl. Where's Peri?"

Harmony's mouth dropped open. Outraged and thinking she'd been betrayed, she turned. "You son of a bitch!"

Make the smart move, Jack, Bill thought, and then Jack relaxed, his aim falling from Bill.

"Sorry, Bill," the man said, gun pointing to the floor. "Peri turned rabbit. I got her newest best friend, though."

With a cry of rage, Harmony launched herself at Jack.

Bill hit the floor, rolling into thin cover as Jack howled in pain and Harmony in rage. "Michael, get down!" he shouted, but it was too late as Harmony wrestled Jack's gun away, and, that fast, shot Michael in the chest.

The pop sounded ridiculously small for the damage it did. Michael fell. Gun in hand, Harmony bolted for the door. Bill let her go, crawling to Michael as five more shots rang out.

"You stupid fool," Bill muttered, his hands bloodied as he turned Michael over, praying he was still alive. "Don't you die on me."

From the lot came an apologetic "Sean got her! Sorry. She's, ah, dead."

Michael made a weird, choking laugh, bloody froth at his lips. Bill pulled him up, his hands stained, warm and sticky. "Draft, Michael. I need you alive."

"Bill!" Jack hovered close, shoving hotel towels at him to try to stanch the bleeding. "I was bringing Peri in, but I had to draw WEFT away, and I lost her."

Bill said nothing, pressing towels into Michael, waiting for the bastard to draft. Jack was making this up as he went along, lying to him. What was it with his people turning on him? Had he ever been unfair or dishonest in his requirements?

"Say it," Michael demanded, his face pale under his dark hair and blood. "I want to hear you say it."

The towels soaked up the blood, making Bill's hands sticky. "Say what? Pretty please?"

"Say . . . you need me," he gasped, his long hands gripping Bill's over his shattered chest. The team was gathering at the door now, and if Michael was going to draft, it would be soon.

"I need you?" Bill said. "Of course I need you, you little pissant!"

"Just making sure you knew it," he said, and then Bill clutched at him, vertigo taking him as his mind disconnected from the present.

More like rubbing my nose in it, Bill thought as his balance reset. His grip on his Glock tightened, and he found himself standing outside the motel's door. Fifty seconds, he estimated. Peri's best was forty-five. But her reach was almost a half mile and Michael's was limited at hardly a block.

"Take Jack down, but do not kill him. Do you under-stand me, Michael? I want him alive!" he hissed at Michael beside him.

"If you touch my mind, I'll fucking kill you," Michael said, his eyes mere slits. Teeth clenched, he slammed his foot into the door. Harmony shrieked as Michael stormed in. She screamed again at the sudden pop of Michael's weapon.

Frowning, Bill lurched through the door, glad to find Harmony alive and clutching her arm. Sloppy. Michael was getting sloppy. This shouldn't have needed a draft. "Jack!" he shouted at the closed bathroom door, knowing the anchor would remember the past they were rewriting. "She's down. Come on out."

Harmony's face went livid as the lie took hold anew and she believed Jack had betrayed her. It was sweet irony it was really the other way around—and she'd never know.

Michael stood over Harmony, his Glock pointed down at her. "I hear you're on unpaid leave from the CIA. Doing a little Dirty Harry with Jack to bring me in? There's a good idea," he said, and Bill winced, jolted into motion when his foot thumped into her.

"Michael, stop it," he demanded, then louder, "Jack? Let's go!"

Curled in a ball, Harmony looked up, clearly in pain, both from the kick and the bullet. "You son of a bitch! This was a setup?"

It hadn't been, but no need to let Jack think he knew otherwise until Jack was down. The door to the bathroom cracked open, and Bill's pulse jumped when he came out, his weapon dangling from a finger. "Bill. I've got this. She trusts me now. I just need a little more time."

Bill's gaze flicked to Michael, and the taller man lashed out, knocking the weapon from Jack's hand, then slamming Jack into the wall. The smaller blond man grunted as he hit, sliding down only a few inches before Michael shoved him again, cuffing him as he held him against the wall. Harmony didn't move, pinned by Bill's weapon. Jack was compliant, knowing if he died while within a draft, there were no second chances.

But that didn't mean he wouldn't keep trying. "Bill, I can explain!" Jack exclaimed as Dan came in, taking Jack when Michael pushed him at him. "I had to leave Peri to keep WEFT from catching her," Jack said even as Dan yanked him out onto the raised walkway. "As soon as she runs out of the Evocane, she'll come running. I promise you, Bill. She wants to come back. She just doesn't know it yet. I'll get her. I have to."

"Isn't that the truth," Bill said, but Jack was

gone. Bill held his hand out for the duct tape, giving his Glock to Michael as he dropped to kneel before Harmony.

"I should have listened to Peri," Harmony said as Bill wrapped her wrists in front of her. "You're lying bastards. All of you."

Truer words have never been spoken, Bill thought. But the danger was over. All that was left was the haul-away. "Michael, go wait in the van."

"The van?" he echoed incredulously as he picked up Jack's Glock. "Are you fucking kidding me? This is my task."

Bill rubbed his forehead. God help him, he was going to shoot this stupid kid in the head just for the hell of it. "I'm not going to let you knock me unconscious at the end of your draft so you feel safe. Go wait in the van."

Clearly frustrated, Michael spun, pushing Sean out of the way to storm out.

"Don't touch me. Don't you touch me!" Harmony shouted, furious when Bill tried to get her to stand up. Eyebrows high, Bill ripped a second piece of tape free and taped her mouth shut. Her fury was suddenly muffled.

"Give me a hand here, Sean," Bill said, and the man gingerly took her feet and they lifted.

The draft ended almost without notice, Sean stumbling slightly on the stair as time meshed and the old timeline where Michael lay dying was rubbed out by the new. The van was already pulled up. They only had to get her to it.

Together they tossed Harmony into the back to slide into a silent, white-faced Jack. Furious, the woman kicked at him until he pulled himself away. Michael was already in the front seat, and Bill ignored him.

"Good man." Bill clapped Sean over the shoulder, shutting the van and motioning Jillian to head back to Opti without them. He needed some time to think about how to handle Michael. This attempted end run had him worried. "You want some coffee?" he said to Sean, leading him away from the van. "I need some coffee. Did you have fun? How did it feel to fire that gun for real?"

Sean's eyes flicked over his shoulder to the van, and then to his hands, spotted with Harmony's blood. "I don't know, sir. Can I get back to you on that?"

Bill laughed, but inside, he stewed. It was obvious that Jack had teamed up with Harmony to put an end to Michael, changing his story when it suited him to keep his ass out of a cell. Bill couldn't fault him for that. He wanted to put an end to the dangerous, fickle man himself. But not yet. Not yet.

He needed Peri first.

CHAPTER THIRTY-TWO

Jack stumbled when the guard shoved him. His hands were cuffed in front of him, and his shoulder hurt. That Bill hadn't believed him wasn't a surprise, but it left him thinking he should have shot Bill when he'd had the chance. Even with Michael drafting to rub it out, he would have had the satisfaction of having done it.

Even if it didn't change where I am now, he thought as the man behind him jerked him to a stop before the first of two cells. His head came up, and he stiffened. Harmony was in there.

"Oh, hell no," Jack said, turning to the guard. "I want my own cell."

Harmony sat up from the single cot, rumpled in her black suit and smiling in a not very nice way. "Hello-o-o-o, *Jack,*" she said, hitting his name hard.

"I'm serious!" Jack protested, and the guard unlocked the door and pushed him in.

"Bill doesn't want you to get lonely," the man said, ignoring Jack's cuffed hands as he wedged them through the bars to be unlocked. "Have fun," he called over his shoulder as he left.

It felt as if something was crawling down his spine. Cuffs clinking, Jack turned to find it was Harmony's stare.

She stood at the back of the one-person, ten-by-twelve cell, her hip cocked and her arms over her chest. "Wishes do come true," she said lightly, a seriously pissed look in her eyes.

"Harmony," he said, trying for calm but knowing it probably came across as pleading. "You don't know what's going on. I can explain," he said, cuffed hands up in placation.

"Yeah." She let her arms dangle, hands clenching into fists. "I want to hear that." Expression ugly, she came at him, aiming a side kick at his gut.

"Hey!" Jack hopped back, cuffed hands trying to block it with some success. "Will you just listen?"

Eyes wide, he back-pedaled, but there was nowhere to go, and her roundhouse hit his arms, which he'd brought up to save his face. He was too slow to react, and her back kick slammed into his middle, flinging him into the wall.

Eyes watering, he slid to the floor, clutching his chest and trying to breathe.

"Are you okay?"

Bleary, he looked up, seeing Harmony leaning close over him.

"I said, are you okay?" she repeated, touching his shoulder. "Are you all right?"

He managed a breath, trying to smile. "Yes. Damn woman. What is wrong—"

He gasped, ducking as she hauled off and hit him right in the jaw. "Ow!" he shouted, cowering as she smacked him again. "What the fuck?"

"How about now?" Again she leaned over him, her anger easier to see now that he could breathe. "You still okay?"

"No!" Pissed, he pushed her away and she shoved him back, thumping his head into the wall.

"You sure?" she asked. "You look okay to me."

"Knock it off!" he shouted, swinging his legs to cut her feet out from under her. She fell with a little shriek, and he decided to stay where he was on the floor. "Shit, woman. I was trying to save your life!"

Still on the floor, she kicked at him. "You never had any intention of helping me get Michael."

Feeling like a school-yard bully, he kicked back, but it was more threat than action. "I never promised I'd help you get Michael. I told you I was after Peri. If I'd taken a shot at Bill or Michael, Michael would have drafted. Fixed it." She'd gotten to her feet, and he looked up at her. She was still mad, but at least she wasn't kicking him. "And that's exactly what happened when you shot Michael in the chest. He drafted. Me pretending to be there to give you up was the only way I could think of to stay at large." His eyes fell. "And even that didn't work."

"Always thinking about yourself." Harmony felt her side where she'd fallen. "I didn't shoot Michael. If you're going to lie, at least make it believable."

"You did." *Shit, she loosened a tooth.* Disgusted,

he spit out a wad of blood. "In the first draft. Next time aim for his head or he'll just jump to fix it. The only other way to kill a drafter is to do it in a rewrite. I was trying to save your life. Both our lives."

Harmony paced, arms over her chest. "My first husband was good at lying," she said, motion slowing. "My anger at him was what got me through the crap the CIA makes their women recruits swim through."

Jack stiffened as she dropped to crouch before him, grabbing him by the shirtfront. But he'd lived his life with volatile women, and he knew if she wanted to hurt him, she'd still be kicking him.

"I can smell a lie before it comes out of your mouth, white-bread boy," she said, squinting evilly at him.

"Yeah?" he panted, uncomfortable in the angle at which she was holding him. If she had cracked a rib, they'd take him to the infirmary, wouldn't they?

Harmony dropped him with a huff, drawing back to stand over him. "But I can't tell with you." Her head tilted, and she eyed him again. "You need some help with those cuffs?" she asked, her voice softening.

Jack looked at them, then back at her. "Sure?" he said hesitantly, and held them out.

Sighing heavily, Harmony slid down the wall to sit beside him. Drawing her knees to her chest, she hid her face.

Jack let his hands fall. Wincing, he felt his ribs. Maybe he deserved it.

"I don't like feeling stupid," Harmony said, voice muffled.

"I didn't lie to you. I came here to kill Bill. It's the only way Peri will believe I love her."

Harmony snorted and pulled her head up. "You don't love her."

He took in her fatigue and weary uncertainty, seeing in her that she'd given up almost everything. "You want to hear what happened?" he asked, and she dropped her head back to her knees. "When they came in the door the first time, they were surprised to find me. If I had shot Bill, Michael would have drafted, and it would have been for nothing, so I said the only thing that would keep them guessing."

"Yeah, and here you are. In a cell."

"I lied to them," he said, trying to make her believe it. "I still had my gun, and you took it from me. Shot Michael in the chest." He took a slow breath. "I told you to shoot him in the head."

"I wanted him alive," she complained.

Jack wiped the blood from his nose, then smeared it off onto the hem of his pants. "If you had shot him in the head, we wouldn't be here. You can't take a resisting drafter alive without drugs." He sighed heavily, satisfied she was listening now. "But you shot him in the chest and ran out the door thinking I had betrayed you.

And then you died in the parking lot with Sean's five bullets in your chest."

Her eyes were high in disbelief. "Five? You can call me superwoman."

"But all you remember is me giving you up."

"Yep." Harmony arranged the laces of her boots to make them lie perfectly.

Bringing his feet forward, Jack awkwardly worked the plastic pin out of the hem of his slacks. "I was hoping that if you shot Michael in the first draft that you'd do it again in the second. I hadn't counted on him downing you so fast." He gently bit his lip as he got the pin in the cuff lock. "And you're mad at me?"

"You're blaming me for this?" she said incredulously, then chuckled when she realized he was trying to be funny. "You are a lying bastard, Jack, and I don't trust you."

But she *had* laughed, and he shrugged, struggling with the cuff pin. "You can't bring down a drafter without a lot of planning, and they caught us off guard." His chest hurt, and he gave up on the cuffs, easing the strain on his ribs as he took a break. His thoughts drifted to Peri, and he sighed.

For a moment, Harmony was silent, her eyes flicking to his cuffs. "How long do you think they'll keep us here?"

He lifted a shoulder and let it fall. "Until Peri shows. Then they'll hurt or kill us to make her draft so they can scrub her."

Harmony eyed him. "You seriously think she'll show? She hates you. If it were me, I'd be half-way out of the country by now with my sexy psychologist."

"You think Silas is sexy?" he asked as if affronted. "The man is all brawn and—" He hesitated. "Yeah, okay."

She laughed, turning to take the cuff pin. In three seconds, it clicked open. Relieved, he took the cuffs off, biting his tongue when Harmony tucked them in her pocket along with the key. "She'll show," he said as he rubbed his wrists. "If only to kill me, she'll show."

And that, of course, was why Bill had stuck him here instead of killing him outright. His only hope now was to convince Harmony he'd done it for Peri. For love.

CHAPTER THIRTY-THREE

The soft alert ding from her car was as subtle as the predawn morning light, but it rang through Peri like a shot, jolting the mild highway hypnosis from her in a spark of adrenaline. Silas was asleep against the door, never having heard it. The last of the stars were fading in front of her, and she was beginning to smell salt. A steady hum from the engine had her in a light, meditative state, and she hadn't even noticed when the GPS system had flicked on the car's front display. But there it was, a bright pink line superimposed on the map to Newport.

"Prepare to exit right in one mile," her car said, the male voice soothing in its proper British accent.

I didn't set the GPS. Peri frowned, then hit a few buttons to pull the display back and see that her car wanted her to exit onto Gilbert Stuart Road instead of continuing on 138. ETA was eight minutes, but it looked like it ended at the middle of a wetland and nowhere near Newport. Concerned, she reached out and nudged Silas.

His soft groan was achingly familiar, and he stretched, his long legs jerking back when they hit the underside of the dash. "How close are we?" he asked, peering at the predawn sky, and then his watch. "I told you I'd drive the last leg."

"Did you set the GPS?" she asked, pointing it out with her chin.

Silas exhaled heavily, still not fully awake. "No." Thick finger extended, he toggled through the touch screen to find the destination. "And again no. Where the blazes is Nokewa?"

Lips pressed together, she drove past the exit. Her computer told her it would recalculate, and the screen shifted to show her getting off at the next exit.

Silas ran a hand over his sleep-mussed hair. "I thought this was an unregistered car."

"It is," she said, then jumped as her phone rang. Uneasy, she looked at the screen. The number was coming from . . . Uruguay? Clearly it was being rerouted to hide its location.

"You going to get that?"

"Reeves. Answer the phone," she said loudly, and when nothing happened, she said it again, this time using a fake accent. "Reeves. Answer the phone."

This time it worked, and her grip on the wheel tensed. "Hello?"

"Peri Reed?" a woman said, the sound of wind and ducks behind her.

Shit. "Sorry. Wrong number." Peri reached for the disengage button.

"This is Helen Yeomon. Bill works for me," the woman said, and Peri jerked her fingers back. "I've heard you're wanting out and not averse to causing a significant amount of damage to achieve it. Would you be available to talk with me about it?"

His head going back and forth, Silas touched her knee.

"I'm not coming back," Peri said, her voice holding all her determination.

"That's why I want to meet," the woman said. "I'm loath to lose you, but I understand that when it's time, it's time, and perhaps after we talk, I'll be better able to convince Bill that this is the right direction for everyone. Do you have the morning free?"

Do I have the morning free? She looked at Silas in disbelief, but he was pointing at the screen. They'd found her car. Set her GPS. They couldn't gain control of her vehicle, but clearly they knew where she was. "You want me to follow your bread crumbs so you can bury me in a salt marsh?" she said, sifting through the options. "Not a high enough payout for so great a risk."

"Risk?" Helen made a disparaging noise. "If you want to *risk* Bill sticking his nose into it, we can meet at my office. I thought you'd prefer open space and many exits. Bill is unaware I'm meeting with you today, and I promise to keep it that way."

But a marsh, a true marsh, wasn't open *or* easy to exit. And still, even as she thought it, the curiosity wound through her. Hesitating, she looked at Silas for his opinion.

"We should stash the Evocane," he mouthed, and she held down the toggle that would normally put her flashers on. The car's onboard monitor whined, lifted, and slid back to show the car safe. Silas turned awkwardly in his seat to open the through-hatch to the trunk, pulling her short-job bag forward and onto his lap. There were only four doses left now, after she'd shot up last night at a rest stop.

"I'm trying to find a gracious compromise," Helen said as if growing impatient. "That, and perhaps stop throwing good resources after bad.

Bill is very good at what he does, but he doesn't know when to let go. Can I expect you and Dr. Denier this morning?"

His thick fingers were nimbly filling two syringes with Evocane as Silas shook his head no, but Peri liked Helen's no-nonsense approach. "You understand it's not my habit to take people at their word," Peri hedged.

Helen chuckled. "Neither do I. But we both got where we are by taking risks. I'd like to meet you. See firsthand what Bill has developed with you. You're important to me. If I meant ill will, I would've given Bill your car's address and had him bring you in, but as it is, I'd rather have a quiet chat. I hope you decide to come."

With a click, the connection ended from Helen's end. Focus distant in thought, Peri used her thumb to open the safe, but she frowned when Silas put the syringe of accelerant and the two Evocane syringes he'd just made inside. It wasn't truly secure. Anyone with a Mantis catalog would know it existed, and she didn't like putting them together like that.

Taking the accelerant out, Peri twisted the knob off the drive shaft and dropped the syringe into the column, leaving only the two syringes of Evocane in the safe.

"That's not very secure," Silas said as she recapped it, twisting it slightly to make sure it was aligned properly.

“It’s also not in the manual,” she said, and he nodded in understanding.

“Which is why I want you to carry half the Evocane,” he said, handing her the original vial with only two doses left in it. “In case we have to run.”

She dropped the heavy glass into her jacket pocket, seeing the wisdom in it even as she loathed carrying it to a meeting with the money behind Bill. Peri looked at the screen as it slid back down. The GPS wanted her to exit. Without a word, she did.

Silas straightened in his seat, clearly uneasy. “This is so bad for my asthma,” he said, the familiar phrase coming from him startling her.

“She’s like eight minutes away.” Peri gestured at the road ahead of them, silent and empty at the early hour. “If she wanted me dead, there’d be a car behind us ready to shoot out my tires. You see anyone back there?”

Grunting, he turned in the small seat to look. “I still don’t like it,” he muttered when he spun back and began searching the glove box. There was a set of needles and a ball of yarn in there, and Peri’s head started to hurt. “You got any more weapons in here?” Silas muttered.

“I wouldn’t take one even if I did,” she said. There was a stop sign before the right onto an even smaller road. “They’ll only confiscate it. All the Glocks stay in the car.”

Clearly peeved, Silas leaned back into the seat,

big arms over his chest. "What does Jack say?" he asked, and she felt herself warm.

"He hasn't weighed in," she said, not sure whether that pleased her or not. "But this woman is holding Bill's purse strings, and I want to talk to her." They had left the cluster of commercial buildings beside the expressway behind, and it had gotten wild surprisingly fast with winter-bare trees and scrub. *Carr Pond?* she thought as they passed a "Natural Resources" sign. "If I can convince her that I'm not going to go *work* for anyone else, she might get him to back off. Bill is a dick. If anyone can get him to back off, it'll be the one paying his rent." *And then maybe I won't have to kill him.*

A left at a blinking light put them on a dirt road, and she followed it past the wetland preserve sign. The headlamps began to show on the vegetation pushing up against the car, and though it wasn't anything she recognized, it reminded her of her grandparents' farm. The old woods was damp and broken from years of high water alternating with decades of drought. "If I don't like what I hear, I'll be no worse off than I am now."

"If she lets you walk out of there, sure. But what if she doesn't?"

"Silas," she complained as the trees dwindled and vanished, replaced by tall scrubby brush. "If she wanted me dead, there are easier ways to do it. Would you rather spend the morning trying to break into Opti and risk capture there? Or talk to a woman who is so wealthy she thinks she's bulletproof?"

He chuckled. "Who are you, and what have you done with my Peri?"

She gave him a good-natured smack on his shoulder, idling the car forward over a packed dirt road elevated a foot or so above the marshy surroundings. There were dead trees among tall grasses, and she could smell decay even in frozen cold. They wobbled over the ruts, and she slowed when they found a man in camouflage standing beside the wooden, easily surmounted gate. It was pulled aside to let them in.

Silas whistled in surprise when the narrow road expanded into a wide turnaround. Three identical vans were parked in the center of the large lot, and a comfort station set up with a cook and an open fire. Three happy Labs watched in interest as they pulled in, their tails wagging. "I'd say this is it," he said as he jabbed a thick finger at the car's screen and dismissed the GPS.

Eyes searching for the hidden snipers, Peri parked for a fast exit. Putting the car in park, she didn't get out, searching her gut to find there was no answer. She was willing to talk to Helen, but trust was another matter.

"What do you think she's doing out here?" Silas said, squinting at the brightening sky.

Peri looked through the skylight at the flock of

birds overhead, and then the familiar *pop-pop* of a rifle. "Duck hunting?" she guessed, and then got out, hesitating just outside the car to take a deep breath, pulling the smoky air deep into her lungs and feeling it relax her. There were eyes on her, but they only made her feel daring, and she stretched like a lioness, showing her fangs to those who might test her. Her boots scuffed, and she collapsed in on herself. Her black jeans and the turtleneck sweater she'd put on this morning would make it easy to get lost, hard to find in the predawn gloom.

"There," Silas said softly, and she turned to follow his gaze. A man had come out of one of the vans, bundled up and carrying what looked like coats and boots. He had a dog with him, and her eyebrows rose when the man hailed them.

"Agent Reed? Dr. Denier? Ms. Helen took the liberty of arranging for the proper attire!" he called out, red-cheeked from the cold as he came to a confident halt before them.

Peri dropped her hand for the dog to sniff, feeling the lingering cold on his fur as she gave the happy animal a quick ear rub. He was a hunter, not security, and he liked his people. Silas cleared his throat, and she shrugged, reaching for the smaller of the two coats.

"Thank you." It smelled new, and she tugged it on over her WEFT jacket, feeing the warmth of the rich wool immediately, but Silas shook his head, content with his long coat—as out of place as it looked amid the broken marsh grass.

"I'll take you out to where she's at when you're ready," the man said sociably. "Would you like a coffee? Ms. Helen insists the ducks can smell it, so we can't take it to the blind, but there's no hurry."

So she really is duck hunting, Peri thought as she glanced at Silas, then answered for both of them. "No. Thank you."

The man set the boots down, eager to please. "You'll find the boots are sized as well."

Silas looked at his inappropriate dress shoes still holding the salt from Detroit's streets, and Peri wasn't surprised when he shook his head again. "I'll keep my boots, too. Thanks," she said.

"Then let's head out," the man said, and the dog trotted ahead of them, clearly knowing the way. Walking slowly behind, Peri wrapped the scarf that had come with the coat around her neck. It didn't smell like anyone, which said that they had been expected for at least a day. Ms. Yeomon, whoever she was, was a planner, and concern stole around Peri's heart.

But the gloves she found in the coat's pockets were warm, and she put them on as their guide led them deeper into the marsh. They had a removable flap for the fingertips—shooting gloves.

Silas leaned close as they found the boardwalk. "They didn't search us."

"You don't think we were scanned?" she said

softly. “Probably before we even got out of the car, at the bridge we had to go over. My car is bullet resistant, not scanner proof.”

“I suppose.”

Her pulse jerked at the sound of another shot, and the dog with them whined eagerly. The scent of gunpowder was strong as they came out onto a cleared platform that was probably used for observing wildlife on less dangerous days. Though they were near the ocean, it was a fresh-water pond, and she squinted at the puddle ducks still flying in, the lure of a resting spot over-riding the obvious danger.

Silas nudged her, and she brought her gaze back to the two people standing at the blind at the edge of the structure—one man, one woman. Helen, obviously. The dog trotted ahead, getting a fond ear rub, shortly followed by a command to sit—which it did without hesitation.

Peri exhaled slowly, not sure what she had expected. The woman was older, in her late fifties, probably, despite the well-done efforts to keep her face from showing it. She was dressed in camouflage-colored fur and held an open twelve-gauge shotgun over her arm. Seeing Peri and Silas, she smiled and beckoned them forward, her hands sleek within her shooting gloves.

“If you don’t need anything,” their guide said, but it was clear he’d been dismissed.

“Thank you, no,” Peri said distantly, wishing

Silas would quit scowling. "Smile, will you?" she said out of the side of her mouth as they crossed the worn planks.

"I don't like that they're the only two people with a weapon."

True. "Relax. If anyone can get Bill to back off, it will be a rich, attractive, powerful woman. He's a sucker for powerful women."

Silas dropped his head. "I've noticed."

"Agent Reed." The woman beamed as she handed her shotgun to the athletic-looking man beside her, taking her glove off before extending her hand to grip Peri's. "Can I call you Peri? Please, I'm Helen. I was so pleased when I heard you and Dr. Denier had arrived. Thomas, give her your weapon. It's more fun being cold when you can shoot at something."

"Yes, ma'am."

The woman's grip was surprisingly strong, and Peri took the shotgun when her security passed it reluctantly over. It was still warm from his hand, and she knew that it had shot in it; he hadn't wanted to give it up. *And yet he did without complaint,* she thought, wondering at the woman's personal power. "It's been a while since I've shot," she said, looking the gleaming steel over and calling it good.

"You never forget." Helen dropped two shells into her gun and locked it up. "At least, that's what I've been told. I've not missed a year since my husband died." Her gaze went distant out over the marsh, and Peri saw the age at the corners of her eyes in the new sun just rising. The woman's lips twitched, and then she turned her gaze to her security. "Thomas. A moment, please?"

Silas rocked from foot to foot, clearly uneasy. Thomas, too, hesitated until Helen's expression shifted to one of irritation, whereupon he turned and walked away to stand at one of the cold-looking benches surrounding the platform. Her gaze lost about half its ire, and she forced a tight smile at Silas.

"I'll be fine," Peri said, and his eyes went to the shotgun. "I'm here to talk. That's it."

Helen's smile became real. "Thomas, take Silas up and get him some coffee. He looks half-asleep." Neither man moved, and the woman leaned toward Peri. "I'm not stupid. There are six people watching you through scopes."

"I'd be offended if it were any less." Peri uncocked her gun and hung it over her arm.

Helen laughed, touching Peri's shoulder familiarly. Peri didn't mind, liking the woman's personal power. Slowly the two men moved off. At her feet, the dog swished his tail.

"I regret that I hadn't taken the initiative to meet sooner, and now having done so, I understand Bill's continued reluctance to let you leave. But I also understand about the desire to retire—to perhaps pursue one's own plans. Is this your intent?"

Is this my intent? Peri brought her gaze back from the silver and gold the marsh had become in the new light. "One's benign, not politically involved plans," she hedged.

Helen frowned. "Do you truly wish to retire, or are you standing your ground, obstinate in the face of Bill's continued insistence?"

Warning tightened in her, but it wasn't an unexpected question. Her thoughts went to the Evocane vial in her pocket, and she wondered whether they were trying to search her car even now. It would take her living thumbprint to open the safe.

"Bill's clumsy attempt to force your hand by hooking you on Evocane was ill thought out," Helen said, clearly adept at reading people. "You stole his accelerator. You want to remember. Be your own anchor, yes?"

"I kept it to force him to leave me alone, Ms. Yeomon, not to become addicted to a new leash holder. Replacing anchors with a chemical shackle is what has been ill thought out."

Helen huffed, her gaze drawn by the incoming birds. "Why? Chemicals are not greedy as many anchors are. They don't think they're anything other than a watchdog or ask for more as their faulty view of themselves grows. They do not fall in love, look the other way. They do not lie to you or manipulate. They are clean and pure."

The memory of Jack rose, a fractured sensation

of emotion that made Peri's chest hurt, and she studied Helen's profile against the rising sun, memorizing it, wondering whether that smooth, surgical perfection had ever twisted in love or passion, anger or hate.

"Look," Helen said, chin lifting, "here comes another flight. Get ready."

Helen put the shotgun to her shoulder with a smooth expertise. Still, there were six rifles pointed at her if she was to be believed, and Peri didn't move.

"You have nothing to gain by killing me, and everything by cooperating," Helen said, sighting down the barrel. "Shoot a bird. I insist."

Motion laughingly slow, Peri readied her weapon. The world seemed to fall away as she sighted down the barrel, finding a bird intent on landing with the rest. Still, she held off, waiting for Helen to shoot first as was polite.

The twin pops of Helen's gun echoed, numbing Peri's ears, and Peri let her gun droop.

"You had a great shot," Helen said, and Peri handed her the shotgun, done with games.

"They were mergansers. They taste like fish." Bitter and oily, like the remnants of her feelings for Jack. She couldn't decide which was worse, a leash that pretended to love, or one that was unfeeling and oblivious.

Helen frowned. "And you keep what you kill. I appreciate that." Eyes narrowed, the woman brusquely motioned for the dog to retrieve her ducks, and the Lab launched himself off the dock. Helen's fingers were white with cold as she reloaded her shotgun and snapped it shut. "Are you steadfast on retiring, Reed? Yes or no."

Peri felt better not holding a weapon. "Yes." Anger and disappointment rose up anew, drowning out her wary caution. "Dr. Denier has developed a substitute Evocane. You left a big hole in your fence, and I'm taking it. Using addiction to control your drafters instead of anchors is only as good as your chemists, and I've got a better one."

Helen's breath steamed in the bright light, obscuring her face. "A hole in my fence indeed. Thank you, Peri. This is why I insisted Bill use his best for the live trial."

The woman motioned, sharply, and Peri jumped when a dart hit her arm, stabbing through the thick wool and the WEFT jacket underneath without hesitation.

"Y-you," Peri stammered as she pulled the dart out, feeling it slip from her fingers. Her arm was numb even before the metal dart clattered on the wooden dock. "I won't draft so you can scrub me. I'll die first." Shit, she had trusted this woman, and why?

"I'm not scrubbing you. I'm scrubbing the program. If Denier can synthesize an Evocane substitute that easily, then any agent under its influence can be hijacked with a minimal investment. We need, as you say, a better chemist."

Lips pressed together in annoyance, Helen took a step back when Peri fell and Michael paced onto the platform. It felt as if knives were being slid in and out of her muscles every time she moved. "She won't flip. Dispose of her," the woman said, her expression peeved as they both peered down as if Peri were a marvelous bug.

Dispose? Peri blinked, trying to grasp what Helen was saying. She'd found the flaws in Helen's system, and her reward was to be . . . disposed of? *Silas will never let me live this down.*

"I regret your sacrifice in the matter," Helen said, her boots planted firmly in front of Peri's face. "But I needed to know where the holes were, and you found them."

"Go . . . to hell," Peri managed as the platform shook, sending spirals of painful sensation up from where she lay against the wood. Then she screamed, knives stabbing through her when Michael spun her around to cuff her hands behind her, almost passing out when he shoved her back down, hands searching for any lumps or bumps that could mean a weapon.

"You should have done this before she was allowed near you," the dark man muttered as he found the vial of Evocane and tossed it to Helen when the woman insisted.

“She’s not dangerous unless threatened.” Helen eyed the blue liquid. “And I didn’t threaten her.”

Peri lay on the wooden planking, afraid to move. It felt as if she were breathing glass, each rise and fall of her chest slicing her. It was the drug. She couldn’t draft. She couldn’t move! *What the hell is this stuff?* Face against the wood, she searched out Michael’s face from the blur. Somehow she managed a grim smile. “You’re afraid of me,” she whispered, and his eyes met hers. “I’m the better agent. Say it.”

He kicked her. Again the knives sliced through her, and she curled into a ball, riding it out, holding her breath until she could get tiny slips of breath into her.

“Michael, you assured me you would practice restraint,” Helen said with a sigh.

“This isn’t restraint, this is common sense. You should kill Denier, too.”

“No, I need him. She found me a better chemist if nothing else. Take Reed somewhere and dispose of her. This as well.”

The clink of the vial hitting Michael’s ring pulled Peri’s attention up, and she looked at his satisfaction through blurry eyes. *Thank God I don’t have the accelerator on me.*

“Yes, ma’am,” he said enthusiastically as she stood up over Peri. “I’d like to be accelerated first.” He nudged Peri, rolling her over, and she gasped as pinpricks turned to knives. “I might have to kill her twice, and it would be a pleasure to remember both times."

"No," Helen said, her disappointment obvious. "I'm suspending the program."

The dog scrabbled back onto the dock, shaking the water from itself in little drops that burned when they hit Peri. In its mouth was a duck, still alive but dying.

"Suspending? How long?" Michael asked, voice heavy in frustration.

But Helen lavished praise only upon the dog, taking the duck and walking off with it to leave Michael standing over Peri, little pinpricks of pain radiating into her from the vibrations of Helen's steps.

Peri began to laugh, the sound low, as even that caused pain. Furious, Michael turned to her, the rising sun making his hair into a halo. "What did you say? Why did she end the program?" he snarled, and Peri laughed even more, the sound turning into a guttural groan when his foot lashed out, making shards of broken glass cut into her middle. His foot connected again, and she stared at the sky, breathing them in. They cut her lungs, and she choked, sending more through her as his foot hit a third time.

And finally, she passed out.

CHAPTER THIRTY-FOUR

"Where's my Evocane!" Peri shouted at the shadowed stacked boxes and clutter just outside her makeshift cell, her forehead pressed against the cool chain links. She knew someone had heard her; voices had gathered behind the windowless steel door. Her pulse raced, and counting herself lucky she was alive, she let herself sink to the frigid cement floor. It was cold, even with the coat Helen had given her, now smeared with old oil and grease. Withdrawal was hours away, but Michael didn't know that. She just wanted some interaction with someone other than illusionary Jack perched on a stack of boxes on the other side of the fence. She had to discover where she was—and maybe find a way out.

"Michael will let you rot in here," Jack said, giving voice to her darkest fears. "Turn you into his own private Evocane experiment."

It took everything she had not to fling the bucket she'd found in here at him. "I liked you better when all you did was warn me one of my old boyfriends was in the vicinity."

Shrugging, Jack tugged down the cuffs of his best Armani suit. Crossing his arms behind his head, he leaned back against the stacked boxes as if settling in to wait. He looked better than good with his clean-shaven cheeks and pressed pants, an illusionary bug-out bag beside him, untouched by the cold. She wondered what it said about her state of mind that he was on the opposite side of the chain-link fence with everything she would ever need to escape—there in his imaginary bag.

I'm not looking for Jack to save me, she thought, though she'd admit that the rush had been real enough when they'd escaped WEFT together. He was a good partner—smart, fast-thinking, versatile, and dependable—apart from the betrayal thing. But even that wouldn't help her now.

Helen had closed the entire program down. An entire decade of work mothballed because Peri had done her job and found the holes. "That will teach me to be efficient," she said, looking up at the bank of grimy windows when the gleam of headlights passed across it.

The narrow, high-ceilinged room smelled like oil and hot metal shavings, making her think she was at one of Helen's shipyards. Boxes and equipment were piled haphazardly against the far wall. She guessed that until recently, everything had all been in the cage, locked up so it wouldn't wander off with an employee. Her cell might be makeshift, but it was tight.

Frustratingly tight, she thought, tucking her sock feet under her. Someone had taken her boots, and her feet were like ice. Her shooting gloves, too, were gone along with the scarf.

"If I don't get my Evocane, you're not going to have much left to interrogate!" she shouted, stiffening when Jack sat up as the metal door screeched open. A dark factory floor was quickly eclipsed by an Asian man in a lab coat.

"Oh, look, it's your meds," Jack said when Peri saw the syringe in his hand. Her pulse raced, and she stood, not sure she liked this. It might not *be* Evocane.

"We didn't expect you to be awake for another hour," the technician said as he came forward and stopped before the fencing.

"She's a light sleeper." Jack ambled forward to peer inquisitively at the syringe.

"What's on the menu?" Peri asked, not sure she'd believe him even if he told her.

The technician hesitated. "Your fix."

"Evocane?" Peri looked past him to Jack, who made a "why not?" expression. Taking off Helen's coat, then the WEFT jacket, she pushed her sleeve up and pressed her shoulder to the chain link. Someone had just arrived and withdrawal was mere hours away. If they wanted to drug her, they only had to wait until she collapsed.

The tech roughly swabbed her shoulder, and her chin rose. "I didn't ask for this," she said.

His eyes flicked up to hers. "You didn't want to be a god?"

"Is that what he told you it is?" she said, stiffening against the prick of the needle and the sudden ache of pressure. "They forced it on me. All of them. I wanted to retire."

He pulled the needle out with a shade more gentleness. Eyes averted, he rose. "He knows I have two kids. I can't help you. Don't ask."

Leaning to see his watch, she put Helen's coat back on, grateful for the warmth. *Two hours until midnight.* "Can you at least tell me where I am?" Peri asked, and his ears reddened. A pleasant lassitude was spilling into her, but it was only relief that she had another twenty-four hours before her demon would show again. *Isn't it?* "Hey, what did you give me?"

"Something to make the next hour more tolerable," he muttered. Again the door screamed a torturous squeal of metal on metal, and Peri backed up as Michael deliberately pushed the technician aside and came in, eyes roving over the space to tell Peri he hadn't been here before, or at least not with the boxes on the wrong side of the fence. His dress shoes looked odd on the cold cement floor, his tailored suit and coat even more so among the industrial grime and dust.

"Out," Michael said, and the technician obediently left. Peri chuckled when Michael shut the door, sealing the two of them in the cold silence lit by a bare bulb at the ceiling. Eyeing her, he swung a metal chair from the pile and set it down before the chain link. “You find being confined amusing?” There was a bottled water in his hand, and she licked her lips. “The evening shows promise.”

“Oh, God. He’s going to monologue,” Jack said as he tried to follow the technician out, but the door didn’t budge. “Just shoot me now.” He hammered on the thick metal, the echoes of sound that weren’t really there making Peri jump. “Hello? Hey! I’m not supposed to be here. Can someone let me out before Major Delusion starts talking?”

Peri pulled herself out of the shadows and into the bare bulb’s light, not happy her sarcastic humor was showing itself through Jack. “I think it’s sweet you spent last week trying to kill me, and now that you’ve got me, you’re keeping me alive against Helen’s wishes.”

Jack quit hammering on the door, turning to lean against it as a faint hope sparked through her. Bill probably didn’t know about this. He wanted her alive. She was his girl. Every moment she sat in one spot, the stronger the signal of that radioactive tracer he gave her last spring would become. Perhaps she should play nice—stall for time. “Sorry about this. I didn’t know I was running a double-blind study. But that’s Opti for you.”

Michael smiled without mirth, pulling the chair back another three feet before sitting. “It’s fixable, and with Helen thinking you’re dead and Bill thinking you're missing, we've got time. And speaking of dead, what's your car's pass code?"

Eyebrows high, she snorted. "It hasn't been searched yet? Opti is getting slow."

He brought an ankle up to a knee, reclining as he checked his phone and set it on his upraised leg. "They cleared out the safe behind the communications screen before we left that swamp. Your thumb turned everything on but the engine." He took a sip of water and wiped his mouth. "What is that? Voice activated?"

"No," she said, wondering why Jack was so fascinated with his hand all of a sudden. "One of the drugs you gave me must have registered over the legal alcohol limit." She couldn't help but wonder whether her car was anywhere close—or at the bottom of a cliff with a dead woman who looked like her in it.

"Your car is a Breathalyzer? Damn. That's rough." Setting the water down, Michael leaned toward the fence, his smile wicked. "If the lock pad didn't require living, oxygenated tissue, I would've cut your thumb off. Made it into a car fob."

Close, she guessed, disgusted at the mental image his words had evoked, but thankful someone had known about the Mantis's living-tissue lock.

Michael's smile faded. "That was Evocane in the safe, wasn't it."

She nodded, remembering Helen giving him the vial she'd had with her and telling him to dispose of it. Peri had just been given one dose. That left twenty-four hours—best case. "Few days' worth," she said, knowing she had to be out of here before then. "Why do you need the pass code if it's been searched?" she asked, the beginnings of a plan trickling into place. She didn't even know whether Silas was alive. If he was, she would get him free. If he wasn't, she'd send Michael to join him.

"To reset it to me," he said slyly. "Some idiot put it into lockdown trying to drive it out. Helen thinks it went into the Atlantic with you, but you don't throw something that beautiful away. At least not until you've used it up."

Her lip curled. "Stay out of my car."

Chuckling, he looked at his phone again. It was starting to irritate her. "You might change your mind." Apparently satisfied, he put his phone away and took another swallow of water, eyeing her as if waiting for something. A flicker of unease rose as she realized Jack was still staring at his hand in fascination, his fingers going see-through. What's more, a pleasant lassitude was filling her. Evocane wasn't supposed to do that.

Something to make the next hour more tolerable. Shit, they'd laced her Evocane.

Peri took a step back, alarm pulling through her like a hot ribbon. Her muscles were beginning to feel warm even in the chill of the back room. A faint buzz sounded between her ears, and her fingertips were numb when she pressed them together. The tech had laced her Evocane with something to get her talking. Seeing as she didn't have a reason not to, she would.

"She never will, you know," she said. "Accelerate you?" she added when Michael's eyebrows rose in a request for explanation. "Even if I hadn't found that big old hole in her plans and blew myself through it. Want to know why?" Pulse fast, she carefully walked to the front of her cell and sat down on the discarded WEFT jacket before a wobble showed. "Because she wants the best. And you're not it. I'm the better agent. Say it," she mocked.

"You're not as bulletproof as you think." He stood so fast that the chair scraped backward.

Head resting against the fencing, she sighed, not needing to breathe again for at least four heartbeats. She couldn't take her eyes off Jack, now spinning in a circle like a dog after his tail, watching himself go transparent under the effect of the drugs. "Hey, uh, babe? I don't feel so good," he murmured.

"I'm not surprised," she whispered when he vanished with a tiny pop. Apparently she had no intuition under the influence of whatever drug Michael had forced on her. *Curious.* "Where are we? Newport?"

Michael ignored her, fiddling with his phone.

"Is Silas okay?" she asked, slurring to make him think she was deeper than she was. Three more minutes and it might be real. "If you hurt him, I'll be pissed. You won't like me when I'm pissed."

He looked up, his dress shoes scraping on the old cement. "I don't like you now."

She chuckled, feeing the chemicals taking a stronger hold. Her obstinate nature gave her some resistance, but with no stake in the outcome, she was going to talk. She needed to talk now, before she lost all control.

"You want to know my secrets," she said, letting her chuckle turn into a giggle-laced sigh. "It looks like you do." Her head lolled, and she squinted up at him through one eye. "What's your plan here, Major Delusion? I'm surprised you didn't just let me slip into withdrawal. Force the truth out of me that way. Why all the drugs?"

Michael looked down at her with the keen sharpness of gauging her high. "Because anything gained under duress is not going to be the truth." His legs folding gracefully, he sat down on the cement right before her, nothing but chain link between them. "You would tell me only what you think I want to hear so I will stop the pain. We proved that in the sixties. Torture is just an old white man's need for revenge." He picked a piece of gummed label off the wire between them and flicked it away. "I'm trying to be more forgiving to the people under me. You can't help it if you're ineffective. Besides, we have very good drugs these days."

She blinked at him, hoping she wasn't too far gone. "How big of you, Michael. Tell you what. Just for that, I'll tell you what you want to know. For free."

"I know you will."

"But I want some assurance that Silas is okay first," she said, eyes closed as she put her face against the fencing. "I want to talk to him."

"No," Michael said shortly. "Helen has Denier tucked into one of her labs. I don't have easy access."

Good to know. Peri lazily opened one eye. "Jack could do it," she taunted. "You just don't want to. Lazy ass."

A jolt of adrenaline pulsed as she heard the fabric of his suit sliding as he eased closer, almost whispering, "Why did Helen suspend the program? How did you fail?"

She blinked slowly. "I didn't fail. I succeeded. I've got a renewable source of Evocane that she can't control, and I got it in a week while under fire." His eyes narrowed and she added, "And that's a problem, because if you take the anchor out of the equation, we are all loose cannons." She smiled with half her face. "It makes for a very unsecure workforce. But you don't plan on working for her, do you."

"Now, why would you say that?" he said as he lifted his phone to take a picture of her.

"Because I don't care," she said, laughing sloppily and making a peace sign as the camera clicked. "You deserve it, Michael. If anyone does, it's you. But you'll never get it. She ended the program. Just like that. The thing is, I think you knew you'd never get it. That's why you're pissed all the time." She squinted one eye shut. "Caught in her web. The bitch."

"Where is the accelerator you stole from Bill?" he said tightly. "Does WEFT have it?"

"What, and have you kill me if I tell you?" she said, smiling cattily as the beginnings of a plan formed. She didn't want out of her cage until keeping her alive was a priority for him. "Tell you what, though. I'll take you to it. It gives me a fair shot. If you're the best, then I won't be able to slip you and you'll deserve to be accelerated and I deserve to die." Snuggling into Helen's coat, she closed her eyes and leaned her head against the fencing again. "And if I escape, which I will, you'll spend the rest of your life getting cats out of trees."

Peri gasped at the sudden pain, never having seen the slap coming. Scooting back out of his reach, she put a hand to her face. The adrenaline cleared her mind for an instant. "Is that a no?" she said, thinking she'd won some points. Trying to hit her through the chain link had probably hurt his hand more than he'd hurt her face.

"I'm not letting you out. Tell me where it is, or that is the last Evocane you get."

There was that, and she pulled the air into her, feeling it swirl in her lungs. *Damn, I am so high right now.* His threats meant little. She was a dead woman talking unless she could get herself out of here in the next twenty-four hours.

Seeing her pantomime zipping her lips shut, he stood, clearly confident things would be different when withdrawal set in. A fear born in self-preservation slid through her as Michael sauntered to the door, icing her mild buzz away. She had to keep him there, engaged. If that door shut, she was sure he wouldn't open it until she was in withdrawal.

"You're never going to get it, Michael," she said, feeling drained as the words passed her lips. "Helen is holding your leash now instead of Bill. Kill me, and your chance for acceleration is gone. I can give you what you want, but you're too scared to take it," she accused, and he turned stiffly. "You're afraid. Just like those old men you hate so much. You hear me? I got what you want, and nohow are you going to get it unless Silas is safe. Never."

He pointed a finger at her, a lifetime of being told no on him. "I'm not letting you out."

Because he was afraid of her. "Send Silas for it," she said, concentrating on making the words come out right. *Please stay alive, please.*

"He knows where it is. He can put it somewhere only I know about." She forced her wandering gaze back to him. "And when I'm sure he's safe, we'll go collect it and see just who is the better agent, Mickie."

Michael didn't move, poised in the center of the room, thinking. Scared he wouldn't go for it, she blew him a kiss and eased herself all the way down to the cold floor, pillowing her head on the wadded-up WEFT jacket. She had no intention of getting Silas involved other than getting him free. But the seed had been planted. It would fester until he pulled it out or it grew into full paranoia.

"I don't have access to Silas," he said. "I'll send Harmony instead."

Tension zinged through her. "No." She rolled over onto her back, feigning indifference as relief swept through her. There was a grate in the ceiling, too tiny to fit through. "I'm not getting her involved anymore."

"Harmony tried to kill me yesterday and got herself caught." Michael ambled back to her fencing. "She's involved up to her cornrows."

Shit. Peri turned her head, a wave of dizziness blurring her vision. When it cleared, Michael was swiping through his phone, smiling as he turned it to show her a picture. Peri's eye twitched as she took in Harmony's anger and frustration in what looked like an Opti cell. *Damn it all to hell and back.*

Silas was bad enough, but Harmony? Harmony hadn't asked for this. She had not only helped her stay out of Steiner's cage but had risked her career doing it. Peri didn't care Harmony's motive had been to bring in Michael and save her career—she had trusted Peri to remain true to her word when she had every reason to think otherwise. That this trust had put her in danger, a cage like the one she'd gotten Peri out of, was intolerable. Peri never abandoned those she worked with. Jack didn't count. He had turned his back on her first.

Michael turned the phone and studied the photo. "She'd be fun to play with." Smiling, he closed out the app and tucked the phone away. "Here's the deal," he said as he crouched before the fencing and Peri sat up. "You stay right here. I send Harmony and Jack—"

"Jack!" she blurted, and Michael grinned at her sudden flash of anger.

"He was with Harmony. I'm guessing they were aiming for you? But Jack is good backup. He'll continue to play both sides of the fence," he said smugly. "You gotta love Opti conditioning. They collect the accelerator. Bring it to me. And if it works, I let you all go."

Fat chance. Even higher than a cirrus cloud, she knew better than that. "They collect the accelerator, call me, and I tell them where to drop it. Once I know they're safe, I'll take you to it,"

Peri countered. *I'll get you out, Silas. I promise.*

Michael inclined his head in thought. "Okay." He took a surveillance camera from his pocket, one suitable for tucking atop a blind or under a TV. "But if your friends show up, I'm killing them all," he said as he toggled on the tiny battery with a pen tip.

Peri grimaced. Harmony wasn't getting anywhere near the accelerator currently tucked into the gearshift of her Mantis. "What about Silas?"

"Your credit isn't that good. I can get you Harmony. That's it. Yes or no."

Peri grasped the chain link, trying to think around the drugs he'd pumped into her. She had little time to figure out how to get Silas in the mix to even the odds, but she wasn't giving Michael anything unless Silas had a chance. "You give me no choice," she finally said.

He shifted the chair back another foot, eyed her, then pulled it back some more. "Good."

Her pulse quickened as he set the camera up on the clutter and strode to the door, his pace fast with intent. It screamed a protest as he opened it, but then the door slammed shut and the light clicked off, leaving her in thick darkness broken by the muffled sound of Michael giving orders.

Peri let go of the fencing. Slowly a crack of light showed from under the door as her eyes adjusted. Slumping, she sat where she was, pulling Helen's coat tight around her again.

Evocane shot—check. Implant the idea I'm Michael's ticket to remembering his drafts—check. Ascertain where Silas is . . . unknown but currently alive. He was alive. Her first hour of captivity had gone as well as she could have hoped.

Somehow, though, as she thought of Silas and Harmony, it didn't feel like a win.

CHAPTER THIRTY-FIVE

Somewhere between searching for Peri's cell tower pings and scanning blurry plates from the tollbooth records, it had gotten dark. Bill pushed back from his desk, eyes smarting from the bright glow of his laptop. Past the big plate glass windows, Boston was just beginning to glitter against the bay. He cracked his neck, thick fingers pushing his notes and maps aside so he could think.

The afternoon spent looking for shadows of Peri on the I-95 corridor had been met with minimal success. It was as if she had dropped off the face of the earth, even his request for a ping on her radioactive tag culminating in nothing. He couldn't believe she'd gone into hiding. Not to mention giving up on her revenge against Jack. It wasn't like her and would mean she'd not only bucked the deep-set conditioning he'd installed that she never be alone, but she'd divorced herself from her ingrained loyalty to those she worked with as well. It was the loyalty that made her the perfect, easy-to-manipulate agent, but it was her need for revenge that convinced him she hadn't given up and simply gone ghost.

"Maybe I'm going about this the wrong way," he murmured, reaching for the intercom. "Sean? Are you here?"

"Yes, sir," Sean answered back, his tone weary but still anxious to serve. "Would you like me to order something in?"

Priceless, Bill thought. "Might not be a bad idea. Whatever you want is fine. Could you run a check on Dr. Silas Denier for me as well? Same depth that you gave me for Peri. I may be going about this wrong."

"Yes, sir. Michael is here to see you."

Michael? Bill's eyes flicked first to the early evening, then the papers on his desk. Michael never came to him. It was always the other way around. *Except when Helen is involved.*

Focus blurring, Bill calmed himself. Perhaps it was the endgame. "Send him in."

He bent to his papers, shuffling them into order and pretending indifference as Sean opened the door. "Michael!" he called cheerfully as the tall, swarthy man edged in around Sean's distrustful stance. "Come in. I've been getting a bead on Peri. This was easier when I had an entire team."

"Did Peri get something other than Evocane?" Michael said point-blank, still standing just inside the door. "Either when she stole the original supply or with what we gave her in the arena?"

Truly surprised, Bill looked up, noticing he'd shut the door behind him. "No," he said carefully. "My intent had been that she accelerate herself. Giving her fake Evocane would be counter-productive. Why?"

Silent, Michael sat in one of the overstuffed chairs. An ankle went atop a knee, his focus becoming distant.

This is not like Michael, Bill thought, and then a wash of heat took him as he realized that the reason he couldn't find Peri was that Michael and Helen had her already. They had her, and hadn't told him. They were cutting him out. Fortunately for him, Michael couldn't read her, even with the drugs they'd probably been pumping into her. She'd said or done something to get the man confused, and he'd come to Bill to figure it out.

It was time.

Bill's pulse quickened. With one swipe of his hand, he pushed the papers on his desk into the wastebin. "I've got Peri's phone pinging towers all the way to Cleveland, and then nothing. Damn dead zones."

Michael said nothing, fingers steepled and

covering his lips in thought. His hands dropped and he took a breath. “Did you know how easy it was to duplicate Evocane?”

“It isn’t.” Bill hid his confusion, aiming for irritation instead. “Did Helen tell you that? Getting it to balance with the accelerator is almost impossible. She only thinks it’s easy.”

He could hear whispers of Peri’s plan in Michael’s questions, the way he was puzzling through it. Second-guessing Peri was usually a losing proposition. It was better to give her a goal and let her work it the way she wanted, but his life was in the mix this time. Perhaps she wanted Michael to believe she had a supply of it and was willing to share the accelerator she’d stolen in return for her life. But even Peri had to realize that Michael could achieve the same ends by simply killing her, riding out Helen’s wrath for the ultimate goal.

Unless upon gaining Peri, Helen let it slip that Michael would never be accelerated. Bill’s tension rose until he hid his agitation behind a sip of that cold, overly sweet coffee Sean kept pushing on him. If Helen had her, there was a danger that Peri would be wiped. But he knew his girl. She’d never cave. Not for pain, not for love. Not for anything.

He needed more. “What is this about, Michael?” Bill prompted, and Michael pulled himself out of his thoughtful stare.

"Nothing. What do you want me to do with Harmony and Jack?"

Interesting topic shift. Perhaps Peri had offered Michael her original vial of accelerator, telling him she had a ready supply of Evocane to go with it, and she needed someone to fetch it for her. If so, it wouldn't hurt to further Peri's aim and confuse the man a little more.

"Why don't you move them into a more permanent installation?" he said lightly, wanting to give Peri the help she was asking for. "We can't trust Jack anymore, and it's time to start thinking about the possibility that Peri isn't going to come around. Hell, Michael," he said with a chuckle. "At this point, if I had any accelerator, I'd be tempted to give it to you myself."

Michael's frown deepened, and a secondary thrill rose up in a whirlwind through Bill. Giving Michael access to the accelerator she'd stolen was exactly what Peri had offered him. If Bill could verify that she had the only viable stash, Michael would act on it. Taking on a bland look, Bill took another sip of cold coffee to hide his rising excitement. "Helen confiscated my entire store of it when we shut down the med wing. I got nothing, Michael, and that's likely not going to change. She's turning me into a damn administrator."

Michael didn't move, and Bill spun his Opti ring, stopping when he realized he was doing it. It had been the right thing to say. *And now a layer of bullshit to hide the poison pill,* he thought. "Speaking of which, I want your help tomorrow. I've got Peri's location narrowed to a hundred-mile circle, and I need feet on the ground."

"Where?"

Bill stifled a smile at the hint of angst in his voice. He had made these gods, and they were his to control. "I'm sending you to Buffalo," he said, putting the search far away from where Helen had probably stashed her. "She'd go where she could duck over the border if she needed to." Which was a lie, but Michael wouldn't know that.

Michael's sudden disinterest hit Bill like a slap. "Sure," the tall man said, his subtle shifting as telling as the incongruity of Michael coming to see him at all. "You want me to move Harmony and Jack tonight so I have tomorrow free?"

How cooperative of you. "If you like. I'm in no hurry." He stood to force Michael to stand as well. He wanted him out. Out and gone so he could put his own plan into action. "Sean is bringing up Denier's info. It might help narrow her position down."

"Sounds good," Michael said, but the usual cocky man was hunched slightly, and Bill's jaw clenched. *Son of a bitch.* Helen had Denier as well. If Peri didn't take care of this in twenty-four hours, he'd be dead in forty-eight. But he didn't think it would come to that. He was betting his life on it.

"Okay. I'll call you tomorrow," Michael said, jerking Bill out of his thoughts. "I'll be on the road if something comes up between then and now."

"Thank you, Michael. Leave the door open, will you?"

Bobbing his head, Michael left. Bill stood at his desk, unmoving as he listened to the two men in the outer office exchange a word, and then Michael's shoes on the imported tile. Finally the hermetically sealed door in the outer office hissed shut.

"Sean!" he shouted, making a fist when he realized his hands were trembling.

"Sir, I've got the first of Denier's info," the small man said as he hustled in. "And Chang's is on the way. I've got an ETA for dinner of forty minutes, but I promised them a twenty tip if they could make it in thirty."

"I want you to shred this," Bill said as he gathered up Peri's info. "Shred the office. Everything. We are out of here in twenty minutes. You're driving."

"Sir, what about Chang's?"

Bill hesitated. "Thirty, then. Start with these," he said, handing him Peri's info.

"Yes, sir." Juggling the papers, Sean turned and calmly walked out of the room.

The adrenaline tingled down to his toes, and Bill went to stand before the window, smiling when the shredder whirled to life. Helen was cutting out the middle man. Thank God Michael was as simple as a four-year-old when it came to office politics. Thirty minutes was a negligible risk; chances were good that Michael wouldn't tell her of this meeting at all since he was probably thinking of betraying her himself.

Money, he thought, running through his own checklist as he twisted his Opti ring, working it over his thick finger to try to get it off. *Resources. Places I've cleared but never used, and one kick-ass assistant who knows the power of a cup of coffee and blind obedience.* A smile began to grow, and he spun, anxious to wipe the room and shut the door for the last time. Tomorrow he would be free of Michael and have Peri back at his side.

It's going to be a good day, he thought as his Opti ring finally worked over his knuckle and he set it on the empty desk as if it were a resignation letter. And the best part? He didn't have to do a thing but sit back and watch.

CHAPTER THIRTY-SIX

It wasn't the first time Jack had been cuffed and thrown into the back of a panel van with no seats, but it was the first time fear, real fear, had been a part of it. He and Peri had never been caught outside of a few training tasks where the odds had been intentionally stacked against them to see how they'd respond. Now, in the middle of the night with nothing between him and the cold metal wall of the van but a wrinkled Armani suit, he knew the meaning of doubt.

He could hear Harmony breathing in the far corner, see the darker slump her body made. Neither had said much after the first few minutes of being bundled inside, and the silence had held as they spent by his reckoning at least an hour on an expressway, the turns so gradual that trying to figure out their final destination was chancy at best. He figured they were going to their deaths. Clearly their usefulness was done, meaning Peri was likely dead.

Jack found he was more troubled about that than he ever expected he would be.

The hum of the van muted, and he felt it slow. Harmony stirred. His pulse quickened, and he shifted his hands, fingers swollen from the tight band of plastic. There was no whoosh of passing traffic, meaning they were on a deserted stretch, or more likely, it was just because of the late hour.

"Harmony?" he hazarded, knowing the proud woman was likely more inclined to kick him than talk to him.

"This really sucks," she said, her voice resigned. "I had always hoped I'd be buried next to someone I actually, you know, liked." She sighed, adding, "What do you want."

It was flat and emotionless. Much better than the hysterics he half expected. But then again, Peri liked her, and Peri was a great judge of character.

Usually, he thought, surprised at the flash of guilt.

He gathered himself, training and a steadfast refusal to simply give up demanding he do something. "Hey, don't hit me. I'm coming over."

"Why?" she asked, but he was already moving. "What is your problem!" she exclaimed when his shoulder knocked hers as the van turned and he fell into her. He settled himself, awkward because of his bound hands. Peri would know what he was doing right off. Hell, Peri would have asked him.

"I'm going to try and get your cuffs off," he said, and she snorted, not moving.

"I'm not cuffed," she said, and he jerked upright.

"Excuse me?"

"I snapped it an hour ago," she said. "Come on. Show me."

Jack stared at her in disbelief, her shadowy silhouette showing her confident amusement. "Why didn't you say something? It's been over an hour."

"Because you're a tool and I don't like you," she said, finding his hands in the dark and jamming what looked like a hairpin into the workings of the cuff.

Immediately it released, and Jack freed himself, rubbing the circulation back into his hands as he scooted to the opposite corner, not believing she'd left him like that.

"Hey, if you're going to pout about it, I'm sorry," she said, and his mood worsened. "You didn't say anything, and I assumed you had gotten yourself free."

"Yeah, okay." But it sounded sullen even to him. Frustrated, he thumped his head back against the van, little more than an uncomfortable, rolling box. He had known he wasn't going to die in bed, but he'd thought he'd have more time. What rankled was that he hadn't gotten sloppy; he'd gotten replaced by a chemical soup.

"They're taking us to a big field, aren't they," Harmony said softly.

"Or a short dock." He looked toward the front of the van, the partition between them and the driver nothing more than a thin piece of metal. "It's quiet, though. No conversation. Only a driver." Which was curious in itself.

Harmony's laugh was bitter. "How many people does it take to put a bullet in someone's head?"

Jack scratched his bristles, estimating it to be about one in the morning. "They usually have two for this kind of thing. Easier to move the bodies."

"Nice to know there's an SOP." Harmony

stretched only to fall into a dejected slump. "I never thought I'd be on this end of a murder investigation. My brother would laugh his ass off."

They both stiffened as the van slowed, turned, and stopped. Jack's pulse hammered, and he flexed his hands, trying for more mobility. He'd have maybe three seconds, tops, but they'd probably go for him first, cutting that to one.

The front door to the van slammed shut. Only one pair of boots paced to the back, and Jack stood. Harmony rose to stand beside him. A pang lifted through him. He appreciated that someone was here with him, even if she didn't like him.

Never had he thought he'd die like this, pinned down like a bug. Peri's ability to rewrite a mistake had given him a sense of superiority that he only now was willing to admit had been borrowed. A fleeting wish passed through him that he could go back and rewrite the last three years. He'd tell Bill to shove it up his ass, or maybe help Peri blow the whistle the first time she figured it out. She deserved better than him. *Why hadn't I loved her back?* Had being second best to her abilities been that hard to stomach? It wasn't as if she rubbed his nose in it.

They both jumped at the knock at the door.

"I have a gun, but I won't use it unless you do something stupid," a low voice said, and Harmony's lips parted, her eyes wide in the dim light.

“That’s Michael,” she said, and Jack pushed her behind him, not knowing why except it was habit. *Protect your partner, and she will protect you.*

“You’re out of your cuffs, yes?” Michael said. “I can’t believe I’m saying this. Peri needs your help. Will you do something for her? Yes or no. Right now.”

Peri is alive? It shocked through Jack, a slurry of emotion rising up too fast to realize.

“Yes!” Harmony shouted, and Jack jumped when she elbowed him. “Say yes,” she demanded.

But his first rush of relief had vanished, drowned out by three bitter years of lies and hidden resent-ment. “Let me think about it,” Jack muttered, then gasped when Harmony shoved him into the side of the van. He hit with a thump, his shoulder taking most of the force.

“I’m not dying in the back of a van for you,” Harmony said. Head high, she strode to the van’s back door. “We’ll do what she wants.” Angry, she looked at Jack. “I’ll make sure of it.”

Jack pulled himself upright, tugging his suit straight and missing his Glock. This didn’t sound like one of Bill’s games, and the thought that Michael was running his own task was chilling. Bill liked his pieces, cherished them and lavished a manipulative love on them like favorite toys. Michael sacrificed with no thought of tomorrow.

He knew his face still showed his thoughts as the door swung open. Michael was there alone with a bug-out bag in his hand, his lanky, tall outline fuzzy against a black background of light commerce at the edge of an interstate. There was no light in the sky, the stars washed out in the noon glare of the security lights. Here, though, on the weedy, cracked-pavement outskirts, it was dark.

Jack pulled the chill air deep into him, wary upon seeing Michael's sour expression. The man was tired, angry, and pushed to the edge, where chancy decisions were made with snap judgments. Dangerous.

"This is as far as I take you," he said, and Harmony pushed past Jack, sliding out of the van with a hasty rush. Her bare feet hit the ground hard, stumbling on the pebbles until she caught her balance. Michael watched in cool disinterest, never taking his focus off Jack as he slowly levered himself out.

"I want to talk to Peri," Harmony said, her confidence thin and misplaced.

"There's a bus leaving for Detroit in twenty minutes." Michael tossed the bag to Jack. "Be on it. Peri says you know where that vial of accelerator she stole is. You're going to get it for me."

Is that so. The bag was comfortably heavy in Jack's hands, but not heavy enough to hold any firepower, and so he let Harmony take it. "Bill told you to kill us," he said as Harmony began looking through it. "What are you doing, Michael?"

Michael shifted slightly sideways, the tell screaming volumes to Jack. "Actually, his words were to relocate you to a more permanent situation."

Jack laughed, and Harmony looked up from the bag of water and food bars. "You're going rogue," he said, knowing he was right when Michael frowned. "Why?"

"He's leaving Opti?" Harmony asked.

"No, just Bill," Jack guessed, head cocked. "Has Peri turned? Is that why you want the accelerator?"

Harmony went still, all interest in the bag gone. "She wouldn't." But there was doubt, and it fed Jack's indecision.

Michael's jaw clenched. "I'm taking what I was promised. That's all."

Jack turned to Harmony, and the woman blanched under their joined attentions. He could almost see her thoughts calculating to a probable end. Lie? Tell the truth? Play along for more information? *Had Peri really turned? Without me?* he wondered, his own feelings of self-doubt growing. Maybe someone had scrubbed her.

"Do you know where it is or not?" Michael shouted, and Harmony jumped, catching the bag when it slipped from her.

"I . . . Yes. I know where it was when I left.

There's no reason for it to have been moved."

Harmony held the bag close. "I want to talk to Peri," she said, but it was a cautious demand. "I have only your word she's alive. We don't do anything until I know she's alive."

Clearly satisfied, Michael watched a woman in a red sports car pull up at the nearby gas station, her car vivid under the full-spectrum light slicing the night into jagged sections. "Making demands?" he asked mockingly.

Jack's tension slammed back into him as Michael shifted his coat to show the holstered handgun. "Don't speak for me," Jack said, hands up in placation. "She doesn't speak for me."

"You are a prick, you know that?" Harmony said to him darkly. "Am I going to have to babysit you the entire time? Michael, shoot him, will you? Save me the trouble. I'll get the accelerator by myself."

Michael chuckled, seeming to like that Jack was making an impossible task harder. "No. Jack is going to do exactly what I tell him. He knows he's less useful than a second-hand condom without Peri. He'll do just about anything to keep her alive," he mocked, and Jack's face warmed. "Isn't that right, Jack." Michael's eyes tracked the woman in her holographic miniskirt as she left her car at the pump to go into the service station. "I have one dose of Evocane left," he added, throwing the keys to the van at Harmony. "So if you don't want Peri to suffer, be wise with your time. I'll let you talk to Peri then so she can tell you where to leave it. You can have the van. I've got another ride."

Jack watched unbelievingly as Michael turned on a heel and headed for the gas station. His mistrust flared, fueled by his indecision and doubt. "I don't think she's alive," Jack said. "I don't trust you. I want to hear her voice. I hear it now or I don't go."

Michael's expression was cross when he spun back around. "Fine," the taller man muttered as he took his phone from a pocket and hit an app. Eyes on the screen, he cleared his throat. "Good morning, Peri. It's time to prove you're alive. Say something."

Jack's pulse quickened at her familiar voice, groggy with sleep. "Harmony?"

Harmony's brow furrowed, the woman understandably torn by betrayal and wanting to trust.

"Harmony, I didn't mean for this to happen. Jack got himself out. It didn't go like I planned."

Michael smiled. "Really? You didn't plan on being caught, incarcerated, and drugged? But you do it all the time. Say hello to Jack. He's here, too."

"Jack?" Peri's voice came small over the speaker, freezing Jack's first words. She sounded annoyed. "Let me talk to him."

"No." He went to end the call, Peri's voice

shouting, "Let me talk to him! I want to tell him where to leave it! Michael, don't you hang up on me. You want the accelerator, let me talk to Jack!"

Eyebrows high, Michael looked from his phone to Jack. "She wants to talk to you."

Jack's fingers shook as he took the glass phone. Swallowing, he whispered, "Hello, Peri."

There was a short silence, then Peri said, "I had a hundred things I was going to say to you, all of them thought up in the last six hours."

He licked his lips and turned away. "I only have one thing to say to you. I'm sorry."

"Oh, yes," she said tartly. "Now I remember. One: you are a son of a bitch. Two: if I ever see you again, I'm going to kick you so hard you can use your balls as your Adam's apple. Three—"

"You're right," Jack said, ears warming as Michael laughed. "I'm scum. Lowest of the low. I could have had everything—I did have everything—and I pissed it away. But you let me do it to you. Admit it, Peri. You're partly responsible. You let me make you into it."

His pulse hammered at her silence. She might hang up, not willing to trust him, her pride not allowing that she had a part in her own betrayal. He was almost afraid of what she might say next. "I know you never loved me," she said softly, "but if you ever had one ounce of respect, or honor, or decency . . ." She hesitated, and Jack waved Michael back, sure she was going to tell him. "I swear, Jack, that I will come for you if you betray me again."

"Promise you'll come for me if I don't," he whispered.

His head hurt, and he waited, knowing she'd tell him. She'd trust him. God knew why.

"You son of a bitch," she whispered. "Michael thinks I'm telling you where to put the accelerator."

"Which is . . ." he prompted.

"Unnecessary," she said. "This is a ruse to get Harmony free. Take her and go, okay? Get her to safety. Think you can do that for old times' sake?"

Harmony, not himself. He wasn't the reason for the subterfuge, but an afterthought, an also-ran. *I can live with that,* he thought sourly. An also-ran was still in the race. "Sure," he said flatly, ending the call.

Michael's shit-grin as he handed him his phone burned to his core.

"Bill always claimed it was just as easy to condition two agents as one," Michael mocked. "You hate her, betrayed her, lied to her, and yet you're not going to bring it to me directly or tell me where she wants you to put it, are you. Pathetic."

Angry, Jack flicked his gaze to the gas station. "Your ride is leaving."

Michael spun, pulling himself upright as the

woman walked out the door, her long legs eating up the pavement. "Twenty-four hours," he said. "Get the accelerator. If you go ghost, I kill her. If you don't check in every four hours, I'll let her go into withdrawal. If you contact Bill, I'll not only let her go into withdrawal, but I'll send you a copy of the video. If you get caught by WEFT . . ." He smiled. "Don't get caught by WEFT."

Turning away, he jogged to the woman's car, hand waving. "Yo! Beautiful! Wait up! Which direction are you going?"

Jack didn't move as Harmony came even with him, both watching as the woman let Michael in her car and they drove off.

"Think he's going to kill her?" Harmony asked.

Jack shook his head, not believing how indestructible people thought they were. "No. Unless she reminds him of someone he doesn't like." They tracked the red car as it got on the expressway and roared off.

Harmony eyed him as she picked up the short-job bag and jiggled the van's keys. "I meant, do you think he's going to kill Peri."

Jack glanced at her and away, taking a deep breath as his world shifted a hundred and eighty degrees. "No. She's going to kill him first."

Hesitating, Harmony looked between the van and the interstate. "Where?" She turned back to Jack, eyes wide. "How? We've got to help her."

But Jack scuffed the pavement, head down. “How,” he said flatly. “I have no way of even finding out where she is. You know what she told me to do? Get you to a safe place.”

“The little bitch,” Harmony swore, clearly frustrated. “I do not need saving!”

“I know how you feel,” Jack said around a sigh. “But that’s Peri for you.” Opti had ingrained a need for her to put her anchor’s safety before her own, and seeing as Peri had been working with Harmony, the woman now fell into that category. But Jack knew this was more than Opti conditioning. It was just how Peri was.

“I can’t sit and do nothing,” Harmony muttered. “What are we supposed to do?”

Jack turned to the van and opened the door. “Watch the obituaries.”

CHAPTER THIRTY-SEVEN

Her arm hurt where the cold metal of the fencing bit deep. Coat bunched up at her elbow, Peri forced her hand farther out through the chain link. Her fingers were losing their feeling from the cold or, more likely, from the lack of circulation as she angled the thin piece of metal into the lock. The "key" was a piece of the chain-link fence, wiggled off with metal fatigue and filed flat on the cement floor. It was only a matter of time before she got the lock picked. Time, though, wasn't an asset she had.

Worried, she glanced up at the ceiling grate, estimating it to be nearing five or six by the fading light. She had a few hours left before withdrawal became an issue, but she hadn't heard anything in the last twelve hours or so since the camera Michael had left had run out of battery. No food, no water—she was cold and out of sorts. It was likely someone would come soon if only to taunt her. She almost had it, almost . . .

But her fingers slipped, and the makeshift lock pick fell to the cement floor.

"Damn it!" she hissed, drafting to fix her mistake.

• • •

Blue sparkles hazed her vision, and she breathed them in, then out as time reset. Angling her fingers a different way, she maintained her grip on her key, and with a soft and certain click, the lock disengaged.

"Yes!" she hissed as the draft ended, her two-second confusion so brief as to be nonexistent. The key dropped, pinging to the floor, but the lock was open. Adrenaline pulsed through her, and the fencing scraped her arm as she unwedged it. Pulse fast, she picked up the key, tugging her coat sleeve down when the bare-bulb light flicked on, warning Peri before the door screeched open.

The sharp piece of metal went into her jeans pocket as a faint glow of sunlight from the silent manufacture floor spilled over her and Michael came in. He had a briefcase in his hand, his face showing a five o'clock shadow. He was clearly not in the best of moods; his steps were fast and his expression tight. *This is so bad for my asthma,* she thought, backing from the chain-link fence and praying he didn't rattle the door to prove it was still locked.

But Michael clearly had other things on his mind as he all but threw the briefcase atop the clutter before the bars. The open door behind him said more than the heavy silence and distant hoot of a train or boat that he was alone, and she stood, feeling the aches the hard floor had given her. She could smell gunpowder on him, and her thoughts went to Harmony.

"There are quicker ways to kill me other than freezing me to death," she said, finding hope in his bad mood. With some luck, Harmony was gone and safe. Jack, she didn't care beyond wanting to kill him if he'd told Michael her instructions to get Harmony safe. It didn't look as if he had. Michael was too pissed for that.

"I've got a bullet if you prefer," he said, and she moved farther from her unlocked door.

"Did they get the accelerator?" she asked innocently.

Michael frowned. Arms over his chest, he stood before her, his long face dark in anger. "Where did you tell Jack to leave it?"

Yes! "I didn't tell him to leave it anywhere. I told him to get Harmony the hell away from you." And Jack had. Why? Because it got Jack the hell away from Michael, too? Or had it been more, perhaps?

"You scrawny little nothing!" Michael hit the chain link, and Peri's eyes flicked to the wiggling door. "You will die here, Reed. You will die in agony. I've seen the med wing, and they all died in agony. How long until your next shot? Hours?"

But his fury only filled her with calm. She might die before the sun came up again, but it wasn't going to be in this cruddy cage. "I told them to run because I already know where the accelerator is, and it isn't at WEFT."

He turned his vehement expression to her, dress shoes scraping. "Lies don't work anymore."

"Oh, get over yourself." Peri sauntered closer, feeling powerful despite being in socks and having nothing in her pocket but a sharpened piece of metal."I told you before, string bean. I don't care if you get accelerated or not. But asking me to believe that you were going to let Harmony walk away after she made the drop was insulting. I bought her freedom with a few hours is all. I'll take you there now."

Michael's lip twitched. "Where is it?"

Smiling, Peri brushed her coat off. "The same place it's been for the last twenty-four hours. Get me to my car, and I'll take you there."

He laughed, but it wasn't a pleasant sound. Turning his back on her, he picked up the camera, dropping his briefcase in its place. The snap of the fasteners opening was loud, and she wasn't surprised when he took out a pair of cuffs.

"Put them on," he said, throwing them to her. They hit the fencing and dropped.

Peri stood unmoving. She'd caught a glimpse of a packaged syringe and a vial in there as well. *Evocane. One more dose, and he'll need it for the accelerator. None for me . . .* A sliver of need rose and fell, but it was only a memory—so far.

"Put them on . . . or you don't get out," Michael reiterated.

She was going to get access to her car and, if she played it right, to Silas. And with that, she had another twenty-four hours to kill Michael and end this. There was no way in hell she was going to let him live.

Peri rolled her shoulders, stretching them. With a single foot, she reached out and pushed the unlocked door open.

Michael snarled, reaching behind his coat for his Glock. "Let me rephrase. Put them on, or you die. Right in the head."

Sighing, Peri went to the cuffs, leaning over to angle them in through the holes. "Chicken ass," she grumbled, the need to get to her car an ache. The cool steel ratcheted about her wrists, the alien feel of them never becoming familiar.

"Where is the accelerator?" Michael put his Glock away, and feeling as if she were still in a cage she stepped out, her feet cold on the bare cement.

"I'll take you there," she said. "You still have my car, yes?" God help her, if he didn't, this was going to be the lamest jailbreak ever. His eyes lit up, and she added, "You wanted the pass code. I'll put you into the system myself."

A sly grin stole over him. "I'm driving," he said as he snapped his briefcase shut and gestured for her to go first.

Stocking feet silent on the grimy cement

floor, Peri proudly walked through the defunct manufacturing plant, through the break room with its posted signs about employee rights five years out-of-date, past old offices with computers bigger than a microwave . . . all the way to the covered garage. She couldn't help her smile at the sight of her car parked sideways to the lines, a power-saving white this far away from the sun, but a frown took its place at the marring scratch on the bumper. "You towed it?" she asked incredulously. "You *towed* my car?"

Michael shoved her toward the passenger side, and she stumbled to catch her balance. "I didn't have a choice. Someone locked it down in their efforts to shut off the alarm system."

The car beeped a welcome as she put her cuffed hand to the driver's-door handle and it read her thumbprint. "Don't mess with my settings. It took me a week to get them perfect," she warned as Michael pulled the door open wide, slipping his briefcase into the door's panel pocket before manhandling her around the front of the car to the passenger's side. Again he put her hand to the lock, shoving her into the front seat and slamming the door.

"Good evening, Peri," the car's computer said when her weight hit the seat. "There have been several incidents since you have left. Would you like me to detail them?" *Ding.*

Michael hustled back around to the driver's side before she could stretch to close his door.

“That’s going to change,” Michael said as he got in behind the wheel.

“I’m sorry, could you please repeat that?” the car said, and Peri grimaced.

“Shut up for a moment,” she said, not liking Michael touching her car. “Reeves,” she said, affecting an accent. “Cancel incident report. Disengage audio. Accept new driver as all-access. Assign new driver the name Mr. Asshat.”

The car dinged its acceptance and clicked off, and Michael stared at her. “Asshat?” he said, and the console lit up, recognizing him.

“You can change it after I’m dead,” she said, pulse quickening.

“Yeah? Well, my Aston will leave your girl car in the dirt,” Michael said, grabbing Peri’s wrist and angling her thumb to start it.

Her eyes closed in bliss at the aggressive *barummm* of the warming engine. “Silly boy. Fast doesn’t impress a woman,” she said, yanking her hand back. “Only power. And you don’t need my thumb anymore. It recorded your print when you opened the door, Mr. Asshat.”

“God, you are an insufferable bitch.” Michael adjusted the mirrors and fixed his settings as the primary driver. “Where are we going?”

She stifled a quiver, a thrill of would-he, wouldn’t-he be that dumb. “You brought a syringe, right? You’re going to want to shoot up with Evocane first.”

Michael thought about that for half a second, and then he smiled, getting it. "It's here? In the car? They searched it."

"They searched the safe," she said, reaching for the shift stick.

"Hands off!" Michael exclaimed, and she jerked back before he could hit her.

"It's hidden in the shift stick," she said. "Lighten up."

His hand came up fast, smacking her away again when she reached once more. "And engage your lame-ass emergency signal?" he said, and she sucked on her scratched knuckle.

"Oh, if only it *was* an emergency signal," she mocked. "You want it or not?"

He studied her, then nodded. Adrenaline a sweet seep through her, Peri untwisted the knob, praying it was still in there. The knob came free, and she awkwardly reached two fingers in, angling like chopsticks, fishing. "Got it," she said around a long exhale, then gasped when Michael snatched it from her.

"This is it?" he breathed, eyeing the capped syringe of pink-tinted accelerator.

She nodded, curling her fingers into a fist to hide their trembling. Hunger pinched at her, and withdrawal threatened, but right now, she was calm as she waited to see if everything lined up. She wasn't going to let Michael kill himself before Silas was free. But the timing would have to be perfect.

"You need to shoot up with the Evocane first," Peri said, trying not to show her tension.

"I know that." Adjusting his seat back, Michael moved his briefcase onto his lap and opened it, setting the pink syringe of accelerant out of her reach in the door pocket. Her gut ached when she saw the single dose left in the Evocane vial, there among his pens and notepads. She wanted it, needed it, and, fingers trembling, she began to count the seconds.

"I must remember to thank Bill next time I see him," Michael said as he filled his syringe with the Evocane. "All that Opti conditioning makes you very compliant."

"Hey, how about topping me off here?" she asked, awkwardly shifting her coat sleeve up to expose her shoulder. "I scratched your back, you scratch mine."

"There's only one dose," he said as he rolled up his sleeve. "God, I can't tell you the last time I shot up in someone's car," he said, almost laughing as he jammed it into his bicep. "I've got to wait two minutes before I can inject the accelerant, right?"

Thank God for mistrusting fools. "Yeah, but in three seconds, it's not going to matter."

Michael's eyes widened, but it was too late, and she breathed in, willing the blue sparkles that filled her sight to move faster, spilling through the car and coating the underground garage and tainting the setting sunlight spilling in the open door.

"No!" Michael howled, but with a smug certainty, she flung them back to the instant he had opened his briefcase to make his source of Evocane vulnerable.

Michael froze, squandering a vital half second, torn between her and what he thought was her goal. Terrified he was going to lose what he'd worked so hard for, he scrambled for the accelerant in the door pocket, too late and too stupid to stop Peri as she lunged, cuffed fingers grasping for the vial of Evocane.

Grinning, Peri showed him her cuffed hands, the Evocane tight in her grip. "You are such a dumb-ass," she said, popping the soft plastic top and spilling it.

"You little bitch!"

A fist exploded against her face. Cowering, she hunched over the vial, breath held against the stars as she shook out every last drop, soaked up by the thick mats.

"You stupid fucking bitch!"

She gasped as he gripped the back of her neck and yanked her upright. Unable to focus, she bared her teeth in a grimace, her breath exploding out when he backhanded her middle with a heavy hand.

"Take your accelerator now, Mr. Asshat," she gasped, eyes watering. "Oh, that's right, you can't," she said, throwing herself against the door as he swung at her again. His fist hit her cheek, and pain radiated all the way behind her eye. "Go ahead and kill me!" she raged. "You do that, and Silas will never give you any of his Evocane. Ever! I told you I wanted Silas." She stared at him. "And I will have him."

Expression ugly, Michael let his hand drop. Peri's heart raced, waiting for his next blow.

Michael hit the dash instead, and the car flashed a warning. "Yeah, that's right," Peri said raggedly as she wiped the blood from her nose with her sleeve, her hands still cuffed. "You either take me to Silas and let him go in return for your Evocane, or you get nothing." Frustrated, she took a breath. "You hear me!" she screamed, fed up with dealing with him. "Nothing!"

But Michael was busy with his notepad, scribbling frantically before the fifteen seconds ended and they both forgot.

"I will kill you someday for this," he whispered, going still when the world shifted red and time caught up and meshed.

Her eye hurt, but her gut was agony. Peri pulled herself out of her hunch, carefully touching her cheek to estimate the damage. She was still in cuffs and was missing the last fifteen seconds, but there was an empty vial at her feet. Michael's confusion turned to virulent anger as he read a note, and she guessed that her idea to force him to take her to Silas for a new source of Evocane had worked. *Please be close,* she thought as the memory of withdrawal drifted through her.

Michael ripped his note free from the pad and crumpled it. Expression stoic, he clicked the pen closed and dropped both it and the notepad into the briefcase beside the unused syringe. The capped syringe of accelerant went into a front shirt pocket, and he put his hands on the wheel. It had worked. *Hadn't it?*

"Well?" she said as they sat going nowhere, thinking that not remembering seemed like a small price to pay compared to her freedom. Her face and gut hurt from a beating she didn't remember, but inside, she was singing. She'd forgotten, and it was like sweet water on a hot day.

Michael put the running car into drive, his hands gripping the wheel with a white-knuckled strength. "I get you to Silas. He gives me the Evocane. If you don't run fast enough, I kill you both."

"That's all I wanted in the first place," she muttered, wincing when they drove out into the setting sun and her eye ached. Shit, it was going to purple up. She just knew it.

CHAPTER THIRTY-EIGHT

There were at least three people at the fueling station that she could have signaled for help, but she sat meekly in her seat, pride and the shadows from the overhead light keeping her cuffs hidden. Michael slammed the quick-charge plug away, tapping his card to pay for it and striding back to the driver's-side door with an air of excitement. The accumulated insults of alarms and security measures had left the batteries so low that the solar paint couldn't keep up with the demand.

The sun was down, but fortunately they were only a few miles from Helen's research facility. Getting to Silas was her main goal. After that, she'd be going by feel.

Michael opened the door. Peri turned to him, jumping when he shot her with a dart.

"Hey!" she exclaimed, plucking it out and throwing it at him. "Show a little class."

Grinning, he slipped in behind the wheel, starting the car with an obvious satisfaction. She pulled back in a huff, scrunching into the corner to sulk. One thing was certain in her nebulous plans. Michael wouldn't survive them.

"You were a good girl," Michael said, tossing her a candy bar.

It was an insult, but she said nothing, afraid he might take it away, and she was starving. Awkward from the cuffs, she tore the crackling cover off, the tingle of the antidrafting drug in the dart making the chocolate taste funny. The first hints of a headache had joined the faint tremor in her fingers. Withdrawal was coming. A few hours, maybe. That early dose yesterday had shifted her due time. She hadn't been sure until just now.

Disgusted, Peri put her head against the window. She was going to kill Bill for this. Helen would be a nice second. Michael didn't know it, but he wouldn't live out the night, either.

His mood insufferably cheerful, Michael looked both ways before gunning into traffic. It was busy, and she held on to the door and he changed lanes and made a nuisance of himself. "Your girly car is starting to grow on me. Maybe I'll keep it when you're dead. Get it repainted."

Peri wadded up the candy wrapper and swallowed the last bite. "Reeves. Change amplitude thirty down."

The car made a pleasant ding. She almost could feel the electric blanket running through the car change as, outside, the car shifted from white to a steely gray.

Michael grunted. "Remind me to beat the master code out of you so I can reprogram it."

Peri gazed listlessly at the entrance to the industrial park in all its bland grandeur. "Michael, honey, you're not going to survive the next twenty-four hours."

He chuckled. "I'm not the one slipping into withdrawal."

Newb, she thought, rubbing a hand under her nose. "I'm not going to die of withdrawal, and you won't live long enough to have to worry about it."

Michael glanced at her, then back to the big three-story cube of a building they were aiming for, the landscaping lit up by flood lamps to show stark branches waiting for spring. "You still think you're going to kill me?"

She shook her head. "No. I don't think you'll give me the chance."

"Got that right."

The sign on the lawn said YEOMON INDUSTRIES. There were three cars in the lot, and Michael pulled into a spot at the outskirts, worried about a possible ding, perhaps. Peri watched Michael check his clip, watched as his game face settled in: a blank nothing holding his tension in check. "We're just going to go in?" she asked.

He nodded. "I'm not letting you stay in the car like a golden retriever."

"Good, because I'm not going to." Even with the cuffs on, she got out before he did. Worried, she looked at the receptionist behind the window of glass. There was only one end here.

Feeling ill, she sent her gaze to the cameras focused on the lot and the front door. Helen would be coming, called when someone she had asked to be killed walked in the front door of her research facility. Peri would have to have it done by then, or the woman would take steps to scrub her. Evading that would be a pain in the ass, and she was tired. *This is so bad for my asthma.*

Michael grabbed her arm, yanking her into step beside him. "Keep your mouth shut," he said, weapon hidden by his leg as he strode forward to the door. "We are not a team, and I'm not going to draft if you get shot. If you die, it's your own fault."

A new feeling of vulnerability slid out from the cracks of her ill-defined plan. "Is that your new mantra?" she asked, hating that she got flippant when she got scared. "If you die, it's your own fault?"

The door was locked and, ignoring her, Michael tapped on the glass.

Inside, the receptionist hit the intercom. "I'm sorry, but we're closed. If you'd—" The woman's eyes widened. She made a gasping scream, ducking as Michael shot the door.

Peri covered her face with her arm, stumbling when Michael dragged her inside. Heart pounding, she watched, disgusted as he leaned over the reception desk.

Again, the gun rang out with two short pops. The woman stopped screaming.

Angry now, Peri stood in the center of the lobby, turning to show the recording camera her cuffed hands. "That wasn't necessary."

With a familiar, intent focus, Michael wiped the splattered blood from his face and scanned the monitors behind the desk. "Upstairs. This way."

Her mind went to the three cars in the lot, three people who wouldn't make it home this morning. Sure enough, Michael detoured first to the break room, where he shot the security guard in the back as he ran for the alarm. The third person on-site was in a lab coat, and he died in the hall, his soda spilling a fast vanguard to his slowly seeping blood, his sandwich scattered across the floor in a fantastic pattern of lettuce and tomato mixed with the gray and red of his brain.

"You are a one-man killing machine," she said, convinced Michael liked it too much. "Not a lot of finesse here, though."

"I'm working, not making art." Michael dragged her down the hall, her stocking feet sliding as he pulled her past a series of locked glass doors. Behind each one was an empty lab. "There he is," he said, stopping before the last.

Fear slid through her as Peri looked in to see Silas standing at a lab bench, horrified as he watched the monitors in the ceiling corners showing three dead people.

Saying nothing, Michael shot the lock, and Peri's nose wrinkled at the scent of burned electronics. Kicking the disengaged door in, Michael yanked her after him.

Silas already had his hands up. "Don't shoot. I'll do whatever you want."

"You think?" Michael shoved Peri at a lab bench, well away from the open door. "I'm sure they didn't give you any weapons, but it's a lab and there's all sorts of things in here that can kill you." Holstering his weapon, he lit a Bunsen burner with an Opti lighter. "This has possibilities."

Eyes roving the lab for assets, Peri pushed the hair out of her eyes, her cuffs clinking. Silas might be in Helen's lab, but she was betting Silas wasn't making Evocane. No, if she was lucky, he was making the modified version with all the addictive properties and none of the active ingredients. All she had to do was get Michael to take it. *Too many ifs. I'm tired of this.*

But a pang went through her, guilt that she was going to kill Michael with the very thing he most desired—what they both did.

"Peri? You okay?" Silas asked, not moving from where he'd been when they had come in.

Smile mocking, Michael pushed her toward a high lab stool. "Sit," he said. "Stay."

Lips pressed together, she did, able to feel the heat from the burner five feet from her.

"Now." Michael turned to Silas, his fake smile gone. "Evocane. She said you had some."

"Ah, I don't—"

Peri gasped as Michael wrapped an arm around her neck, pulling her off the stool as he reached for the burner. It glinted six inches from her eye, and she tensed, ready to act as a strand of hair smoldered. *Okay. Maybe killing him with what he wants will be easier than I thought.*

"Wait!" Silas took a step forward. "Don't hurt her. Please. I don't have the accelerator. Evocane won't do you any good!"

Peri struggled to breathe, pulled off balance and her back twisted. "He has the accelerator. Give him the stuff you made for me, Silas. I'll be okay!" she choked out, and then she could breathe as Michael shoved her up and away.

She hit the bench. Turning, Peri tossed her hair out of her eyes. Silas stared at her, knowing what she was asking. His eye twitched when she nodded. Let him die from a psychotic episode of remembering twin lines. The bastard deserved nothing less. "Peri, it's for you," he said, his reluctance obvious, but not for the reason Michael probably thought. Silas was going to feel responsible for his death, but it wouldn't be his doing. Peri had planned this, twisted Michael into it.

"So where is it, little professor?" Michael said pleasantly as he adjusted the burner. It made a dry hiss. Silas's big hands clenched, and Michael cocked his head in warning, daring him to try anything.

"Give it to him," Peri said. "I made a deal. If I got him accelerated, he'd let us go."

"And we're trusting this?" Silas grumbled, but he turned, his lab coat furling as he went to a glass cabinet. Unlocking it, he brought out a palm-size, white plastic bottle.

"Try again, little professor," Michael said, taking a new grip on her. "I'm not snorting that."

"It's Evocane." Silas's jaw was clenched at the half lie, and Peri hoped Michael thought it was only Silas's reluctance in handing it over. "If it is a maintenance drug, it should be less obtrusive. Ideally it will be a pill. I haven't had enough time with it is all."

Michael's brow furrowed in mistrust, his gaze flicking to the monitors still showing an empty parking lot and bloodied lobby. "A pill?" Michael questioned, and Peri jerked herself free of him when his grip eased. She pulled herself up against the lab bench, not moving as Michael set the burning flame aside.

"You expect me to trust that?" Michael said, gesturing with his Glock. "When you're sitting in the middle of your lab of poisons?"

"I'll take it," Peri blurted, hoping she didn't look desperate, but the pinch of withdrawal was becoming more insistent.

Michael gave her an askance look, his thin lips quirking in an odd smile. “Feeling a little anxious, are we?”

“I said I’d take it,” she repeated. “It’s the only way you’ll know that it’s the real stuff.”

“I suppose it’s better than you drooling all over the counter.” Michael gestured for Silas to back up. “Tell me how much she needs,” Michael said, and Silas glanced at the scale, focus going distant as he mumbled his way through a weight calculation. “How much!” Michael shouted, and Silas jumped.

“Six grams. About six grams. You need six and a half,” he said, clearly worried as he started to sweat.

“Six grams.” Michael tared the scale. “I haven’t used one of these since high school.”

Peri tried to catch Silas’s eye as Michael began tapping powder onto it. That she was going to ingest it first was suddenly not that appealing. It *was* the modified Evocane, right?

“Here you are, Peri. Time for your meds.”

Her hands shook as she took the little wax paper tray, suddenly unsure. But Silas wouldn’t give her anything to hurt her. “You aren’t funny. You know that, don’t you?” she said. “The reason anyone laughs is because you’re the only one with a gun.”

Silas’s foot scuffed, and Michael’s head snapped around. Eyes wide, Silas said, “Put it under your tongue. Like glycerin.”

Head hurting, she folded the paper into a funnel and angled it in. It hit with a soft hush and flash of warmth. Another breath, and her headache vanished. She straightened from the hunch she hadn't known she was in, shoulders easing as the last of the grit dissolved to nothing. The relief had been immediate. "Thank you," she said softly, and Silas flushed. It wasn't just for this, but what it meant. If they managed to survive the next few hours, she'd have her freedom back—such as it was.

"That's good enough for me," Michael said as he angled his head back and dumped it in. "No one move," he mumbled, looking at his watch as the powder dissolved. "We'll just wait the required two minutes. You do realize I have no need of either of you anymore?"

Silas glanced at the monitors. "That's why I hit the silent alarm when you busted through the front door."

"Shit," Michael swore as he saw Helen striding through the building, at least six armed people with her, two in combat gear. "Damn it," Michael added as he took the syringe with the accelerator from his front pocket and flicked the cap off. "That woman has the timing of a seventeen-year-old. Both of you." He looked up, motioning with his head. "Over there where I can see you both."

Peri obediently moved, her resolution beginning

to waver. He was going to push poison into his veins thinking it would make him a god. It was going to kill him even as it gave him everything he wanted. Was it wrong to want something so bad you were willing to kill for it? She wanted her freedom. Was it any different from what Michael desired?

"Is there a back door?" she whispered as she and Silas backed even deeper into the lab.

"No. If there was, I would have been through it five minutes ago."

His expression was grim, and she found his hand, giving it a squeeze. "This isn't your fault. I did this, not you. I wanted you to be safe, and this was the only way I could think to get to you."

Silas's attention jerked from Michael to her, the man currently staring at his watch and cursing. "Trapped in a lab with a crazy man is safe?" Silas asked.

"I won't let you die," she said, and his expression blanked.

"Don't promise me that," he said, but it wasn't his decision.

"I'm sorry for leaving you with LB," she whispered. "I shouldn't have done that. I was scared."

"*You* were *scared?*" he echoed, but his wonder vanished when Helen came in, flanked by her security. Brow furrowed, he edged in front of Peri. "There's a cuff key on my key chain," he said. "Back pocket."

Thank God, she thought, fingers awkward as she fished for them.

Michael grinned, tossing the used syringe of accelerator away. It was done.

For three long seconds, Helen stood there in her pristine white dress suit, seeing the facts and trying to guess what had transpired. "I told you to retire Reed. Explain this," she said, motioning for two of her security to circle around behind them. Peri reluctantly dropped back, the key still in Silas's pocket.

Michael stood unmoving, his expression slack as he listened to his body, feeling the change, exalting in it. "I will retire her. I had some unfinished business first."

Helen's brow furrowed as she looked from Michael to Peri and Silas. "I had been hoping that you would fill her place, Michael, but I can see you aren't ready for even that yet. Security, put Reed in my car. I will take care of this myself."

But the sound of Michael's weapon cocking stopped everyone, and the half-mad look in his eye kept them unmoving. "After I finish talking to her," Michael said. "You should be pleased. I'm thinking for myself, ma'am, just as you suggested."

Irritation flickered over Helen. "No one shoot him. You understand me?" Helen pushed forward, seeing as he was aiming at the men, not her. "What did she tell you? Lies to manipulate you into making a mistake, I'm sure."

Peri's lip curled up. This was the person behind everything Bill had done to her. It had taken two years, but she'd found her. "I told him nothing," Peri said. "You did this yourself by suspending the program after promising to accelerate him. You really think you can string one of us along, then fail to make good on a promise and live to complain about it when we force the issue?" Peri said bitterly. "As much as we hate each other, we share a common thread you will never comprehend."

Helen went white as she reassessed Michael's smug satisfaction. "Accelerated," she breathed, her eyes dropping to the used syringe. "What did you do?"

Peri had delayed long enough. Even if someone drafted now, they couldn't erase the past. Michael was accelerated. Catching Michael's eye, she tapped her wrist. Michael smirked. "It's done," she said, and Helen flushed, livid.

"I told you to wait!" Helen exclaimed.

Silas took Peri's arm, trying to get her to back up with him. "Ready or not, here he comes," Peri said. "And you're stuck with him. I'm out of here."

"Dart him!" Helen shouted, and Peri gasped as everyone moved. "Both of them!"

Peri flung herself at the floor, but she never hit as the air was suddenly flooded with blue sparkles. The world froze for an instant: Silas's worry, Michael's satisfaction, Helen's ugly expression as she pointed . . . and the dart gun being raised a half second too slow.

And then Michael breathed them all in, resetting the world.

Peri stumbled, putting a hand to her middle as vertigo flashed and was gone. Her head throbbed, and she almost passed out as Michael pushed her farther back in time than she could manage on her own. *I'm still by the lab bench,* she thought, looking at the monitor where Helen was coming through the building, her security in tow. He'd have to take the accelerator again so he wouldn't rub it out, but even as she thought it, Michael shot up with it and threw the empty syringe into a corner. Grinning, he used the handgun to motion them to the door.

"Out. Now," he demanded, and when neither of them moved, he shot the floor. On the monitors, men began running. "Now!" Michael shouted. "Or the next one will be in Denier!"

Silas took her elbow and dragged her to the door. "This isn't going to end well," he whispered as they hustled into the hallway.

"Stairwell!" Michael demanded, and Silas made a fist and hit the fire alarm.

Alarms started honking. Michael pulled the gun up to shoot him, and Silas stepped into it, expression twisted as he got in Michael's face. "I shut down the elevators, you idiot!" Silas exclaimed, toe to toe with Michael. "If we're lucky, they are stuck between floors, and if not, they'll have to use the stairs, too." Silas yanked the door to the stairwell open. "Dumb-ass," he muttered, pushing Peri in. He hustled her down the steps, turning to look behind him. "Think you can jam that door, string bean?"

"You need to shut up," Michael said, but he was breaking the fire hose station for the ax.

"When did you become so good at this?" Peri said, and Silas bent close.

"When the draft ends, we have to get out of here," he whispered.

"Isn't that the point?" Peri asked.

Silas yanked her back out of the way as Michael ran past them."I made the pill for you, Peri," Silas said as Michael shot out the lock on the second-story landing. "No buffers, just the addictive properties. He's going to MEP thirty seconds after the draft ends."

"Like I said, isn't that the point?" she whispered, shoving the guilt down. That she was going to kill Michael didn't bother her as much as she was going to do it using his desire—a desire they both shared.

Silas grimaced. "Who do you think he trusts more? You or Helen? He's going to kill you."

Peri pinched the bridge of her nose, tired.

But Silas was right. The man wouldn't go down easy. He'd retain the ability to act for a while, time when she'd be vulnerable as the focus of his feelings of betrayal. She was going to forget, but Michael . . . he wasn't. And she could use that.

"Promise me you'll go. You can make it if you go alone," Silas said even as they hustled down the stairs to Michael.

She gave Silas's hands a squeeze. "It's both of us, or neither." She smiled. "I have a plan."

Silas's expression blanked.

Michael's feet scuffed on the stair as they joined him. "Don't fall behind, or I'll shoot you myself."

Peri squared her shoulders, jealous that in a few seconds, Michael would remember while she'd be left with hearsay and best guesses. *And it is going to save my life.* "I'm not the enemy, Michael," she said as she made her methodical way down the last flight of stairs. "Helen tried to dart you so she could put you in a cage. She's using you like they used me. They made you, Michael, and they know exactly what buttons to push."

"Why are you still talking?" he snarled, giving her a shove to stay behind him.

"Because you aren't thinking," she said as Silas caught her elbow, saving her from a fall. "You saw Helen's face. She was pissed that you worked around her. As far as she's concerned, you fucked up. She didn't want you accelerated because now you're going to remember, and with that, they can't lie to you anymore. They're going to lock you up, Mr. Asshat."

A door above them blew apart, and they all looked up, pressing to the walls when debris rained down. "Or they could blow the door open and come down the stairs anyway," Silas said, taking Peri's shoulder and pushing her toward the door to the lobby.

Vertigo hit her as she stumbled into the empty lobby. The sky past the broken glass door was black with night, and as she watched, it paled, flickered, and flashed clear.

"Go!" Silas shouted, pushing her to the parking lot, and she balked, trying to find herself.

She hadn't drafted, but Michael had. She was missing the last minute and a half. She was running. Helen was here. They'd made it out of the lab. Someone had pulled the fire alarm by the sound of it.

"Run, Peri!" Silas was at the door, gesturing for her to go. "I'll catch up."

But she wasn't going to leave him. Not now. Not ever. "Where's Michael? Is he accelerated?"

Silas tried to drag her to the lobby's shattered door. "He's in the stairwell. I gave him your fix, not Evocane. He's going to MEP. We have to get out of here."

But they both jerked when a gun popped and a slug buried itself in the door before them.

"Stop right there!" Helen demanded as she strode out of the stairwell, her security and a dazed Michael behind her. "That was a warning. The next puts you down."

"Three seconds too short," Silas swore, turning with his hands high and wide.

Peri shook her head; the Amnoset Michael had given her at the gas station was still holding force. She tried not to look at the blood splattered on the wall behind the desk. That wasn't her fault. Michael had done it. But it still felt as if she'd failed somehow.

"Someone turn that alarm off," Helen said irately as two men grabbed Peri and Silas, cuffing Silas and pushing her into a corner.

Did it work? Peri wondered, cursing her missing memories. *Will I survive if it did?*

Grimacing, Helen scooped up the receptionist's scarf. The fire alarm finally ceased hooting, and, heels clicking, she walked to where Michael sat in a glass-covered chair. Snapping the scarf out, she used it to stanch the blood flowing from Michael's shoulder. "The live trials were suspended," she said as she roughly tended him. "I told you to stay away from Denier," she muttered, clearly angry. "Look at you. This is going to take weeks to heal. What am I supposed to do in the interim?"

Does he remember? Breathless with the need to know, Peri tried to tug away from the man holding her. "Michael," she said, not caring whether her quavering voice gave her away. "Do you remember? Michael! Do you remember!"

Someone jerked her back, and Helen gave Michael a little pat before rising and turning to her. "You, Agent Reed, are astounding. I don't know how Bill managed you. The amount of damage you can inflict in your ignorance is breathtaking. If Michael fails to metabolize the Evocane well, I will have no choice but to wipe you and start over." She frowned. "You are apparently more valuable when you can't remember. Bill will be so pleased," she finished sourly.

Fear swamped her jealousy that Michael might have what she wanted, but she couldn't move, fixed by the need to know whether it had worked. His face pale, Michael had begun to shake. "Did you hear that, Michael?" she said, hoping he hadn't gone too far to reason. "I'm valuable because I forget. She doesn't want you anymore."

"Did you really think he was going to let you walk after you gave him the accelerator?" Helen said as she checked her watch and brusquely motioned for her security to take care of the body behind the desk. "Michael said what was needed to get what he wanted. Lesson one." Her amuse-ment faltered when she noticed Michael was trembling, white-faced and shaky. "Get them out of here. All of them. Put Michael in my car. We need to talk." She frowned at him. "Don't we, Michael?"

"He deserved to know," Peri said over her shoulder as a nameless guard pulled her to the door. Two more men had the body of the receptionist. "You were never going to accelerate him, and now that he is, you're going to shove him in a box with no windows. Tell him!"

It took the remaining security to get Michael upright, the drafter muttering incoherently. They didn't know he was struggling to reconcile two timelines, but Peri did, almost feeling sorry for him as she remembered the chaos, the confusion, the simple one-plus-one not equaling two any-more.

"Put him in a cell?" Helen said, waiting for them to get him out first. "Why? He's my best agent. Or he will be, once we get that shoulder fixed up."

But Michael was falling apart before her eyes. "He never was your best," she said. "And he certainly isn't now."

"Ma'am?" one of the guards holding Michael said when he began to violently shake.

Helen turned, her irritation shifting to confusion when Michael looked at her, his lips moving slowly as he tried to form words. "You sent Peri to retire me," he said, voice thready.

"I told you to kill her," Helen reasserted, and Michael moaned, holding his head. "You've really messed this up. Not a feather of patience in you."

"I see everything. *Everything!*" he exclaimed, and his security struggled to hold him, their efforts stifled by Helen's earlier demand to not hurt him. "And now you're scared."

"Of you?" Helen laughed, not seeing the death in his eyes, watching her from under his lowered brow and sweat-soaked hair. "I made you. Go wait in the car."

"Peri," Silas muttered, his newly cuffed hands before him, the nervous security man holding his shoulder watching Michael, not him. "Get out. Right now."

But Peri couldn't move, riveted. He remembered, and it was driving him insane.

"You kept the accelerant from me. Why!" Michael shouted, finding the strength to stand.

Helen looked him up and down, still confident he was her toy. "You weren't ready."

"Peri, go," Silas begged even as he quietly worked the cuff key out of his pocket and got himself free, but she couldn't move, fixated on Michael.

Michael laughed, the evil sound tripping over the bumps in her spine to make her shudder.

"I think you weren't ready for me," he said, shuffling toward Helen.

"You have had—" Helen said, and then Michael backhanded her.

The woman fell against the reception desk, crying out in affront. "Don't shoot him!" she exclaimed when the patter of safeties going off tripped through the air. "He's worth more than all of you combined. Use your darts!"

"You weren't ready for me!" Michael shouted, her security too slow when he drew his Glock and fired into her.

"Out!" Silas grabbed Peri and dragged her to the door, but she twisted out of his grip, unable to leave the thunderous sound of three Glocks unloading into Michael.

Falling to his knees, he slowly collapsed onto Helen. Someone rolled him off her, and he lay on his back, forgotten as they clustered around the dying woman. It was too late.

"Peri . . ."

Pulling free of Silas, she went to Michael. He was still alive, trying to laugh as blood bubbled about his lips. She fell to her knees, awkward with her hands cuffed. "Michael." She grabbed his shirtfront, shaking him until his eyes focused on her. "Michael. Is it worth it? Is it?"

He blinked, taking a racking breath. "To remember?" he said, shaky hand touching her face, the slickness of blood separating them. "Oh yes," he said, voice becoming thready. "Don't forget. If you die . . . it's your own fault."

His hand fell from her. The warm smear of blood he'd marked her with quickly turned cold.

The sound of Helen's security trying to keep her alive had gone frantic. Numb, Peri let Silas pull her away. She stumbled beside him into the parking lot, hardly recognizing it when he took the cuffs off her. She went without protest into her car, and he drove her away.

CHAPTER THIRTY-NINE

Lloyd Plaza was busy with giggling kids running from kiosk to kiosk for their games and activities. At the far corner under the massive monitor, a band was setting up for tonight's party. The beer tent and dance floor had been in place since last night as the city tried to pull as many people off the streets as possible and into a controlled environment for the last day of Detroit's yearly music/cabin fever festival. Tonight would be capped off by coordinated fireworks at the casinos as local and international bands "broke winter's back," but right now the kids held sway in the plaza, enjoying their January candy-fest under the faultless blue of a late winter sky.

Peri lingered at the outskirts, clearly not a parent and feeling out of place as she scanned the large square with its permanent tables and benches bolted to the cement tilework. It was hard to get a good fix on anyone with the kids milling about, and she forced herself to relax when Silas eased up beside her, handing her a hot coffee that smelled of warm milk and caramel.

"Thanks," she murmured, her cold fingers appreciating the heat as she took it.

"This is a weird place to pick up your cat," he said as he fidgeted beside her, and Peri glanced at her glass phone, thinking the same thing. Cam had never left her a text before—the man preferred the intimacy of a call—but maybe he was trying to distance himself. The coffee shop had a Realtor sign in the window when she and Silas had driven past it earlier today. Her chest hurt every time she thought of the peace she'd had there. She kept telling herself it hadn't been false, but why couldn't she make it last?

"Maybe," she whispered, remembering Silas had said something.

"I mean, why an open plaza?" he insisted. "In the middle of the afternoon? Surrounded by kids? Is the guy a perv, or paranoid?"

"That's why," she said, nodding at a familiar hefty figure in a suit sitting alone at a canopied table, a cat carrier conspicuously on the table.

Silas followed her eyes, going still when he saw

Bill. "God bless it," he whispered, taking her elbow and trying to draw her back. "He's just a cat. Let's go. Now!"

Peri jerked out of his grip, sure there were other sets of eyes already on them. Jack's perhaps. She hadn't seen her illusionary partner since he'd spun in a circle and vanished, but she wasn't taking any chances and would unload her Glock into a shadow if she thought it was really him.

"Carnac is not *just* a cat," she argued. "He's *my* cat. And what about Cam?" Worried, she dropped her gaze to her phone, scrolling to find Cam's number. She hit connect, and sure enough, Bill shifted to reach for his phone. Peri ended the call before it could complete.

"Watch my back," she said, pushing her hot coffee into his hand and starting over.

" 'Watch my back'?" Silas echoed, jerking her to a stop. "Peri, this is nuts."

She sent her gaze to the children running amuck, to the benevolent-looking but heavy police presence enjoying the day as much as the kids. "I want my cat, and I want to know he didn't hurt Cam. I promised him he'd be safe."

But Silas's frown only deepened. He wanted her to turn around and walk away, but she couldn't. "I have to do this," she said, and he let go. "Watch my back," she said again, forcefully. "Jack is probably somewhere. If you find him, you have my permission to kill him." She hesitated in thought. “As long as no kids are watching.”

“I can do that,” Silas said, voice low and threatening, and she smiled.

But it faded as she wove her way between the running kids and the store-themed treats being handed out like the advertisements they were.

Warned by her incoming call, Bill had pulled himself up to his full, considerable height, casting about until he spotted her. His somewhat water-fat face widened in an honest smile, and he stood, knowing better than to spread his arms wide for their usual hug.

“Hey, kiddo,” he said, gaze warm and inviting. “I’m glad you decided to come over.”

She stopped before him under the shade of the canopy, hand on her hip as she took him in. He’d lost some weight, gained some muscle, and his finger was bare of his precious Opti ring, showing a faint lighter band of skin that had yet to darken. Otherwise, he looked the same in his thousand-dollar suit that could never quite hide his thug background. “Whatever you did to Cam, I’m going to do to you twice, and unlike me, you’ll remember it.”

Bill chuckled, gesturing for her to sit down. On the table, Carnac meowed for her attention. “Cam is fine,” he said, reaching his thick fingers through the grate to give the cat something to rub up against. “I left him a note in your handwriting. Have a seat. Let’s talk.”

She didn't move to sit, crossing her arms in front of her and feeling as if scopes were trained on her. "No," she said, then extended her hand. "Give me his phone so I can return it. He lives on that thing."

"So I noticed." Bill shook his head in warning. "I took the opportunity to go through it. He's a bad man, Peri. No good for you. Don't let the boyish charm fool you." His eyes narrowed. "Sit. Down," he demanded.

She sat as he knew she would. Her head came up, focus landing on Jack clear across the plaza, right in her line of sight. His hands were empty, but she felt better when Silas caught up to him and spun him around, threatening violence. *Not illusion Jack, then.* "What did you do to Cam?"

"Nothing," Bill said, voice sounding hurt. "He never even knew I was there."

He? As in Cam? Her eyes flicked to Bill's, reading the truth of it.

Bill sighed, settling in and smiling at the trio racing to a display of candy, their mother trailing along behind with a bookseller tote filled with goodies. "Do you know how hard it is to find a good cat sitter? He took good care of our cat, and you're going to need him again."

Peri's eye twitched. "He's not your cat," she said as she pulled the carrier closer.

"I always felt as if he was."

Which begged the question of how many bugs

and trackers Carnac had in him now. Her head was hurting, and she put her fingers through the mesh, knowing she'd take that risk. "Thanks for nothing, Bill," she said, gathering Carnac to her and standing.

"Ah, wait up. This belongs to you," Bill said as he reached behind his jacket to take out a manila envelope.

Peri looked at it, gauging its thickness. She'd gotten a lot of envelopes from him, and after a quick look around to make sure no one was watching, she took it and lifted the flap with a finger.

It was cash. A lot of it.

Bill smiled up at her, his hands laced comfortably over his middle. "There's half a mil for taking out Michael and Helen for me. Thank you. Well done," he said, inclining his head. "Another two hundred thousand that was originally Michael's cut for procuring Everblue's carbon tree. I have no use for his share, and you were there. Books have to balance, so . . ."

Peri dropped the envelope onto the table. "I don't work for you."

"Really?" Bill barked, irritation crossing his face for the first time. "You think *all that* was happenstance? Don't insult me trying to play dumb. Michael and Helen had outlived their usefulness and I needed them out of the way. I set you on them with the scent of revenge and moral outrage, tempered with blind anger." His expression softened. "You did good, kiddo."

Peri rubbed her forehead, not caring whether he knew she was tempted. She needed money to resettle herself, buy a cloak that even death couldn't find her under. The coffee shop was a loss, and now she had Silas with her. Two people meant four times the cost.

Flushing, she took her eyes off the envelope. "I don't kill for money."

Bill pushed it forward. "You don't kill for kicks, either."

"I did it to be free of you," she said, wanting to point at him but not willing to give the maybe-scopes trained on her an excuse. "All of you. Be careful, Bill. Walk away, or you'll move to the top of my list."

Still, Bill smiled as he stood and put his sunglasses back on. "You are free. You just don't know it yet. Is Steiner giving you flack?"

Not understanding, she shook her head, his faint tone of protection familiar. "Nothing I can't handle," she said softly.

"Because I'd take care of that for you," he added. "Let me know if that's not enough to get you and your new anchor settled. I can float you whatever you need until the next task worthy of your talents comes in."

Her eyes narrowed. "You aren't listening, Bill. You got me hooked on a drug that makes me into a tool. You think I'm going to forgive you for that?"

His gaze shifted to the nearby people, silently telling her to lower her voice. "You already have, or I'd be dead," he said, then softened. "Peri, Peri, Peri, I got you halfway to remembering your drafts. If you aren't ready, I respect that."

"Ready?" she said, flustered. "I'm not doing it."

Still standing over her, he frowned, a worry line pressing into existence over his eyes. "Perhaps it was a mistake. I am sincerely sorry if it was." He turned to look behind him at Silas and Jack, both of them waiting at the outskirts. The kids had saved his life, but that's why Bill had wanted to meet here. "How long until you're off it, then?"

None of your business, she thought, saying, "Just about the same time your chemical tracker runs out."

Again he smiled. "Atta girl. Enjoy your down-time. I'll be in touch."

"I'm done, Bill," she said as he began to walk away. "Call me again, and I'll kill you."

But all he did was turn to give her a smile. "Life is boring," he said, focus distant as he buttoned his jacket. "You need me to feel alive." His eyes fixed on hers, and her mouth went dry at the truth of it. "It was a real pleasure working that closely with you again. You did a lot with half an anchor. Think of what you could do with a whole one."

"Silas is a good anchor," she whispered, stomach rolling.

Shrugging as if it didn't matter, Bill turned and walked away, catching a little girl who had barreled into him and solicitously making sure she had her feet before letting her go.

He had left the money behind, and she took a breath to call out after him, swallowing it back. She had to move. Silas would be with her. Two were harder to hide than one, but they didn't need Bill's money to do it.

She watched Jack say his final words to Silas and jog across the plaza to join Bill, but her thoughts had gone to her goal of sedate days. That they would safely turn into sedate weeks of inaction, and then sedate months of boredom, suddenly had less appeal.

Slowly she tucked the fat envelope into a pocket. Picking up Carnac, she crossed the plaza to Silas, squinting when the bright sun hit her. She wasn't taking Bill's money as a promise to work for him. She was taking it to help hide herself and Silas.

But as she lifted her head and smiled at Silas in the new sun, she wasn't sure she believed herself.

Center Point Large Print
600 Brooks Road / PO Box 1
Thorndike, ME 04986-0001 USA

(207) 568-3717

US & Canada:
1 800 929-9108
www.centerpointlargeprint.com